Autism and Gender

Autism and Gender

From Refrigerator Mothers to Computer Geeks

JORDYNN JACK

UNIVERSITY OF ILLINOIS PRESS

Urbana, Chicago, and Springfield

Library of Congress Cataloging-in-Publication Data
Library of Congress Cataloging-in-Publication Data
Jack, Jordynn, 1977-
Autism and gender : from refrigerator mothers to
computer geeks / Jordynn Jack.
pages cm
Includes bibliographical references and index.
ISBN 978-0-252-03837-2 (hardback)
ISBN 978-0-252-07989-4 (paper)
ISBN 978-0-252-09625-9 (ebook)
1. Autism—Sex factors. 2. Autism in children—Etiology.
3. Sex factors in disease.
I. Title.
RC553.A88J327   2014
616.85'882—dc23   2013040756

Contents

Acknowledgments

This book began in 2009 at the Rhetoric Society of America Summer Institute at Pennsylvania State University, where I joined seminar leaders Lisa Keränen, James Wynn, and an august group of scholars in the "Science and Its Publics" workshop. It was Lisa who suggested that my project—then a hodgepodge of case studies of public science controversies—might best become a book about autism. I am thankful to Lisa and James and to the members of my working group, Jason Kalin and Kim Thomas-Pollei, for their helpful comments on my project as it stood then.

I thank Jack Selzer for the idea of focusing on gender. When he read an early description of this book, he asked where gender figured in. After all, much of my previous research included a gender focus—why not this one? Using gender as a lens proved remarkably helpful in shaping this book, and I thank Jack for his ongoing career counseling, pep talks, and publishing advice. I also thank my mentor and fashion role model, Cheryl Glenn, for her advice and support throughout this project—including her wonderful title suggestions in the eleventh hour. I also received valuable input and support from my colleagues in the field of rhetoric including Peter Cramer, John Duffy, Jessica Enoch, Bernice Hausman, Karen Foss (who read a version of Chapter 5), Paul Heilker, Jodie Nicotra, Tom Miller, Marika Seigel, Stuart Selber, Scott Wible, and Melanie Yergeau.

At the University of North Carolina, Chapel Hill, I received generous support from the Department of English and Comparative Literature, the College of Arts and Sciences, and the Institute for the Arts and Humanities (IAH). In particular, the John W. Burress III Fellowship from the IAH allowed me to make final revisions to this manuscript and to prepare it for publication. I am most grateful for the support of my colleagues at UNC, including Beverly Taylor, Jane Danielewicz, Todd Taylor, Daniel Anderson, Darryl Gless, Jennifer Ho, Heidi Kim, Laurie Langbauer, Mai Nguyen, John McGowan, and especially my writing partner, Katie Rose Guest Pryal.

The three reviewers of this manuscript provided indispensable advice, which strengthened this book considerably. Cynthia Lewiecki-Wilson and the two anonymous reviewers were most generous in their comments and guidance, and I am grateful to them. Of course, I thank Larin McLaughlin for her faith in this project and the team at the University of Illinois Press for their support.

Some material in this book has been published previously in article form, and I have expanded that material into book-length chapters. Parts of Chapter 3 appeared in *Disability Studies Quarterly* 31, no. 3 (2011), as "The Extreme Male Brain? Incrementum and the Rhetorical Gendering of Autism." I thank *Disability Studies Quarterly* and the Society for Disability Studies for permission to include this material in Chapter 3. Parts of Chapter 5 appeared in *Women's Studies in Communication* 35, no. 1 (2012), as "Gender Copia: Feminist Rhetorical Perspectives on an Autistic Concept of Sex/Gender." I thank Taylor & Francis for permission to include this material in Chapter 5.

My family, especially my mother, Barbara Jack, has provided support and a sounding board throughout this project. During the last year of this project, I benefited from the moral support of my new family: my three furry writing buddies, Leo, Ricky, and Cooper, and my husband Ryon Chao. Baby Penelope arrived just in time to provide companionship during the final stages of manuscript preparation.

Autism and Gender

Introduction

Autism's Gendered Characters

Autism has become a controversial subject in the past few decades. What was once considered a rare condition is now estimated to affect one in eighty-eight American children,[1] with similar rates appearing in other industrialized nations. Scientists, psychologists, and doctors debate the relative influence of genetic, neurological, and environmental factors in the dramatic increase in autism diagnosis since 1990. These experts are joined by parents, talk show hosts, and popular science journalists who haggle over what causes autism, as well as appropriate treatments, educational supports, and healthcare policies for autistic children and adults. Autistic self-advocates and spokespeople now appear frequently in print, online, and in the media, offering their perspectives on what autism is, what it feels like, and what (if anything) they think should be done to help autistic people. In short, autism has become a site of controversy and contestation, a scene of rhetorical action, a "rhetorical phenomenon," as Paul Heilker and Melanie Yergeau have noted.[2] Without a clear biological marker (such as a genetic test), a clear understanding of what causes autism or how it progresses, or a clear indication of how to treat it, numerous gaps exist in which different speakers seek to intervene.

Given the gaps in scientific knowledge about autism, this controversy entails more than just arguments about scientific facts, but stories as well: stories about children affected, about parents struggling to come to terms with a diagnosis, about autistic individuals and their lives. There are cases in which parents narrate a course of events in which a typically developing infant became autistic following a vaccine reaction. There are stories of mothers heroically penetrating the so-called fortress of isolation that autism creates, battering down the walls in order to "rescue" the child inside—a dubious narrative for those who see autism as a neurological difference to be accepted, rather than a scourge to be fought. There are stories written by autistic individuals who have "overcome" or "emerged from" autism, and stories written by autistic individuals who celebrate autism and the unique perspectives it provides. The autism narrative is fundamentally a rhetorical narrative, or as the rhetoric scholars John Lucaites and Celeste Condit describe it, one that "exists for a purpose beyond its own textuality," or a story that "serves as an interpretive lens through which the audience is asked to view and understand the verisimilitude of the propositions and proof before it." Autism narratives are rhetorical in that they seek to advocate for something beyond the story itself, whether that is a specific theory about what causes autism, a new understanding of autistic people, or a type of therapy or treatment program.[3] In order to do so, rhetors create, describe, and perform stock characters: typified roles that allow individuals to gain authority, to understand autism as a condition, and to intervene in debates about autism. Whereas rhetoric scholars often link character with *ethos*, or credibility and authority, I describe characters as stock roles or personae that appear in autism discourse. These roles may be performed by rhetors or assigned to others (including autistic people but also the doctors, parents, and experts who speak about them).

Scholars of rhetoric have shown that characters play several important rhetorical roles. As Mark D. Jordan has argued, "Characters surround acts of persuasion—in the audience and the performer as much as in the figures that are presented for admiration or insult."[4] Characters are useful to rhetors because they "condense plots," indexing longer narratives, lines of arguments, and events that are recognizable to an audience. These characters can be deployed across different genres, Jordan notes, "migrat[ing] across all the tidy boundaries of speech, as mobile and insistent as our languages."[5] It is not surprising that rhetorical theories from ancient times onward have included advice for constructing and describing characters, including the techniques of *effectio* (description of physical appearance), *notatio* (description of a character's nature), *prosopopoeia* (imitation of another character), *prosopographia* (sketches of a real person), and character description as an element of *conformatio,* or "that by means of which our speech proceeding in argument adds belief, and authority, and corroboration to our cause."[6]

One way to study a rhetorical controversy or issue, then, is to follow the characters that appear, examining the ways they are named, invoked, and deployed by different speakers for rhetorical effect in different times and places. For instance, Christian rhetors deploy various characters in debates about same-sex love. According to Jordan's account, these characters, such as the adolescent, are often implicitly gendered—it is the male adolescent, especially, who is depicted in religious rhetoric as vulnerable to homosexual thoughts and desires.

Along similar lines, Lisa Keränen, who studies the rhetoric of science, explains that science-based controversies "create, modify, and extend rhetorically constituted characters in order to maintain, undermine, or rehabilitate reputations; to challenge or defend scientific norms and knowledge; and to invigorate and resolve disagreements over scientific knowledge, policy, and values."[7] As Keränen indicates in her book, *Scientific Characters: Rhetoric, Politics, and Trust in Breast Cancer Research,* scientific experts as well as breast cancer patients craft characters that help influence debates about surgical treatments (lumpectomy and radiation versus mastectomy). These characters are not simply creations of individual speakers or writers but are "constructed personae that emerge in interaction between broader culturally derived stereotypes . . . and individual linguistic tendencies."[8] Participants in the breast cancer debate drew upon culturally available stock characters such as the good doctor or the breast cancer patient in order to influence others. In autism controversies, rhetors similarly draw upon culturally recognizable characters.[9]

In this book I examine the way they do so using gendered characters, in particular, as a rhetorical resource. Because gendered characters are readily available in cultural narratives and discourses, they can easily be adapted to rhetorical situations involving autism. Speaking roles, or characters, are constituted in part by power relations, and, as Cheryl Glenn has noted, gender offers one index of power relations within a rhetorical situation.[10] By taking on a particular type of gendered character—or assigning it to another individual—a rhetor is staking a claim to power. For instance, by describing mothers of autistic children as "refrigerator mothers" (who purportedly encouraged their child's withdrawal via emotional frigidity), early autism experts claimed authority for themselves. In order to gain authority to speak about autism, mothers had to generate new roles, drawing on a different type of character, the mother-as-hero who could help "save" her child from autism. I show that gendered characters are especially common in autism discourse because they help fill gaps in knowledge or authority about autism.

I am not the first to pay attention to this phenomenon; other scholars have noted that gendered characters animate autism discourse. In *Understanding Autism* Chloe Silverman notes that "ideas about gender color ideas about 'autism moms' and dads who 'fix things'" and that the kinds of labor associated with autism retain "gendered associations."[11] In a similar vein, Stuart Murray remarks in *Representing Autism* that both fictional and nonfictional accounts of autism tend to highlight males, especially boys, as though "their autism, their masculinity and their youth combine to form the key contemporary autistic character."[12] Females and adults, according to Murray, do not figure into this dominant depiction: "Autism, it appears, can be understood best when seen in terms of the male character, and while its presence within females cannot be denied, it seems more difficult to map an idea of the condition on to the generalized sense of what we believe girls and women to be."[13] To date, no book-length studies consider autism and gendered characters. Autism moms, fix-it dads, and autistic boys are three of the characters invoked in autism discourse, but they are not the only ones: scientific experts evoke the paternal figure of the good doctor, popular texts stereotype autistic people as adult male computer geeks, and autistic individuals themselves seek out gendered characters on the basis of which they may claim authority over their own lives and experiences. A sustained study of these gendered characters helps show why and how they emerged in particular rhetorical contexts, how they are used, and how they continue to affect autism research and treatment, the families of autistic people, and autistic individuals.

Gendered characters in debates about autism do not emerge from nowhere. Instead, they develop from existing narratives and characters, which have already gained cultural acceptance. As A. Cheree Carlson argues, "Uncovering the roots of particular narratives is vital if we are to learn how new narratives are created and judged within their cultural context."[14] Accordingly, in this book I trace the roots of gendered characters that animate debates about autism, beginning in the 1940s, when it was first identified as a separate condition, and leading up to the present.

These characters emerge from and circulate within a rhetorical culture. The rhetorical theorist Thomas B. Farrell defines *rhetorical culture* as the "*common definition of places for the invention and perpetuation of meaning.*"[15] Gendered characters form part of that common set of definitions of places for such invention. As I show, researchers seeking to understand autism have often drawn on those stock characters to theorize what autism is and what causes it. Others seeking to intervene in autism debates, especially parents, have turned to stock characterizations of mothers and fathers for this purpose. Such characters are useful because they can help persuade others to adopt a certain view—a theory of autism, a course of treatment, or a view of the speaker's ethos. The rhetorical theorists Chaïm Perelman and Lucie Olbrechts-Tyteca write that "every social circle or milieu is distinguishable in terms of its dominant opinions and unquestioned beliefs, of the premises that it takes for granted without hesitation: these views form an integral part of its culture, and an orator wishing to persuade a particular audience must of necessity adapt himself to it."[16] Stock characters help speakers and writers adapt to the rhetorical milieu in which they write in order to persuade audiences who also participate in that culture.

Gendered characters are constructed using what rhetoricians would call commonplaces, or *topoi*: culturally available ideas and images. Carolyn R. Miller defines a *topos* as "a conceptual place to which an arguer may mentally go to find arguments," or "a point in semantic space that is particularly rich in connectivity to other significant or highly connected points."[17] When constructing characters, writers or speakers can draw on topoi associated with certain character types. For example, in his study of characters in legal discourse, Marouf Hasian Jr. notes that recurring ones "provide us with enduring cultural exemplars" that influence legal trials.[18] In his case study of a trial in Georgia, he describes how a rape and murder victim, thirteen-year-old Mary Phagan, was characterized as the "embodiment of Southern womanhood," while Leo Frank, the defendant, was portrayed according to racial and gendered stereotypes as a Jewish (hence nonwhite), northern, lascivious male.[19] Participants in the trial drew on commonplaces attached to gendered characters such as the topoi of purity and innocence attached to southern women and the lasciviousness and immorality attached to Jewish men. Here, purity, innocence, lasciviousness, and immorality can all be considered gendered topoi connected to character types. All of this material was readily available for the lawyers in the trial. Frank was convicted in part because the prosecution drew effectively on characterizations already in place in the rhetorical context of Georgia in the early twentieth century.

As a method of study, rhetoric allows researchers to identify the way topoi are invoked in the discourse of autism in a particular context. A theory of autism that invokes, for instance, commonplaces about anxious mothers may seem persuasive if the audience accepts those commonplaces because they are part of the rhetorical culture. In this book I show how gendered characters such as the refrigerator mother from the 1950s and 1960s and the autistic computer geek who appeared between about 1990 and 2010 fit into the broader rhetorical cultures from which they emerge.

The central argument of this book is that gendered characters help construct what autism is and who has authority to speak and write about it. I argue that gaps in scientific knowledge and authority over autism enable gender to become a salient rhetorical force: where knowledge or authority is lacking, gendered characters often fill in. In the remainder of this introduction, I first describe what autism is, how it has been defined, and how those definitions have shifted over time. Next, I explain how I am theorizing gendered characters as a concept and tool for my analysis, and then how I am drawing on research in rhetoric, science studies, and disability studies to support my investigation of gendered characters in the discourse of autism. Finally, I outline the contents of the remaining chapters, each of which takes up a different gendered character that animates controversies about autism and a different rhetorical function served by gendered characters. They include the refrigerator mother, the mother warrior (and her counterpart, the fatherly doctor), the autism dad, the computer geek, and finally, the neurodiverse, often nontraditional gendered characters some autistic people rely on to make sense of their experiences.

Definitions of Autism

It is difficult to provide a single definition of autism that would be accepted by all of the stakeholders involved in the debates about autism. Different stakeholders tend to prefer different models or definitions of autism. My goal in this book is not necessarily to side with any of those groups but, rather, to examine the ways they use gender as a resource to constitute their characters (or how they are constituted by others as gendered characters), whether those characters align with mainstream science, psychiatry, neurodiversity, or alternative health movements.

SCIENTIFIC DEFINITIONS

Within the scientific or medical model, autism represents a puzzle to be solved through continued research. This model depends heavily on the value of scientific progress, the belief that science will eventually provide answers to the "enigma" of autism. Researchers seek out neurological and genetic changes that can be used to identify autism definitively, but they do not yet agree about what those markers are or what their underlying mechanisms might be.

Neurologists tend to define autism as a brain-based disorder, and they accordingly seek to identify differences in the brains of autistic individuals. For instance, some research indicates that autism is associated with large head circumference or brain volume, an indicator of atypical brain growth.[20] Others have identified differences in specific brain regions such as the amygdala and in the connectivity between those brain regions. In a review of brain research on autism, for example, Nancy J. Minshew and Timothy A. Keller argue that autism can now be defined as "a disorder of underconnectivity among the brain regions participating in cortical networks."[21] Researchers in this field use brain imaging tools to try to determine which regions are affected and why.

Geneticists, of course, are likely to view autism as a genetic condition. Researchers report that genetic factors are important in autism, since co-occurrence rates are high in twins (70 to 90 percent in identical twins) and since there is a twentyfold increase in risk for first-degree relatives of someone who has been diagnosed with autism. Despite these findings, though, no single gene accounts for autism; researchers have identified 103 genes and 44 genomic loci that correlate with it, but these genes overlap considerably with other conditions, including epilepsy, schizophrenia, and attention deficit hyperactivity disorder.[22] Researchers in one study detected 126 severe, *de novo* mutations (that is, mutations appearing for the first time in a family member due to a mutation in a germ cell) in a sample of 209 families with a member diagnosed with Autism Spectrum Disorder (ASD). Of those 126 mutations, however, only two genes were present in multiple individuals, indicating "the heterogeneity of the genetic component of ASDs."[23] Given the variability in the genes identified by such studies, according to the psychiatrist Valsamma Eapen, autism does not follow simple patterns of Mendelian inheritance, as in single-gene disorders, but probably represents "a complex disorder resulting from simultaneous genetic variations in multiple genes as well as complex interactions between genetic, epigenetic, and environmental factors."[24] While genetic researchers argue that autism is primarily genetic, others, like Eapen, leave open the possibility that environmental triggers may be at play.

PSYCHIATRIC DEFINITIONS

In the United States, autism diagnosis is based on the *Diagnostic and Statistical Manual* (*DSM*) of the American Psychiatric Association (APA). The fourth edition of the *DSM* lists several criteria, including "impairment in social interaction," such as lack of eye contact or difficulty forming peer relationships, "impairments in communication," such as delayed, absent, or repetitive speech, and "restricted, repetitive, and stereotyped patterns of behavior, interests, and activities," such as adherence to rigid routines, a tendency toward repeated motor movements (for instance, hand flapping), or restricted patterns of interest.[25] The fifth edition, *DSM-V*, revises that definition. Whereas the previous edition distinguishes among Autistic Disorder, Asperger's Disorder, Pervasive Developmental Disorder Not Otherwise Specified (PDD-NOS), and Childhood Disintegrative Disorder (CDD), the *DSM-V* includes only Autism Spectrum Disorder. The new definition names social difficulties and restricted or repetitive behaviors as the main criteria but adds that these symptoms must be present in "early childhood" and that the "symptoms together limit and impair everyday functioning."[26]

In his book *Autism*, Murray argues that "the idea of autism as a problem or deficit is in fact built in, during diagnostic evaluation, to the definition of what the condition is perceived to be."[27] By defining autism as something that "limit[s] and impair[s] everyday functioning," the *DSM* seeks to fix autism and stabilize it so that it can be defined, thereby participating in what Françoise Castel calls the "psychiatrization of difference," or a tendency to impose categories on the range of human behaviors, sorting individuals into "normal" and "abnormal."[28] This psychiatric language functions rhetorically, in Rick Carpenter's terms, as "a mechanism of power used to marginalize some while privileging others through the fabrication of rigid categories/dichotomies."[29] The diagnostic language that frames autism discourages people from understanding autistic individuals as capable, rational, or intelligent as opposed to sufferers of a mysterious and devastating condition.

In this model, autism is often portrayed as a deficit, disease, or disorder. These depictions align with what disability studies scholars would deem the "medical model" of disability, in which the condition in question is described in terms of limitations and lack. This model, according to Tobin Siebers, positions able-bodiedness as "the baseline by which humanness is determined, setting the measure of body and mind that gives or denies human status to individual persons."[30] In scientific descriptions of autism, especially, able-mindedness (understood in terms of how non-autistic brains work) becomes the standard against which humanness is determined. Individuals who do not communicate according to "normal" standards, who are nonverbal, or who demonstrate other autistic behaviors (such as "obsessive" interests or repetitive speech) are depicted as abnormal, abject, and in need of fixing or solving (as a puzzle).

NEURODIVERSE DEFINITIONS

Whereas the APA definition portrays autism as a dreadful disorder of communication and social interaction, autism is increasingly recognized as part of the variable spectrum of human neurological conditions. Those who espouse this view often employ the term *neurodiversity* to refer to the value they place on understanding human brains and thinking styles as different and diverse rather than impaired. Autistic individuals describe a range of differences they experience, which may include sensory differences (such as higher sensitivity to light or sound), synesthesia (the blending of one or more senses, such as sights with sounds), an ability to focus on a single sensory input (rather than many inputs at once), greater attention to detail, an ability to focus intently on a subject or topic, or the ability to remember visual and aural information. In his book *Born on a Blue Day*, Daniel Tammet describes how synesthesia leads him to link numbers with shapes, colors, and textures: "thirty-seven is lumpy like porridge," for instance, while "89 reminds me of falling snow." This ability to visualize numbers helps Tammet perform complex calculations in his head "without any conscious effort."[31] Amanda Baggs describes her sense of the world as involving recognition of patterns: "Everything I perceive—from the movements of my body to the smells in the air—goes into my mind and sifts itself into similar kinds of patterns. Some of them correspond to what other people are usually aware of, and some of them don't."[32] Granted, some autistic people describe the challenges they experience with everyday tasks, such as problems coordinating body movements or decoding visual or aural stimuli.[33] A difference framework, however, allows autism to be understood as a way of experiencing the world that may include both challenges and benefits—not unilaterally as a deficit (a devastating disorder) or gift (as it is sometimes depicted in "savants").

As an alternative to the ability-disability binary that often character-izes descriptions of autism, Heilker and Yergeau posit that it should be understood as a rhetoric, "a way of being in the world through language, a rhetoric we may not have encountered or recognized fre-quently in the past nor value highly in academic contexts, but a rheto-ric nonetheless."[34] Such a concept draws attention to autistic thinking and communication as valuable and potentially transformative of our rhetorical theories and assumptions, as opposed to the deficit model in the *DSM* definition, which assumes that autism represents impaired communication and that autistic people are therefore in need of re-mediation. For instance, Heilker and Yergeau explain that echolalia, or repetitive speech, is often seen as a marker of autistic impairment. From a rhetorical viewpoint, though, "this repeated use of stock mate-rial starts sounding more like a traditional and valued kind of inven-tion."[35] In some circles, then, autism is increasingly recognized as a valid, alternative form of interaction, thought, and communication.

BIOMEDICAL DEFINITIONS

Other groups (often composed of parents of autistic individuals and some scientific and medical experts) reject both mainstream scientific definitions and the neurodiversity approach in favor of alternative health claims: that autism may be caused by vaccines or other environ-mental triggers, that it is precipitated by gastrointestinal disturbances or mitochondrial disease, or that it constitutes a sensory disorder, to name a few theories. For these individuals, autism constitutes a bio-medical condition; it is not primarily a psychiatric or brain-based dis-order but one involving the whole body. One proponent of this view is Martha Herbert, a Harvard University neurologist, who has argued that autism should be understood not as a "brain disorder" but as a "disorder that affects the brain," or a "*behavioral syndrome with a bio-logical basis and systemic features, influenced by genes and gene-environment interactions.*"[36]

Those advocating these explanations cannot be considered a mono-lithic group, but they tend to share a definition of autism as a bio-medical condition characterized by vitamin deficiencies, food allergies, microbial infections, mitochondrial deficiencies, or immune system dysfunction.[37] This definition leads some to embrace alternative (and often controversial) treatments ranging from vitamins and other sup-plements to hyperbaric oxygen therapy. Even "mainstream" autistic spokespeople such as Temple Grandin and Donna Williams mention that dietary restrictions have helped them. Williams, for instance, believes that her autism is worsened by allergies to phenol and salicylate and follows a special diet to avoid those triggers.[38] In her autobiography Grandin refers to severe attacks of colitis that limited her diet to yogurt and gelatin for several weeks at a time.[39]

A subset of this group includes those who believe that vaccines cause or contribute to autism, either directly or by triggering food allergies and gastrointestinal disorders like the ones described by Williams and Grandin. In the early twenty-first century these individuals banded together and gained international attention for their cause, mainly with a series of lawsuits in the United States Court of Federal Claims seeking reparations for children whose parents assert that they were harmed by vaccines. Scientific data do not support the vaccine hypothesis, but some parent groups have continued to lobby for research into vaccines, drawing on emotional stories about how their children have suffered because of them. I explore how mothers, in particular, have crafted their characters in order to participate in those debates in Chapter 3.

HISTORICAL AND CULTURAL DEFINITIONS

More broadly, it is important to recognize that definitions of autism depend on the cultural and historical context. In her work on intellectual disabilities, Licia Carlson notes that "the etiology and treatment for it [intellectual disability] have depended as much on social trends, stereotypes, and discriminatory practices and assumptions as they have on hard science."[40] Similarly, autism has been understood in different ways depending on the social context. Majia Nadesan has argued that autism is fundamentally a "disorder of the early twentieth century," while high-functioning variants such as Asperger's are "fundamentally disorders of the late twentieth and early twenty-first centuries."[41] Although there have, presumably, always been individuals who might now be categorized as autistic, that category did not itself emerge until the twentieth century because it required "standards of normality" and specialized knowledge regimes (such as child psychiatry and educational testing) in order to be identified as a "disorder."[42]

In addition, researchers have shown that autism is understood differently today in different national contexts. For example, as the anthropologist Roy Richard Grinker notes, in South Korea, children who might be classified as autistic often receive a diagnosis of Reactive Attachment Disorder (RAD), a failure to bond appropriately with the primary caregiver (usually the mother). Despite its devastating implications for mothers,

RAD is considered a more socially acceptable diagnosis in South Korea than is autism.[43] Carlson argues that disabilities are shaped rhetorically through "prototype effects," or the ability of one particular portrait of a condition to dominate in particular historical moments.[44] For example, autism has been figured as a condition affecting children, in particular, a tendency that the rhetoric scholars Jennifer L. Stevenson, Bev Harp, and Morton Ann Gernsbacher argue infantilizes it and elides the concerns of autistic adults.[45] The philosopher Ian Hacking would go so far as to suggest that these dominant depictions of a condition like autism can even interact with autistic individuals, who "find the current mode of being autistic a way for themselves to be."[46]

The scholars cited here, including Nadesan, Grinker, Murray, Hacking, and Heilker and Yergeau, have all examined the social construction of autism in discourse, whether fictional, scientific, or popular. In the collection *Autism and Representation* (2007), edited by Mark Osteen, contributors examine portrayals of autism in literature, film, and culture. Stuart Murray's *Representing Autism: Culture, Narrative, Fascination* takes a similar approach. These scholars have demonstrated that representations of autism *matter*, insofar as they influence how autistic people are treated in real life. This book extends this historical and cultural research by offering the first sustained gender analysis of autism, as well as the first book-length rhetorical analysis of autism.

Autism's Cast of Gendered Characters

Throughout this book I use the term *gender* to refer to identities that specify characters portrayed according to a sex/gender binary such as male or female, masculine or feminine. Feminist scholars have typically distinguished between sex (male or female) and gender (masculine or feminine), drawing on Gayle Rubin's theorization of gender as a marker of socioeconomic structures.[47] For these scholars, *sex* refers to the differentiation of the biological body (namely via genitalia), while *gender* refers to the social and cultural ascriptions laid onto that body (including behaviors, beliefs, and material practices such as clothing choice and use of makeup).

More recently, though, gender scholars have questioned this assumption that gender (masculine or feminine) is socially constructed, while sex (male or female) remains biologically neutral. For the feminist theorist Judith Butler, sex, too, is materialized through the repetition of regulatory norms, especially the norms of heterosexuality.[48] As an example, feminist scholars often point to the way intersexed individuals are forced into one sex or another, often via mutilating surgeries that make ambiguous genitalia unambiguously male or female. More generally, feminists note that cultural practices literally change men's and women's bodies. For example, bone density varies across gender, ethnicity, and culture, in part owing to culturally specific patterns of diet and exercise. Anne Fausto-Sterling argues that bones offer one indication that sex and gender blur, since bone density and development bears evidence of "a gendered division of labor, culture, and biology intertwined."[49]

The discourse of autism provides another example of the blurring of those two terms. In scientific discourse, researchers sometimes muddle sex and gender together. For example, theorists might reason from the sex ratio of autism diagnoses to theories of autism that reflect gendered norms, as is the case when autism is portrayed as somehow linked to male technological aptitude, computing, or geekiness. According to this argument, the unequal sex ratio in autism diagnosis (which is usually four to one, male to female) must mean that autism is caused by some sexed difference (such as heightened testosterone levels). Yet, as evidence for this claim, scientists point to the preponderance of gendered masculine interests among autists (such as computing, engineering, and other technical interests). In this case, scientists do not distinguish between sex and gender but, rather, subsume one into the other.

Gender, Butler reminds us, is constituted differently in different historical contexts, and it always intersects with other "modalities of discursively constituted identities" such as race, class, sexuality, region, and ethnicity.[50] In this book I examine how gender intersects with other discursively constituted factors: parenthood (maternity and paternity), expertise (especially technical, medical, and scientific expertise), occupation, social status (popularity and geekdom), and neurological conditions. It is important to note that most (but not all) of the individuals featured who speak and write about autism are white, and their characterizations therefore reflect hegemonic white constructions of gender.

Gender theorists are often set on determining how gender operates for individuals. For example, Butler emphasizes that gender is something performed in accordance with discursive norms that materialize bodies. The sociologists Candace West and Don H. Zimmerman emphasize that gender is something one does, or as "an accomplishment, an achieved property of situated conduct."[51] In this book I claim that gendered discourses circulate in part through characters that enforce norms of behavior, appearance, and interaction. Gendered characters constitute part of the discursive norms Butler describes, and they may serve as models for the accomplishment of gender described by West and Zimmerman. When autism dads write about their struggles, for example, they often confront the models of father characters that serve as norms for most men and often have to adapt those norms, reject them, or refashion them in order to perform an appropriate father character.

This book also extends research in women's rhetorics, a field of study that has traditionally sought to recover the rhetorical contributions of women throughout history. In rhetoric and composition, gender has been understood to be enacted through writing, as in Elizabeth Flynn's early text "Composing as a Woman." Scholars have also sought to understand gender as a quality presented rhetorically through language, performance, and appearance, as in Carol Mattingly's study of women rhetor's costumes in *Appropriate[Ing] Dress* and Lindal Buchanan's study of how women adapted masculine speaking styles in *Regendering Delivery*.[52] These authors and many others have established the centrality of women's rhetorical contributions and the uniqueness of the rhetorical situations they have confronted throughout history.

More recently, scholars have examined how discourses about sex and gender circulate, focusing less on particular rhetors than on arguments about gender. Rather than studying women rhetors, these writers might be described as inquiring into rhetorics of gender. In this vein, Robin Jensen's *Dirty Words: The Rhetoric of Public Sex Education, 1870–1924* discusses female educators' lobbying for sex education in the Progressive Era. Although she focuses on some individual women, Jensen also examines the gendered characters featured in sex education posters and pamphlets. Those designed for soldiers, for instance, featured two gendered characters: the temptress and the sweetheart. The temptress caricatured foreigners whom men might encounter overseas as "'evil,' sexually available women" (also known as "'hardened prostitutes,' 'Come-on Queens,' 'she-hookers,' 'Chippies,' 'Harpies,' and 'Molls'"). In contrast, American sweethearts were depicted with features such as "a lack of make-up, conservative clothing, and a submissive personality."[53] Soldiers were exhorted to consider their modest, wholesome sweethearts and to eschew the temptresses they encountered in order to avoid venereal diseases. Similarly, in *The Crimes of Womanhood* A. Cheree Carlson demonstrates how male lawyers depicted women on trial for violent crimes using specific characters, such that "virtuous women are betrayed by libertines, and innocent men are seduced by fallen women."[54] These gendered characters were deployed to prosecute and defend women in ways that squared with culturally available narratives and gendered ideologies.

Scholars have also examined how genders are established and maintained in rhetorical terms. In his book *Disciplining Gender,* John Sloop studies cases wherein public rhetorics have functioned "to reify binaristic expectations of gendered behavior."[55] For instance, in the famous case of John/Joan (a biological male who received surgical reassignment as a female after a botched circumcision and then was raised as a girl), scientific and popular texts fixated on John/Joan's gender identity and performance as either male or female, masculine or feminine. These discourses discipline gender insofar as they force individuals into distinct, gendered roles and interpret behavior through a binary, gendered lens.

This project also contributes to scholarship in the rhetoric of science, which examines how scientific discourse functions, how it persuades audiences, how it circulates among public audiences, and how even the process of scientific research reflects rhetorical dimensions.[56] In particular, I draw on insights by Keränen on the role of character in scientific argument, but my project contributes to this research, more broadly, by showing how gender matters in scientific discourse. Not only do gendered characters circulate in popular discourse about autism, but they also affect scientific knowledge and rhetoric. For this reason, this book also contributes to work in feminist science studies, which argues that gender (among other factors) influences (and often biases) scientific knowledge and that gender analysis can contribute to stronger science.[57]

In this book, then, I examine the way rhetors deploy gendered characters in discussions about autism, and in doing so, I trace a rhetorical history of gender in autism discourse. As Jessica Mudry describes it, a rhetorical history considers how "persuasive discourse has been shaped over a long period of time, and how, in the past, symbolic performances have influenced, or attempted to influence" audiences.[58] In this study, gendered characters provide a central rhetorical element to track across time, from the earliest accounts of autism in the 1940s to the present day. Gendered characters emerge throughout this history, often in keeping with the cultural preoccupations of each time period. In order to examine these characters, I follow them across rhetorical contexts, exploring how they move through and between scientific and popular constructs.[59] Indeed, it is often difficult to pin the origin of a specific character on a single text or author; instead, characters often emerge in concert from available rhetorical materials in a particular context or rhetorical culture.

Each chapter explores a different mode through which gendered characters work within a rhetorical culture. While I do discuss individual women rhetors, I also focus on how mothers have been depicted in theories about autism's causation, how fathers confront hegemonic masculinity and family roles in their writing about autism, how male computer geeks come to stand in for all autistic people, and how autistic individuals deploy gendered characters to invent alternative identities. Most often, both scientific and popular rhetorics about autism enforce a gender binary, in which stereotypical gender roles are enforced, represented, or assigned to individuals. Ironically, though, many autistic individuals write about their own understandings of gender as complex, multiple, or ambiguous—a finding that draws attention to the rhetorical construction of the binary gender system itself.

Gendered Characters in Early Autism Research

The first autism researchers relied on gendered stock characters as a means with which to distinguish autism from previously identified conditions. In the 1940s, Leo Kanner, an American who defined infantile autism (or Kanner's syndrome), and Hans Asperger, who independently published his findings in Austria, both believed autism to be hereditary. Both identified what they saw as a novel disorder, distinguishing it from existing categories of inherited mental disability such as "feeblemindedness" and "degeneracy." Coincidentally, they both used the term *autistic* to identify this new subset of children—a term they drew from Eugen Bleuler, who used it to describe the schizophrenic's withdrawal from the outside world.[60] Because they believed autism to be genetic, Kanner and Asperger scrutinized mothers and fathers for hereditary clues to its origin.

In order to establish the existence of a new childhood condition, both would have to carve out a new definition and distinguish it from competing conditions and definitions, including definitions of mental illness and intellectual disability. Kanner notes that most of the children in his original study "were at one time looked upon as feebleminded."[61] Part of his rhetorical task was to distinguish these children from that group and their description from psychiatric terms then in use for children who seemed withdrawn or emotionally disturbed, such as childhood schizophrenia, childhood psychosis, and symbiotic psychosis. The sociologist Gil Eyal has shown how experts put autism forward against these competing diagnoses to occupy the "ecological niche" between mental disability and intellectual disability.[62] In his 1943 article Kanner sought to develop that niche for autism. He begins with a claim for novelty: "Since 1938, there have come to our attention a number of children whose condition differs so markedly and uniquely from anything reported so far, that each case merits—and, I hope, will eventually receive—a detailed consideration of its fascinating peculiarities."[63] Kanner casts this condition as both new and "fascinating," making an argument for its relevance to the scientific readers of the journal.

Part of the success in differentiating autism from these other conditions lay not only in Kanner's and Asperger's initial efforts to distinguish autistic children from children deemed schizophrenic or feebleminded but also in their efforts to distinguish the *families* of autistic children via their social class, appearance, and gender. In particular, they drew on character descriptions of parents, arguing that the features they saw in a subset of children stemmed from traits found in successful middle-class parents. In rhetorical terms, they used effectio (descriptions of physical appearance) and notatio (descriptions of a character's nature) to create character sketches, or prosopographia. They used similar strategies to describe the children they examined. In so doing, they demarcated both parents and children as being from a class background and lineage superior to that of the feebleminded, who were usually depicted as poor, slovenly, and dimwitted.

Both researchers may have been eager to distinguish autism from feeblemindedness because the latter was linked to eugenic practices including sterilization in the United States and outright murder in Eastern Europe, where eugenic theories advanced alongside the growing Nazi movement in Germany. The Germans founded the Kaiser Wilhelm Institute for Anthropology, Human Heredity, and Eugenics in 1927, and scientists explored theories of "racial hygiene" that supported the Nazi regime.[64] German eugenic researchers sought out the genetic influence on mental illness and disability as well, an obsession that led to some bizarre research studies, including one that involved analyzing handprints of children and teenagers to look for signs of neurological difference in the papillary lines.[65] Tragically, the Nazi concern with mental conditions led to the Law on the Prevention of Genetically Deficient Progeny, which authorized the sterilization of more than 400,000 individuals (including those in annexed areas) and, eventually, the mass murder of thousands.[66] Those subjected to sterilization included individuals with "congenital feeble-mindedness," "manic depressive insanity," "serious alcoholism," and hereditary blindness, deafness, and epilepsy, as well as individuals who did not graduate high school, did not have a job, or had an illegitimate child.[67] Pursuant to this law, then, individuals from many different groups were rhetorically linked as exemplars of degeneracy.

Asperger did not espouse such theories, but they clearly shaped the context in which he lived. Austria was annexed to Nazi Germany in 1938, and the Law on the Prevention of Genetically Deficient Progeny was applied there as well. More than six thousand Austrians were forcibly sterilized. In 1939 euthanasia replaced sterilization, leading to the deaths of more than twenty-five thousand.[68] Doctors and midwives were ordered to report cases of physical and mental disabilities to the authorities. In Vienna alone more than 976 children were murdered, often starved or frozen to death, and then subjected to autopsies to seek the causes of mental disability.[69] Establishing Asperger's syndrome as a separate disorder would have had the benefit of cordoning off those individuals from the broader category of the feebleminded, who were subjected to these horrific outcomes.

Kanner may have had similar motivations. In the mid-nineteenth century, American physicians began to advocate sterilization in order to prevent the inheritance of "degeneracy," a term they used to refer to "anyone who exhibited diminished mental, moral, or sexual capacities."[70] They gained support from biologists in the twentieth century, when the rediscovery of Mendelian genetics coupled with evolutionary theory sparked widespread interest in eugenics. In his history of eugenics in the United States, Mark A. Largent notes that "it is difficult to find many early-twentieth-century American biologists who were not advocates of eugenics in some form or another" and that they were supported by "politicians, social activists, philanthropists, educators, and assorted do-gooders, racists, and utopians."[71] More than sixty-three thousand people had been sterilized in the United States by 1960, and sterilization laws were passed in two-thirds of the states.[72]

The American Association for the Study of the Feeble-Minded (AASFM) categorized the feebleminded into three grades: "idiots," "imbeciles," and "morons."[73] These terms were assigned to individuals on the basis of their performance on the newly developed intelligence tests, with *idiots* being used for those with the lowest mental age (that of a one- or two-year-old) and *morons* for the highest level in the group (those with a mental age between eight and twelve).[74] However, the AASFM indicated that intelligence metrics, alone, did not completely capture what was meant by the term *feebleminded,* since the term was to be used "generically to include all degrees of mental defect due to arrested or imperfect development as a result of which the person so effected [*sic*] is incapable of competing on equal terms with his normal fellows or managing himself or his affairs with ordinary prudence."[75] Feeble-mindedness had a social and economic dimension as well, since those who could not support themselves financially or demonstrate prudence in other areas of life could be slotted into that category. To make the link more explicit, in a 1914 report the Eugenics Record Office listed ten "cacogenic varieties" that were targets for eugenic measures, includ-ing, alongside the "feeble-minded class," the "pauper," "inebriate," and "criminalistic" classes as well as the "insane," the "epileptic," the "de-formed," and so on.[76] Thus, proponents of eugenics used vocabulary that linked these neurological and physical differences with social and moral conditions, namely, criminality and poverty, creating characters (or caricatures) of feebleminded individuals.

These characters were often gendered. Licia Carlson shows that females with intellectual disabilities (ID) came to stand in for those disabilities as a whole, especially when the category of "moral imbecil-ity" emerged after the 1880s. For females, moral imbecility included "ability to bear illegitimate children" and other sexual or reproductive concerns. Women deemed feebleminded were portrayed as disease carriers, as sexually prolific, and as threats to the purity of the race.[77] Notwithstanding, women have also been positioned as caregivers for people with ID, Carlson notes, owing to their supposed natural ability to care for others. Some institutions for people with ID replicated a patriarchal family structure, with a male superintendent, female ma-tron and attendants, and inmates positioned as children. In some cases, female inmates were trained to care for other inmates.[78] Paradoxically, though, women were also portrayed as responsible for feebleminded-ness because of either their genetic inferiority or their poor parenting skills[79]—a trend we shall find in the case of autism, as well.

Intellectual disability also intersected with the masculine gender. The term "moral imbecile" in fact replaced an earlier term, "moral idiot," which was typically associated with males. According to the historian of social policy James W. Trent, accounts of idiocy often featured boys who had improved under strict training and supervision and who would after-ward be able to work outside the institution.[80] The emphasis on training for employment favored males, although some accounts also mentioned the suitability of feebleminded girls for domestic employment.

The descriptions in nineteenth- and early twentieth-century accounts seem to suggest that at least some of the individuals then categorized as feebleminded might today be considered autistic. In his 1858 account of children at the Pennsylvania Training School for Feeble-Minded Children, Isaac Newton Kerlin describes several children who had speech difficulties, avoided eye contact, and preferred to play alone, yet also demonstrated "*intelligent thought*," excelled at arranging "geometric boards" and blocks, and showed excellent visual acuity.[81]

Those singled out as exemplars of the feebleminded differed from those later represented as exemplars of autism, however, in that the latter were usually individuals from lower social classes, and they were represented verbally and visually with commonplaces that signified poverty and degeneracy—topoi that related to appearance, class, and gender. To take one example, in 1912, Henry Herbert Goddard published a study of a single family, producing a series of character sketches of its members. Titled "The Kallikak Family: A Study in the Heredity of Feeble-Mindedness," the report was based on qualitative data gathered by a team of researchers, many of them women, who tracked down genealogical data and then conducted site visits and interviews with 480 impoverished descendants of one Martin Kallikak Jr. (a pseudonym). The researchers determined that 143 of those 480 descendants were feebleminded.[82] On the basis of his genealogical work, Goddard argues that one branch of the family possessed "good English blood" but that in "an unguarded moment" Kallikak's father met a "feebleminded girl" and sired "a line of mental defectives that is truly appalling," a line that began with Martin Kallikak Jr.[83]

In the report, Goddard repeatedly describes members of the Kallikak family using detailed sketches of characters (prosopographia). Goddard drew on commonplaces (topoi) of physical appearance, or effectio, that he associated with the feebleminded. In the case of one family, he writes that the children "stood about with drooping jaws and the unmistakable look of the feeble-minded."[84] Another group of individuals had a "fixed, stupid stare."[85] In these descriptions the faces of Kallikak family members were read for signs of feeblemindedness or degeneracy, and some features—eyes, jaws—were singled out, especially, as symbols of mental disability.[86] Since Goddard himself did not witness these family members but relied on the reports of his field researchers, it is quite possible that his verbal descriptors also depended in part on rhetorical conventions in the depiction of mental illness.[87]

In addition to reading mental disability into physiognomy, Goddard described the Kallikak family members' material conditions: clothing, cleanliness, furniture, and the homes themselves were read as stigmata of mental disability. Children in one family were described as "scantily clad and with shoes that would barely hold together."[88] One woman answered the door for a researcher wearing "tawdry rags, her hair unkempt, her face streaked with black, while on the floor two dirty, half-naked children were rolling."[89] In another home, the researcher found a room containing "a few chairs and a bed, the latter without any washable covering and filthy beyond description. There was no fire, and both mother and babies were thinly clad."[90] In another site, "heaps of junk . . . cluttered the room."[91] These material conditions actually index social class, not mental disability per se. But, in Goddard's formulation, poverty and feeblemindedness were so closely associated that the condition of Kallikak family homes and the clothing they wore were taken as evidence of mental disability.

Although Goddard's report describes male and female members of the family, females were often depicted as being "sexually immoral" (Goddard identified thirty-three such individuals, either by virtue of being prostitutes or by the presence of illegitimate children, as was the case with Jemima and Old Moll, to name two.)[92] (Male members were occasionally called "sexually immoral," although it was not clear from the report how that diagnosis was made.) According to the cultural historian Patrick McDonagh, the representation of feebleminded women as sexually "undisciplined" is a "historically resilient" construct, appearing across many cultural locations and time periods.[93] Allison C. Carey notes that the character of the feebleminded woman was represented as "without the ability to reason, unable to protect herself, and guided purely by her emotions, uncontrolled sexuality, and animal instinct."[94] The association between feeblemindedness and sexual immorality led to a paternalistic attitude that females, especially, should be either institutionalized or raised by "good families" in order to protect them from sexual depravity.

In contrast, male members of the Kallikak family are most often portrayed as financially irresponsible—also a tradition McDonagh finds across cultures and time periods but one that he considers rooted in the cultural emphasis on men's "participation in the world of work and commerce."[95] The originator of the family, Martin Kallikak Jr. (nicknamed "Old Horror"), was "always unwashed and drunk. At election time, he never failed to appear in somebody's cast-off clothing, ready to vote, for the price of a drink, the donor's ticket."[96] While Kallikak women are often described as sexually immoral or as incompetent mothers, then, Kallikak men are depicted as drunkards and deadbeats. In both cases, these feebleminded individuals are marked by appearance, class, and gender.

Early reports such as Goddard's illustrate some of the stock characters used to describe the feebleminded. To set autism apart, Kanner and Asperger needed a new set of stock characters. Kanner's "Autistic Disturbances of Affective Contact" was published in 1943 in the journal *Nervous Child*. Asperger published "'Autistic Psychopathy' in Childhood" in 1944, although the text was not translated into English until 1980. There was little communication between researchers in Austria and the United States in the 1940s.[97] For this reason, we cannot assume any vectors of influence between the two, nor can we consider their rhetorical situations as exactly equivalent. Yet I consider both articles here in order to highlight that Kanner and Asperger both used gendered characters to differentiate autism from other diagnoses that were, in the 1940s, being used to justify sterilization, institutionalization, and murder of children deemed feebleminded. They described the profile of the autistic child using similar rhetorical appeals and a similar rhetorical structure: prosopographia.

Whereas Goddard had deployed visual description to associate Kallikak family members with topoi of intellectual disability, Kanner and Asperger described their patients as the healthy, good-looking, and well-cared-for sons and daughters of upstanding citizens. Kanner describes the children in question as "endowed with good *cognitive potentialities*," with "strikingly intelligent physiognomies" and faces that "give the impression of *serious-mindedness*."[98] Using effectio, Kanner describes one child, Paul, as a "slender, well built, attractive child, whose face looked intelligent and animated." In contrast to the feebleminded with their slack jaws and dull eyes, Kanner's Virginia is "a tall, slender, very neatly dressed 11-year-old girl," and Charles was a "well developed, intelligent-looking boy." Another boy, Herbert, "showed a remarkably intelligent physiognomy and good motor coordination."[99] These descriptions help constitute a new character type that could, in part, be distinguished from feeblemindedness by differences in physical appearance.

As was the case with depictions such as that of the Kallikak family, in Kanner's article appearance is a proxy for class. Take, for instance, Kanner's patient Frederick, born in 1936, who grew up with his mother, a college graduate and former director of secretarial studies for a girl's school, and his father, also a college graduate and a plant pathologist. His family tree featured a medical missionary, a best-selling author, a singer, a writer for adventure magazines, and a painter.[100] Frederick was one of the eleven patients Kanner originally identified in 1943, and this pedigree (and that of Kanner's other exemplars) led Kanner to note that perhaps there was something particular about autism that targeted the middle class.

In contrast with the unemployed, criminalistic parents profiled in Goddard's study, the parents in Kanner's study are well-educated, upstanding middle-class citizens. Instead of painting them as lascivious or louche, Kanner uses descriptions of parents' personalities (notatio) to depict them as obsessive, anxious, or introverted. For instance, he observes that the mother of one patient, Richard M., "brought with her copious notes that indicated obsessive preoccupation with details and a tendency to read all sorts of peculiar interpretations into the child's performances."[101] The father of Donald is described as a "successful, meticulous, hard-working lawyer who has had two 'breakdowns' under strain of work," as a hypochondriac who took doctors' orders very seriously, and as somewhat absent-minded: "When he walks down the street, he is so absorbed in thinking that he sees nothing and nobody and cannot remember anything about the walk."[102] Kanner interprets these parents' characteristics as signs of "a great deal of obsessiveness," classified here as evidence of a genetic link rather than a psychological influence on the child.[103] Kanner also notes that most of the patients he studied had "highly intelligent parents"[104]—they included a psychiatrist, a lawyer, a chemist, a plant pathologist, a physician, and a psychologist. In his careful descriptions, Kanner builds up detail. After reading eleven examples, the reader is led to accept the claim that autism seems somehow linked to intelligence and upper middle social class. Kanner uses prosopographia, then, to offer a new characterization of these parents.

Asperger employs similar strategies. In his 1944 account, he presents case studies of four boys he examined at the University Pediatric Clinic in Vienna. He describes the first boy, Fritz, as the latest in a long line of eccentrics on his mother's side, which included "one of the greatest Austrian poets" as well as a number of "mad-genius[es]" or "intellectuals."[105] Asperger notes: "The mother herself was very similar to the boy. This similarity was particularly striking given that she was a woman, since, in general, one would expect a higher degree of intuitive social adaptation in women, more emotion than intellect."[106] Like Kanner, he employs prosopographia to help his readers imagine the kind of person in question—a strange loner with an odd demeanor. This comment also implies that gender mattered in Asperger's interpretations of parents; mothers who demonstrated odd social behaviors were not only deviating from social norms but from gender norms. Meanwhile, the boy's father is described as "a withdrawn and reticent man who did not give much away about himself," was "extremely correct and pedantic," and "kept more than usual distance."[107] In Asperger's account, like Kanner's, both parents are described as a new kind of character: intelligent and absent-minded, eccentric and anxious, obsessive and withdrawn. Asperger's character sketches contribute to the reader's acceptance of this new condition, one that could be associated with a different class of parents.

Kanner's and Asperger's characters were also cast in different gender roles from those of the feebleminded. Neither figured his young cases as sexually immoral or fiscally irresponsible. While Kanner did not remark on the gender ratio among his cases (eight boys to three girls), Asperger noted that the condition he observed seemed to represent an "extreme variant of male intelligence."[108] Accordingly, autism came to be represented in both works by innocent, middle-class boys, the scions of intelligent, professional fathers and cold, obsessive mothers—a far cry from the poverty-stricken ragamuffins depicted in earlier studies of the "feebleminded." In the ensuing years, this depiction lent support to psychoanalytic theories premised on the mother-son relationship, to theories suggesting that autistic children represented the results of nerd in-breeding, and to the involvement of middle- and upper-middle-class parents in discussions about autism. The chapters that follow explore how this cast of characters emerges from autism discourse and the broader rhetorical culture.

Methodologies

This book draws on research in the areas of feminist science studies, cultural and rhetorical studies of medicine, and disability studies, all of which seek to understand how language shapes our conceptions of health and wellness. The area of feminist science studies demonstrates that gender matters for the practice of science and the knowledge claims it produces. Researchers have considered, first, how and why it is that women have been historically underrepresented in science,[109] second, how the very character of "scientist," especially the ideal of objectivity, has been defined in contradistinction to that of "woman,"[110] and third, how both of these factors, combined with cultural factors, result in scientific theories or knowledge claims that are biased by gender.[111] I examined the first of these areas in my book *Science on the Home Front,* where I considered how genres of scientific writing entrained women to a system that did not always favor their advancement or their unique perspectives. This work examines the second and third areas of feminist science studies.

Scholars including Evelyn Fox Keller and Donna Haraway have shown that, historically speaking, science was defined according to values associated with masculinity (objectivity, disinterestedness, reason) whereas values linked with femininity (subjectivity, bias, emotion) were excluded. Women were barred from science (mostly) because they were associated with these undesirable values. By defining science in this way, male scientists claimed authority. Keller writes that "the sexual division of emotional and intellectual labor has provided a readily available and much relied upon tool for bolstering the particular claims that science makes to a univocal and hence absolute epistemic authority—not only in the contest between scientists and nonscientists, but equally, in contests internal to science."[112] Part of the struggle I track in this book involves attempts by female nonscientists—namely, mothers—to gain epistemic authority over their children's condition.

Others scholars assert that gendered metaphors shape scientific discourse and knowledge. For instance, in an influential essay Emily Martin examines how traditional scientific descriptions of conception gendered eggs and sperm, positioning eggs as passive recipients of the active, aggressive sperm. They are personified as stereotyped feminine and masculine characters.[113] Drawing on this work, I argue that gendered characters have shaped scientific investigations into autism, often resulting in inaccurate characterizations of autism and its causes.

I also draw on insights from work in rhetorical and cultural studies of medicine that examines women's experiences with medicine and the gendering of illness. Scholarship in this field has long stressed that health and medicine have rhetorical dimensions, following the literary theorist Susan Sontag's preeminent book *Illness as Metaphor.* Sontag writes that consumption became associated with femininity in the nineteenth century, such that "the tubercular look . . . became more and more the ideal look for women" since it symbolized key feminine qualities of passivity, vulnerability, and sensitivity.[114] More recently, others have examined how

HIV/AIDS has been socially constructed as a gendered illness, often in ways that characterize patients as gay men, prostitutes, and intravenous drug users, thereby neglecting others, such as heterosexual men and women.[115] These studies indicate that representations and experiences of illness intersect with gender and that illnesses are often represented by gendered characters. This insight applies to autism, as well, which is primarily depicted as a condition affecting male children. Women and girls (along with adults in general) tend to be elided. Part of my task in this book is to understand how autism has come to be associated so strongly not only with males but also with masculinity, especially by connecting autism with high technology culture.

I extend these analyses by taking a historical and rhetorical approach and by focusing on gendered characters employed in public debates about theories concerning autism: what it is, what causes it, and how it affects people's lives. My aim is to examine why particular characterizations of autism and gender emerged in particular historical moments, and I draw on scientific accounts as well as those by parents, health practitioners, and autistic people. Throughout, I seek to show why certain kinds of gendered characters and characterizations have been persuasive, in part by connecting discussions of autism to cultural discourses about parenting, gender, economics, technology, and the like.

For this I use key insights from disability studies, which, according to Siebers, examines "the social meanings, symbols, and stigmas attached to disability identity and asks how they relate to enforced systems of exclusion and oppression."[116] Disability theorists have argued that disabilities are socially produced, in part through the barriers and hindrances we construct in social and built environments, and that disabilities are not static, pre-existing conditions but social constructions whose meanings change across time and place. James W. Trent Jr. contends that the meaning of the term *mental retardation* (no longer considered an appropriate term) varied with the social, institutional, and administrative context in which it was used.[117] Intellectual disability, he continues, has been viewed variously as "a disorder of the senses, a moral flaw, a medical disease, a mental deficiency, a menace to the social fabric, and finally as mental retardation."[118] Disability is also discursively constructed. Tanya Titchkosky argues that "words on disability are themselves a doing, are themselves a way of knowing; such words reside among us and help to make our fate as embodied beings." Most often, Titchkosky claims, disability is represented as a problem to be surmounted, rather than a natural part of human variation.[119] The language used to describe disability might be internalized in individuals, materialized in physical spaces, or institutionalized in the practices of psychiatric, educational, and legal discourse. Such is the case for autism, a neurological condition that is often presented as a crisis, a disaster, or a sentence to a life of devastating isolation. The disability studies scholar Bill Rocque argues that "the insistence on pathological meanings of ASD [Autism Spectrum Disorder]—as producing tragic isolation, for instance—creates the need for the kind of authoritative truth claims that science generally makes."[120] Framing autism in this way, as a mystery or a threat, tends to support intensive behavioral therapies, mandate insurance coverage of those therapies, and authorize attempts to gain more funding for special education. How we speak and write about autism matters in important ways to all concerned.

Representations of autism also matter because they tend to support problematic narratives that position it as something to be overcome or beaten, rather than a neurological difference that can be recognized and even celebrated. The autistic individuals who are most often featured in popular rhetoric are those who have "overcome" autism to become successful artists, professors, or performers (such as Temple Grandin, the well-known animal science professor and author) or as autistic savants, characters who are portrayed as "profoundly autistic" but who possess unusual talents, such as the artist Steven Wiltshire or Kim Peek, the man who inspired the character Raymond Babbitt in the film *Rain Man*. In this way, portrayals of autism in popular media echo tendencies in portrayals of people with disabilities more generally. In general, popular media tend to favor portrayals of individuals who have overcome their disabilities through tremendous force of will, such as the sprinter Oscar Pistorius, who used two prosthetic legs but recorded times rivaling those of top nondisabled sprinters, or geniuses like Stephen Hawking, who has motor neurone disease and uses a wheelchair but has made major scientific discoveries. Disability studies scholars and advocates call such individuals "super-crips"— people who are celebrated for surmounting disabilities but who do so by creating an impossibly high standard for other people with disabilities. The *but* in these sentences reflects the logic of super-crip narratives—these individuals have accomplished major achievements despite their disabilities, not because of them. In some cases, though, autistic individuals are depicted as achieving phenomenal feats *because* of their neurological differences, as is the case with savants.

Disability advocates resent these "super-crip" narratives because they send the message that people with disabilities are valued only if they accomplish great things or if they possess remarkable skills. Further, as Joseph P. Shapiro has indicated, these depictions promote an individualistic, medicalized model of disability rather than a social one, since "the overcoming is not connected to facing a societal barrier; the individual is not seen as taking part in any larger civil rights or social movement of people with disabilities."[121] The autistic super-crip is one rhetorically constructed character that is common in fictional and nonfictional accounts of the condition.

Although I point out such constructions throughout this book, I am particularly interested in the gendered nature of constructions of disabilities, especially intellectual disability and mental illness. The area of feminist disability studies examines what Rosemarie Garland-Thomson refers to as "gendering of disability—and th[e] disabling of gender."[122] For instance, Diane Price Herndl has examined how the character of the invalid woman circulates in literary texts from 1840 to 1940, drawing on and encouraging a "cult of female frailty" that emphasized characterizations of women as delicate and susceptible to illness.[123] The historian Daniel J. Wilson points out that, in the 1950s, polio became associated with masculine characters such as the warrior or athlete, characters that helped some to "recover maximum physical function and to make their way in an often hostile world" but also served to diminish those who did not fully recover.[124] It is in this vein that I examine how characters related to autism emerge and circulate, and to what effect, from the 1940s onward.

Much of the work on which I draw relates to intellectual disability. Yet autism does not fit easily among the categories of ID. Though some autistic individuals are also diagnosed as intellectually disabled, many score within or above the normal range on standardized tests of intelligence. Furthermore, some researchers argue that these tests fail to capture the true intelligence of autistic individuals, because those tests rely on verbal abilities. Whe, Isabelle Soulières, Michelle Dawson, Morton Ann Gernsbacher, and Laurent Mottron deployed an alternative test for intelligence (Raven's Matrices, which does not place as many demands on receptive language skills), they found that autistic individuals' intelligence scores increased dramatically.[125] For this reason, I use scholarship on ID when it helps illuminate the rhetorical function of discourse about autism, but I do not subscribe to the view that autism can be considered, straightforwardly, an ID. Instead, autism can coincide with ID, but perhaps in ways that are more complex than is indicated by IQ tests.

If anything, gendered characterizations of autism often emphasize superior intelligence, especially in figurations of the male computer geek as typical of Asperger's syndrome. Professed "Aspie" characters are usually depicted as a professionally successful yet socially inept geek or nerd. Examples include the character of Sheldon Cooper on the television show *The Big Bang Theory* or Temperance Brennan on *Bones*. Cooper is a theoretical physicist, Brennan a renowned forensic anthropologist. Both characters are portrayed as lacking in fundamental social skills—they are (at least initially) uninterested in romantic relationships, they do not understand irony or sarcasm, and they tend to speak in a pedantic monotone. Brennan is a female character, but her portrayal on the show often emphasizes masculine traits such as a matter-of-fact, unromantic view of sex or a lack of interest in typically feminine activities such as gossip (despite her stylish wardrobe of tailored trench coats and funky necklaces).

Gender also becomes relevant when the focus extends beyond depictions of autistic individuals to those who speak on their behalf—parents, doctors, therapists, caregivers, and other "experts"—through what Cynthia Lewiecki-Wilson calls "mediated rhetoricity." The term refers to "language used for the benefit of the disabled person that is (co)-constructed by parents, advocates, and/or committed caregivers."[126] In the competition to speak for the autistic individual, gendered positions become important conveyors of authority as mothers, fathers, and experts enter the fray.

As Linda Martín Alcoff has argued, "the practice of privileged persons speaking for or on behalf of less privileged persons has actually resulted (in many cases) in increasing or reinforcing the oppression of the group spoken for."[127] Unfortunately, this mediated rhetoricity becomes possible only because autistic people have largely been constructed as lacking in rhetorical agency, either because they are depicted as children or because they are depicted as silent, nonverbal, or intellectually disabled. Although some have difficulty communicating, many others do so effectively through a range of media, whether in traditional verbal or print formats or through tools such as facilitated typing or speech software.

The problem of rhetorical sovereignty for autistic individuals is exacerbated by the characterization of autism as a condition affecting children. In their study of popular representations of autism, Stevenson,

Harp, and Gernsbacher found that children were featured on 95 percent of home pages for parent-run autism associations, in 90 percent of fictional books, and in 68 percent of films or television programs. Children also dominated news articles about autism, outnumbering articles featuring autistic adults by a factor of four to one.[128] These depictions contribute to a tendency to devalue the rhetorical agency of autistic people.

Apart from fictional depictions, though, autistic individuals may actually be dismissed as too high-functioning, as "shiny Aspies" unable to speak for or understand "low-functioning" autistics, or as individuals lacking in empathy or audience awareness. Yergeau writes about this experience on her blog, Aspie Rhetor: "I have gotten used to not existing, rhetorically speaking. I will say something about autism, and someone will assert that nothing I've said matters or applies to anything. Because I'm self-centered. Because I don't have the capacity to intuit other minds or understand others' life experiences. Because it's just my autism talking."[129] The characters of the autistic child and the Aspie both make rhetorical participation difficult for actual autistics seeking to engage in debates about autism.

Because they are disempowered rhetorically, autistic people have struggled to make their voices heard in the fervent debates about autism that I examine. Accordingly, whenever possible I have sought to incorporate perspectives of autistic people throughout the text, while also striving not to give the impression that there is a single, agreed-upon stance of the "autistic community" on any one issue.

By focusing on gender, I have paid less attention to other issues about autism and rhetoric that interest me, such as how autistic rhetorical practices might enrich rhetorical theory and how, as educators, we might challenge our pedagogies to better support autistic students and help develop their abilities.[130] I have also paid limited attention to how and why autism is deployed as a rhetorical resource in debates over the environment, health, and science. All of these projects certainly merit attention from scholars interested in autism.

Outline of Chapters

The first chapter, "Interpreting Gender: Refrigerator Mothers," explores how the gendered character of the refrigerator mother offered an interpretive lens through which experts viewed autism when it was first identified as a unique disorder. I examine accounts from the World

War II era of "maternal deprivation," popular childrearing handbooks, and advice columns that generated the character of the absent or cold mother, one that autism researchers such as the notorious Bruno Bettelheim drew upon to theorize causes of autism. Character sketches of these early "autism mothers" emerged from a set of topoi about mothers in the 1960s and were found lacking compared to the standard of a warm, devoted, and loving mother. This chapter shows that typified gendered characters can be interpreted as explanations for autism, thereby functioning as heuristics for scientific theorizing. It then considers the ways mothers began to counter this character and construct a new one that would grant them greater epistemic authority.

Chapter 2, "Performing Gender: Mother Warriors," deals with individuals' performance of gendered characters in more recent debates about vaccines and autism. Drawing on memoirs and congressional testimony, I argue that mothers engaged in these debates perform traditional feminine characters in order to claim epistemic authority over their children's diagnosis and treatment and to argue against the scientific establishment, using character as an element of conformatio, or as support for a cause. Mothers who actively argue for increased research funding or for specific theories of autism's etiology (including vaccines) draw on topoi of experiential knowledge, caregiving, and maternal instinct, sometimes embracing the character of mother warrior or autism mother. They are countered by experts, most often males, who take on the character of the good doctor or father figure to argue against the vaccine theory. In books and magazine columns, they, too, perform a role to ground their arguments. This chapter shows how gendered characters can be used for strategic persuasive effects. These performances involve actions that signal a specific gender expression or performance, including choice of dress, makeup, and styling as well as words.

Chapter 3, "Presenting Gender: Computer Geeks," offers a rhetorical history of the male computer geeks, engineers, and other high-tech types who came to epitomize autism in the late 1990s. This chapter employs rhetorical analysis of key texts, including Simon Baron-Cohen's book *The Essential Difference*, a *Wired* magazine article titled "Silicon Valley Syndrome," and a series of articles diagnosing Silicon Valley titans such as Mark Zuckerberg and Bill Gates as autistic by drawing on topoi of technology, geekdom, and cognitive capitalism, or the "knowledge economy." I study how this character emerged in autism discourse and why it continues to circulate in discussions of high technology. As presented, gendered characters help make a cultural phenomenon seem livelier and more immediate to readers, often in ways that stereotype people (in this case, autistic people) in order to make a larger rhetorical point.

To a certain extent, rhetors can rehearse new gendered characters through their language. Chapter 4, "Rehearsing Gender: Autism Dads," discusses "autism dads" who write about their children. By analyzing memoirs written by several fathers of autistic children, I show how fathers rehearse topoi related to fatherhood, masculinity, the family as an institution, and their professional or disciplinary identities in order to rhetorically constitute roles for themselves.

Although fathers refigure available characterizations of fatherhood, few reject that role entirely. The final chapter, "Inventing Gender: Neurodiverse Characters," shows how individuals may invent alternative gendered identities from available gender topoi. Drawing on memoirs by Donna Williams and Dawn Prince-Hughes, along with blogs and online forum posts, reveals that autistic individuals offer alternative understandings of gender, using and combining disidentificatory or idiosyncratic terms such as *nongendered* and *third gender* or combining terms such as *trans, gay, lesbian, bisexual,* and *androgyne*. As the gender scholar Myra J. Hird notes, the experiences of transsexual and transgendered individuals, in particular, can "reveal the regulatory mechanisms through which sexual difference is enforced" at the same time as they might "disturb the infallibility of the binary" of male-female or masculine-feminine.[131] In a similar way, I argue that when autistic individuals write about feeling nongendered or ungendered, they contest hegemonic genders and develop new types of gendered characters with which to present themselves and their experiences. I illustrate that genders can be invented using available terms, in that some autistic individuals employ a gender copia, or multiplicity of gendered topoi, to understand themselves and their roles in the world.

In each chapter, I examine how these gendered characters show up in scientific discourse, including articles, handbooks, and outreach materials for parents. This analysis shows not only where these gendered characters come from, and how they circulate, but also why they matter for scientific research and practice. That they *do* matter is the fundamental insight of this book.

CHAPTER 1

Interpreting Gender

Refrigerator Mothers

June Francis was a refrigerator mother. When her son was diagnosed with autism in the 1950s, she was told that she "had not connected or bonded with the child because of inability to properly relate to the child." The doctors she consulted prescribed psychological therapy—for her, not her son. "I couldn't quite see how that could happen," she states in a documentary called *Refrigerator Mothers*. "But here's someone of authority saying that it had happened."[1]

In the 1950s and 1960s, shortly after Leo Kanner first identified autism as a unique psychological condition, experts drew upon psychoanalytic theories to explain the apparent detachment of autistic children from their parents. One particularly notorious expert was Bruno Bettelheim, a survivor of the Nazi holocaust who operated as a child psychiatrist using fraudulent credentials. In his book *The Empty Fortress* and in numerous columns and television appearances, Bettelheim insisted that cold, emotionless mothers could provoke an autistic response in their children. Despite his questionable credibility, Bettelheim became a minor celebrity and spokesperson for autistic children, claiming that he could effectively treat them using the psychoanalytic methods he used at the residential Sonia Shankman Orthogenic School in Chicago. Bettelheim has since been widely condemned for the damage he caused to children and to parents and for the false image he helped generate of autism as a child's withdrawal from uncaring or cold parents. The most thorough critique of Bettelheim is by Richard Pollak. In *The Creation of Dr. B.* Pollak reveals that Bettelheim fabricated both his credentials and the results he claimed for his methods in treating autism.[2]

This chapter examines the reasons why Bettelheim's theories became so influential despite these fabrications. One explanation for this phenomenon centers on Bettelheim as a particularly persuasive figure. In this view, the refrigerator mother theory was a hoax, and a rhetorically savvy charlatan had hoodwinked unsuspecting doctors and parents into accepting it. Katherine DeMaria Severson, Denise Jodlowski, and James Arnt Aune claim that Bettelheim used "clever" rhetorical strategies to persuade popular audiences of this theory despite his "shoddy" science.[3] Similarly, Roy Richard Grinker argues that, while other theories about autism were in play during this time period, Bettelheim was "simply too good a writer, and with his Viennese accent—the sign of an authentic expert in psychology—too good a self promoter" for his theories not to take hold.[4] Yet pinning the circulation and persuasiveness of the refrigerator mother entirely on Bettelheim does not fully explain why he was so readily believed or why other psychologists supported similar theories. After all, the term *refrigerator mother* stems from a statement made by Kanner, not Bettelheim, and similar theories of parental causation were applied to an array of childhood disorders, not just autism.[5]

Rather than locating the popularity of Bettelheim's theory solely in his rhetorical prowess, in this chapter I examine the rhetorical characters that gave it persuasive power. I argue that Bettelheim's theory of autism was convincing because it drew on extant characterizations of cold, emotionless mothers and the narrative of maternal deprivation, in which a child deprived of a mother's presence or affection could develop psychological problems.

Theories of autism premised on this hypothesis were persuasive because they drew on a set of culturally available topoi. The commonplace of the absent, anxious, or cold mother became a heuristic through which Bettelheim and other experts could interpret autism. I first examine some of the scientific and popular sources of those topoi and show how they informed theories of autism from the 1940s to the 1960s. I then discuss the ways mothers countered the figure of the refrigerator mother. By interpreting their characters differently, mothers found an alternative position from which to argue. Rather than accepting the guilt and blame placed upon them by this theory, mothers took on the character of heroines and saviors of their children. In doing so, they configured their children, reciprocally, as damsels in distress—vulnerable figures that only mothers could save. Finally, I consider how the character of the refrigerator mother continues to haunt some contemporary autism research, especially research into parent-child interactions, bonding, stress, and attachment.

Interpreting Mothers

In an article in a 1961 *Saturday Evening Post*, Rosalind C. Oppenheim offered her story as the mother of a nonverbal son, Ethan, who was diagnosed with autism as a toddler. Faced with changes in her son's behavior, she cast about for explanations, especially because her son seemed to have been developing normally until he was two years old. Oppenheim wonders whether Ethan changed after she was hospitalized for a few days after a miscarriage: "Perhaps it was this enforced separation from me that triggered the change in Ethan that followed—we will never know."[6] Like many other mothers whose children were diagnosed with autism in the 1950s and 1960s, she questioned her own contributions to Ethan's condition. Mothers, after all, were depicted as anxious and controlling or cold and unaffectionate, and according to psychoanalytic theory, their personality could severely affect their children's emotional development. This view is most commonly attributed to Bettelheim.

Bettelheim's theories of autism did not necessarily posit that these mothers caused their child's condition. Notably, he points out that, while "the mother's pathology is often severe" and may offer "a fascinating example of abnormal relations," it does not follow that the mother was to blame.[7] Instead, for Bettelheim, it was more apt to say that the child's reaction to the mother, and the mother's reaction to the child's reaction, can lead to autism. In other words, it is the relationship between the two that is at issue. Furthermore, Bettelheim argues that "the figure of the destructive mother . . . is the creation of the child's imagination, through an imagining that has its source in reality, namely the destructive intents of the mothering person."[8] These caveats do not absolve Bettelheim, but they demonstrate that his view of the mother-child relationship is somewhat less rigid than is often supposed. Also, *refrigerator mother* was not a term he used. Instead, it took on force owing to the rhetorical context within which it emerged. It became aligned with previous descriptions of the character of the bad mother, the anxious mother, or the ineffective mother that had been circulating decades earlier and continued to hold sway in the 1960s.

In *The Empty Fortress* Bettelheim offers extended case studies of three of the children under his care: Laurie, Marcia, and Joey. In each case he describes the parents, especially the mothers, using topoi drawn from the rhetorical culture of America in the years following World War II. This section first examines the topoi Bettelheim used to construct the rhetorical character of the autism mother, and then considers some of the sources of those topoi and how they were deployed in the rhetorical culture of the 1930s to the 1950s.

BETTELHEIM'S CHARACTERS

Bettelheim describes all of the mothers in his case studies as anxious, with emotional problems that began before their children were born. He describes Laurie's mother as an unhappy woman who underwent a nervous breakdown after her first marriage ended in divorce.[9] Marcia's mother's difficulties, he contends, stemmed from a troublesome childhood in which she assumed responsibility for the family at the age of eleven, after the death of her father. She "felt a great deal of resentment at being a girl, growing into a woman" and became severely depressed after the death of her first husband, who was killed in action in World War II.[10] Joey's mother had had a "stormy" adolescence, including periods of truancy and psychological troubles. Like Marcia's mother, Joey's mother lost her first love in the war and suffered emotionally as a result.[11] It is difficult to ascertain whether the mothers in question would describe their earlier experiences in this manner. In each case study, then, Bettelheim interprets information gleaned from interviews as evidence of emotional instability or anxiety. His character descriptions form part of his rhetorical strategy of conformatio, as evidence to support his authority and claims. While the fathers in question are sometimes also read as anxious or emotionally volatile, those features are read as more significant in the mother, perhaps because of a longstanding history portraying women as psychologically vulnerable. Emotional instability and anxiety become interpretive topoi Bettelheim uses to characterize the mothers in his study.

Another topos in these case studies is the mother's dissatisfaction with marriage. In all three, the parents married shortly after World War II, while on the rebound from an earlier marriage that ended in divorce (in Laurie's mother's case) or death (in the case of Marcia's and Joey's mothers). Bettelheim characterized Laurie's mother as ambivalent about marriage and children, noting that she had planned to delay Laurie's birth and that, to escape her household duties, she continued working from the time Laurie was six weeks old, turning Laurie over to a young nurse.[12] In the case of Marcia's mother, Bettelheim reports that the parents married after a "short and indifferent courtship," both of them still attached to their first love.[13] Perhaps because her husband also suffered from anxiety and depression, the mother "felt trapped in her marriage, resented husband and child, thought of leaving them both, and would have done so except for Marcia." Like Laurie's mother, Marcia's mother went back to work shortly after Marcia's birth, leaving the infant's care to various baby sitters.[14] Joey's mother also felt "'trapped' in her marriage"; she, too, and had sought out her second husband to forget the "private, unshared hurt" and "hardships of a wartime existence."[15] In all of these cases, Bettelheim employs the topos of the troubled marriage, one inflected by the upheavals of World War II, including emotional trauma and shifts in gendered divisions of labor. The troubled marriage forms part of his descriptions of each character's nature, a technique he uses to establish the grounds for his suggestion that maternal attitudes and behavior could contribute to autism. It is not difficult to catch Bettelheim's implication that these mothers acted selfishly by returning to work after childbirth, for instance. Nor is it difficult to miss the suggestion that the mother's absence played a role in her child's condition.

To make this connection clearer, Bettelheim describes each mother as detached from her child. Laurie's mother was "well pleased with her plump healthy baby, who was pretty enough to win first prize in a baby beauty contest," but her interest in Laurie is described as largely superficial, since she employed nurses to take on most of Laurie's care.[16] Marcia's mother is portrayed as brisk and businesslike in her care of her daughter; Bettelheim quotes her as saying that what she did do for Marcia, she "'did in a hurry. I'm a busy person.'"[17] He describes her as "estranged and resentful" of her family, noting that when she cared for Marcia, she did so out of guilt: "The more the mother rejected Marcia and the sicker Marcia got, the more guilty the mother felt."[18] And Joey's mother, according to Bettelheim, was strangely indifferent when she talked about her son, speaking about him more as a "vague acquaintance" than a person in his own right.[19] She admitted to feeding him on a strict schedule and leaving him to cry for hours in between, calling Joey a "good baby" for being quiet and undemanding.[20] In all three cases, then, Bettelheim interprets the mother's character as lacking because of her improper handling of her baby, including rigidity and emotional detachment. These characterizations lent support to his definition of autism and its causes.

Yet to ascribe mother-blaming to Bettelheim alone may actually downplay the extent to which the character of the anxious, cold, emotionless mother permeated all kinds of psychological inquiry in this time period. As A. Cheree Carlson has argued, characterizations are believable only when there is "correspondence to 'truths' already held by the audience."[21] Bettelheim's depictions of mothers drew upon existing characterizations whose roots lay deep in American rhetorical culture.

PSYCHOANALYTIC CHARACTERS

Evidently, one source for Bettelheim's characterizations of mothers came from psychoanalytic theory developed in the 1920s and 1930s. As an aspirant psychoanalyst, Bettelheim would have been well steeped in this language. In classic psychoanalytic theory, mothers represented the fulfillment of innate infantile drives such as the drive to cling, suck, and bite. While Sigmund Freud emphasized these acts as part of the infantile oral stage of development, it was Melanie Klein who concretized the mother's role in infantile development. In her object-relations theory, Klein hypothesized that the mother-child relationship was fundamental to a child's development. The mother represented the infant's first "object," which it used to develop its own ego by "splitting off parts of the self and projecting them into objects." The mother's breast represented an especially important early object, and failure to properly engage in this process with the mother-as-object could lead to both mental and psychological problems: Klein insisted that "in considering mental deficiency in children at any age one should keep in mind the possibility of schizophrenic illness in early infancy."[22] Not surprisingly, these arguments provided material for researchers in the developing fields of child and developmental psychology.

Drawing on this line of work, Margarethe Ribble published a series of articles and books arguing that ineffective mothering could lead to emotional and psychological disturbances. Her articles characterize ineffective mothers as withdrawn, careless, and resentful, and their attitudes are shown to generate similar attitudes in their babies. Ribble used these portrayals to support her claim that early maternal care (or lack thereof) had profound effects on the child's development. For instance, she claimed that a mother's touch "has a definite, biological implication in the regulation of the breathing and nutritive functions of the child," not just his or her emotional development. On the basis of a study of newborns and their mothers, she concluded that "mothers who make a practice of speaking softly or singing to their infants while holding them have a much better relationship to the child."[23] Ribble describes this relationship with the term *symbiosis*, a state in which "two organisms with essentially different needs profit by the relationship, the mother getting the satisfaction of completing the creation of her child, the infant not only receiving food but getting a primary form of experience which helps to bring his sensory nervous system into functional activity."[24]

Ribble was not invested in psychoanalysis per se, but in her research she located an inventory of potential transgressions in everyday mothering tasks that would upset this symbiotic relationship. She described one mother who was "sexually infantile both physically and mentally," lacking "the usual breast development" and not wishing to nurse.[25] The mother would even "brag[] to the neighbors about how 'good' her baby was and not awaken[] her for feedings."[26] (This description is remarkably similar to Bettelheim's description of Joey's mother, who considered her son good for being quiet.)[27] As a result, the baby was "listless and apathetic," and her attention "was fleeting and was not directed exclusively toward the mother."[28] Here, we see precursors to the type of character Bettelheim described—mothers who did not want children, were perfunctory in their care, or who were ill-prepared for raising children.

Although Ribble does not discuss the status or class background of the mothers in question, she does suggest that infants are most likely to suffer when the mother often left the house or when there was "a continuing shifting of nurses."[29] Such mothers seem likely to be middle- or upper-class women—those who could afford a nurse. They left their children in the "isolated seclusion of the modern nursery," a descriptor also less likely to apply to lower-class mothers living in a cramped tenement.[30] A nursery implies a home with a separate room for the infant. The mothers in question, then, are not the same as those characterized in nineteenth-century depictions of the feebleminded, which often featured several children of various ages in a single room, under the care of a disheveled mother. This character appears, similarly, in Bettelheim's accounts, since all three of the mothers he profiles went back to work shortly after giving birth.

While Ribble focused on bad mothers, others focused on the effects of an absent mother, especially during and after World War II. In 1943 the American psychiatrist William Goldfarb published a series of studies comparing the outcomes in orphans of institutional and foster home settings, concluding that those who lived in institutions during their first few years were "less secure, more isolated from other people and less capable of entering into meaningful human relationships" than were those placed in foster care. The emotionally starved children in these studies were often "hyperactive," exhibiting "bizarre, disorganized, unreflective behavior" or "emotional unresponsiveness."[31] Because Goldfarb was interested in children, we learn less about the mothers in question—they are notable mostly for their absence in the text. He notes, however, that "the mothers of the institution children are significantly superior to the mothers of the family children in occupational background."[32] The explanation for this discrepancy, according to Goldfarb, lies in the fact that parents of higher status were likely to anticipate that their children could return to home care at some point, whereas parents of lower status were more likely to place their children in permanent foster homes.[33] In Goldfarb, as in Bettelheim, the absent mother is figured as one of higher education, likely one who worked outside the home, as did the mothers of Laurie, Marcia, and Joey.

In Goldfarb's studies, the children placed in institutions demonstrated intellectual and emotional difficulties not present in those raised in foster homes: they were "less well adjusted to the demands of the community group, more simple in their mental organization, less capable of making reflective or complex practical adjustment as in school, and, most important, less capable of normal human relationships." These observations led Goldfarb to question whether children diagnosed as schizophrenic, in general, should also be investigated for signs of early maternal neglect.[34] After the war, he went on to direct the Henry Ittleson Center for Child Research in the Bronx and devoted much of his career to studying childhood schizophrenia—a term some initially used to describe children we might now consider autistic.

The character of the absent mother gained even more currency as World War II came to a close and child psychologists began to take stock of ways in which the war had affected children. In England, the psychologist John Bowlby began research into the effects of separation on children at the Children's Department of the Tavistock Clinic. Trained in developmental psychology and object-relations psychoanalysis under Klein, Bowlby was inclined to reject theories that linked childhood disorders to internalized fantasies and libidinous drives, instead preferring theories that emphasized the child's fundamental attachment to its prime love object, the mother. At Tavistock he joined the Canadian researcher Mary Ainsworth, who had trained in "security theory" under William Blatz at the University of Toronto.[35] Together, Ainsworth and Bowlby developed what is now known as attachment theory, according to which the character of the bad or absent mother becomes especially important.

In 1952 Bowlby published a report commissioned by the World Health Organization (WHO) titled *Maternal Care and Mental Health.* He coined the phrase "maternal deprivation" to describe the range of situations in which children might be denied a warm, loving relationship with his or her mother, whether due to institutionalization, separation from the mother, or an inadequate relationship with the mother.[36] He distinguished between partial deprivation, which could bring on "acute anxiety, excessive need for love, powerful feelings of revenge," and "guilt and depression," and complete deprivation, which could "entirely cripple the capacity to make relationships." Children raised in orphanages were separated from both their mother and their father, but mothers, in particular, received attention in Bowlby's study. Fathers played a role, Bowlby conceded, but that role was primarily to furnish material and emotional support. For the child, the "father plays second fiddle," so his presence and emotional contributions are considered only minimally in the theory of maternal deprivation.[37] Like Ribble and Goldfarb, Bowlby presented the absent mother as the primary threat to a child's development, arguing that "the infant and young child should experience a warm, intimate, and continuous relationship with his mother (or permanent mother-substitute) in which both find satisfaction and enjoyment."[38]

In many ways, Bowlby's claims differed little from those found in previous work by Ribble, Goldfarb (both of whom he cites) and others, who had already drawn attention to the effects of institutionalization on children's development. What differed in Bowlby's case was not content but timing and genre. For one, Bowlby's book was published in 1952, when the upheaval of war had drawn attention to the plight of children who were either orphaned or placed in institutions owing to the demands of wartime employment on their parents. In addition, the book carried the imprimatur of the WHO. As a commissioned report it fit into a system of genres that would be used to set policy, and it carried the authority, or *ethos*, of expert judgment. As Stephen Hilgartner notes in his discussion of National Academy of Science consensus reports, the rhetoric used in expert reports "presents conclusions as the rational and carefully considered opinions of qualified experts who have carefully reviewed the evidence."[39] Bowlby was able to draw on such institutionalized authority. It seems likely that the WHO's influence helped popularize Bowlby's study. The book was translated into fourteen languages, and the English paperback version alone sold 400,000 copies.[40] In 1965 Penguin published a popular version, *Child Care and the Growth of Love*. Bowlby's theories also inspired "attachment theory," a parenting style popularized by William and Martha Sears that still holds appeal for some parents today. Bowlby's report was cited in *New York Times* articles debating the role of the career woman and the wisdom of parents' taking a vacation without their young children.[41]

Ribble, Bowlby, and Goldfarb did not deal with children then termed autistic, but the framework they developed nonetheless prefigured early understandings of autism. These and other works about maternal deprivation laid out the topoi that grounded the character of the absent or ineffective mother, they posited the importance of a reciprocal mother-child relationship as key to development, and they figured the mothers in question as belonging to the middle class. In these ways, the work on maternal development shifted the focus from the hereditary blight of the feebleminded among the lower classes to the potential transgressions of the middle-class mother whose child's impairments were primarily psychological and not simply intellectual.

In the case of autism, the type of maternal deprivation considered relevant was mainly emotional, not physical. Autistic children profiled in early studies were most often raised at home with both parents, not in an institution. In some cases short separations could be identified, as when a mother was in the hospital having another child. But in most cases physical separations could not be considered likely causes of autistic behavior. Instead, researchers began to consider whether emotional separation might cause autism.

In 1944 Kanner noted that, among the parents of the autistic children he had documented, "there are very few really warmhearted fathers and mothers," and he wondered "to what extent this fact has contributed to the condition of the children."[42] By 1956 he had revised his earlier view that autism was primarily a genetic condition. In an article written with Leon Eisenberg, he posited that the "emotional frigidity in the typical autistic family" indicated an environmental and experiential genesis for autism.[43] Kanner and Eisenberg described a case in which two graduate students raised their child Brian using rigid scientific principles, imposing a strict schedule, and avoiding unnecessary contact because of concern for "bacteriological sterility";

it was here that the term "emotional refrigeration" first was identified as the "common lot of autistic children."[44] Notably, they cited maternal deprivation studies, including those of Goldfarb and Bowlby, in this article, concluding from that research that consistent, affectionate mothering was necessary for proper emotional and psychological development.[45] For the authors, postwar maternal deprivation studies offered rhetorical resources for understanding autism. That is, prior to these wartime studies Kanner had considered autism to be primarily genetic; it was only after the war, when theories of maternal deprivation began to circulate, that he began to consider "parental refrigeration" as a possibility. The character of the absent mother seems to have offered Kanner one new way to interpret autism.

CHARACTERS IN CHILDREARING BOOKS

The refrigerator mother character also emerged from childrearing advice and discussions about the effectiveness of different methods of childcare. Kanner and Eisenberg note that Brian's mother imposed a strict feeding and sleeping schedule according to what they term "naïve behaviorism applied with a vengeance."[46] (Bettelheim notes that Joey's mother followed similar advice.) But they do not explain why she might have felt compelled to do so. In addition to theories of maternal deprivation, depictions of autism mothers also drew from the legacy of childrearing advice books, which helped establish obsessive and anxious mother characters in language that moved beyond professional psychology texts.

As Rima Apple demonstrates in her study of parenting advice, in the twentieth century the tenor of mothering advice shifted from a focus on the mother's innate authority to a focus on scientific motherhood. By the 1920s mothers were expected to follow the advice of a range of experts: doctors, nurses, teachers, psychologists, guidance counselors, and scientists.[47] In keeping with the "scientific" orientation ascendant at the time, advice books approached child rearing as a rule-driven enterprise. One text, John Lovett Morse's *The Care and Feeding of Children*, advocated "five feedings, at three-hour intervals, beginning at six in the morning"; these consisted of a small, gradually increasing set of bland foods such as "barley jelly," strained oatmeal, and farina. Morse warned against all manner of liberal childrearing errors, from offering tastes of attractive food items to picky eaters, allowing children to eat too quickly or too slowly, and giving up on afternoon naps prior to school age to allowing meddling grandmothers to interfere with the carefully constructed feeding and care schedule.[48] In practice, of course, women tempered this advice with their own beliefs and expectations, but rhetorically speaking, such texts diminished maternal authority and increased scientific authority over childrearing practices.

This development was bolstered by national government policies and organizations begun in the early twentieth century. In 1912 the United States established the Children's Bureau, which focused studies and outreach efforts on nutrition, infant and maternal mortality, and provision of care to children with special needs. By the 1920s, the government had funded initiatives to improve pre- and post-natal care across the country, circulating free pamphlets, enrolling new mothers in correspondence courses on infant care, and the like.[49] Given this deluge of advice, mothers had plenty of reason to seem obsessive.

By the 1940s, when autism was first conceptualized, some experts such as Kanner wondered whether this emphasis on scientific motherhood had produced anxious mothers whose obsessive behavior harmed their children. In a 1944 article he included prosopographia of the obsessive, cold mother who depended too much on scientific advice. This mother, whom he calls the "smother mother," slavishly follows the rules laid out in handbooks that tell mothers "when and how they should, or preferably should not kiss a child, how spankings should be administered and dosed, how a child's bath should be made 'a serious but not gloomy occasion.'"[50] Such books claimed that by knowing all the rules, Kanner writes, "you will be able to manage your child as, with the help of a good cookbook, you manage your cuisine."[51] The emphasis on quantification, expertise, and regulation, he argued, led to anxious mothers who, while "forever occupied with the child," overlooked the most basic childhood need: maternal affection. This "smother love" (and its cousin, "schoolmarmitis") had replaced maternal instinct and affection.[52]

According to Kanner, these smother mothers are "painstakingly punctilious" and take the form of a "punitive, retaliating authoritarian" when the child inevitably fails to live up to the standard of behavior outlined in the handbooks she reads.[53] He relates the case of a college graduate whose insecurity and lack of independence from her own parents led her to reject her child—even attempting to abort him for fear that she and her lawyer husband could not adequately provide for him, despite their "spacious home and adequate domestic help." When the child arrived, the mother atoned by "thrusting all her energies upon him," slavishly enforcing rules of parenting and leading to her son's rejection and withdrawal.[54]

The stock character of the smother mother, like others featured in accounts of maternal deprivation, is clearly a middle-class woman who can afford domestic help and has a college education. Earlier in the article, Kanner addresses such mothers in ways that clearly delineate their class status: "[I]s there any reason why you shouldn't turn over your nursery to a well-instructed governess, as you delegate your kitchen to an efficient cook? You could then enjoy your game of bridge and your other social affairs, with the reassuring knowledge that all the rules are carried out to the dot."[55] Middle- and upper-class mothers, then, who were conscientiously trying to follow the expert advice doled out to them, are here lampooned for their anxiety and overwrought solicitude, made into stock characters in discourse about childrearing advice.

Kanner's article participates in a conceptual shift away from scientific motherhood toward what Barbara Ehrenreich and Deidre English deem "libidinal motherhood," which emphasized, above all else, maternal love. In such a conception, the anxious or cold mother functions as a stock character contrasted with the loving mother. Rather than rigorously quantifying their child's activities, the libidinal mother was to carefully observe her child's needs and to calibrate her responses accordingly.[56] This version of motherhood stressed that mothers would naturally find fulfillment in childrearing, and it found a fast friend in psychoanalytic theory, given its emphasis on the emotional bond between mother and child. For instance, Helen C. Goodspeed, Esther R. Mason, and Elizabeth L. Woods advised in *Child Care and Guidance* (1948) that "the baby's hunger and need for love is quite as urgent and necessary as his need for food," citing "modern research" (namely, Ribble) that has "shown that babies can be love-starved and that such deprivation can warp their entire being."[57] Maternal deprivation theorists supported this approach to childcare, as is evident from the title of Bowlby's advice book *Child Care and the Growth of Love* (1953). This text built on Bowlby's maternal deprivation studies, arguing that a sustained, loving relationship with a mother or "mother-substitute" is essential for psychological health.[58] Whereas experts once recommended imposing a rigid schedule, they now counseled mothers to respond to their child's signals, offering food, rest, and affection as needed.

The characters of the obsessive mother and its foil, the libidinal mother, were already in place, then, and available as commonplaces for autism theorists seeking to understand autism as a disorder of the mother-child relationship. Most often, mothers of autistic children were portrayed as falling into the category of the scientific mother, rather than the more flexible and affectionate mother now consti- tuted in advice books. In a 1958 article, James Anthony argued that mothers of autistic children tended to be "domineering, rigid, con- trolling and criticizing" or "immature and perplexed." Such women seemed "to lack 'an instinct for mothering,'" and, especially among middle-class parents, seemed to rely too heavily on the advice found in books.[59]

Such depictions also participated in broader debates about women's economic roles, which continued after World War II, when, contrary to expectation, many women remained in the workplace. The mothers profiled in Kanner's original paper are often described according to their occupational and education achievements. The mothers of Donald and Frederick were college graduates, and Barbara's mother was "well educated."[60] Kanner was not alone in noting the tendency for autistic children to have parents from the middle or upper middle classes, al- though Anthony contended that there might be a certain "snobbish- ness" at stake. One mother, he noted, was relieved to find out that her child had autism and not some other mental condition: "I just knew he couldn't be an ordinary defective," she reportedly stated. "His father is a statistician."[61] Nonetheless, the perception that women with successful careers lacked the emotional skills necessary to raise children lent cre- dence to the conservative view that women should remain at home with their children. Overly educated mothers might also be overly anxious. As a stock character, the anxious mother was useful to autism theorists because she provided a potential theory of causation.

Of course, alternative explanations were also available. Autism moth- ers might instead represent the unfulfilled housewife—a new character profiled in Betty Friedan's *Feminine Mystique* (1963). Indeed, Friedan described the rise of "autistic" or "atypical" children, some of whom she had visited at a famous clinic, as a response to the discontented house- wife's smothering care. These children, she noted, were "arrested at a very primitive, sub-infantile level,"[62] perhaps due to the "omnipresent care" they received from overly solicitous mothers who were "following 'the picture of what a good mother should be.'"[63] Denied a chance at a full life of their own, Friedan hypothesized, these mothers directed their energies into their children, who, as a result, retreated as a matter of survival. This emphasis counters the emphasis on maternal affection put forward only a decade or so earlier. A different character led to a different interpretation of autism.

Thus, Bettelheim, though rightly demonized for his mother-blaming, was not alone in this kind of thinking. As I have shown, the character of the inadequate mother was readily available in other cultural sources, from the absent mother of Bowlby's theories to the overly solicitous mother in Friedan's formulation to the anxious, obsessive mother in Kanner's. All of these sources *interpreted* the mother character according to certain culturally available characters.

Note that the character in question is implicitly white, middle to upper-class, and well educated, and it had material effects for actual mothers of autistic children. In the film *Refrigerator Mothers*, Dorothy Groomer recounts how her son was refused an autism diagnosis because she did not fit the picture of the autism mother: "I was not white, and it was assumed that I was not educated. Therefore, he was labeled emotionally disturbed." As an African American, Groomer was excluded from the category of autism mother. She notes wryly that she was not even good enough to be considered a refrigerator mother, given the racial and class-based assumptions that defined autism as a disorder of the white middle class.[64] Even today, African American children are likely to remain undiagnosed with autism later than their Caucasian counterparts,[65] perhaps in part because the condition tends to be constructed as one affecting white parents and children.

These characterizations have left an indelible mark on the rhetorics of autism. For mothers raising autistic children in the 1960s and 1970s, *The Empty Fortress,* especially, was often one of the first books to consult, perhaps the only one in a local library. In her memoir about her daughter Georgie, *The Sound of a Miracle,* Annabel Stehli relates her early encounter with Bettelheim's work in the Sunday paper: "My heart sank as I read on, trying to absorb Bettelheim's conviction that autism was caused by mothers who either ignored or overpowered their babies." Stehli would deal with this "profoundly unsettling news"[66] for years, reinterpreting events in Georgie's early life—her strained marriage, her doubts about wanting a second child, her belief that Georgie had suffered anoxia at birth, her failure to eat properly in the first trimester—and wondering about their effects. Once mother blaming is imposed as a framework, it can recolor all sorts of perceptions and events as potential causes of autism.

Despite the prominence of such theories, there were naysayers in the 1960s as well. In *Infantile Autism: The Syndrome and Its Implications for a Neural Theory of Behavior* (1964), Bernard Rimland argued that autism's causes were organic rather than psychological. As a parent of an autistic child, he, too, hoped to absolve parents from guilt. Yet the chapter titled "The Parents of Autistic Children" concludes that the evidence "overwhelmingly supports Kanner's unprecedented early report that the parents of autistic children form a unique and highly homogeneous group in terms of intellect and personality," namely, highly educated, bookish types of primarily Jewish and Anglo-Saxon origin.[67] Rimland differed from the late Kanner only in his interpretation of this evidence as indicative of a genetic origin for autism, rather than an environmental one. In 1969, Austin M. DesLauriers and Carole F. Carlson published a rejoinder to Bettelheim in *Your Child Is Asleep: Early Infantile Autism,* in which they insist that children do not become autistic for any of the reasons Bettelheim identifies: "The early infantile autistic child is not a product of a death wish; nor do his behavioral deficiencies result from an impoverished environment, lacking in sensory stimulating qualities, or from a rejecting environment, offering little affective and emotional gratifications."[68] Instead, DesLauriers and Carlson insist, autism stems from an "inborn functional neurophysiological imbalance," absolving parents from blame.[69] Any signs of parental coldness, they argue, should be considered as a normal reaction to a child who seems unable to respond to them. Nonetheless, it was Bettelheim's interpretation that haunted mothers of autistic children in the 1960s and 1970s, perhaps because that interpretation featured stock mother characters and assumptions about the mother-child relationship that circulated in that time period.

Interpreting Authority

Elly was a fair-haired, placid sprite, a "tiny, golden child." As a toddler, she would quietly sit for hours, contemplating the links of a piece of chain or "circling a spot on the floor in mysterious, self-absorbed delight."[70] Content in her play, she was described as dwelling "in a solitary citadel, compelling and self-made, complete and valid."[71] Elly's mother, Clara Claiborne Park, relates this behavior in *The Siege: The First Eight Years of an Autistic Child* (1967), one of the first book-length accounts written by the parent of an autistic child.[72]

Ethan, too, lived in a world of his own. He would spend hours rolling a ball and retrieving it but did not make eye contact or respond to his parents' attempts to engage him in other activities. Ethan's mother, Rosalind Oppenheim, wrote in the *Saturday Evening Post* in 1961 about her work to help Ethan: "Watching him progress, seeing his intelligence emerge from behind the wall of silence that still holds much of his personality captive[,] has been immeasurably rewarding."[73]

In these accounts, autistic children are held hostage, trapped in citadels or behind "walls of silence." They have withdrawn from the world, and only their mothers can get them out. Mothers who write in this manner reinterpret the figure of the mother and child, forging a new narrative in which mothers are not the cold, frigid women who cause their child's condition but saviors working to free their children from isolation. In order to do so, they invent a new stock character that they can use to write persuasively about their children and to gain authority to contradict harmful depictions of anxious, cold autism mothers.

The philosopher Ian Hacking has argued that contemporary novels featuring mothers and their autistic sons "provide an image of the mother-child pair as being a unit coming into contact with the larger world." For Hacking, this figure offers a way of "talking and feeling that simply did not exist some years ago."[74] This character still draws on elements available in the rhetorical culture, however. As A. Cheree Carlson notes, new narratives must also gain adherence through links to "preexisting stories."[75]

In particular, writers of this new kind of autism story adopted the form and character of the quest narrative. The mother takes on the character of the savior or romantic hero who batters down the walls her child has constructed. This character provided mothers with a new way of interpreting their roles, a point of intervention, and a way to challenge experts who deemed their children hopeless or who blamed the mother for her child's apparent withdrawal. One of the key purposes of accounts such as Park's and Oppenheim's was to disprove theories such as Bettelheim's. Like any narrative, these serve as rhetorical actions, or, in James Phelan's terms, "an author's attempt to harness all the resources of storytelling for the purpose of evoking a set of effects (cognitive, emotional, ethical) in an audience."[76] Constructing a new character for the autism mother proved a central part of that rhetorical action.

THE HERO CHARACTER

In order to understand the new character that mothers developed, it is important to consider the genre from which they adapted it. Mother's narratives frequently take up what literary critics call the quest myth, perhaps the most prevalent theme in human literary production, from foundational cultural myths to contemporary adventure or science fiction films. The quest, or romance narrative, features a hero pitted in a battle against an enemy. In medieval romances such as *Sir Gawain and the Green Knight* or *La Morte d'Arthur*, the hero must demonstrate his valor in a series of challenges in order to attain a reward (honor or the favor of a lady). This form of the romance reached its apogee in the medieval period, but it has been repurposed in productions of more recent vintage, from the *Harry Potter* and *Lord of the Rings* series of books and films to parodic versions such as *Forrest Gump* and science fiction versions featuring female heroes such as Madeleine L'Engle's *A Wrinkle in Time* and the *Buffy the Vampire Slayer* television series. All of these examples include a hero (most often male, but not always) who must undertake a series of trials in order to win a prize or save the victim (usually female, but not always).

Perhaps the most famous of these early autism narratives is *The Siege*. Park's narrative sets up many of the elements that are now paradigmatic of autism memoirs and the new discourses they engendered. First, the metaphor of the fortress or citadel under siege gives the narrative a clear link to the romantic quest: the goal of the hero, in this case Park herself, is to chip away at and eventually destroy that fortress, to enter into the inner sanctum of her daughter's world and rescue her from autism. The title also evokes the title of Bettelheim's book *The Empty Fortress*. In short, the fortress becomes one of the key symbols that takes on what Kenneth Burke would call "generative force," becoming "a relationship to be repeated in various details" within the form of the quest.[77] It also helps construct the mother's character as a hero, since the fortress constitutes the major trial or challenge she must overcome in order to save the victim, her child.

The symbol of the fortress propels what Burke would call a "*logical consistency*" in the rest of the narrative, a "terminology of thoughts, actions, emotions, attitudes, for codifying a pattern of experience."[78] Yet in order to employ the quest form, mothers must reinterpret the character of the male hero, recasting it in maternal terms. Typically, the romance quest features a young man or single woman as the hero figure seeking out adventure in a distant place; seldom is she a mother whose quest takes place in the quotidian setting of the home. In general, this exclusion may stem from the stereotypical roles female characters take on in literature, where, as Kathryn Hume notes, they are rarely depicted as sufficiently sturdy for battle.[79] If the mother is the hero, then the autistic child (in this case Elly) takes on the role of the damsel in distress, the sleeping beauty who has been stolen by fairies and must be awakened. Notably, the reward for the hero is traditionally a bride who, according to the literary critic Northrop Frye, is revealed through "[t]he removal of some stigma."[80] When transposed into a maternal autism narrative, the reward is a normal child, the one who has been "stolen" by the autism fairy.

Park's use of the fortress metaphor reflects available characterizations of the autistic child, especially Kanner's 1943 article describing the condition for the first time. Kanner provides a useful set of phrases to describe such children, whose parents use phrases such as "self-sufficient," "like in a shell," "happiest when left alone," "acting as if people weren't there," "perfectly oblivious to everything about him," and "giving the impression of silent wisdom." Kanner sums up such descriptions in his own phrase: "*extreme autistic aloneness* that, whenever possible, disregards, ignores, shuts out anything that comes to the child from the outside."[81] The figuring of autism as *aloneness* or as being *locked in* makes possible the attack or battle, the attempt at rescue, or an "emergence from solitude."[82] Aloneness frames Park's interpretations—Elly "seemed to live in isolation," according to Park, and a doctor remarked that Elly "'seems like a child who has been raised very much alone.'"[83] This isolation represents the challenge for the heroine, the defect to be removed. The fortress symbol comes to epitomize it but also represents the challenge the hero faces. Given its prominence in quest narratives, the fortress, Burke might say, "attracts us by its power of formula."[84]

Of course, if the child needs to be rescued from the fortress, it is because he or she has been kidnapped by the enemy. As Frederic Jameson points out, the enemy in a quest narrative need not be pure evil; most often, what is considered evil is that which is "Other, alien, different, strange, unclean, and unfamiliar."[85] From the start of Park's narrative, Elly is positioned as other, a "fairy child" whose "eerie imperviousness" and "serene self-sufficiency" were those of one who could "live somehow untouched by the human experience."[86] Her otherness is constituted primarily in comparison to other children, including her three older brothers and sisters, and neighborhood children of a similar age. Unlike them, Elly did not point to draw someone's attention or to ask for objects, she did not imitate words or actions, she did not seem to see or hear. Although not malicious or evil, Elly is other, and it is a belief that this otherness can somehow be removed from an underlying normal child that enables Park's quest to begin.

In these narratives, autistic children are commonly characterized as captives being held hostage by autism, the true enemy. According to Alicia A. Broderick and Ari Ne'eman, "autism is seen as an invasion of a diseased alien entity, to which parents or society must respond by engagement in militaristic intervention operations."[87] Autistic children take on a role similar to that of Sleeping Beauty or Rapunzel, having been poisoned or held hostage, waiting for the prince to rescue them. The metaphors of the fortress and the siege align not only with dominant theories about the causes of autism—the psychogenic idea that children actively withdrew from the world—but also with Park's idea of the appropriate response as a parent. As Broderick and Ne'eman have argued, these metaphors "create a commonsensical narrative congruence between common understandings of autism and currently dominant notions about appropriate responses to or interventions for autism."[88] Yet they also reflect the genre of the quest form itself, which depicts mother, child, and autism using the stock characters of hero, victim, and enemy.

In addition, it is possible to portray autistic children as actively withdrawing from the world, and hence as reachable through intervention, because they have been depicted as *appearing* intelligent. Park draws from Kanner's distinction between retardation (the term then in use to describe individuals with ID) and autism. The children he profiled, Park writes, were "like and yet not like the psychotic, neurotic, brain-damaged, and retarded children" with whom Kanner was familiar—a line that echoes Kanner's pronouncement that the children in question were remarkable because their "condition differs so markedly and uniquely from anything reported so far."[89] Park relates glimpses of ability that lend credence to this belief, such as the times Elly took a dustpan and brush and swept the floor, "just like any little girl who wants to be like her mother," or suddenly pronounced the word *scissors* upon seeing a pair in the playroom—both isolated moments that were not repeated but that, nonetheless, intimated to Park that her daughter might not be retarded.[90] After all, Kanner proposed that autistic children often possessed "good cognitive potentialities," a fact that differentiated them from feebleminded children.[91] This appearance of intelligence provides hope for rescue or transformation, an option Kanner did not seem to suggest in the case of a feebleminded child, whose disability was presumably stable and unchangeable (even if that is not the case in reality).[92] By distinguishing autistic children from other children with ID, Kanner's original description of autism opened up new representational possibilities, new narratives of rescue.

The quest genre provides a structure and set of stock characters for Park's book and for others that followed it. Frye argues that the romance traditionally involves three stages: the *agon,* or conflict; the *pathos,* or struggle; and the *anagnorisis,* or discovery and triumph of the hero.[93] These three stages have been alternatively delineated as the call to adventure, initiation, and return, or as equilibrium, struggle, and higher harmony, in psychological terms.[94] In the paradigmatic autism romance, the first stage involves the hero's gradual recognition of the other, the difference in her child's behavior compared to a norm, which usually shifts to the second stage upon diagnosis. The struggle features the mother's attempts to rescue her child from the throes of autistic solitude. The concluding portion may feature anagnorisis—the child successfully emerges from autism, becoming the reward much like the lady or princess in a classic tale or "higher harmony"—a level of acceptance or peace, which usually occurs when the hero has not successfully rehabilitated the child. This form is persuasive because, as Burke argues, any work's form "leads a reader to anticipate another part, to be gratified by the sequence."[95] The agon calls forth the struggle, which calls forth a desire for resolution on the part of the reader.

In accordance with the structure of the quest narrative, the first part of Park's book describes how Park seeks help for her daughter but finds herself stymied by the complicating force: doctors and experts who are unable to offer any meaningful assistance. The ignorance and arrogance of these figures leads Park to develop her heroic persona, which, as is typical of the romance narrative, is thrust upon her. After several disappointing visits with specialists, Park writes, she and her husband "began to feel angry and resentful, to react as intelligent adults, not as obedient children in the hands of those wiser than we."[96] Thus Park's narrative rejects the refrigerator mother character that, circa 1967, was attached to mothers of autistic children, writing that "[r]efrigerator professionals create refrigerator parents, if the parents are strong enough to keep command of themselves at all."[97] Park recasts this aloofness as stoic strength.

In the second part, Park shifts into the hero character when she decides to become her daughter's teacher and therapist. This character grants Park ethos, or authority; it becomes a persona she can use to speak and write authoritatively and to take control of her daughter's care. Park found her own ways to help her daughter, primarily through little games she invented. Her book justifies this approach and provides a rationale for granting authority to mothers. In a chapter called "The Amateurs," Park explains why parents might be particularly adept at helping their children when experts could not. She argues that parents possess "total familiarity with the case since birth," while experts had to rely on what the parents told them. Parents, therefore, had insight into facets of their children's behavior or communication not available to therapists, who often had to rely on proxies for household situations. (For example, a therapist might infer knowledge about the child's family through play with dolls and dollhouses.) This parental authority stems simply from their constant presence. "Parents are *there*," Park writes, and for this reason "they can act when the child is ready." This round-the-clock contact provides a wealth of material for therapeutic activities, which can be blended into daily life rather than abstracted in a separate session at a psychiatrists' office.[98] The parent is in a better position to understand the autistic child's idiosyncratic communication, fears, and desires. Because they "know this language," Park argues, parents have a head start over professionals, who would necessarily require some time to build up an understanding of the child's communication patterns.[99]

Of course, the assumption that parents are in a position to act as therapists for their children relies on gendered and classed situations. Park admits that the price of intensive therapy is often beyond the means of "all but the well-to-do," whereas "every family can afford the services of its mother."[100] The mother, Park assumes, will probably be the one most responsible for the child's care. Although middle-class women in the 1960s were generally expected to stay home while their children were young, not all could afford to do so. Thus, Park contributes to the gendering of the parent therapist as female and as belonging to the middle to upper class, a pattern that continues well into the current era. Single parents or families in which both parents must work full time seldom appear in the typical memoir. Narratives written by lower-class mothers are especially rare, perhaps because of the expense and time required to assume the mother-therapist role.

Burke argued that narrative forms have rhetorical and psychological ends. He defines a form as "the psychology of the *audience*," so that form becomes "the creation of an appetite in the mind of the auditor, and the adequate satisfying of that appetite."[101] Forms like the quest can be particularly satisfying because they first create tensions that, for Burke, "prove to be simply a more involved kind of satisfaction," intensifying the ultimate psychological experience.[102] The trials faced by the romantic hero prior to winning his love object only serve to amplify the emotions readers feel and their satisfaction when the quest finally ends.

Park's narrative does not completely conform to the structure of the heroic quest—and hence, does not completely satisfy the "psychology of the audience"—because she does not reach anagnorisis, or the completion of the quest. She eventually does help her daughter come out of her shell, but she does not claim recovery or a cure, which would be the most obvious form of success according to the quest narrative. Instead, the last portion of Park's memoir is driven by slow, incremental progress, narrated through careful descriptions of such painstaking achievements as drinking from a cup or turning the tap on for the first time. Park continues in these efforts, she writes, on the assumption that even the smallest steps forward would lead the child closer to normalcy, that each new action was "an incursion into that guarded emptiness, an entrenchment of that terrible simplicity" that constitutes autism.[103] At the end of the book, which traces Elly's first eight years, Park concludes that, since the siege, she "has ceased to be autistic" since she is "no longer immured within the self," that she "lives with us now, truly with us, no longer a changeling but a human child."[104] In later editions of the book, Park fills in Elly's progress, noting the increasing self-sufficiency that came in her teenage years, her successful employment in her twenties, and her burgeoning career as an artist, even as Elly continued to live at home. But Park stressed that Elly still exhibited autistic behaviors—idiosyncrasies of language and habits that marked her as different.

The narrative sweep of Park's memoir may seem to some rhetorically unfulfilling, leaving the reader with a lack of closure—at least from the perspective of the genre, which requires a straightforwardly happy ending or resolution. According to Burke, a form "is 'correct' in so far as it gratifies the needs it creates."[105] In the case of the heroic mother's quest, the form itself seems to require a resolution, such as the child's "emergence" or "recovery" thanks to the mother's efforts. Park's narrative does not provide that resolution.

Nonetheless, *The Siege* offers a new, authoritative role for autism mothers. Like any rhetorical narrative, it, in Lucaites and Condit's terms, serves to "compel the audience to a particular understanding of the facts of the case, to a particular point of view."[106] Park provides a prototype for women seeking to claim authority over their children's conditions, to reject the dominant psychoanalytic hypothesis, and to strike out on their own, using their instincts and the expertise acquired through research to develop their own tools to help their children. In doing so, her narrative sets out an argument for maternal expertise that would be taken up by many women in later years; it creates a new character with greater ethos that mothers could use. The genre of the romantic quest provides a source and site for maternal authority and may account for the appeal of Park's book, which has reached the status of a classic among accounts of autism. More than a point of identification, the book provides a template for others seeking to work with their children. The character of the mother warrior becomes a model for readers. In this way, Park's book offers a constitutive rhetoric through a narrative that, in the words of the rhetoric scholar Maurice Charland, "through the identificatory principle shift[s] and rework[s] the subject and its motives."[107] By identifying with Park, other mothers of autistic children who read the book were inspired to wage their own sieges against the fortress of autism.

After writing *The Siege*, Park became an advocate for special education, something that was not universally guaranteed for Americans in the 1970s. In a 1974 article for *Phi Delta Kappan* she writes that experts lack knowledge of children with disabilities because they do not have the experience that comes from living with such children. "If psychiatrists or psychologists . . . seek deeper knowledge of what an autistic child is like," she continues, "I suggest, not very humbly, that they apply to my child's teachers, or to me."[108] In her book she appeals for a rapprochement between parents of autistic children and the professionals who treat them, an end to the tendency for parents to be excluded from therapy sessions and deemed to demonstrate the "cold intellectuality which many professionals expect to find" if they display "the slightest knowledge of their child's problem."[109] Instead, Park established the right of parents to read professional literature and glean useful techniques from it, rather than being excluded.

THE "BEST MOTHER" CHARACTER

The form of the quest narrative began to satisfy the urge for resolution in the 1980s, when mothers began to write about the "recovery" of their children after using Applied Behavioral Analysis (ABA) as a therapy. Designed by O. Ivar Lovaas, ABA involves intensive, one-on-one work that breaks down complex skills into small components and then rewards children for each small step. Lovaas believed that arguments about what caused autism deflected attention away from what could be done about it, and he developed his approach accordingly. In 1987 he presented evidence that his behaviorist methods could help some children (47 percent of his study group of nineteen) successfully complete first grade and score within average or above-average range on IQ tests.[110] His results, Lovaas claimed, supported Kanner's position that autistic children were not intellectually disabled, and promised new treatment options that could reduce the emotional toil of raising an autistic child.[111]

Alicia A. Broderick has argued that Lovaas's rhetorical influence began with this 1987 study, which introduced "the rhetorical construction of 'recovery' from autism.'"[112] Note that a key component of ABA involves training parents to be primary behavior modifiers. This form of therapy offered a new role for mothers, a new authority position from which to speak about autism, and the potential for a new type of story about autism.

This rhetoric of recovery became fundamental to maternal narratives because it helped complete the arc, fulfilling the desire engendered by the quest narrative for a resolution to the child's disability and solidifying the maternal heroine as a stock character. Former patients and autism advocates have questioned the effectiveness and ethics of ABA, arguing that it fundamentally disregards the rights and desires of the autistic patient. Charlotte Brownlow, a child development researcher, claims that ABA is problematic because it legitimizes a discourse within which the autistic person must normalize his or her behavior, leading to "the dominant construction of the person with autism as having a *deficit* rather than a *difference*."[113] In rhetorical terms, though, ABA offered a powerful resolution to the incompleteness of earlier quest narratives. That ABA could be positioned as resolution may, in part, account for its popularity. That is, if autism is depicted as an enemy to be defeated, ABA becomes the weapon leading to resolution, the sword in the mother's scabbard, completing the quest.

As in earlier stories, accounts featuring ABA therapy usually begin with the mother's dawning awareness of her child's difference from other children, followed by a frantic search for a doctor who will listen and for a diagnosis. The difficulties these mothers face in finding a sympathetic doctor often lay the foundation for their self-transformation into the hero figure. In *Autism: From Tragedy to Triumph*, Julia Crowder recounts how her doctor insisted that there was nothing wrong with her three-year-old son Drew, who did not yet speak or make eye contact, saying: "Julia, it's not this child who has the problem. It's you."[114]

Crowder received the same message from a hearing specialist. Similarly, in *Let Me Hear Your Voice,* Catherine Maurice rails against the "paternalistic familiarity" of doctors who failed to address her concerns, insisted that her daughter had no problems, and then claimed that there was nothing to worry about.[115] Both Crowder and Maurice refuse to accept these professional views and instead strike out on their own.

These characters are motivated by urgency as well as guilt, emotions that help flesh out the character but also create dramatic tension and set up the reader's appetite for resolution. Maurice describes scientific research as agonizingly slow, too slow for her and her husband, who were "racing against the days, racing to find some way of halting" her daughter's decline.[116] The hero only has a short amount of time in which to complete her quest. Similarly, we learn of the hero's guilt: even before her daughter's diagnosis, Maurice was wracked with guilty sentiments, the feeling that she was "an extraordinarily bad mother as to have produced a chronically unhappy child." Despite knowing, intellectually, that this could not have been the case, she describes a "gut-level, entrenched, ultimately dangerous conviction that my child was somehow a product of, an extension of, me."[117] Maurice went so far as to seek out therapy with a doctor who espoused the theory that autism was caused by failed bonding between mother and child, one who prescribed "holding therapy" as a treatment program. "I *wanted* Anne-Marie's autism to be the result of nonbonding," she writes. "That way I could do something about it."[118]

Heroes may draw explicitly on models imparted by other autism mothers. Indeed, they may have been impelled or constituted into the character of the autism mother via the narratives of others. Maurice directly credits Park's book with providing the key concept for her struggle via the metaphor of the siege.[119] The book, she writes, provided her with a sense of control and agency that had previously eluded her.[120] In intellectual terms Maurice rejected the metaphor of the fortress. Yet, she argues, "Parents who are going to fight for their child do need the construct, however fictional, of that child imprisoned within, waiting to be reclaimed."[121] Perhaps, this fictionalized metaphor served Maurice not because it accurately described Anne-Marie but because it (like holding therapy) gave Maurice a clear character to assume.

For Crowder and Maurice, identifying as a mother-hero offers a strong position of authority, one they recount in their narratives. Crowder avers that she would pursue any ends that would allow her son to have a "normal" life. When Lovaas tells her that the "best mothers" jump right into the therapy, Crowder does so, too: "I wanted to be one of the best mothers, maybe even the best mother."[122] Maurice describes how her role as mother helped her question paternalistic doctors and take it upon herself to read scientific and medical accounts: "My daughter's health was manifestly my business, and I was going to pursue my questions about her until this aching anxiety went away."[123] In typical romantic fashion, the mother hero finds strength within herself to address her challenge.

In many autism quest narratives, the mother describes her feelings of isolation and aloneness—characteristics of the genre. Crowder describes how her marriage deteriorated as her husband disassociated himself from the family and the intensive therapy in which she was invested, ultimately deciding that she would move back to Oklahoma once Drew had completed his therapy. For Maurice, the isolation stemmed from the fact that she could find no psychiatrist who would treat her daughter Anne-Marie using ABA. Instead, Maurice ordered Lovaas's handbook, *The Me Book,* hired her own staff of therapists, and began running an in-home therapy program. The hero character must take on her feats alone in order to slay the dragon; such is the case for the autism mother hoping to slay the autism dragon.

Crowder and Maurice complete the romantic quest, achieving success when the child has reached a stage when he or she is deemed normal—usually by an outside figure who either never knew the child was autistic or one who had not seen the child for a period of time and who notices the transformation (a teacher, the family doctor). In Maurice's case, resolution occurs when a doctor announces that Anne-Marie has scored within the normal range on a series of tests, finding "no residua of autism."[124] For Crowder, resolution comes one day when she stands in the hallway, listening to her son Drew squabbling with his brothers, a sound that, for her, is akin to "an aria performed by angels." This sound, she writes, "served to liberate me from the prison of foreboding I had built for myself," leading to a feeling of "exultation." At that moment, she knew "as surely as [she] had ever known anything that Drew would have the life every child observed."[125] Narratives that feature ABA therapy, then, offer not just heroism but absolution to mothers of autistic children.

It is worth reiterating that ABA therapy has become a divisive issue for stakeholders in autism policy and treatment. Many parents look to the kinds of narratives offered by Maurice and Crowder and see the possibility of a "normal" child. Maurice writes that she wanted Anne-Marie's autism "to go away and a normal personality to blossom"; as Anne-Marie's therapy progressed, Maurice began to see ABA as "a radical but necessary means of assisting her to form a self," to "free[] her into normalcy."[126] This form of therapy offers a persuasive treatment plan for these parents because, as Broderick argues, it has been rhetorically bolstered by scientific rhetoric—it is often positioned as the only scientifically proven method for treating autism, usually by reference to Lovaas's original 1987 study. Broderick argues that Maurice's account, in particular, helped forge this link by drawing on scientific rhetoric of recovery, using terms such as "facts," "data," "validation," and "empiricism" to describe the ABA method.[127]

Many autistic people argue that ABA pathologizes autistic difference. The researcher and autistic advocate Michelle Dawson argues that this approach fails to acknowledge that "people with differences have abilities and worth, because they fail to be like those self-designated as exemplifying capability and worth," and that, further, this approach constitutes "a denial of basic human rights."[128] Dawson testified against a Canadian proposition to provide government funding for ABA, and she has spearheaded critiques of Lovaas's study methods. While a thorough analysis of this debate is beyond the purview of this chapter, it strikes me that, fundamentally, it revolves around authority. Mothers like Maurice and Crowder found ABA a powerful tool for wresting authority away from psychologists and doctors who had demeaned them. Yet this authority often comes at the expense of autistic people, who, as I show in Chapter 5, often advance very different understandings of their neurology, their ideals, and their life goals.

Quest narratives, then, provided new rhetorical resources for thinking, talking, and writing about autism and new characters for individuals to assume, but did so at the expense of pathologizing autism and foregoing acceptance of autistic difference.

Interpreting Characters in Science

The characters recounted here—mother-heroes and their autistic children—continue to shape scientific research into autism. Although mainstream science now pursues genetic and neurological studies with enthusiasm, some researchers continue to investigate elements of parent-child bonding, often in ways that position parents (especially mothers) as potentially at fault, perilously close to the old refrigerator mother character. These scientific studies continue to describe autism by interpreting the character of the mother in a particular way.

Psychoanalytic accounts of autism did not begin and end with Bettelheim; the mantle was taken up in the 1980s by Martha G. Welch, who promoted "holding therapy," which at its basic level involved the mother forcibly holding the child in her arms. (In her narrative, Maurice recounts how she was drawn in by this theory and by the evidence Welch claimed to have of its effectiveness). Welch developed this approach on the basis of work with autistic children, who, she hypothesized, suffered from "a break or disturbance in the mother-child attachment or bonding process."[129]

Similarly, Frances Tustin, a British psychoanalyst who worked at the Tavistock Clinic under Bowlby, considers autism a response to a sudden separation between a mother and child that gives the child a "traumatic awareness of bodily separateness." This sudden separation can lead to terror and autistic withdrawal because, according to Tustin, "autistic children are not fully born—they still feel part of the mother's body." She notes that such a state is especially common when the mother sought to have a child "as a solace for her loneliness" or to fill a void in her own life.[130] Tustin's writing shows clear similarities to the much earlier work of Ribble, Bowlby, and Bettelheim, which continues to pin autism on failed maternal bonding or care.

Even today, some research circles foreground questions of maternal bonding and attachment in autism. At the time of writing, searching for "autism and attachment" in the PubMed database yielded 181 hits for articles that were published since 1980, 97 of which were published after 2000. While none of these studies directly blames parents, some still tend to employ concepts such as "maternal insightfulness and resolution" or "maternal sensitivity."[131] These concepts mark off gradations among parents in a study, usually mothers, some of whom are inevitably categorized as deficient. One study by the psychologists Lynn Seskin et al. concluded that "children with autism spectrum disorders whose parents demonstrated secure attachment representations were better able to initiate and respond in two-way pre-symbolic gestural communication; organize two-way social problem-solving communication; and engage in imaginative thinking, symbolic play, and verbal communication."[132] Implicitly, the article alleges that parents who lacked secure attachment to their children might have been causing their child's limited communication and imagination, an implication that once again stigmatizes parents. The methods used to make these determinations also have their roots in Bowlby-era studies of infant separation. One technique in use today, the Strange Situation, was developed by Bowlby's colleague Ainsworth with Sylvia Bell in 1970. It identifies children's reactions to being separated from the mother.[133]

These studies fail, for the most part, to keep up with the vast changes in childcare arrangements since the 1960s and 1970s. None of the studies I read acknowledged that children might spend a significant amount of time at a day care or preschool, with a nanny, or with fathers, although many children (if not most) spend at least some portion of their time with a caregiver besides their mother. Yet as of 2010, only 48 percent of children in the United States under the age of four received primary childcare from a relative. The remaining 52 percent, presumably, were cared for either in the home by a nonrelative (such as a babysitter or nanny) or at a daycare center.[134]

Nonetheless, most studies of attachment continue in the rhetorical tradition drawn from psychoanalytic theory, which makes the maternal figure the primary and often the only caregiver of interest. In the articles I examined closely, mothers were involved far more frequently than were fathers. In most cases, fathers made up a disproportionately small percentage of parents or they were not mentioned at all.[135] In rhetorical terms, these studies often employ a slippage or synecdoche in which *mothers* stands in for *parents*. Take this passage from a study of infant-parent affect by Sy-Miin Chow, John D. Haltigan, and Daniel S. Messinger: "Parent-infant interaction involves matches and mismatches in affective engagement. Given that infant and mother interactive behaviors are not deterministic but, rather, encapsulate the stochastic influence of the two partners [. . .] within-dyad variability in synchrony constitutes an important aspect of interaction."[136] The term "parent-infant interaction" is replaced in the second sentence with "mother interactive behaviors," so that mothers stand in for parents. Instances such as this one make it hard to determine whether the authors really mean to refer to both fathers and mothers when they say "parent," since the writers seldom indicate whether their study group included fathers. Similar slippages occur with *caregiver*, as in this passage from a study of expressed emotion (EE) in mothers of autistic children: "more work needs to be directed toward explicating the relationship between EE (and its constituent components) and other *caregiver characteristics*, such as *maternal responsiveness and sensitivity*, thought to be critical in helping children with and without ASD develop and sustain positive ties to their *caregivers*."[137] In work focused on parental attitudes, emotions, and attachment, mothers make up the vast majority of parents studied, but the findings of those studies are cast in gender-neutral terms, a rhetorical move that elides the fact that very little is known about fathers as caregivers to autistic children.

Authors seem to be aware of the stereotype of the cold mother, and often take measures to stave off suggestions that they might be continuing its legacy. In one study Paul Robert Benson et al. assure readers in the discussion section that "despite the many challenges posed by their children's autism, the vast majority of the mothers participating in the present study expressed strong feelings of warmth, appreciation, and love for their children."[138] The authors seem to be concerned with the possibility that readers will interpret them as advancing a "refrigerator mother" type of theory, yet by exclusively focusing on mothers they nonetheless perpetuate the historical tendency to interpret autism via the character of the cold or anxious mother.

As we will see, the legacy of mother blame and the struggle for mothers to claim authority lent fuel to a contentious debate over vaccination and its role in autism and helped mothers articulate and perform a new character in order to gain authority in those debates.

CHAPTER 2

Performing Gender

Mother Warriors

In 2008, Hollywood celebrity Jenny McCarthy led a rally in Washington, D.C., to pressure Congress to require the removal of trace amounts of aluminum, mercury, and other elements that McCarthy claimed could trigger autism. Amid a sea of parents—mostly mothers—clad in green tee shirts, she took to the stage wearing a matching shirt, her hair smoothed into a professional blonde bob. She began her speech by noting that mothers like her had been told "lies" by scientists before: "Do you remember when smoking was actually good for our health? Do you remember when autism was blamed on lazy mothers? We were known as 'refrigerator mothers,' cold and uncaring to our children." One day, McCarthy claimed, the argument that vaccines did not trigger autism would also be proved a lie, and mothers like her would be vindicated. In this speech, McCarthy claimed the authority to interpret scientific evidence, contradicting the professional majority that insists there is no connection between vaccines and autism. She also encouraged those in attendance to take control of their children's health, including their vaccination schedules: "I want to empower parents to educate themselves," she stated, "and take safety back into their own hands."[1] This chapter traces the history of the "mother warrior" character, one that McCarthy, and mothers like her, have used to take a stand in public debates about autism and its causes.

In that role, they argue against the dominant understanding of autism as a genetic neurological condition. McCarthy, and other mothers who agree with her position, argue instead that autism stems from a range of physiological conditions such as gastrointestinal dysfunction, vitamin deficiency, and chronic infections, which they attribute to a range of causes including vaccines, environmental toxins, processed foods, and allergies to gluten or casein. On the basis of this model, which they call the biomedical theory of autism, they focus their efforts on alternative health treatments, from dietary interventions to heavy metal chelation to hyperbaric oxygen therapy, all of which, they say, can help children recover from autism.

McCarthy may have brought the issue of vaccine safety to wider public consciousness, but she was not the first to do so, nor did she single-handedly invent the character of the mother warrior. Mothers before her have argued for funding for more research into the vaccine connection, have lobbied for changes in the composition of vaccines and the vaccination schedule, and have brought lawsuits in the Office of Special Masters of the U.S. Court of Federal Claims (the "vaccine court"), seeking compensation for their children's health issues. This chapter explores how this character emerged and enabled mothers to become influential (albeit controversial) rhetors in public debates about autism.

The term *mother warrior* has been popularized by McCarthy's book of that name; its variant, *autism mother*, derives mainly from the magazine *Autism File*. Women such as McCarthy, Polly Tommey, Katie Wright, and Lyn Redwood encourage mothers of autistic children to envision themselves as fighters, superheroes even, average women who are thrust into leadership roles when they confront the apathy or malpractice of those who are meant to help their children. This character enables them to present themselves in rhetorical terms as tenacious mothers fighting a corrupt medical system, drawing on the topoi of maternalist rhetoric. The maternalist rhetor draws on her status as a mother to claim authority and then extends that authority to a public or civic issue, in this case, vaccines.

These mothers have been dismissed as denialists, conspiracy theorists, or scientific illiterates,[2] but I argue that those who engage in this movement actually participate in the larger scientific trend of "total motherhood," a version of mothering that requires women not only to provide affective and emotional labor but also to manage the mental and physical health of their children.[3] When they take on the character of the total mother, they can tap into this broader cultural trend as a persuasive resource, but they have also themselves been constituted by the cultural discourses that position mothers as managers of their children's health. Autism mothers are, in some ways, not so different from other total mothers; they simply apply that expertise in a more intensive way, compelled to treat a condition that has been portrayed as devastating to parents and families.

In this chapter, then, I first examine total motherhood and its sources. I then deal with the character of the total autism mother, in particular, and how it has been constructed and circulated, by examining some of McCarthy's precursors: mothers who began to speak and write about vaccines in the 1980s and 1990s, including Barbara Loe Fisher, Lyn Redwood, and Sallie Bernard. These women performed the role of the mother warrior mainly in scientific texts and in congressional testimony. After the year 2000, this character began to circulate more widely. Thus in the second section I treat memoirs by mothers of autistic children including McCarthy, Leeann Whiffen, and Christina Adams, mining them for clues about how they perform a character, one that becomes a model for readers. In the third section I illustrate the mother warrior character as it has circulated in blogs, magazines, and Web sites. The final section considers why responding to their arguments has proved difficult for the scientific community, which has had to counter the rhetorical force of the mother warrior character with that of the paternalistic good doctor and to rely on emotional appeals not usually considered appropriate for scientific discourse.

Performing Total Motherhood

The current vaccine debate gained international attention in 1998 when Andrew Wakefield and several co-authors published a report in the medical journal the *Lancet* implying a possible link between the measles-mumps-rubella (MMR) vaccine, gastrointestinal disease, and autism.[4] Wakefield hypothesized that affected children's symptoms may have been due to exposure to the live measles virus in the MMR vaccine. Subsequent studies failed to substantiate this link, and the article was eventually retracted. While parents concerned about vaccines and autism had been sharing their anxieties prior to this event, Wakefield became a key figure in the debate, a hero to some and a villain to others. In recent years, he has been publicly pilloried for a number of ethical violations, notably the fact that his original study was paid for by lawyers seeking to sue vaccine manufacturers on behalf of parents of autistic children—and the fact that Wakefield took blood samples for the study from children attending his own child's birthday party.[5] Despite these allegations, Wakefield has also become a hero to anti-vaccine campaigners in the United Kingdom, who have focused their efforts on trying to prove a connection between exposure to measles via the MMR vaccine and autism.

In the United States, meanwhile, lobbyists have focused their efforts mainly on the preservatives used in vaccines, especially thimerosal. Many narratives by American parents also feature their children's receipt of the MMR vaccine as a turning point, after which parents noticed symptoms of autism. Mothers, especially, have formed a formidable lobbying group supported by several well-funded associations and a small number of celebrity advocates, including McCarthy and actress Holly Robinson Peete, both mothers of autistic sons. As a precaution, thimerosal was banned in vaccines in the United States in 1999, although scientific evidence had not shown a conclusive link between thimerosal and autism. After the ban, mothers nonetheless continued to lobby for changes such as those McCarthy advocated in her "Green Our Vaccines" rally, noting other trace chemicals and minerals in vaccines, the continued use of thimerosal in the flu vaccine, and the possibility that the vaccination schedule overloads the immune systems of young children.

On both sides of the ocean, Wakefield served a crucial rhetorical function: for those opposed to the vaccine theory he was a scapegoat, and for those who support the theory he was an authority figure. As is the case with other unsupported health claims that Elaine Showalter has studied in her book *Hystories,* (such as those for Gulf War Syndrome and Chronic Fatigue Syndrome), the vaccine theory "needs a doctor or theorist, an authority figure who can give it a compelling name and narrative."[6] Wakefield did just that. Indeed, he moved to the United States and ran the Thoughtful House, a clinic in Texas, from 2004 until 2010.

The rhetorical momentum behind the vaccine movement stemmed in large part from stories: stories told in speeches, on blogs, and in YouTube montages, stories that dramatize a child's shift from being a "normal" baby to one who was "damaged" by vaccines. One explanation for the rhetorical success of vaccine activists, then, lies in the emotionally charged language used to describe purported cases of vaccine-induced autism. Steven Schwarze has argued that environmental debates often follow the genre of melodrama: they create victims and villains, introduce moral and emotional dimensions, and polarize groups rather than unifying them.[7] The vaccine narrative similarly operates as melodrama: it names innocent children as victims and vaccine manufacturers and government regulators as villains. These stories are highly emotional, portraying the devastation of family members, the lost potential of previously healthy children, and indignation at the lack of understanding within the medical establishment.

Accordingly, critics have contended that these emotional stories constitute fear mongering. As Paul A. Offit, author of *Autism's False Prophets* and frequent spokesperson against the biomedical theory, explains, "People are far more likely to be swayed by a personal, emotional experience than by the results of large epidemiological studies."[8] Michael Specter, author of the book *Denialism*, puts it this way: "The fear of a common disease like autism will almost always outrank a fear about something like measles that people no longer take seriously."[9] Yet such stories' persuasive appeal stems not simply from emotionality, as some critics assert, but also from the character mothers perform in those debates, one with deep roots in American rhetorical culture: the total mother.

Total motherhood involves managing a range of interventions meant to optimize the child's body and mind, and it impels all mothers, not just autism mothers, to do so. According to Joan S. Wolf, this cultural formation "obligates mothers to be experts in everything their children might encounter, to become lay pediatricians, psychologists, consumer products-safety inspectors, toxicologists, educators, and more."[10] Within this logic, mothers can be held accountable for any "defects" in their offspring. Even the earliest texts devoted to midwifery and pregnancy warned women against behaviors that might lead to physical and mental defects. For instance, Alexander Hamilton's *Treatise of Midwifery* (1781) advises women against "crowds, confinement, every situation which renders them under any disagreeable restriction; agitation of the body, from violent or improper exercises, as jolting in a carriage, riding on horseback, dancing, and whatever disturbs either the body or mind."[11] By the twentieth century, growing attention to intellectual disabilities led to what Licia Carlson calls a "cult of proper motherhood," in which mothers were encouraged to "be vigilant at every stage in order to prevent feeblemindedness in their offspring: in proper procreative habits, low stress and appropriate care during

pregnancy, and attentiveness to signs of idiocy in the newborn."[12] Today, amid fears of environmental pollution, movements encouraging
organic food, and an increased emphasis on individual responsibility,
mothers are still more likely to develop this character in order to engage in debates related to children's health.[13]

The rhetorical climate of current health discourse is one characterized by doubt and mistrust, and this affective predisposition must be
understood in the broader context of the risk society. As the sociologist Nikolas Rose explains, contemporary citizens are encouraged to
understand themselves as invested in what he calls "biopolitics," or
"our growing capacities to control, manage, engineer, reshape, and
modulate the very vital capacities of human beings as living creatures."[14]
Because public health discourse increasingly stresses active engagement on the part of patients, individuals now expect access to scientific
information, experimental therapies, and legal recourse when those
expectations are not met. As a result, somatic expertise has become
a public imperative and "a key element in contemporary ethical regimes."[15] Total motherhood is one prominent way in which somatic
expertise manifests itself.

For instance, the total mother must actively scrutinize her children
for evidence of Attention Deficit and Hyperactivity Disorder (ADHD),
various learning disabilities (dyslexia, hyperlexia, and so on), autism, and
more. Her somatic expertise involves overseeing the choice of medical,
dietary, and pharmaceutical products for families, finding counselors, fit-
ness coaches, therapists, and specialists, and ferrying children to a range
of lessons and classes, from, for example, gymnastics to math tutoring
to Mandarin lessons. All of these interventions are meant to produce
optimal children and to remediate the suboptimal—whether that refers
to a child with a diagnosed disability or one with a weight problem or
less-than-stellar grades.

Mothers of children with disabilities, however, seem especially likely to
be saddled with the duties of total motherhood, since within the regime
of somatic expertise there is the expectation that any disability can be
eradicated (if not prevented) given the proper treatment and dedication.
The autism mother is a particular version of the total mother, and she
takes part in a particular community of somatic expertise, with its own set
of assumptions, lines of argument, and valued explanations for autism,
different in degree but not in kind from what any mother is expected to
do for her children. Often, this includes enacting a complex set of dietary
and behavioral interventions, overseeing a staff of therapists, consulting

with experts in gastrointestinal disorders, neurology, and pediatrics, attending conferences to learn about new treatments and supplements, and participating in support and advocacy groups. In this way, the autism mother is similar to the ADHD mothers whom Claudia Malacrida describes in her study—mothers who are considered "responsible for all aspects of their children's lives," including both physical and moral development. These mothers are considered to be "both consumer of and handmaid to disciplinary knowledge, including medical knowledge about raising a healthy child, social work knowledge about ideal socialization and emotional wellbeing of the child, and educational knowledge about rearing an intellectually developed and occupationally prepared child."[16] As a result of these general tendencies, mothers of children with a disability are especially likely to be targets of this disciplinary knowledge and expected to master and enact those precepts.

Total motherhood is part and parcel of the shifts in healthcare discourse in the late twentieth and early twenty-first centuries. As Sara Henderson and Alan Peterson argue, this time period witnessed a shift away from the notion that the state should provide healthcare for its citizens and increasingly emphasized the notion that "citizens should play a more active role in caring for themselves as 'clients' or 'consumers.'"[17] This consumerist model places responsibility on individuals, especially women, to make healthcare choices for their families. From this perspective, it is not surprising that mothers of autistic children would consult the World Wide Web for information: neoliberal healthcare policies have encouraged them to do just that.

In the 1990s, about the time parent-led organizations were raising questions about the link between autism and vaccines, healthcare policy in the United States was increasingly taking on the rhetoric of consumer choice and responsibility. In 1997, President Bill Clinton endorsed the Consumer Bill of Rights and Responsibilities, which was premised on the notion that "the best role for government in the Information Age is to create public institutions that empower citizens to act for themselves."[18] Such language persisted throughout the following decade, and it made its way into books and magazines targeted to mothers.

The magazine *Mothering*, for instance, provides advice to new mothers in articles such as "Your Child's First Healer." In this piece, Peggy O'Mara describes the new role mothers undertake with the birth of their first child. As healer, O'Mara claims, the mother is responsible for choosing a range of treatments (herbal, homeopathic, acupuncture, massage), and for picking "health consultants," which might include a

pediatrician, chiropractor, naturopath, acupuncturist, or family-prac-
tice doctor. When confronted with a major health issue, she advises,
"You will be wise to get a couple of different opinions and to do your
own research. You can see such professionals more as counselors helping you to make a choice than as managers telling you what to do. It's
a sure thing that having your own experience of healing your child
helps you better negotiate with professionals."[19] Clearly, this kind of
advice encourages readers to take on the role of total mother.

Mothering is clearly focused on alternative health, green living, and
the like (and often carries stories questioning vaccine safety), but more
mainstream publications echo the rhetoric of total motherhood as well.
The popular magazine *Parenting* features an online "Family Health
Guide," with information on conditions from ADHD to wheezing.
Though slightly more skeptical of alternative health treatments, *Parenting*'s guide still offers advice that assumes readers are total mothers
seeking to evaluate and make choices about their child's health. The
page for ADHD, for instance, provides the following advice: "If you do
wish to explore complementary therapies (those done in conjunction
with, rather than as an alternative to, conventional medicine), try those
that are first of all harmless, and second can benefit health in some
way, even if they're not proven for ADHD. Examples include yoga or
eliminating food additives in your child's diet."[20] Here, the parent is
constituted as one who is making such interventions in her child's life
with the goal of optimization—even if she is advised to consult her
doctor before making such changes.

Similarly, Parenting.com advises parents who suspect that their child
may be autistic to "keep a journal of their child's symptoms and patterns
of behavior if there's any doubt he's developing normally. Bring notes,
listing your concerns about your child's odd symptoms or behaviors,
including when they started and how they're affecting his ability to
function in his young life."[21] This level of surveillance is not limited
to autism: the total mother should be on the lookout for depression,
dehydration, weight gain, ADHD, sleep problems, and food allergies,
to name a few.

Within this framework, mothers who have children with disabilities
can be discursively constructed as careless usurpers of maternal duty.
According to Claudia Malacrida, "mothers of children who are different
are suspected of poor prenatal practices, including alcohol and drug use
during pregnancy. They are also criticized for providing inadequate nutrition, relying on fast foods, working too much outside the home, and of

laying inadequate moral, psychological, and emotional foundations for their children because of single motherhood."[22] Perhaps to compensate for this, some mothers turn away from mainstream medical and psychiatric practices and toward alternative theories and treatments, which allow them to still perform a character grounded in somatic expertise and to claim rhetorical authority over their children's condition.

By using the term *performance*, I am evoking—but not entirely subscribing to—Butler's concept of gender performativity. Butler argued that gendered identities are constituted by a continuous process of stylized repetition: "If gender is instituted through acts which are internally discontinuous," she writes, "then the *appearance of substance* is precisely that, a constructed identity, a performative accomplishment which the mundane social audience, including the actors themselves, come to believe and to perform in the mode of belief."[23] Butler's term refers to the process by which gendered identities are reproduced, internalized, and circulated. By focusing on gendered characters, though, I am taking on a more rhetorical viewpoint. I am less interested in the internalized identities of mothers, less interested in how much they believe in their roles (although it seems that many mother warriors do incorporate the character into their core identities), than I am in the persuasive effects of the characters they portray. A rhetorical understanding of gender performance, then, considers how a gendered character such as the mother warrior offers a resource for the construction of a rhetorical persona and ethos.

Performing Warrior Motherhood

American women have a long tradition of evoking gendered characters to achieve rhetorical ends. From the very start, women in the new American republic sought to extend their roles in public rhetoric by aligning childrearing with politics. For example, early American feminists argued that, as mothers, they needed education and voting rights in order to be better able to educate their sons and daughters.[24] In making this argument women drew on the character of the "Republican mother," one that developed from Enlightenment-era political thought but that continued to be used into the twentieth century by women arguing for a range of issues, from urban sanitation to food and drug laws.[25] The Republican mother character allowed women to position themselves as mothers looking out for the best interests of their children, and by extension, their communities. In doing so, they avoided being positioned as overly radical women seeking to usurp male authority.

In the twentieth century, female labor activists styled themselves as maternal rhetors—most notably Mary Harris "Mother" Jones, who clad herself in "matronly black silk and white lace" and responded only to "Mother." As Mari Boor Tonn points out, Jones was joined by a number of other figures in the labor movement, including Ella Reeve "Mother" Bloor, Leonora "Mother" O'Reilly, and Mary "Mother" Skubitz.[26] Tonn shows that these rhetors were successful because they could connect their claims for labor rights to maternal characters.

Much like these exemplars, mothers active in vaccination rights campaigns stake out new roles by aligning motherhood with deeply rooted libertarian principles of responsibility and choice. In doing so, they can portray themselves as nurturing figures looking out for the good of the nation's children and fighting against injustice. I next examine three of the first mothers to become active in the vaccine movement because they helped invent the modern autism mother or mother warrior character.

The contemporary vaccine safety movement traces its roots back to the early 1980s, when a group of parents led by Barbara Loe Fisher argued that their children had developed learning disabilities after receiving the diphtheria, pertussis, and tetanus (DPT) vaccine. Fisher founded the official-sounding National Vaccine Information Center to forward her case and published a book with Harris L. Coulter called *A Shot in the Dark* (1991). In part because of the pressure brought by Fisher's organization, the United States switched to a new type of DPT vaccine in which the pertussis portion (the one thought to cause increased side effects) was reformulated.

As part of her campaign, Fisher has testified often at state and national hearings related to vaccines, and her statements usually begin with her credentials as mother and founder of the NVIC. In a 1999 statement before the United States House Government Reform Committee, she introduces herself as "the mother of a vaccine injured child and co-founder and president of the parent organization that launched the vaccine safety and informed consent movement in America."[27] Next, she relates her son Chris's story in great detail, describing how, within hours of his DPT vaccination, Fisher found her son "sitting in a chair staring straight ahead, his face pale and drawn," before shuddering and falling into a deep sleep—symptoms Fisher later identified as typical symptoms of a reaction to the DPT vaccine. In the following weeks, she states, Chris stopped smiling, lost interest in books and identifying letters and numbers, cried frequently, and had persistent infections and gastrointestinal trouble. Ultimately, she claims, "Christian never returned to the child he was before the vaccination that changed his life forever."[28] By narrating her personal witnessing of her son's deterioration, Fisher couches her claims in maternal language.

Only then does she shift to the thrust of her argument: that the federal government needs to support better reporting of vaccine injuries, do more research on the cumulative effects of multiple vaccines, and support scientific research that will identify those most susceptible to vaccines' side-effects. Toward the end of her testimony, Fisher switches to more scientific language:

> Because studies used to license vaccines only require a limited follow-up period to evaluate for adverse events (in some cases only a few days); because vaccine studies are often conducted in populations which do not reflect the genetic diversity of the US population; because once a vaccine is licensed, it is often administered at the same time as many other vaccines without credible corroborating scientific evidence to prove it is safe to do that; and because no case controlled, long term studies have been conducted to measure for all morbidity and mortality outcomes over time, mass vaccination with multiple vaccines has become, in effect, a national medical experiment on our children as well as on our men and women serving in the armed forces.[29]

Fisher speaks as someone who has read and evaluated scientific evidence, and her claims are no longer tempered by appeals to her maternal authority. In rhetorical terms, we might describe this passage as prosopopoeia, or imitation of a character, insofar as Fisher is adopting the language and manner of a scientist. Because total motherhood, as Wolf puts it, "obligates mothers to be experts," it is not surprising that sometimes mothers like Fisher take on the character of scientific expert despite not possessing, in point of fact, the credentials of a scientist.[30]

Toward the conclusion of her testimony, though, Fisher shifts gears again, to language of choice and private rights. She notes that the current vaccination policy "has placed many American parents in the difficult position of having to choose between obeying their conscience or obeying the law," that the database of adverse vaccine events maintained by the United States Department of Health and Human Services is "not open to public oversight," and that vaccination programs lead to "erosion of privacy and informed consent protections."[31] Thus, Fisher's testimony blends maternal rhetoric with scientific and civic rhetorics, creating a character on the basis of which she can claim authority.

Her son was not autistic, but Fisher nonetheless provided an early model of the total mother as a character to be performed in specific settings, especially congressional hearings. Later, other mothers took up a similar performance. By incorporating scientific discourse and rhetorical strategies into their self-presentations, they sought to influence not just other mothers but also policy makers and researchers. Historically speaking, scientific discourse has been viewed as the sovereign province of male doctors and scientists. Keller notes that the natural philosophers who formed the first scientific societies explicitly argued for a "masculine philosophy," aligning passion, emotion, and desire with irrationality and, by implication, femininity.[32] The values and characteristics associated with scientific discourse draw on such resources of upper-class male culture as independence, disinterestedness, and discretion.[33] Despite their heavy reliance on emotional appeals, autism mothers also appeal to scientific expertise, objectivity, and standards of proof. In this way, they use the historically masculine authority position of scientists and doctors to become biopolitical rhetors, skilled in scientific discourse as well as the emotional and ethical discourses usually attached to motherhood.

Two mothers of autistic children, Sallie Bernard and Lyn Redwood, formed the organization SafeMinds in 2000. To call attention to concerns about vaccines and autism, Bernard and Redwood channeled their maternal authority into scientific discourse but, like Fisher, they also took on the character of the scientist, using prosopopoeia. In their writing, Fisher, Bernard, and Redwood incorporate features of scientific writing and common lines of scientific argument, or topoi. In 2001 they co-wrote an article with A. Enyati, H. Roger, and Teresa Binstock titled "Autism: A Novel Form of Mercury Poisoning," published in the journal *Medical Hypotheses*. The article provided the impetus for much of the furor surrounding vaccines in the years following Wakefield's controversial article, and it is cited among anti-vaccine activists as scientific evidence. For detractors, though, the article smacks of pseudoscience—it is published in a journal with a low impact factor whose most frequently cited article offers a protocol for medical marijuana use.

Medical Hypotheses is an unusual journal in that it eschews peer review in favor of editorial review. According to the editorial statement, the purpose of the journal is to "give novel, radical new ideas and speculations in medicine open-minded consideration, opening the field to radical hypotheses which would be rejected by most conventional journals." Despite the speculative nature of the articles published, it takes a "standard scientific form in terms of style, structure and referencing," such that its content *appears* to be scientific. In this way, the journal takes on the mission of constituting "a bridge between cutting-edge theory and the mainstream of medical and scientific communication, which ideas must eventually enter if they are to be critiqued and tested against observations."[34] The purpose of an article published in *Medical Hypotheses* is somewhat different from that of a traditional scientific article, which usually serves to advance, however incrementally, an established line of research. For this reason, writers of research articles typically situate their work in relation to an ongoing research program, citing other scholars in the field to show how their work contributes. Research articles also tend to avoid strong statements of proof or causation, instead preferring to qualify their claims with hedges and modifiers: the results *may suggest* or *possibly indicate* a certain claim, but they seldom *prove* a theory or *show* that x causes y.[35] In contrast, writers of *Medical Hypotheses* articles are encouraged to be speculative and provocative.

Accordingly, the article co-written by Bernard and Redwood mixes traditional scientific style with the more speculative style of the journal itself. The article begins with a clinical description of autism followed by a paragraph outlining the diverse presentations of mercury poisoning, which they draw from historical examples—Minamata disease in Japan, poisoning from grain in Iraq and Russia, or pink disease caused by teething powders. The hypothesis appears in the third paragraph: "It is hypothesized that the regressive form of autism represents another form of mercury poisoning, based on a thorough correspondence between autistic and HgP traits and physiological abnormalities, as well as on the known exposure to mercury through vaccines."[36] As is common in scientific style, the hypothesis appears in an impersonal or "dummy" clause ("It is hypothesized that" rather than "We hypothesize that"). The remainder of the article uses a comparative approach in which the writers align symptoms of autism with symptoms found in cases of known mercury poisoning. They identify behavioral traits and physiological abnormalities common to both, which they describe in paragraph form and list in two tables—again, a feature of scientific articles. The rhetorical effect of the article is cumulative: in each section, the authors pile up parallels between the two disorders (mercury poisoning and autism)—yet they do not suggest alternative explanations or point out significant differences between the two.

At the sentence level, the article deploys the nominalizations and complex noun phrases often found in scientific discourse: "In the developing brain, mercury interferes with *neuronal migration,* depresses cell division, disrupts *microtubule function,* and reduces NCAMs [*neural cell adhesion molecules*]."[37] The article also employs scientific acronyms and avoids overtly attributing causality, stating that "other phenomena are consistent with a causal Hg-ASD relationship."[38] Yet in the discussion section, the authors do not modulate their claims, concluding, "We have *shown* that every major characteristic of autism has been exhibited in at least several cases of documented mercury poisoning."[39] A more common approach in scientific articles would be to substitute "suggested" for "shown." Further, the writers state outright that "the standard primary criteria for a diagnosis of mercury poisoning—observable symptoms, known exposure at the time of symptom onset, and detectable levels in biologic samples (11,31)—have been met in autism." Later in the conclusion they temper their claims, stating that "mercury toxicity *may be* a significant etiological factor in *at least some* cases of regressive autism."[40]

Scientific readers of the article would likely critique the kinds of sources the writers cite or the comparative structure of the article, which does not report on original experimental results but instead lines up similarities between mercury poisoning and ASD. Although the article has been cited more than 150 times since publication (according to the science citation index Scopus), these citations fall into two broad categories: low-impact-factor journals that also feature articles positing a link to vaccines (such as *Toxicological and Environmental Chemistry* and *Reviews on Environmental Health*), and articles disputing the vaccine connection, usually in more mainstream scientific journals (such as *Nature, Neuroscience,* and *PLoS ONE*).

Regardless of the scientific validity of the article, though, the writers perform the writing style quite effectively. It would be difficult for the layperson to distinguish this article from any other scientific research paper, especially if one did not investigate the nature of the journal *Medical Hypotheses* or of the scientific response to the article. Moreover, it circulated in autism networks of various kinds. For instance, it appeared in the Families for Early Autism Treatment newsletter on September 20, 2000, and on Web sites with titles such as Health Matrix, Reverse Autism, and HealingArts—all of which might attract parents seeking information about autism. These citations give the authors a public stage upon which to enact the character of the autism mother.

Regardless of its scientific merit, the article helped Bernard and Redwood to gain a voice in government and scientific decision making, a way of promoting their somatic expertise in a scientific context. We might consider the article as what John Lynch calls a *scientistic idiom,* or "a combination of scientific and quasi-scientific rhetorical strategies and key words" that individuals use to "define what counts as real and thus embed their own values and ideological positions into the taken-for-granted assumptions that shape a debate."[41] By combining scientific language and rhetoric with maternal appeals, Redwood and Bernard made parental involvement necessary for decision making about autism funding and made parental appeals (for funding, for treatment, and so on) key factors in those decisions.

Redwood served on the U.S. Department of Defense Autism Spectrum Disorder Research Program from 2007 to 2009 and later became a lay member of the National Institutes of Health Interagency Autism Coordinating Committee.[42] Bernard and Redwood have testified before government commissions, drawing on their maternal character as well as their research. These appearances gave them another public stage upon which to portray the autism mother.

On July 18, 2000, Bernard testified before the U.S. House of Representatives Committee on Reform. Her remarks demonstrate a blend of maternal and scientific appeals. Bernard introduces herself as "the mother of three boys, triplets, age 12—Fred, Jamie, and Billy," and then recounts how Bill, "after meeting all his developmental milestones on schedule and receiving unremarkable pediatrician reports up to age 2 1/2," started to "exhibit slower word acquisition than his brothers, articulation difficulties, and attentional problems."[43] Bill was diagnosed with autism at age four. Her testimony thus begins from the ethos position of a mother speaking out of concern for her son.

Next, though, Bernard invokes scientific authority by referring to the "research conducted by me and others, and summarized in our paper, 'Autism—a Novel Form of Mercury Poisoning.'" She amplifies the strength of the correlation noted in the paper, stating that the article "*has shown* that the symptoms which are *diagnostic of or strongly associated with* autism itself are *found to arise from* mercury exposure," and that this research "*strongly suggests* that mercury, primarily from thimerosal in vaccines, may be a contributing factor in many cases of autism."[44] Whereas the original paper demonstrated parallel symptoms, before the committee Bernard implies a causal relationship.

She evokes another scientific topos, novelty, by citing other recent research such as a "just-released Congressionally-mandated mercury report by the National Academy of Sciences" and "the latest issue of Environmental Health Perspectives." She devotes the bulk of her time to explaining the similarities noted in the paper, yet she ends on a personal note: "What parent will want their baby injected repeatedly with a known neurotoxin? How much confidence will parents have that our national vaccine program really cares about safety? Parents like me already have their doubts that it does."[45] Bernard returns to her status as a mother, evoking not only her personal experience but making herself, synecdochally, a representative of all parents. In doing so, she performs the role of the total mother, one whose interest in a scientific controversy is driven by her identity as a mother.

In her testimony before the Subcommittee on Human Rights and Wellness, Lyn Redwood also performs total motherhood by blending maternal and scientific appeals. She begins by thanking the representatives for holding the hearing, speaking as both "President of the Coalition for SafeMinds, and the parent of an autistic child."[46] Yet she quickly transitions into the scientific portion of her statement, arguing that the Food and Drug Administration (FDA) had failed to adequately address the problems associated with thimerosal content in vaccines. (Although the FDA had banned thimerosal from vaccines in 1999, Redwood states, as of 2004 it still appeared in some products such as the flu vaccine.) Throughout her testimony, Redwood refers to scientific studies: "Just a simple Medline search reveals hundreds of peer reviewed articles which document the toxicity of Thimerosal, including severe morbidity and mortality from high level exposure."[47] Like Fisher and Bernard, she uses the ethic of total motherhood to take on scientific language and even perform a scientific character.

Redwood also deploys the converse strategy of critiquing the scientific studies that discounted the possibility of a connection between mercury exposure and autism. For instance, she points out flaws in one study that examined levels of mercury in the blood of infants who received vaccines containing thimerosal. She remarks that the study used a small sample size, thirty-three infants, that "[b]lood levels for mercury were obtained days and often times weeks after the vaccine exposure," and that the infants studied were not randomly chosen. In addition to these limitations, the objectivity of its authors is questionable: Bernard states that her organization, SafeMinds, notes "their ties to vaccine manufacturers, which may have resulted in a biased study design and biased interpretation of the results."[48]

By adopting features of scientific rhetoric, Bernard and Redwood performed the role of a scientifically literate individual, if not an expert. In doing so, they sought to create common ground with decision makers. As the argumentation theorists Chaïm Perelman and Lucie Olbrechts-Tyteca explain, "A person—whether an adult or a child—who wants to 'count' with others, wishes that they would stop giving him orders and would, instead, reason with him and concern themselves with his reactions. He wants to be regarded as a member of a more-or-less equalitarian society."[49] By couching their claims in total motherhood and by emphasizing the scientific elements of that character, Bernard and Redwood performed a character that can count with decision makers who value scientific expertise as well as civic values.

The effectiveness of vaccines rests largely on popular acceptance of a modernist narrative in which science represents an unequivocally beneficial endeavor, leading to ever healthier, stronger, and happier individuals. Jacob Heller calls this the "vaccine narrative," which contrasts "crippled children [who] remain trapped in metal braces or doomed to live in iron-lung machines" with "happily vaccinated children [who] run and play without fear." This stark contrast leads to an obvious conclusion: "vaccines are cheap, safe, and effective; they rescue us from dreaded infectious disease."[50] Yet acceptance of this narrative requires a public with faith in science, trust in scientists, and belief in authority. Although vaccines have always involved skepticism and attendant risks, in the past they could be promoted to the public using arguments based on scientific progress. By linking their arguments to science, Redwood and Bernard disrupted that narrative and questioned whether vaccines always contributed to scientific progress.

In contrast, the vaccine-autism connection relies on a narrative of conspiracy, distrust, and risk that squares with contemporary understandings of science in what the sociologist Ulrich Beck calls the "risk society." For better or worse, scientists and experts can no longer count on near-universal support for scientific endeavors. According to Beck, we now "find ourselves in a completely different playing field, inasmuch as, whatever we do, we *expect unexpected consequences*," whether environmental, political, or economic.[51] This state of affairs stems not only from actual risks but also from a loss of trust that makes risks seem ubiquitous. This loss of trust, Beck argues, is rhetorically powerful, and it can be "instrumentalized politically" by strong activist networks that challenge even the most powerful corporations and governments.[52] Bernard and Redwood used the rhetoric of risk to disrupt the vaccine narrative, using their maternal characters and the stories about their children to personify those risks.

Fisher, Bernard, and Redwood were actively involved in the early vaccine debates; the character of the mother warrior seems to have developed later, due in large part to McCarthy and her cohort of mothers who combined ABA therapy with biomedical treatments that, they believe, address the effects of vaccine injury. While Fisher, Bernard, and Redwood protested vaccines, they did not claim to have recovered their children. Recovery narratives made the mother warrior character especially powerful—not for decision makers, necessarily, but for other mothers of autistic children seeking a way to come to terms with their child's diagnosis.

MODELING WARRIOR MOTHERHOOD

For this discussion of how the mother warrior developed as a character, I turn to three books written by mothers of boys with autism: McCarthy's *Louder Than Words* (2007), Leeann Whiffen's *Child's Journey out of Autism* (2009), and Christina Adams's *A Real Boy* (2005). All are memoirs written by mothers who used a combination of behavioral and biomedical interventions with their autistic children. These memoirs model the autism mother or mother warrior character for readers, encouraging them to identify with and potentially emulate that character in their own lives (especially if the reader is a mother of an autistic child).

All the books use a similar narrative structure, beginning with a dawning recognition that the child in question was different in some way, leading to a struggle to diagnose the problem, a refusal to accept conventional medical advice, and a description of the intensive treatments the mother undertook. By the end of the book, the mother has developed the character of the autism mother, one that frames her approach to autism, to her son, and to the medical community. By sharing their stories, these mothers model what it means to be a mother warrior to an audience composed primarily of other mothers.

All three women take watchful care of their child's health in accordance with the dictates of somatic expertise. Adams describes how, having had little experience with children prior to the birth of her son Jonah, she pored over parenting books: "At night, while Jonah played with water or paged through his books, I would sit in my white nightgown in his bedroom, poring over the simple-Simon parenting books offered by bookstores. I had checked that, yes, he could use a pincer grip to grasp a raisin between his two fingers. I noted his timely sit-up, his grasp of a spoon, his taste for Plums 'n Chicken baby food."[53] Aside from tracking their children's progress, total mothers are expected to take their children for regular check-ups, including vaccinations. Whiffen notes that she dutifully vaccinated her son Clay according to schedule, relating her comment at Clay's first doctor visit: "'What mother who cares at all about her child would refuse to vaccinate them?' I ask her as I mentally pat myself on the back for being so conscientious."[54] By portraying themselves as good mothers, that is, total mothers, these writers perform an available gendered character.

Diagnosis challenges this performance but does not lead the mother to reject the gendered role of the total mother. McCarthy writes that her "heart shattered" when she realized that Evan's "cute and unique" traits were actually signs of autism. "I almost felt betrayed," she writes, or tricked, as if "I didn't know the child standing in front of me."[55] Whiffen writes that somehow "a switch inside me [was] flipped." Once the diagnosis sank in, she writes, "A part of me withered away today as the formality of the diagnosis crushed my dreams for Clay and what he could become—the barometer from which all parents measure their own successes and failures."[56] And Adams writes that suddenly "the universe was rushing by in black and red. . . . I was plummeting into a dark new oblivion."[57] The metaphors these authors use—a switch, a dream "crushed," a plummet into oblivion—set the stage for a doubling down on total motherhood.

After this profound shift, the mothers channel their despair into an intensified somatic regimen, including diet, vitamins, supplements, ABA therapy, and myriad other treatments. Adams writes that, two days after her son's diagnosis, she eliminated wheat and dairy from her son's diet,[58] McCarthy began a similar regimen after meeting some other "autism mothers" who were treating their children with alternative methods.

In all three cases, this quest becomes all-consuming. "Any piece of information I find that gives me hope is fuel enough to sustain me," Whiffen writes, "driving me to continue searching. I stay up all hours of the night investigating everything related to autism."[59] Similarly, Mc-Carthy spends hours searching Google and combing through books. Adams spends hours implementing her treatment plan: "There are neurologists' appointments to schedule, vitamin supplements to order, bags of rice to boil, delicate cookies with the texture of foam to bake, spice labels to visually dissect for hidden words meaning *gluten*."[60] By their actions these women find models for a new type of total motherhood and begin to perform that role themselves.

They also find psychological succor in their efforts. Whiffen writes that throwing herself into research "gives me control over something that makes me feel so powerless."[61] For Adams, being an "Autism Mommy" stems from her desire to know and understand her son.[62] All three women are transformed from good mothers into autism mothers, performing a new character as mothers of autistic children determined to help their sons recover. In her account of her son Jonah's early years, Adams reflects on her trajectory from typical motherhood to autism motherhood. Once cowed by the stream of information about therapies, diets, vitamins, and medical terms, ten months after her son's diagnosis Adams has become a full-fledged Autism Mommy: "A mild mannered mother by day, I can leap picnic tables to grab forbidden foods in a single hysterical bound. I'm able to lift heavy medical terms like *benign Rolandic epilepsy, immune markers, opioid effect*, and *peptides*. I can diagnose a possible autism spectrum disorder over the phone by asking a few simple questions. When the need strikes, I become . . . Autism Mommy!"[63] McCarthy describes this role as that of the mother warrior, who will sacrifice everything to aid her child. Whiffen tells another mother that her "motherly intuition is screaming at [her] to go, go, go!"[64]

Adams describes four categories of autism parents. Those in the first category, "Special-Needs Parents," simply accept the services offered by the school district, taking no additional measures. For Adams, this approach represents resignation to the diagnosis and, implicitly, a failure on the part of the parents. At level two are those in the "Upgrade Crowd," who might tinker with vitamins or drugs, but still rely on the school district's advice. The third level, where Adams places herself, is the group of women who do "everything that sounds remotely reasonable," such as introducing dietary interventions, having their child's blood tested, running a comprehensive in-home intervention program, and shuttling their child to specialists and therapists.

Finally, the "Autism Super Mommies" are those who outdo even the Autism Mommies:

These mothers cook with the purest, rarest, most clean ingredients. They devote their days and weekends to cooking and activism, their nights to their child, their sleeping time to counseling others. They run

forty-hour-plus home programs. They use speech pathologists, occupational therapists, nutritionists, homeopaths, neuro-feedback providers,
auditory trainers, and the latest therapies from around the world.[65]

Although Adams admits that not all mothers can be Super Mommies,
she certainly implies that all parents should at least aim for level three
since, presumably, only at that level can changes take place. In this
way, Adams's text functions as constitutive rhetoric—it seeks to act on
readers, encouraging them to identify with her version of ideal autism
motherhood. John Hammerback explains that constitutive rhetorics
act on the "character or self-identity of audiences," often in ways that
"impel . . . them to enact the rhetor's substantive agenda."[66] By endorsing a particular way of being an autism mother, Adams works on the
self-identity of the reader, especially if that reader is the mother of an
autistic child.

None of these women can fathom how a mother could fail to perform this gendered role. Adam disparagingly describes mothers "with
solid marriages, money, and time who spend little effort on their kid's
special needs, who refuse to try the diet because, 'We love our pizza and
ice cream,' who feel it is the school's job to salvage whatever parts of
the child can be salvaged."[67] Similarly, McCarthy describes a group of
"'woe is me' moms" who complained about how autism had changed
their lives for the worse, compared with a group of "'I'll try anything if
it will help my kid recover' moms": "I couldn't understand," she writes,
"why *all* the mommies would not be up for something that *could possibly*
help their kid." Even if those treatments and therapies didn't work,
she notes, those who tried everything could at least take solace in the
fact that they had tried their best.[68] These passages suggest that not
all mothers feel compelled to "take on" the orientation of an autism
mother—that some, perhaps, have other orientations in place that do
not require them to take on a new one. Or, they may not experience
an autism diagnosis as a moment of cognitive dissonance that requires
a new role.

Adams, Whiffen, and McCarthy, then, do more than simply perform
the character of autism mother; they implicitly argue that others should
perform that role as well. They support this position by suggesting that
mothers have an innate ability to choose the best interventions for
their children, a maternal instinct that manifests itself not simply as
an affective response but as an ability to make somatic choices. When
Whiffen's son seems more and more remote prior to the intensive

therapy program she started, she notes, "My instinct as his mother tells me he's in there."[69] This instinct grounds the approaches Whiffen chooses: "I'm his mother. No one else knows my son as I know him."[70] Similarly, McCarthy refers frequently to how her instinct or "gut" cued her to act. When Evan began to develop obsessive-compulsive behaviors, she writes, "motherly instinct told me that something was wrong, that I was missing a sign." McCarthy urges readers of her book, likewise, to "trust your instincts, and if something doesn't feel right, ask questions."[71] Instinct offers a powerful justification for parents to question what they hear from doctors and other experts.

Memoirs written by autism mothers do not function simply to tell a story about a kid with autism. Instead, these writers perform a specific gendered character. These texts, in turn, generate networks of affiliation with other mothers. Online evidence provides some indication of how readers interpret the roles offered to them by memoirs. Sometimes, bloggers pay homage to a writer who has inspired her approach to treating her child. For example, one woman, mother to an autistic son named Ty, insists that McCarthy helped save her son, writing, "I shudder to think what my situation would be like without her. She is really a living angel in my eyes."[72] On her blog, this mother chronicles the steps she took to address her son's physical symptoms, following much of the advice given in McCarthy's books.

Similarly, reviews of these books on Amazon.com show that parents of autistic children make up a large portion of the readership and that they largely identify with the presentation of total motherhood offered to them. For instance, one reader, Britt K. Salisbury, writes:

> As a mum of two children diagnosed on the Autism Spectrum, and as a mum who has also watched my children make remarkable progress toward recovery, I could more than relate to Leeann Whiffen & her family's journey! What a fantastic read—it offers hope, while still being brutally honest & sincere. I often had goosebumps while reading! Leeann Whiffen is a true warrior in the fight to help others' [*sic*] affected by autism.[73]

Another self-proclaimed Autism Mommy writes that she found comfort in Adams's book, which she discovered shortly after her child was diagnosed with autism: "She opened my eyes and inspired me to look under every rock and be a REAL advocate for my son. She gave me the greatest gift a new autism mommy could get—HOPE!"[74] Narrative accounts, then, seem to function *rhetorically* to encourage identification between mothers of autistic children, but they do more than that. They offer a particular theory of autism as illness and a specific gendered character for mothers to emulate.

Some reviewers of these narratives find the mother warrior character off-putting, however. For example, one reader of Whiffen's story writes that "throughout the book she portrays herself as the savior, not only of her son, but also other autistic children and their families. She makes sure the reader understands what an excellent mother she is, how proactive and dedicated she is, spending most of her time researching treatments on the Internet and watching Clay's ABA sessions."[75] The mother warrior persona may not only seem self-aggrandizing but also unsympathetic to other mothers. One reviewer of *A Real Boy* on Amazon .com writes, "I admire her single-mindedness but how on earth can all parents of children with ASD's be expected to do this? I'm the primary earner in my family and my husband at present is unemployed. We rely on our school district to provide the services that Stephen needs. I cannot open my home to therapists for 40 hours a week or see the army of specialists that Ms. Adams and her son saw. I have to work and provide for my family! So, I felt like a failure."[76] Here again we have evidence that the autism mother character is not compelling for everyone—that some resist this role and the somatic expertise it entails.

Rhetorically, the total mother character has its limitations. It seems persuasive to some mothers of autistic children, but it is also easily dismissed as lacking in authority—the total mother can be portrayed as overly emotional, neurotic, and overly subjective. For instance, on "A Touch of Alyricism," a blog dedicated to "the equally fascinating topics of autistic advocacy and the 'sisterly sophistries' of radical gender feminism," the author writes that Katie Wright, a prominent autism mother, tended toward "overly florid emotional outpouring untempered by critical thinking skills."[77] McCarthy's views are roundly dismissed as unscientific, not only on blogs but also in mainstream news accounts. A 2010 *Time* magazine article, for instance, recounts that McCarthy "glibly and with irate dismissal of the scientific evidence accused pediatricians and doctors of poisoning children and then withholding the treatments that could save them" during her appearances on *Larry King Live*, *Oprah*, and *Good Morning America*.[78] Given the association between women and emotion, those who take on the mother warrior ethos are susceptible to criticisms on the grounds that they lack objectivity or rationality.

Vaccine theories aside, some commenters also object to the warrior metaphor. One blogger, Julie Boehme, questions whether the autism warrior mothers are really working in their child's best interests, since they seem more focused on changing their children than on loving them the way they are.[79] She argues that this image places the onus on mothers themselves to cure autism, often by endorsing "a sort of mystical sensibility that suggests that we, as mothers, 'should just know' what the problem was, how to treat it, and how to overcome it."[80] The warrior image may also stigmatize people with autism as defective and in need of a "cure" and as perpetual children unable to act on their own behalf.

Indeed, the warrior mom character places a considerable burden on mothers of autistic children. Although it may function rhetorically to give some mothers authority in public discourse, another rhetorical effect is that it superimposes this role onto all mothers of autistic children, whether they embrace it or not. One mother, Kristina Chew, writes that she initially styled herself as "some kind of super mom" whose main obstacle was autism. In "Confessions of a Former Warrior Mom," she relates that her conviction that her maternal instinct would always lead her to the right choice turned out to be false. Later, Chew wondered whether her focus on curing her son had prevented her from recognizing and valuing him as he was.[81] Similarly, Kate Movius found that she was transformed—"hijacked"—from the "Silver Lake Hipster Mom" she thought she was into "AutMom." This role, Movius writes, was exhausting:

> I learn[ed] how to ask for therapeutic services and get them even when I am told no, that's not possible, not in a million years. I [fed] my child no wheat or dairy and defend[ed] that decision to grandparents and strangers. I [was] a full-time chauffeur, speeding daily between the offices of specialists who work with Aidan to teach him to talk, zip, button, cut, follow directions, have those vitally important tea parties. I [did] all of this on four hours of sleep.[82]

These mothers did not invent the character of the autism supermom. Instead, they are interpellated into this role through various autism discourses, from the messages in memoirs such as McCarthy's to self-help books and encounters with other parents at support group meetings. The dominant message in many of these texts is that mothers should do everything to eradicate autism, sacrificing careers, money, and their own personal time (or time with other children or a partner).

Autism researchers often agree with these readers' perspectives. According to Michelle Dawson, a self-advocate and autism researcher, the early tendency for theories of autism to blame the mother has created an opposite tendency in contemporary discourse to praise mothers for their heroic battles against what they see as a debilitating disease. By taking advantage of societal praise for their actions, she writes, autism mothers "have rejected accountability to autistics, and they have taken control of the research and public agendas."[83] For Michael Fitzpatrick, the current image of the warrior mom is "yet another reflection of the culture of mother-blaming and a manifestation of the burden of guilt carried by parents as a result of the influence of pseudoscientific speculations about the causes of autism."[84] From this perspective, total motherhood is an extension of the earlier forms of libidinal motherhood, which constructed the mother's role as emotional and psychological life giver.[85] In either case, a "suboptimal" child represents the mother's failure to appropriately fulfill her duties. Whereas the libidinal mother might have failed emotionally, the total mother has, presumably, failed to be sufficiently engaged or to make the right healthcare choices. Despite these pitfalls, though, the autism mother or mother warrior character continues to circulate in autism discourse.

CIRCULATING THE MOTHER WARRIOR

The April 2009 issue of the magazine *The Autism File* featured six mothers of autistic children on the cover. Dressed in black evening gowns and heels, hands on their hips, these beautifully coiffed women stare accusingly at the viewer. None is smiling. The headline reads: "Delivering Where Governments Have Failed: Autism Mothers." The magazine itself includes little about who they are or how they have fought for their children. They are mentioned in an editorial written by Teri Arranga, who notes that "Autism Mothers have facilitated and discovered answers" where government investigators have not. Arranga emphasizes these mothers' *knowledge*, constructing an authoritative stance from which she and other autism mothers can stake their claims: "We know that children can be helped medically, including safely detoxifying under regular medical oversight. We know that the nation could prevent future cases of autism by preventing toxic insults from the air, water, food, surroundings, vaccines, and other environmental factors. And Autism Mothers want to help everybody's children."[86] In their self-proclaimed battle against governments who have "failed our children," they deploy the supreme rhetorical appeal: love. "The greatest motivation in the world is love," Arranga writes. "And, in the final analysis, it is the effects of love that will endure."[87] As Chloe Silverman has shown in her study of parents of autistic children, love functions as a "form of labor" for parents, as well as a "description of practices that are invisible in biomedical research."[88] That is, love functions as a key motivation for autism mothers, one that grounds their claims to authority, but one that does not usually figure into our understanding of scientific and medical practices.

As Silverman points out, the exercise of love is highly gendered, given that it is imbricated in "gendered structures of labor in American society" such as division of domestic labor and ideologies of motherhood.[89] Not surprisingly, then, *Autism File* features primarily mothers throughout the issue, for example, in profiles of mothers who are treating their children using alternative health techniques and of female therapists working with autistic children.

The *Autism File* cover also evokes the highly gendered visual rhetoric of any women's magazine—hair, make-up, jewelry, and the aloof stare of a cover model. This cover might not be so remarkable were it not for the fact that other autism mothers began to copy it—something *Autism File* encouraged and promoted on its Web site. A subsequent issue of the magazine includes a six-page spread of similar photos sent in by readers. Each photo features five to six women emulating the original cover image to varying degrees. Most wore black, but not all are in evening gowns. The women featured in a photo sent in from northwest Indiana wear black tee shirts with jeans, while women from San Antonio, Texas, wear black cowboy hats, white shirts, and red bandanas. But most of the images imitate the original, each giving a regional spin. The group from southern California poses on the beach, while the women from Seattle hold brightly colored umbrellas. The vast majority of the women featured are young, thin, and white.

On the surface, it is unclear, exactly, what these images seek to accomplish. In the introduction to a follow-up feature, Polly Tommey and Teri Arranga claim that posing for the photograph represents strength in the face of adversity. The message, they write, is this: we "stand united as mothers of autism; we are a powerful alliance, and we do deliver where governments have failed. That—governments' inaction—has to change." The precise actions that they want governments to take remain unstated, except for Arranga's insistence that these mothers want answers for their children's "hopelessness and suffering."[90] The message only becomes clear in the context of *Autism File* magazine as a whole, which advocates for a range of therapies, biomedical interventions, and alternative health treatments, presumably to address the environmental assaults or vaccine damage they understand as causing autism. Within the framework of total motherhood, these images of mothers are understood as visual performances of the autism mother role.

In 2010, one year after the Autism Mothers campaign began, *Autism File* editor Polly Tommey took the message a step further, posing in a black brassiere on billboards posted around London. The stunt worked, insofar as all three of the British party leaders responded to Tommey's campaign.[91] In the United States, artist Jules Burt organized a fundraiser for McCarthy's organization, Generation Rescue, called the High Heel Hike. For this event, "divas of all ages, shapes and shoe sizes" were encouraged to "strap on their favorite stilettos and glam it up" as they walked a one-kilometer "fashion strut."[92] Photos posted on the Web site for the event feature women in feather boas, little black dresses, and, yes, high heels.

Since the women who adopt the glamorized autism mother image seek authority to intervene in government policy, scientific research directions, and the like, their choice of image is in some ways surprising. They are not donning white lab coats in order to appear more scientific. Yet by highlighting their appearance, these women create media-friendly images, the kinds of images that lead to television appearances.

They also echo McCarthy's image. Prior to her fame as an autism mother, McCarthy was a minor celebrity with trademark layered blonde hair who frequently posed in bikinis or low-cut shirts (or less; she is a regular in *Playboy*). When she appeared on television to speak about autism, though, McCarthy cut her hair into a smooth bob and dressed more conservatively, often in black. The *Autism File* cover echoes this style, linking it to the particular character autism mothers perform.

The magazine turned its cover idea into a media campaign and also defined the act of taking a photograph as a political intervention. In this regard, the *Autism File* and the High Heel Hike campaigns draw on tropes of other feminized forms of disease activism, such as the "red dress" campaign for heart disease and the pink ribbon campaign for breast cancer. The main difference, though, is that it is not the mothers who have autism, but their children, who are not pictured. No one is trying to glamorize autistic women by having them pose in little black dresses, nor is anyone turning autistic men into sex symbols. The children of these parents are invisible and, presumably, *children*, not adults capable of making their own interventions.

Beyond spreading the mother warrior image, for many of the mothers engaged in warriorhood, the internet forms a particularly important venue for the circulation of somatic expertise. Not only do mother warriors such as Jenny McCarthy talk about attending the "University of Google," but they also marshal Web resources to share their findings, account for their child's progress, and argue for or against ways of understanding autism. On blogs, these mothers model the warrior mother's actions and emotions, not just her image. They draw on topoi from books, Web sites, and other blogs and recirculate those topoi in order to perform this character for themselves and for others. In particular, they model an attitude of guilt, a stance toward vaccines, an orientation toward experts, and a program for treatment, all of which are key to the performance of this character. Readers of these blogs may be other mothers of autistic children seeking advice; these readers, in particular, might be likely to adopt these character elements themselves.

Blogs written by mother warriors usually include an entry (or set of entries) or separate page describing their child's story, including the mother's theory about what caused her child to develop autism. As Della Pollock has shown, birth stories "(re)produce maternal subjects."[93] In a conventional birth story, a mother might recount the events leading up to the birth of a healthy child, following a linear narrative from conception to delivery and often including, ironically, near-misses or potential dangers that were narrowly averted.[94] These stories constitute performances of a culturally available character, the mother. Autism mothers are denied that narrative because their tales cannot end with the culturally sanctioned outcome, a "good," healthy baby. Instead, they tell a different tale, one in which they develop the character of the mother warrior and aim for a child who has recovered or been cured.

Often, they narrate the story of their child's birth and first few years of life, sometimes starting the tale during their pregnancy. In these entries, mothers implicitly argue that some precipitating factor or factors, besides genetics, led to their child's autism and that those factors could have been eliminated, had they only known. These blog entries constitute a public rehearsal of guilt, a key element of this character. On a blog titled "Recovering Nicholas," one mother ponders whether the second epidural she received while in labor might have affected her son: "Now I sit here and think . . . what the hell was in the epidural? Great, more metal, I'm sure. Injected right into Mommy—and gee, let's guess at how many hours it had to go from me to him."[95] Another mother, on a blog titled "Recovering Ty," offers the following theory:

> I am no scientist, but I am a mother that watched my child's personality slowly disappear until he was so far gone, that at times I hardly knew the boy who was in front of me. First off, I will say that there was a combination of factors that led to Ty's autism, including a genetic predisposition. I'm a bit pissed off at myself for many reasons, one being I was well aware of a possible genetic issue, but not one doctor of mine even gave it a second thought (I should have).

Ty's mother adds that she should have avoided dental amalgam removal during her pregnancy, since amalgam contains mercury, and that she should not have taken Tylenol to mitigate the tooth pain she felt during pregnancy.[96] And Lucy, mother to Alex, writes on her blog that she believes the Pitocin she received to induce labor may have affected her child: "Honestly I was so eager to have Alex also that an induction sounded great to me back then, now after everything I know an induction would not be my first choice or a choice at all. The more natural your child's birth can be the better."[97] Each of these mothers identifies a specific action that she should have avoided, modeling to readers a stance toward autism as something avoidable and an emotional stance a warrior mother should take: guilt. As Pollock explains, birth stories often "displace what is commonly considered the 'birth itself,'" producing "a *reality-effect*: a child, a self, an identity produced and reproduced within given narrative terms."[98] In these cases, the "reality effect" is produced through a narrative of cause and effect—a reflection back on an experience given new insights or questions about the dangers of medicalized childbirth.

In keeping with the dictates of total motherhood, a good mother should be able to identify and avoid potential toxins. Those who have children with disabilities, by extension, are encouraged to reflect on their transgressions and to atone for them. The mother warrior character spurs mothers to identify their wrongs and to alleviate their guilt by pouring themselves into autism recovery. Readers of these blogs might be led to wonder about the prenatal factors that affected their child and to take on the kind of guilt expressed there.

Of course, vaccines are especially likely to be mentioned as causative factors. Writers model a range of stances toward vaccination, some more tempered than others. One blogger named Lori, mother to Dylan, had to reconcile her status as a professional nurse with her concerns about vaccination: "I don't like to be anti-vaccine. I am a nurse and I know they are important. I do think if I had it to do over again, I would not vaccinate until after age five and then only one every few months instead of getting 2–5 at a time. . . . As a mom, I would certainly not have risked it if I had all the information."[99] In order to perform the role of a nurse, this mother had to support vaccination, at least in principle. But the role of mother warrior encouraged her to question that viewpoint.

The decision to vaccinate, for many of these bloggers, becomes a focal point for performing maternal guilt. Ty's mother writes, "I believe the final toxic straw for my beautiful son was his vaccinations. I don't exactly remember which set it was, but a few hours after his vaccinations, I said[,] 'His personality is gone.' I had this awful sick feeling in my gut. It was my motherly intuition telling me something was wrong. I pushed that intuition aside and listened to everyone tell me I was crazy."[100] Similarly, Nicholas's mother writes:

> I really wanted to stop the vaccinations completely . . . but I did not listen to my instincts and I regret that every single day of my life. It's too easy for you to listen to a doctor when they tell you that he's fine, he's normal, he's a typical boy, etc. etc. "Boys later than girls" is one of our former pediatrician's favorite statements. As a parent, you're reassured that everything is ok and you continue on with life with that reassurance—and it's not always correct. Trust your mommy instinct. It's there to protect your innocent children.[101]

Both recount a story in which they ignored their maternal instincts and instead trusted medical experts. Implicitly, these stories argue that readers should learn from these stories and trust their gut in such decisions.

Mother warrior blogs, then, model a particular stance toward medical authority that readers may be encouraged to emulate. The character of the mother warrior requires faith in maternal instinct over and above professional expertise. Lori, the nurse, draws on her professional experience to suggest that readers (other mothers) should be skeptical of medical authority:

> As a nursing student, I can't tell you how many times doctors would ask for my input and advice on a patient. A nursing student barely knows her behind from a hole in the wall so the notion that these doctors (who before this experience held god-like esteem in my eyes) were asking for *my* advice was unsettling to say the least. This experience taught

me how essential it is to advocate for ourselves and for our children in every aspect of life. We need to be informed and be sure that those working with our kids are on the right track.[102]

She argues further that only parents have the motivation necessary to really help their children. Justin's mother, who goes by the initials K.M.R. on her blog, similarly claims maternal authority: "I'm no scientist, I'm no doctor. What I am is a very angry mom with the common decency and sense enough to read; read any and all material I can on the subject of Autism and the debate of who is to blame; the vaccination part of it and whether or not there is a genetic predisposition to equal such a recipe as that of Autism."[103] These mothers all claim authority and urge their readers (implicitly or explicitly) to take ownership of their child's health. Their views may seem unorthodox, but in some ways they merely represent an emphasized version of a character all mothers are expected to perform, the total mother invested in personal responsibility, one of the values of a neoliberal health regime.

Yet the mother warrior character is always vulnerable to critique, and so it must be frequently reinforced. Sometimes, mothers do so by denigrating mothers of autistic children who do not take on this role. One mother, Maryann, writes the following:

> It irritates me to no end when someone can't even try! Do you think I'm something special? That God gave me some gift for being able to doing biomedical [sic]? Well guess what, He didn't. All I have is determination to help my son, and I'll do whatever is in my power to help him. So here is what I have to say to all those parents that "wish" their child was doing as well as Matthew. "Wishes" only work in fairy tales and we live in the real world. Get off your butts, get to work, and put your child on the diet. Then get out there and start researching and figure out what else your child needs.[104]

Similarly, Lori warns readers that "when you're the one who is accountable—you're the one who has to bear the burden of guilt for making wrong choices for your children," implying that those who do nothing should be responsible for their child's lack of progress.[105] Other mothers reinforce their character by reiterating their dedication and the importance of their tasks, creating a mission statement of sorts. On the "About" page for her blog, Alex's mother Lucy states: "Soy una madre en una mision, en la cual fracasar no es una opcion. Fracasar significaria perderlo todo, mi felicidad, mi tranquilidad, mi hijo. [I am a mother on a mission, and failure is not an option. Failing would mean losing everything: my happiness, my peace, my son.]"[106] Both of these acts—denigrating other mothers and posting mission statements—shore up the mother warrior by rehearsing the role.

Some of the mothers whose blogs I've quoted, including the mothers of Justin, Matthew, and Alex, admit that financial difficulties prevent them from performing the character as well as they might. In their blogs, they discuss the financial sacrifices they have made and their sense that they are still not doing everything they could. They feel compelled to perform a character that conflicts with their economic status. After all, McCarthy funded her son's treatments via television and media appearances, and both Whiffen and Adams were able to cover their expenses, in part by borrowing from family members. That character seems to belong inherently to the middle to upper-middle class, though mothers from other socioeconomic backgrounds are drawn to perform the role as well.

The mother warrior character circulates through a variety of performances, including memoirs, images, and blogs. That character allows mothers to rehearse a stance toward autism, one that lets them shore up their authority within a rhetorical culture that would otherwise paint them as ineffective mothers for failing to protect their children from harm. For many mothers, the warrior character is *useful* insofar as it allows them to constitute an identity and to frame the challenges they face raising an autistic child. The usefulness of this character helps account for the tenacity of alternative theories of autism causation and treatment, including vaccine theories, and for the difficulty scientific experts have had in countering arguments that vaccines and other toxins can contribute to autism.

Performing the Good Doctor

In a February 2009 Salon.com essay, the medical doctor Rahul K. Parikh reflected on the reason why the vaccine theory of autism causation had not been quashed in public opinion after ten years of study:

> While it's easy to blame the bad science of the anti-vaccination community, it's not enough. Legitimate scientists must own up to the controversy and learn to communicate better. Too often they use guarded, often complicated language, reflective of their skeptical and cautious perspective. . . . As doctors and scientists, we all have a lot to do to make

our messages stick. By communicating with conviction and compassion, we can only benefit our patients.[107]

Similarly, Steven Novella commented in a blog post that "the efforts to promote vaccines and fight against anti-vaccine propaganda have been lackluster," and Donald G. McNeil Jr. commented in a *New York Times* review that "the response from public health officials has been muted and couched in dull scientific jargon."[108]

Why have the communicative attempts of medical experts proved so dissatisfying? The efforts of (mostly male) experts to discredit the arguments raised by mother warriors have failed to convince those skeptical of vaccines. The inability to locate a point of stasis for this argument rests in part on the neoliberal logic underlying it. Within a rhetorical realm of consumer choice, engagement, and individual responsibility, it becomes difficult for scientists or government agents to present vaccines as a civic, rather than an individual, responsibility. Arguing for the greater good of the nation, or, more strenuously, mandating vaccines, conflicts with that logic. As a result, experts who support vaccination rely on the character of the good doctor who seeks to inform and advise but not to insist on vaccination. This role inevitably teeters on the edge of paternalism and lends itself to critique using the very language of choice and individualism that has been enshrined in contemporary health discourse. Like the breast cancer debates that Keränen studies, these debates rely on the overlooked factors of persona, voice, and ethos, in which the paternalistic good doctor marshals his character against that of the total mother.

By *paternalism* I am referring to the deeply rooted (albeit contested) tradition that emphasized the physician's duty to make decisions on behalf of patients. As a principle, paternalism emphasized that doctors were best placed to make choices in the interests of their patients because of their greater expertise and objectivity. As a *rhetoric*, it is a set of discursive strategies and appeals that continue to guide attempts to counsel and persuade audiences, in opposition to the consumer choice model. A paternalist rhetoric includes three fundamental persuasive strategies:

1. The rhetor writes in his or her role as a medical expert, emphasizing an ethos based on expertise and objectivity.
2. The rhetor makes arguments on the basis of objective decision analysis, an approach that presumably is unavailable to lay audiences.

3. The rhetor argues that he or she, as the expert, has a better perspective on what is in the best interests of the patient.

Although female medical experts can take on paternalist rhetorics, these strategies stem from a particular gendered relation between doctor (as father) and patient (as child). Unlike a maternalist rhetoric, which emphasizes emotional connection, a paternalist rhetoric could be summed up as "Father knows best." Those relying on paternalist rhetoric often present a fatherly character—as do those marshalled by the opposition. Both groups of (usually male) rhetors seek to present themselves as the good father, the one who has the public's best interests at heart.

Paul Offit's 2008 book *Autism's False Prophets* performs these paternalistic rhetorical strategies. Offit argues that scientists are "bound only by reason," and that, quite simply, "good science will be reproduced by other investigators; bad science won't."[109] Meanwhile, he writes, the shift in medical practice toward engagement and participation on the part of the patient, coupled with the rise of internet health pages, leads many parents to seek out information on their own. Yet few, he insists, "have the background in statistics, virology, toxicology, immunology, pathogenesis, molecular biology, and epidemiology" required to understand scientific studies, so they rely instead on "other people's opinions about them on the Internet."[110] This position leads Offit to disparage the scientific knowledge of members of the public, most of whom, he asserts, "don't understand what science is and what it isn't," and accordingly may not understand that science cannot prove the null hypothesis, or the difference between causation and correlation.[111] They might not realize that, over time, "truth emerges" from the scientific method. Given this lack of background, Offit cautions, parents (and many doctors) should rely instead on the expert advice of the CDC, the American Academy of Family Physicians, and the National Vaccine Program Office. While this may seem like solid advice, it unfortunately places Offit in the disadvantageous rhetorical position of advocating against patient engagement and for a return to a more paternalistic model of medicine.

Because he spends much of his argument critiquing the vaccine theory, Offit has little opportunity to forge identification with those he seeks to persuade, aside from another paternalistic appeal to the greater good: "my motivation is the same as theirs. You want what's best for kids."[112] In the case of vaccines, though, what is best for kids may depend on whether one views them in the aggregate or as individuals. From a public health perspective, ensuring high rates of vaccination provides herd immunity, which can ensure that contagious illnesses do not spread. The fact that a small portion of children may have a reaction to a vaccine (aside from the unproven link to autism, there are recognized cases of reactions ranging from minor to severe) seems like a small price to pay for this greater public good. From the perspective of an individual child, though, calculating what's best could be something different. From a purely individualistic perspective, the best-case scenario would be if everyone else vaccinated their child, allowing your child to remain disease-free due to herd immunity while avoiding any risks from the immunizations themselves (however rare). What's best, then, depends on one's perspective. Unfortunately, in an individualistic culture like the United States, arguments on behalf of the public good usually shift the burden of proof onto those who would argue in favor of the public good, not against it.

Paternalistic rhetoric also appears in responses to the various campaigns led by McCarthy, Tommey, and other mother warriors. In 2009, when Tommey launched her provocative billboard campaign, the physician Michael Fitzpatrick argued in an online article that Prime Minister Gordon Brown should not have responded to her requests. He evoked scientific authority, arguing, "Not a single paediatrician or autism specialist practising in the National Health Service supports the unorthodox biomedical approach,"[113] and he also evoked the superior cost-benefit analysis skills of a scientific expert when he argued that "until there is good evidence for such interventions parents should be discouraged from imposing them on their children (and warned to beware of practitioners recommending costly but unproven treatments)."[114] In short, he positioned himself as someone who knows best and can advocate not only for himself and his own son (who has autism), but for other parents of children with autism.

My point is not to dispute Offit's or Fitzpatrick's claims but to show that they both rely on well-worn characters present in paternalist rhetoric. While these arguments can be effective for many, they may not be effective for parents who are skeptical of the medical establishment, one that (from the perspective of many parents) offers few solid treatments or therapeutic resources. Further, these arguments neither engage the emotional appeal of the vaccine-injury narrative nor offer media-friendly images for *Oprah* or *The View*.

If paternalist rhetorics fail to convince some parents, why do medical experts persist in offering them? For one, the notion that facts should speak for themselves is deeply rooted in scientific ideology, as Perelman and Olbrechts-Tyteca have argued:

> [A]uthors of scientific reports and similar papers often think that if they merely report certain experiments, mention certain facts, or enunciate a certain number of truths, this is enough of itself to automatically arouse the interest of their hearers or readers. This attitude rests on the illusion, widespread in certain rationalistic and scientific circles, that facts speak for themselves and make such an indelible imprint on any human mind that the latter is forced to give its adherence regardless of its inclination.[115]

Offit and Fitzpatrick seem to fall prey to this notion that audiences should eschew biomedical approaches once they are shown that scientific evidence is lacking. This assumption fails to adequately address the reasons why some parents may be attracted to biomedical approaches, including the lack of scientifically sanctioned treatments, skepticism of medical authority, and the emotions of guilt or urgency that may accompany an autism diagnosis. As I have shown, these reasons circulate in autism discourse through unofficial channels, and they help explain why the character performed by autism mothers persuades some parents.

This rhetorical situation places scientific persuaders in a bind. To take one example, consider the federal Centers for Disease Control Web site, which now includes a special section devoted to Autism Spectrum Disorders, and the Vaccine section of the site. To begin with, the amount of information on these pages is overwhelming; the Vaccine homepage alone produces a dizzying array of links.[116] Given the glut of information on these pages, it seems that the CDC lacks a coherent vision or frame for its site or a clear idea of a pathway parents might use to navigate the site (see figure 2.1).

Further, the CDC Web site seems to lack a coherent strategy for addressing the emotional (as well as logical) bases upon which people make decisions. Several features of the site purport to address parent's fears, including articles under the heading "Concerns about Autism." The Web site frames this information in the language of risk-benefit analysis, assuming that people make decisions based purely on rational bases: "Remember, vaccines are continually monitored for safety, and

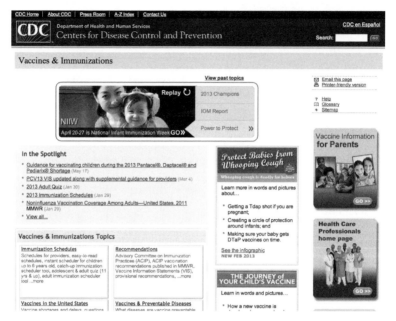

Figure 2.1. A CDC Web site showing vaccine information. From Centers for Disease Control and Prevention, United States Department of Health and Human Services. http://www.cdc.gov/vaccines/.

like any medication, vaccines can cause side effects. However, a decision not to immunize a child also involves risk and could put the child and others who come into contact with him or her at risk of contracting a potentially deadly disease."[117] The page does not provide parents with any guidance in weighing these risks. Instead, it assumes that parents already possess these skills, though few parents are ever taught how to wade through medical information to make their own decisions. The CDC is of little help here. For instance, the MMR section of the site lists potential side effects but does not say anything about the risks of not getting vaccinated—the effects of a child's contracting measles, mumps, or rubella. Since the measles vaccine was introduced in 1963, the incidence of measles has declined dramatically. Parents who have young children today probably have no experience with the disease or its potentially devastating effects. Without information about measles itself—its fatality rate, potential complications, and so on—parents consulting the CDC Web page might have difficulty weighing the risks as presented. Because measles (like other childhood diseases that were once common) no longer weighs heavily in collective memory, concerned parents are more likely to be struck by concern about vaccines. Ironically, the very success of the vaccination program has diminished public concern for the diseases it prevents.

Moreover, the CDC's approach ignores the fact that most parents make decisions about immunizations based on personal experience and belief, not just scientific information.[118] A 2007 study of students, faculty, and staff at three universities found that risk perception predicted whether individuals would get the flu vaccine that year. However, the researchers found that risk perception phrased in terms of a cognitive probability was less predictive than risk perception phrased in terms of feelings. For example, actual vaccination rates were higher for respondents who agreed that they would likely feel regret if they did not get the flu shot and later caught the flu.[119] Possibly, parents make decisions about vaccinations based on similar subjective factors, with questions such as "Will I feel regret if my child gets the vaccination and then develops autism" or "Will I feel regret if I forgo vaccination and my child gets the measles?"

Jessica Mudry might describe the quantified approach as "impoverished because it feeds certain human sensibilities only: rationality, reduction, and objectivity."[120] She is referring to discussion of nutrition by government agencies, but her observation is apt in this case, too. Government discourse about vaccines tends to privilege information and rationality, overlooking the fact that, for many parents, decisions about children's health and well-being are highly emotional and value-laden.

By relying primarily on logical appeals, the CDC website actually misses out on some rhetorical opportunities. In order to persuade the public to reject the vaccine narrative, scientists need to engage in what organizational communication scholars call "boundary spanning." As Mary Lay explains it, boundary spanning, for medical experts, involves transitioning from the scientific sphere of argument into the public sphere.[121] In the case of the vaccine debate, this would mean drawing on emotional and ethical arguments as well as logical ones. The CDC might consider telling the stories of unvaccinated children who have contracted measles in the past decade or so. In a 2008 episode of the popular radio program *This American Life*, Susan Burton interviewed parents of children who caught measles after an unvaccinated seven-year-old contracted the disease in Switzerland, then returned to San Diego. Eleven more children were infected, and more than sixty had to be quarantined.[122] The stories of these parents create a powerful counter-narrative to the vaccine narrative, and they could revive cultural memory about a disease that has otherwise been forgotten.

As I have shown, self-proclaimed mother warriors employ a full range of rhetorical appeals, including strategies that scientists tend to find distasteful or inappropriate given the emphasis in science on cold, hard facts. One doctor, Kevin Pho, writes that "anti-vaccinationists have a compelling story that no physician or scientist can fight against. Indeed . . . competing against the likes of Jenny McCarthy is a 'no-win situation.'"[123] Another medical blogger, a surgeon who uses the pseudonym Orac, laments that what gives the anti-vaccine movement an advantage is "the power of the story": "They routinely present such compelling testimonials of children regressing after a vaccine. It doesn't matter that epidemiology has shown repeatedly that correlation does not equal causation; the story is what matters because we are storytelling animals."[124] Thus, scientists recognize the persuasive power of emotions and storytelling.

Yet these experts are reluctant to employ those rhetorical strategies. The neurologist Steven Novella writes that the tactics of the anti-vaccination movement cause a "serious dilemma for scientists and skeptics—how do we hold true to our dedication to good science and intellectual honesty while still being persuasive?"[125] For Novella, the main difficulty for scientists is that they are constrained by "intellectual honesty," whereas their opponents are not. His proposed solution lies in *more* effort on the part of scientists: op-eds explaining the benefits and safety of vaccines, quicker responses to misinformation, and greater accountability for media outlets. Despite a few cautious recommendations, such as one claim that "it may be possible to use similarly emotive tactics to promote communication,"[126] for the most part scientists have stuck to tactics used in other debates such as those about climate change and evolution. Although scientists consider these tactics to be fact-based, as opposed to the "rhetorical" tactics of the anti-vaccination groups, they are actually no less rhetorical than their opponents. Instead, scientists who do enter the fray rely on their own arsenal of rhetorical appeals, including the traditional image of the good doctor or the disinterested scientist.

Of course, scientists tend to be resistant to emotional appeals because these are strictly barred from the works that scientists write for each other. The scientific orientation emphasizes objectivity as a key rhetorical and ethical value. Stephen Shapin and Simon Schaffer have demonstrated that this value goes back to the eighteenth century, when

Robert Boyle exhorted his fellow natural philosophers to stick to matters of fact in order to avoid philosophical conflicts; these early scientists were encouraged to separate accounts of experiments from reflections upon them.[127] By reintroducing emotional factors, mother warriors have unleashed a powerful rhetorical deluge, long restrained in scientific debate.

Scientists may fear that emotional appeals might dilute their objectivity or that appeals to fear constitute an ethical violation. Emotional appeals are ruled out of court in the scientific sphere, but they nonetheless are central to arguments in the public sphere. Emotional appeals are what get presidents elected, laws passed, social movements started. By focusing only on *logos*, scientists simply waste opportunities to judiciously draw on the full range of rhetorical tools available to them. They overlook the insight of scholars in rhetoric of science, namely that in a controversy, according to Alan G. Gross, "each side challenges the story of the other, adducing facts and argument in its favor. . . . Closure is achieved only when, *and if*, one story achieves consensus."[128] Although public opinion seems to be largely shifting toward those seeking to maintain the vaccine narrative, better stories with more compelling characters and plot lines may be required before those who are skeptical of vaccines may be persuaded of their necessity despite the risks they may entail.

Responding to mother warriors has required scientists and doctors to develop new forms of authority and appeal, including emotional appeals not usually considered appropriate for the character of the paternalistic, disinterested scientist. In his follow-up to *Autism's False Prophets*, Offit does exactly that. Instead of foregrounding his authority and expertise as a doctor, in *Deadly Choices: How the Anti-Vaccine Movement Threatens Us All*, Offit uses a more narrative-driven approach. He begins the book by recounting how a group of unvaccinated children in Minnesota contracted a disease that is preventable by vaccination, meningitis, and how residents of tiny Vashon Island, Washington, suffered 458 cases of whooping cough in 1999 because of low vaccination rates. Offit describes the horrifying effects of whooping cough, which leaves children coughing "until they are literally blue in the face," unable to take a breath due to the gummy, sticky mucus clogging their windpipe.[129] He describes an outbreak of measles in Cincinnati in 2005 and one in San Diego in 2008.[130] Whereas Offit himself was often the primary character in his earlier book, here Offit forwards other characters: parents who chose not to vaccinate, and children harmed by preventable diseases. These narratives draw readers in through emotional appeals and characterizations.

In contrast, the first word in *Autism's False Prophets* is "I." The character sketch Offit draws in the start of that book is of himself. Offit describes how he grew up in Baltimore, decided to become a doctor, and, witnessing children affected by polio, chose a specialization in pediatric infection diseases and invented a new vaccine to prevent rotavirus, an intestinal virus that causes dehydration and, in severe cases, death.[131] He thus tried to ground his rhetorical appeal in his authority as a pediatrician and scientist, using a typical paternalistic stance. His second book demonstrates a shift in rhetorical approach, perhaps reflecting the need for scientific responses to the vaccine debates to engage the emotional and character-driven appeals used by the opposition.

In vaccine debates, then, the autism mother and the good doctor are often pitted against each other, with both using the emotional and ethical appeals that will move audiences to action. I next examine how a different character has been presented as an alternative explanation of autism's causes and nature: the male computer geek.

CHAPTER 3

Presenting Gender

Computer Geeks

In 2010 the film *The Social Network* premiered to wide critical acclaim. Reviewers praised the central irony of the film—that the founder of Facebook, the most popular social network site, was himself "almost completely bereft of people skills."[1] Soon, suggestions emerged that Facebook's CEO, Mark Zuckerberg (either in real life, or as portrayed in the film) had traits consistent with autism or Asperger's syndrome. The *Wall Street Journal*'s reviewer wrote that the character "combines a borderline autistic affect with a single-minded focus on a beautifully simple idea," while the *New York Times* noted that, as portrayed in the film, "Mr. Zuckerberg is a social autistic who pivots between brilliance and hubris on his way to becoming the youngest billionaire the world has seen."[2] The online magazine *Slate* called the Zuckerberg character "a socially autistic, status-obsessed, joyless dweeb."[3] Indeed, even before the film came out, a *Baltimore Sun* article reported that Jesse Eisenberg, the actor who portrays Zuckerberg, studied up on Asperger's because "people have said Zuckerberg may have minor Asperger's syndrome."[4] Debates emerged in the online community WrongPlanet and blog aggregator Autisable, both of which attract autistic participants, about whether Zuckerberg has Asperger's. And in 2012 an article in the online blog *Gawker* "diagnosed" the real-life Zuckerberg as autistic, mainly on the basis of secondhand accounts of his behavior and an analysis of a video interview.[5]

In recent years, similar public diagnoses have been made for Microsoft founder Bill Gates and the inventor and game designer of Pokémon, Satoshi Tajiri.[6] Temple Grandin goes so far as to claim that there would be no Silicon Valley without autistic people: "We called them geeks and nerds. They're the ones that might be good at science but they're not very social. And a lot of those people, they run Silicon Valley."[7] In short, the character of the male computer geek has come to signify "Asperger's." Equating Asperger's with computer geeks has shaped definitions of the syndrome as associated with science and technology—and with maleness and masculinity.

According to Majia Nadesan, "the public's fascination with autism, particularly its high-functioning forms, stems in large part from the idea that people with autism are technologically gifted and are particularly adept with computer technology."[8] The character of the male Aspergian computer geek reflects the ubiquity of technology in our rhetorical landscape. For Nadesan, this character also reflects "social anxieties surrounding technology as a force itself, devoid of concern about the human condition."[9] But she does not explore how, exactly, the association between autism, maleness or masculinity, and technology has become present, rhetorically, and why it seems appropriate— so appropriate that journalists can feel confident enough to diagnose individuals such as Zuckerberg or Gates on the slimmest of evidence and be widely believed. The goal of this chapter is to examine how this stock character emerged from a rhetorical landscape in which commonplaces about masculinity, males, geeks, and technology are already in place and made present in an economic context driven by the internet bubble of the late 1990s. I draw on Chaïm Perelman and Lucie Olbrechts-Tyteca's definition of *presence* as an "essential factor in argumentation" that arises from the "very fact of selecting certain elements and presenting them to the audience," so that "their importance and pertinency to the discussion are implied."[10] By selecting details about computer geeks in order to represent autism, rhetors make technological skill and masculinity essential factors in definitions of autism, making those items commonplace in character sketches of individuals who supposedly have Asperger's. They do so using strategies of representation that help make the character in question rhetorically present, or especially lively and compelling: use of anecdotes, appeals to icons, use of the ironic antithesis, and appeals to the uncanny.

In what follows, I first consider the rhetorical context for these portrayals and then consider how they evolved in four key sites of analysis.
All of these sources make the male computer geek rhetorically present
in discussions of autism by drawing on topoi of technology and geekiness. As Perelman and Olbrechts-Tyteca warn, "Presence, and efforts
to increase the feeling of presence, must . . . not be confused with
fidelity to reality."[11] I argue that presenting autism via the character
of the male computer geek has limited popular and, to some extent,
scientific understanding of ASD more broadly, by focusing attention
away from females with ASD and away from features of ASD that do
not conform to the geek profile.

Presenting the Rhetorical Context

During the 1990s, four key events shaped the rhetorical context from
which the stock character of the male Aspie computer geek emerged.
First, on July 18, 1990, United States president George H. W. Bush
declared the 1990s the Decade of the Brain. "A new era of discovery
is dawning in brain research," Bush proclaimed, one that might make
it possible to address the "compelling" set of neurological conditions
affecting Americans, "from neurogenetic diseases to degenerative disorders such as Alzheimer's, as well as stroke, schizophrenia, autism, and
impairments of speech, language, and hearing."[12] During that decade,
popular science outlets regularly publicized new research findings that
purported to offer new truths about the brain. Often, these findings
heralded new types of brains that represented mental conditions, such
as "the depressed brain." In a 1997 article in the *Miami Herald*, for
instance, Karen Rafinski noted that new brain research showed that
"a depressed brain mimics the patient's sluggish behavior" via "lower-
than-normal brain activity."[13]

Sex and gender offered particularly popular resources for establishing these brain types. Newspaper articles heralding the reality
of sex or gender differences abounded, with emphatic titles such as
"Males and Females Inhabit Separate Brain Hemispheres," "It's True:
Sexes Don't Think Alike," or "Female Brain Structurally Different
from Male Brain."[14] Books appeared such as Anne Moir and David
Jessel's *Brain Sex: The Real Difference Between Men and Women* (1991),
and Deborah Blum's *Sex on the Brain: The Biological Differences between
Men and Women* (1998)—popular science versions of John Gray's

1992 smash hit and perennial bestseller, *Men Are From Mars, Women Are From Venus*.[15] Together, these articles and books reanimated debates about the science of sex differences.[16] The sexed brain became a commonplace of argument.

Second, in 1994 Asperger's syndrome was listed for the first time in the *Diagnostic and Statistical Manual* (*DSM-IV*) of the American Psychological Association. A high-functioning variant first identified by Hans Asperger in the 1940s, Asperger's syndrome differed from autism mainly in its severity. Whereas an autism diagnosis included delayed (or absent) language development, those diagnosed with Asperger's did not necessarily have language delays. Based on the similarities among other features, such as narrow interests and impaired social interactions, researchers agreed that autism and Asperger's could be placed along a continuum, or spectrum, of disorder.[17]

Asperger's was also distinguished from autism by gender. Although gender is not mentioned in the *DSM-IV*, Asperger had linked the condition to male intelligence: "The autistic personality is an extreme variant of male intelligence."[18] Thus, gender lurked at the margins of Asperger's definition and became more prominent as popular representations of the condition emerged.

Once included in the *DSM*, Asperger's not only became clearly ensconced in the rhetorical framework for how we understand autism, but it developed an increasingly public profile through stock characters that linked it to mathematical and technological skills. The 1988 film *Rain Man*, perhaps more than any other rhetorical event, had already made Asperger's present to American audiences through the character of Raymond (played by Dustin Hoffman). In the film, Raymond's brother Charlie (played by Tom Cruise) kidnaps Raymond and takes him on a cross-country trip to Las Vegas, where Raymond's savant abilities help them win big. Raymond is portrayed as both hampered and enabled in specific situations. His life is organized around a rigid television viewing schedule, for instance, but in a Las Vegas casino he uses his rapid-fire mathematical talents to win money.

This film was followed by Oliver Sacks's book *An Anthropologist on Mars* (1996), which introduced Americans to Temple Grandin, an autistic animal scientist and professor who has since become an icon. Like Raymond's skills, Grandin's are depicted as savant-like. Sacks describes her as having "near hallucinatory power of visual imagery" and a memory that was "both prodigious and pathological—prodigious in its detail and pathological in its fixity, more akin to a computer record than to anything else."[19] In part due to these kinds of portrayals, Asperger's became part of the rhetorical culture as a stock character that could be deployed in literature and film as well as in debates about autism itself. Usually, these characters are depicted as possessing astounding technical abilities—a trait that would later link them with the computer economy.

Third, political theorists declared the 1990s the start of a shift in economic organization toward what has been variously called the "knowledge economy," the "network society," or "cognitive capitalism." All of these theories encapsulate shifts in economic production driven by the rise of the internet and the concomitant rise of jobs centered on producing knowledge rather than things. As early as 1967, Peter Drucker argued that in large work organizations, "the center of gravity has shifted to the knowledge worker, the man who puts to work what he has behind his ears rather than the brawn of his muscles or the skill of his hands."[20] Drucker's concept of the knowledge worker has only gained currency with the rise of internet technology, leading economic theorists to argue that cognitive skills were essential for economic success. For Cristina Morini, "cognitive capitalism embodies the era of production of knowledge through making proper use of the cognitive faculties to form relationships and communicate effectively."[21] For Manuel Castells, this period is best captured by the notion of the "network society," in which "the productivity and competitiveness of units or agents in this economy . . . fundamentally depend on their capacity to generate, process, and apply efficiently knowledge-based information."[22] Of course, not all workers in the twenty-first century produce texts, data, knowledge, and the like—the knowledge economy has been accompanied by a rise in service and retail jobs as well. Nonetheless, computer and internet tycoons such as Gates and Zuckerberg became the poster children for this new economic model, men whose information skills catapulted them to the top of the economic heap.

The internet geek gained presence during the period now referred to as the "dot-com bubble," roughly from 1992 to 2002. Beginning in 1992, when Bill Clinton became president, the United States funneled billions of dollars into building an "Information Superhighway," promising new devices and systems that would "flood the economy with innovative goods and services, lifting the general level of prosperity and strengthening American industry."[23] Popular magazines and newspapers touted the coming digital revolution, creating narratives, according to Thomas Goodnight and Sandy Green, that "represented new technology as a bridge to a world where revolutionary changes in the personal and networked practices of communication were in the offing."[24] Soon, companies invested in these new technologies began to go public, leading to widespread enthusiasm and speculation, and later, record-setting prices in initial public offerings for companies with no measurable profits.[25]

These narratives of the internet revolution featured computer geeks as heroes. In the new American dream, the hero is a social outcast, a geek who launches his company from a garage and becomes a multimillionaire overnight: the ultimate revenge of the nerds. The geek became a topos for argument about the ways the new economy was shifting social relationships. Geeks possessed the cognitive skills to thrive in an economy driven by speed, innovation, and global competition; they became present in the rhetorical culture in which they had previously been marginalized.

Fourth, the concept of "emotional intelligence" gained sway alongside the emphasis on high technology in the 1990s.[26] Howard Gardner had introduced the idea in his 1983 book *Frames of Mind: The Theory of Multiple Intelligences,*[27] and the term gained scientific purchase when Peter Salovey and John D. Mayer published their article "Emotional Intelligence" in 1989. In it they define their key term as "*ability to monitor one's own and others' feelings and emotions, to discriminate among them and to use this information to guide one's thinking and actions.*"[28] The idea took off in 1995, when Daniel Goleman's *Emotional Intelligence* hit the shelves. It became a pop culture reference, educational objective, marker of marketability—and something geeks were said to lack. Emotional intelligence (EI), Goleman argues in a follow-up book, *Working with Emotional Intelligence* (1998), may be more important than any other type of ability in determining success on the job. He notes that late twentieth-century workers were "being judged by a new yardstick." Intelligence, training, and expertise no longer constituted the key measures for success on the job; instead, he writes, workers were being judged by social skills, such as "initiative and empathy, adaptability and persuasiveness," which determined "who will be hired and who will not, who will be let go and who retained, who passed over and who promoted."[29] It is not surprising that corporations, business schools, and consultants jumped on the EI bandwagon as traditional manufacturing jobs in the United States all but disappeared. Women had always worked in the so-called service sector—since the start of the twentieth century, at least, they had been funneled into service jobs that at one time were called "pink collar"

jobs.[30] It was men, in particular, who were most affected by the shift towards a service or knowledge economy and who must now develop skills
required to work with people rather than (or in addition to) things. At
the same time, though, cognitive capitalism privileged technological
skills as keys to innovation and global competitiveness.

The computer geek as Aspie character emerges from this 1990s context. On one hand, cognitive capitalism stressed skills typically associated
with geek cognition—categorization, systemizing, and programming. On
the other, the new economy privileged emotional and relational skills
such as leadership and emotional intelligence—skills autistic individuals are said not to possess and that are typically associated with female
cognition.[31] The character of the male autistic computer mogul stands
in for this tension in the logics of cognitive capitalism.

This tension derives from the contradiction between the knowledge
economy and the service economy: male computer geeks are champi-
oned as exemplars of the financial success that can be achieved in the
former, yet feminized skills such as emotional intelligence are lauded
as keys to success in the latter. What is crucial is that traditional hegemonic males are marginalized in both. Those who succeed in the
knowledge economy are geeks, and to protect the character of the
traditional male (now diminished in his economic productivity), those
geeks are repeatedly cast as disabled, autistic, and abnormal. Articles
diagnosing public figures as autistic offer one way for writers to examine this tension and to make it come to the life in the form of a stock
character or icon.

Presenting Computer Geeks as Autistic

Since the 1990s autism has been epitomized not only by young children
(usually boys) who are rescued by their warrior mothers but also by
adult males. In this section, I examine how that icon was popularized
by portrayals of Bill Gates in 1994 and Mark Zuckerberg more than
a decade later. Despite the time lapse, representations of both men
rely on similar rhetorical strategies. I then consider how these popular
diagnoses, dependent on characterizations of computer geeks, lead
some individuals to self-diagnose as autistic.

In 1994, the same year Asperger's syndrome was first added to the
DSM, Microsoft CEO Bill Gates was popularly diagnosed as autistic in a
Time magazine article titled "Diagnosing Bill Gates." The article simply
presents a series of quotations mined from two *New Yorker* magazine

articles published in the first weeks of January that year: Oliver Sacks's description of Grandin (an excerpt from *An Anthropologist on Mars*) and a profile of Gates titled "E-mail from Bill" by John Seabrook. This structure presents Gates as an example of a computer geek with Asperger's using rhetorical strategies of juxtaposition (or parataxis) and anecdote.

"Diagnosing Bill Gates" takes on a paratactic structure, a loose association of clauses or "a pattern of connection based on coordination rather than subordination," in Diane Davis's terms.[32] The article first lists an observation from the Sacks article such as "Some autistics possess an 'excellent ability of logical abstract thinking,'" and then gives a statement from the Seabrook article, such as this: "A Microsoft executive is quoted: 'Bill is just smarter than everyone else.'" Sacks states that autistics avoid eye contact; "E-mail from Bill" states: "He did not look at me very often but either looked down as he was talking or lifted his eyes above my head to look out the window.'"[33] "Diagnosing Bill Gates" accomplishes its purpose in a mere 333 words, simply by juxtaposing quotations from two sources.

The *Time* article does not take the form of a hierarchical, logical organization of claims that we might find in a piece making a more conventional (or hypotactic) argument for diagnosing Gates as autistic. In a hypotactic argument, according to Davis, "one phrase is linked to another phrase in a pattern of subordination. One phrase is subordinated to another, called as supplement to another."[34] With parataxis, Susan Jarratt notes, "the point is not exposing or discovering the unknown, but rearranging the known."[35] "Diagnosing Bill Gates" does just that, rearranging quotations from the source articles to invent a new article. It does little more than list these parallels, aside from giving them a title, which tells readers how we are to interpret them: as a diagnosis. The introduction notes simply that the two *New Yorker* pieces were "strangely and intriguingly similar."[36] Readers are expected to draw their own conclusions from the list of similarities.

The paratactic style of the article works against a more contextualized understanding of the "symptoms" attributed to Gates. It is important to note that the quotations included are several steps removed from either Gates or Grandin. These pieces of information are anecdotes, brief snippets of detail used to represent Gates's character.

Christopher Oldenberg writes that anecdotes are inevitably synecdoches; that is, they epitomize a larger whole.[37] A presidential candidate might use an anecdote to sum up or epitomize his character; similarly,

"Diagnosing Bill Gates" employs anecdotes to sum up the characters of Gates and Grandin. As a result, only some elements of their characters are represented, and some of the context is lost. Further, the *Time* article takes some of these observations out of context. For example, it quotes a former girlfriend of Gates who remarked that "'you have to bring him into a group . . . because he doesn't have the social skills to do it on his own.'"[38] Yet in the full quotation from the Seabrook article, the same girlfriend describes Bill as "an open, emotional guy," one who is "actually more open with his feelings than most men I know."[39] Similarly, the *Time* article mentions that Gates has a habit of rocking side to side that he started at an extremely young age but does not mention that, according to Bill, this habit began because his parents placed him on a rocking horse to soothe him to sleep.[40]

The nature of what was then nascent email technology also figures into Seabrook's account. The point of his article is to marvel at the implications of this form of communication. Some of his observations deal with this new medium, not Gates himself. His observation that "social niceties are not what Bill is about" refers specifically to the fact that Gates's emails dispensed with the formal epistolary conventions of signatures and salutations.[41] For someone new to email in 1994, brevity might have seemed like one of Gate's quirks, not a quirk of the genre itself. Today, we might not think it unusual for someone to write short emails devoid of complimentary closings, since email has evolved to embrace brevity.

A hypotactic article seeking to diagnose Bill Gates might have to take on these potential objections, subordinating them to the main claim, but the paratactic and anecdotal style of the article enables the authors to avoid addressing those objections. This style allows the article to pass as conjecture, even humor; indeed, the subject terms given to it in the academic database I consulted were "WIT & humor"—not autism.

Although "Diagnosing Bill Gates" may have been facetious in nature, it later became commonplace to claim that Gates was autistic. Temple Grandin herself contributed to the notion in *Thinking in Pictures* (1995), suggesting that Gates "has some autistic traits." Grandin cites the *Time* magazine piece in her book: "His voice lacks tone, and he looks young and boyish for his age. Clothes and hygiene are low on his list of important things."[42] In this way, Grandin employs a rhetorical strategy Katie Rose Guest Pryal calls "laying claim," or the tendency to diagnose others with a mental or neurological condition in order to create rhetorical authority.[43] Laying claim, Pryal argues, functions as more than simple name-dropping; it helps rhetors to normalize a condition. However, it can also require the writer or speaker to retroactively diagnose long-dead individuals who were never officially diagnosed or to diagnose those, like Gates, who have not publicly claimed that diagnosis. By diagnosing Gates, rhetors do the same for autism: they seek to normalize it or even praise its cognitive and economic benefits.

Yet doing so risks presenting autism via stock characters that turn into stereotypes, deflecting attention away from a wider range of actual autistic individuals, not all of whom are computer geeks. By claiming Gates and a handful of other technological geniuses, rhetors let the part stand in for the whole. In "Four Master Tropes," Kenneth Burke notes that synecdoches are often reductive, although they claim, rhetorically speaking, to be representative.[44] To choose Gates as a representative of autism involves reducing the full range of autistic individuals to those who fit Gates's profile: a male computer geek with highly developed technological skills and poorly developed personal skills.

Burke reminds us that synecdoche, as a trope used to discuss something "in terms of something else," is always "determined by the particular kind of interest uppermost at the time."[45] Given the particular interest in technology in the mid-1990s, it is not surprising that writers began to epitomize autism in the figure of the male computer geek. During that decade, networked computer technology helped give new meaning to "geek" as a social identity, which crystallized in online chat rooms, multiplayer role-playing games, and popular memes such as the Geek Code or Geek Test. Both detailed the qualities and skills that made up the geek as an identity position.[46] Although it is possible to "geek out" on any number of interests, popular representations from the 1990s reinforce the image of what I am calling the hegemonic male geek, the one with stereotypical interests in *Star Trek*, *Star Wars*, computers, role-playing games, and the like. The comparison to Bill Gates published in *Time* only crystallizes the existing conflation of geekiness, social ineptitude, and computer skills, but crucially, it adds the element of a diagnosis.

Presenting Geekiness as Autism

Portrayals of individual computer geeks such as Gates and Zuckerberg as autistic have led to characterizations of autism itself as fundamentally a disorder of geekiness. Sometimes, this redefinition emerges in the public sphere, but the hypothesis has also circulated in scientific theories, in particular, those of the psychologist Simon Baron-Cohen. In this section I examine his work as well as that of author Steve Silberman.

DEFINING THE GEEK SYNDROME

The connection between ASD and geekiness was cemented by Steve Silberman's 2002 article in *Wired* magazine, "The Geek Syndrome." Silberman claims that America's center of technological development was becoming a center for autism, owing to the selective mating practices of Silicon Valley's geeks (formerly isolated geeks were now meeting each other, falling in love, and having geeky offspring). He warns that "something dark and unsettling is happening in Silicon Valley," citing "spiraling" rates of autism in California.[47] The word *dark* portends doom, while *unsettling* suggests more particularly the uncanny—the feeling that the German psychologist Ernst Jentsch described in 1906 as resulting from events that make one "not quite 'at home' or 'at ease' in the situation concerned."[48]

For Jentsch, the word *uncanny* (*unheimlich* in German) "suggests that *a lack of orientation* is bound up with the impression of the uncanniness of a thing or incident."[49] Silberman's writing evokes the uncanny by implying that geeks and nerds—formerly social outcasts—were taking on economic and social capital, an unsettling thought for those used to a different socioeconomic hierarchy. It may also be unsettling to think that the offspring of those geeks and nerds might shift the kinds of social values neurotypical individuals take as the norm. For individuals used to a different state of affairs, in which economic and social capital lay in the neurotypical country club set or Old Boy's network, in systems of labor and capital in which social and leadership skills prevailed, not technical skills, the rise of the technical class might indeed seem uncanny. Silberman invokes an audience that lacks an orientation in which to understand the technological shifts that were, by 2002, changing everything from the way people shopped to the way they communicated with each other and acted at work. For many, this new technical class might indeed present a shift in orientation, a sense of unease, that can be personified (or perhaps scapegoated) in the autistic computer geek.

Silberman's article relies on this sense of the uncanny to create rhetorical intrigue:

> The Valley is a self-selecting community where passionately bright people migrate from all over the world to make smart machines work

smarter. The nuts-and-bolts practicality of hard labor among the bits appeals to the predilections of the high-functioning autistic mind. . . . The chilling possibility is that what's happening now is the first proof that the genes responsible for bestowing certain special gifts on slightly autistic adults—the very abilities that have made them dreamers and architects of our technological future—are capable of bringing a plague down on the best minds of the next generation.[50]

The Silicon Valley article envisions a plague of nerds wreaking havoc on normal American culture by breeding with each other. It also educes a sort of post-human future, a race of geeks who will somehow hack into and destroy America.

The central rhetorical figure Silberman employs to express this discomfort with the new economic order is what I am calling ironic antithesis. It is usually expressed in two opposing clauses, as in "the genes responsible for bestowing certain special gifts on slightly autistic adults . . . are capable of bringing a plague down on the best minds of the next generation." Ironic antithesis works by opposing benefits of slight cognitive differences with the purported drawbacks present when those differences are too pronounced. The comparison evokes the uncanny, highlighting the tensions and unease embedded in a system of cognitive capitalism.

The ironic antithesis used here reflects fears about technology and the cognitive skills it privileges—those traditionally found in nerds and geeks. When computers were first introduced in the years following World War II, such fears were located in computers themselves, "electronic brains" that many were afraid might replace the chemical brains of humans. In a 1964 article in *Fortune* magazine, for instance, Gilbert Burck pondered whether such machines might "outperform" human cognition, wondering, "Is man falling behind in a race with machines of his own creation?"[51] As computers became part of our everyday lives, these apprehensions of being taken over by computers were (largely) displaced by fears of being taken over by humans with advanced computer skills. Works aligning autistic people, especially, with technical proclivities serve to personify this fear. Lurking in Silberman's and similar articles is a dread of neurological difference as well as of technology; indeed, the two become merged into a sort of neuro-technophobia.

Silberman also evokes the uncanny with the language of crisis. He describes the increase in autism diagnoses in Silicon Valley as a "significant surge" and later describes the "surging influx" of autistic children into area schools. This influx is "cause for alarm and for the urgent mobilization of research." Autism becomes not just a learning disability or neurological difference but a threat. Silberman describes, for instance, its "insidious style of onset" as especially worrisome.[52] By framing the increase in autism diagnoses in the language of crisis, he aligns it with an uncanny, dystopian vision of a technological future.

After Silberman's article was published, many of its ideas were repurposed in accounts seeking to link high rates of autism to other high-tech regions. For example, a 2002 Toronto *Globe and Mail* article by Carolyn Abraham titled "Is There a Geek Syndrome?," though it places the central term in the form of a question, remediates much of the content of the Silberman article and places it in a Canadian context. Abraham refers to assortative mating theories to account for the rise in autism cases in Ottawa's technology corridor, mentions icons such as Gates ("the best-known public face of Asperger's"), and evokes the uncanny nature of the phenomenon. The blurb uses similar language, describing the piece as a rumination on the theory that "people with superior technical ability but poor social skills are meeting and mixing genes in high-tech centres, and having offspring susceptible to a disorder whose traits hold up an eerie mirror to our computerized culture." Later Abraham reflects on whether this "all leads to an eerie image of the tools remaking their makers." And she notes, with some trepidation, that "Silicon Valley has celebrated its idiosyncrasies with . . . exuberance, in offices where employees can ride between cubicles on pink bicycles, or descend floors on slides instead of elevators."[53] This sentence clearly displays the lack of orientation Jentsch associated with the uncanny: for outsiders, these behaviors seem unusual, even threatening.

Both Silberman and Abraham use anecdotes to constitute the uncanniness of the autistic boy geek. Silberman's article begins with a profile of eleven-year-old Nick:

> Nick is building a universe on his computer. He's already mapped out his first planet: an anvil-shaped world called Denthaim that is home to gnomes and gods, along with a three-gendered race known as *kiman*. As he tells me about his universe, Nick looks up at the ceiling, humming fragments of a melody over and over. "I'm thinking of making magic a form of quantum physics, but I haven't decided yet, actually," he explains. The music of his speech is pitched high, alternately poetic and

pedantic—as if the soul of an Oxford don has been awkwardly reincarnated in the body of a chubby, rosy-cheeked boy from Silicon Valley.[54]

In Abraham's article we read a profile of Sean McRae:

> At the basement computer in a bungalow just outside Ottawa, Sean McRae is designing a town. Eyes glued to the screen, hand to the mouse, he is holding forth on the cost-benefit ratios of various municipal infrastructures. . . . Sean is eight years old. Before his fascination with civic planning, it was clocks, right down to their pinion springs. Before that, it was world calendars, then National Hockey League arenas—he can name the seating capacity of every one.[55]

Part of the rhetorical intrigue generated by these anecdotes lies in their ability to produce a feeling of the uncanny by sketching out Sean and Nick as characters.

Authors accomplish this by using ironic antithesis to contrast the singular abilities of such subjects with the difficulties they face in "normal" human interactions: "Sean could read by the age of 3, and recite numbers in five different languages. But even now he can't brush his teeth, or play with other kids at birthday parties."[56] Like Sean, Silberman's Nick is described using these antithetical comparisons between highly developed abilities and challenges. Nick is "infatuated with fantasy novels, but he has a hard time reading people"; though "bright and imaginative, he has no friends his own age."[57] Each of these sentences contrasts an unusual ability with an equally unusual deficit (at least according to the logic of the article).

Jentsch reminds us that "in storytelling, one of the most reliable artistic devices for producing uncanny effects easily is to leave the reader in uncertainty as to whether he has a human person or rather an automaton before him in the case of a particular character. This is done in such a way that the uncertainty does not appear directly at the focal point of his attention, so that he is not given the occasion to investigate and clarify the matter straight away."[58] By using antithetical terms, Silberman and Abraham depict Nick and Sean as automatons, as not-quite-human in some fundamental way. In another instance, Abraham describes technological virtuosi who "can devote endless hours to writing code and design silicon chips the size of quarters, but are often more comfortable with computers than with people."[59] Writers come close to aligning autistic individuals with computers in these kinds of formulations, describing them as somehow lacking in fundamental human qualities, a tendency that is troubling because it dehumanizes autistic people.

Burke would remind us that anecdotes, when they seek to ground a theory or system of thought, should be representative of that which they seek to describe. Otherwise, "if the originating anecdote is not representative, a vocabulary developed in strict conformity with it will not be representative."[60] By beginning with anecdotes of these young male children of technologically oriented parents, who live in technological centers and have the requisite interests, Silberman and Abraham cast autism in a vocabulary linked to masculinity and technology. These anecdotes represent not the full range of individuals with autism or Asperger's but a subset thereof. By characterizing autism via anecdotal descriptions of children such as Nick and Sean, Silberman and Abraham reduce the range of definitions and meanings that can be attached to autism, selecting one set of meanings, in particular, that resonates with the cultural preoccupations of that time period.

In order to do so, each article positions its subject within a distinct geographical location. Both sets of parents work in the high-tech industry—Nick's in Silicon Valley, Sean's in Ottawa's "tech corridor." Burke might suggest that these anecdotes narrow the "circumference" of autism, placing it in "geographically local scenes" that constrain the way it is understood and where it is understood to exist.[61]

Silicon Valley Syndrome continues to circulate as an explanation for autism. For example, in a *Time* article from 2002, "The Geek Syndrome," J. Madeleine Nash and Amy Bonesteel call Silberman's article "basically a bit of armchair theorizing about a social phenomenon known as assortative mating" and speculate that other issues such as prenatal factors or birth trauma may be in play. Yet the authors cannot resist ending with the same rhetorical flourish used by Silberman and Abraham, the ironic antithesis: "Filtering the geeky genes out of high-tech breeding grounds like Silicon Valley . . . might remove the very DNA that made these places what they are today."[62]

Despite popular acceptance of the idea, to date scientific studies have not supported the notion that autism can result from geek mating. A 2009 study of families in the San Francisco Bay Area found that fathers with technical backgrounds were no more likely than were controls to have children with autism.[63] Other studies have likewise turned up no evidence of assortative mating as a factor in ASD.[64] Nonetheless, the association between male geeks and autism has taken on a life of its own, making it possible for Gates and Zuckerberg to be popularly diagnosed as autistic without any substantiation and leading to popular representations of autistic people as computer geeks.

The author of a BBC News article "Autism Link to 'Geek Genes'" connects the Silicon Valley situation to the high-tech "Silicon Fen" region surrounding Cambridge, England, and cites someone who would take the Silicon Valley theory a step further, professor Simon Baron-Cohen. The article posits that ASDs may be "manifestations of a kind of 'extreme maleness'—an amplification of a slight natural bias in many boys favouring analytical skills rather than social abilities."[65] Baron-Cohen's "extreme male brain" theory would soon become a favored paradigm—at least in popular discourse—within which to understand autism. And that theory was based on the stock character of the autistic male geek as its representational anecdote.

The kinds of children featured in these articles appear in television and films in which autistic individuals have become popular stock characters. In some cases, these characters are used for comedic purposes, as in the popular television series *The Big Bang Theory*. The show features a group of four male geeks, all of whom work in the physics department of a university in Pasadena, California. All share difficulties in social communication, affinities for technology and other geek paraphernalia (comic books, *Star Trek* figures, video games, and so on), but one is portrayed as especially Aspergian: Sheldon Cooper. Cooper is seen struggling with social interactions, sarcasm, and humor, in particular, and his rigid routines and idiosyncrasies are regularly deployed for comedic effect. Other comedies, such as the film *Eagle vs. Shark* (2007), even celebrate the quirkiness of their characters. In comedy, the strange is made familiar and laughable, and hence feelings of uncertainty or unease are softened.

More commonly, though, autistic characters are used to evoke the uncanny, especially in dramas. In the television series *Touch*, Keifer Sutherland plays the father of Jake, who has selective mutism and a propensity for numbers and patterns; although he is not officially described as autistic, many audience members (including participants in online autism communities) interpret the character as such. Most likely, prior characterizations of autistic boys with mathematical or technical talents allow viewers to fill in the blanks—Jake can be understood as autistic without the actual label because he exhibits the traits that have come to be associated with autism since the late 1990s. In the show, however, Jake's traits are used to evoke a more uncanny suggestion; a professor tells Sutherland's character that his son represents a "shift in consciousness," an "evolutionary step."[66] The tone of the show evokes other fantastical or uncanny elements from hit science fiction shows such as *Lost* and *Fringe;* including an autistic (or seemingly autistic) character adds to the sense viewers get of being disoriented or out of place.

DEFINING THE EXTREME MALE BRAIN

In 1997 Baron-Cohen introduced his "extreme male brain" (EMB) theory of autism, according to which autism is an augmented example of the typical male brain, a brain preoccupied with technology, systems, and classifications to the exclusion of social and emotional concerns. The EMB theory posits that people with autism possess more masculine brains than do normal men or women. In particular, they excel at what Baron-Cohen terms systemizing—an ability to understand systems, organize information, and make classifications that he defines as inherently male, since men are more likely than women to enjoy this type of activity. Women, in turn, are more likely than men to excel at what Baron-Cohen calls empathizing—a tendency to valorize social interactions, sharing feelings, and caring for others. He admits that some men may be empathizers, that some women may be systemizers, and that some people may be equally good at both.[67] On the whole, however, he insists that men tend more toward systemizing skills and that individuals with autism and Asperger's syndrome reflect an extreme version of that typical male interest, or the EMB. As Kristin Bumiller has noted, Baron-Cohen's "explanation for autism has the twin effect[s] of normalizing the condition (by suggesting it includes all of us) while essentializing gender differences (by rooting the condition in biological maleness)."[68] But how does Baron-Cohen accomplish this in rhetorical terms?

Although he published scientific articles on the topic, Baron-Cohen also sought to make his theory rhetorically present by writing a popular book, *The Essential Difference.* The book draws on gendered characters and topoi that are already present in the rhetorical culture and uses them to put forward a theory of autism. In a popular book Baron-Cohen can use gendered topoi, as well as the genre of popular gender-based books often used for self-help or advice literature. In this way, *The Essential Difference* shares rhetorical features with perennial bestsellers such as Deborah Tannen's *You Just Don't Understand: Women and Men in Conversation* and John Gray's *Men Are from Mars, Women Are from Venus.* These wildly popular books give Baron-Cohen's book much of its structure, tone, and style, as well as its rhetorical effect.

Books in this subgenre of self-help employ two fundamental strategies: a tendency to admit differences while writing as though generalizations are universal, and a tendency to constitute sex or gender binaries using anecdotal evidence or fictionalized examples. In this way, such books help constitute the differences they purport to explain.

The first rhetorical strategy, admitting difference while constituting categories, involves acknowledging that individuals are diverse but then arguing that *groups* of men and women tend to display clearly dimorphic patterns. For instance, Tannen admits that generalizations, "while capturing similarities, obscure differences," noting that communication patterns are also shaped by "ethnicity, religion, class, race, age, profession," and so on. However, Tannen argues, she focuses on gender and language because "the risk of ignoring differences is greater than the danger of naming them"—ignoring language differences would be a form of denial, which can ultimately "compound the confusion that is already widespread" between men and women. Then, Tannen affirms that "there *are* gender differences in ways of speaking, and we need to identify and understand them."[69]

In his book, relationship advisor and psychologist John Gray outlines a binary that sounds remarkably similar to what Baron-Cohen later described as systemizing and empathizing. Martians, Gray insists, value "power, competency, efficiency, and achievement"; they are "more interested in 'objects' and 'things' rather than people and feelings"; they "fantasize about powerful cars, faster computers, gadgets, gizmos, and new more powerful technology."[70] In Baron-Cohen's terms, they would be type S brains. Meanwhile, Gray insists, Venusians value "love, communication, beauty, and relationships" and spend their time "supporting, helping, and nurturing one another."[71] In Baron-Cohen's terms, they would be type E brains. Although "we are unique individuals with unique experiences," at heart, men are men and women are women, Gray asserts. Failure to embrace those identities is due simply to "role reversal" or denial. Gray advises women who don't identify with stereotypical feminine traits to simply "look deeper inside" themselves to discover their true core identity.[72] Alternatively, Gray argues, the ten percent or so of women who identify more strongly with Martian attributes may simply have higher testosterone levels than other women. Men who identify with Venusian qualities are not mentioned. Despite acknowledging that men's and women's interests and abilities may overlap, Gray proceeds to elide these similarities in the rest of the book, stating: "Men and women differ in all areas of their lives."[73]

Similarly, Baron-Cohen admits that when he writes about brain differences, he is "dealing only with statistical averages" and that the very topic he has chosen is likely to bring him "straight into the heart of the political correctness debate."[74] He decries the stereotyped gender differences outlined in Gray's book and others of that ilk, but he insists that a "serious book on this topic is needed" in order to show that biology does play a role in determining brain sex—despite the variability between brains on an individual level.[75] He claims only, he avers, that "*more* males than females have a brain of type S, and *more* females have a brain of type E."[76] From the perspective of statistical averages, then, brain types should mean very little for a single individual, just as individuals are likely to display a range of influences on their conversational style.

Yet despite these admissions, Tannen, Gray, and Baron-Cohen all proceed to portray sex and gender differences as universal. By rising to the level of the "statistical average" or category (male or female), they can simply recognize individual differences and then ignore them by focusing on categories. By the second chapter, Baron-Cohen has mostly excised any mention of statistical averages (although the term "on average" appears occasionally). In the main, we read sentences such as "Boys seem to love putting things together" or "Girls often extend dialogue by expressing agreement with the other person's suggestions."[77] These sentences elide the variability admitted earlier, constituting sex differences as natural and universal.

In contrast, gender scholars insist that these sex differences should be recognized as culturally and discursively constituted, as multiple, and as historically situated. What is usually meant by "masculinity" or "femininity," in the singular, might more accurately be called "hegemonic masculinity" or "emphasized femininity."[78] As the gender scholars Raewyn W. Connell and James W. Messerschmidt argue, hegemonic masculinity refers to "the pattern of practice (i.e., things done, not just a set of role expectations or an identity) that allowed men's dominance over women to continue."[79] Although the precise associations attached to hegemonic masculinity may change in different times and places, today we might associate this form with sports, cars, heterosexuality, aggression, power, authority, and the like. Yet hegemonic masculinity is not the only gender men can perform. For example, men who identify as nerds or geeks might adopt some elements of traditional masculinity (such as an affinity for technology) but reject others (such as sports or physical aggression). The "metrosexual" identity also represents an alternative form of masculinity, insofar as metrosexuals embrace activities normally considered feminine, such as caring about one's skin, using hair products, and wearing well-pressed striped shirts in pastel colors. Popular books such as Baron-Cohen's, Grey's, and Tannen's tend to portray hegemonic masculinity only, and to take that as representative of all males' behavior.

Similarly, "emphasized femininity" refers to the practices that support men's dominance over women by portraying women as weak, frivolous, and emotional. Today we might associate emphasized femininity with all things pink (as in Disney princess mania or pink ribbon breast cancer campaigns) or with interests in shopping, celebrity culture, and similar values shown in popular magazines. As is the case with masculinity, though, femininity comes in a range of hues, although perhaps not as wide as some would like. More frustrating is that alternative representations of femininity tend to be pathologized or denigrated. For instance, women who take on powerful positions in business or politics are often assessed as "dragon ladies" or "iron ladies," the only sanctioned role for a politically minded woman. It is not necessarily the case that women said to perform those genders—such as Condoleezza Rice or Madeleine Albright—would themselves identify with those qualities. In popular books, though, "emphasized femininity" tends to be the only available way in which women are (positively) portrayed.

The language used in popular books tends to elide differences among individuals in order to highlight differences between men, as a group, and women, as a group. Depictions of hegemonic masculinity and emphasized femininity help make that difference more stark. In such books, readers are not given the information necessary to determine exactly how strongly gender differences emerge. Baron-Cohen states that boys are "more likely to brag, dare each other, taunt, threaten, override the other person's attempt to speak, and ignore the other person's suggestion."[80] He does not indicate where this information came from, although previous passages referred to several books by Eleanor Maccoby published in the 1960s and 1970s such as *The Development of Sex Differences*. Baron-Cohen does not indicate the kinds of studies Maccoby performed, of which children, or when. He does not state *how much* more likely these behaviors are in boys or whether those differences reach statistical significance, nor does he provide warnings about the biases apparent in observational studies, whose results depend heavily on what observers are looking for, and in whom. Instead, the sentence exchanges a group of particular boys in a particular time and place (perhaps from the 1960s) with the universal boy, a synecdoche for both the particular boys in a study *and* the full range of boys who exist in all their particularity now.

Another rhetorical strategy, anecdotal evidence, comes into play here, as it did in Silberman's article. In *The Essential Difference,* this strategy parallels those used in popular gender-based books. In the first chapter of *You Just Don't Understand,* Tannen introduces readers to a couple, Linda and Josh, and their disagreement over whether Josh should ask Linda first when he makes plans with an old friend visiting from out of town. Linda thinks she should be consulted, while Josh feels that checking with his wife would imply he is not fully independent. From this example Tannen concludes that "many women feel it is natural to consult with their partners at every turn, while many men automatically make more decisions without consulting their partners."[81] The passage moves from the particular to the general, with the characters Linda and Josh standing in for "many women" and "many men," respectively.

Similarly, Baron-Cohen devotes an entire chapter to the account made by one mother of her two children, a boy and a girl. The boy, Alex, "loved miniature tractors, fire engines, and cars. . . . At the age of three he loved to collect small toy bicycles. . . . His favorite video was *Thomas the Tank Engine*—he knew the names of all of the trains backwards."[82] In this mother's story, Alex goes on to various collections—soccer stickers, soccer players, *Top of the Pops,* and the like, which are presented as examples of systematizing. Meanwhile, the daughter, Hannah, "was just so sociable. She would smile at new people, and take them one of her toys or show them a drawing she had made."[83] Hannah acted out scenes with her teddy bears, played games and flirted with adults, and loved brushing her dolls' hair and changing their clothes. These activities are interpreted as "empathizing." This interpretation might be considered, in Burke's terms, "over-simplification and analogical extension": "We over-simplify a given event when we characterize it from the standpoint of a given interest—and we attempt to invent a similar characterization for other events by analogy."[84] Baron-Cohen (via the mother he quotes in this chapter) seeks to interpret two children's behavior from the standpoint of an interest in biologically based gender; in order to do so, he characterizes these children's interests from the standpoint of his interest in empathizing and systemizing. All of these children's activities are placed in one of those categories via analogical rhetorics. For instance, brushing a doll's hair might be considered empathizing mainly because it is analogically related to other activities deemed girlish and hence associated with empathizing in Baron-Cohen's scheme. Hannah may have had other reasons for enjoying that activity, such as the sensory appeal of repeatedly running a brush through the soft, silky doll hair or the way that activity might remind the girl of having her own hair brushed.

As gendered characters, Alex and Hannah perform an important rhetorical function in the text. They act as synecdoches for the typical boy and typical girl and, by extension, for the Type S and Type E brains. The representative of the extreme male brain comes later in the book, when Baron-Cohen profiles Richard Borcherds, a prominent professor of mathematics who "was puzzled by his sense of alienation from people."[85] We learn that Borcherds often retreats to a separate room with a book when his wife has company, that he avoids phone conversations, and that, as a child, he was obsessed with the game Battleship and with chess.[86]

To characterize Borcherds, Baron-Cohen draws on the same rhetorical strategies used in the articles discussed above. In addition to anecdote, he relies on ironic antithesis and negation. His language reflects the pattern of ironic antithesis used in "The Geek Syndrome": "Here was a man who could fathom any mathematical problem you could throw at him, but who was unable to work out the basics of friendship or how to have a phone conversation."[87] This basic pattern comes up time and again in discussions of autism: this person can do complex technological feats, but is stymied by simple communicative tasks.

Baron-Cohen recounts meeting Borcherds at his office, noting that "basic greetings or social niceties were clearly not part of his routine behavior" after the professor failed to offer him a chair. His language echoes Seabrook's observation that "social niceties are not what Bill is about."[88] This language of negation phrases Borcherds's characteristics as deficits or diagnostic features. One might have also described him (or Gates) as "a strong, silent type" or a "man of action, not words." Yet those characteristics, which might previously have been typical, even expected, of men in another time and place, are here portrayed in negative terms, as a lack or a sign of neurological difference. These descriptions reflect the expectation that men should possess emotional and social intelligence in order to participate fully in the knowledge economy.

I do not disagree that Borcherds, as portrayed by Baron-Cohen, probably represents an individual on the autism spectrum. It is Baron-Cohen's choosing him as a "representative anecdote" that can be problematic. Burke warns that an anecdote is, after all, "a *summation,* containing implicitly what the system that is developed from it contains explicitly."[89] Borcherds, used here as a representative anecdote for autism, evokes gendered assumptions about technology and assumptions about autism itself.

Baron-Cohen takes a further step to solidify the male autistic computer geek character by including a series of quizzes readers can take to determine their own type, including the Systemizing Quotient (SQ) test and the Empathizing Quotient (EQ) test. The SQ test reflects the gendering of computer and electronic technology as masculine, especially in the prompts relating to computer processing speeds (item 20), wireless communication (item 57), and reading about new technology on the World Wide Web (item 11).[90] These technologies emerged from male-dominated spaces such as video arcades and computing labs, both of which tended to be "highly competitive and aggressive context[s]."[91] As the high-tech industry surged in the 1980s and 1990s, computer expertise seeped into what the sociologist Marianne Cooper calls a "newly constituted masculinity," one that stressed competition based on long work hours and technical ability, combined with creativity and adaptability to a quickly changing workplace.[92] Of course, this trajectory could have differed; indeed, the first computer programmers were women. Originally seen as an extension of the calculations work women performed during World War II, programming of the ENIAC computer was assigned to six women.[93] Only later, when it became apparent that programming was to be a high-status activity, did it come to be considered a man's job.

Yet the specific kinds of interests included in the SQ test obscure the historically and culturally specific discourses and practices that define technology. Most often, the technologies included in the SQ test elide those typically associated with women (sewing machines, dishwashers, blenders).[94] In her book *Making Technology Masculine,* the historian Ruth Oldenziel shows that the term *technology* itself only gained popularity in the United States in the 1930s. In the previous century, the more capacious terms "useful arts" or "applied science," which included innovations, tools, and techniques in fields such as agriculture, textiles, and metalwork, prevailed.[95] *Technology* gained favor as engineering became professionalized, laying an exclusive claim to technology, now defined more narrowly to refer to machines and as the purview of white men.[96] The term *technology* excluded the broader range of useful arts in which women's inventions and objects (quilts, corsets, and so on) were included.[97] This history, Oldenziel argues, "is essential for our current understanding of who is believed to be a true technologist or an inventor" and, I would argue, for who is considered to possess a systemizing brain.[98] As a representative anecdote, Borcherds embeds these culturally specific assumptions about what counts as systemizing skill or technological interests.

Indeed, Baron-Cohen found that he could change the results of the SQ test—the proportion of men and women who were counted as possessing SQ brains—based on how technology was defined or how broadly he drew the circumference around the term. In 2006 Sally Wheelwright, Baron-Cohen, and their collaborators published a revised version of the SQ, the SQ-R, which included a wider range of questions about systemizing. The original SQ prompt, the authors admitted, "were drawn primarily from traditionally male domains." For this reason, the SQ-R included "more items that might be relevant to females in the general population," a feature that would allow the researchers to determine whether men would continue to score higher on the SQ "even with the inclusion of items selected from traditionally female domains."[99] Some of the new prompts included "When I have a lot of shopping to do, I like to plan which shops I am going to visit and in what order" and "My clothes are not carefully organised into different types in my wardrobe" (answering "no" on this prompt presumably indicates an S type brain).[100] The SQ-R successfully shifted the results. In the original SQ, men had a higher mean score on 86.6 percent of the questions, while women had a higher mean on only 13.2 percent. In the revised version, men scored higher on 68 percent and women on 32 percent—a rather dramatic shift in the sex ratio.[101]

While the SQ-R attempts to offer a wider range of prompts, it now includes prompts that might be considered to be gender-neutral. One might hypothesize that the SQ could be revised even further in ways that would equalize the scores. For example, knitting, sewing, and crafting involve spatial reasoning, understanding or designing patterns, and seeing how pieces fit together, which are systemizing activities. Yet none of the questions on the SQ or SQ-R tap into these skills. Table 3.1 presents a list of selected questions from the SQ that might be rewritten to reflect typically feminine interests.

Table 3.1. Selected questions from the Systematizing Quotient test in standard and feminized versions

Item #	Current Version	Feminized Version
5	If I were buying a car, I would want to obtain specific information about its engine capacity.	If I were buying a new dress, I'd check to see the fabric content and care instructions.
7	If there were a problem with the electrical wiring in my home, I'd be able to fix it myself.	If I lost a button on a shirt, I'd be able to fix it myself.
11	I rarely read articles or Web pages about new technology.	I rarely read articles or Web pages about new fashion.
13	I am fascinated by how machines work.	I am fascinated by how the human body works.
20	If I were buying a computer, I would want to know exact details about its hard drive capacity and processor speed.	If I were buying a computer, I would want to know exact details about its size and weight.
25	If I had a collection (e.g., CDs, coins, stamps), it would be highly organized.	If I had a collection (e.g., dolls, books), it would be highly organized.
26	When I look at a piece of furniture, I do not notice the details of how it was constructed.	When I look at a piece of clothing, I do not notice the details of how it was constructed.
29	When I read the newspaper, I am drawn to tables of information, such as football scores or stock market indices.	I am drawn to tables of information, such as sizing charts or nutritional information.
32	I do not tend to watch science documentaries on television or read articles about science and nature.	I do not tend to watch science documentaries on television or read articles about health, animals, or nature.
33	If I were buying a stereo, I would want to know about its precise technical features.	If I were buying a sewing machine, I would want to know about its precise technical features.
35	I am not very meticulous when I carry out do-it-yourself projects.	I am not very meticulous when I carry out craft projects.
57	I am not interested in understanding how wireless communication works.	I am not interested in understanding how baking powder works.

This example illustrates how the wording of specific quiz prompts draws different circumferences around the term *technology*, potentially skewing the reported sex differences between men and women. The SQ-R demonstrates that these sex differences may in fact be artifacts of the testing prompts and the specific mix of questions included. Yet the authors conclude from the revised study that "in the typical group, more than twice as many males as females had a Type S brain, and more than twice as many females as males had a Type E brain," a finding they interpret as upholding Baron-Cohen's EQ/SQ theory.[102]

In rhetorical terms, the tests themselves might be understood as forms of constitutive rhetoric, in that they "change the character or self-identity of audiences" or encourage test-takers to assume the characteristics they purport to simply describe, rather than being simply diagnostic.[103] In her book *Delusions of Gender*, Cordelia Fine shows that individuals are subconsciously primed to respond to psychological tests in certain ways, depending on the testing situation. For instance, researchers asked university students to state whether they were male or female before completing a survey ranking their verbal and math abilities. In the control condition, students had to select their ethnicity. When asked to provide their sex, female students rated their math ability lower than when asked to indicate their ethnicity. When sex is made salient in a testing situation, researchers hypothesize, students are likely to unconsciously evoke gendered commonplaces, such as the notion that males are better at math than are females.[104] In the case of a self-test for empathizing or systemizing, those who design the test might not be knowingly seeking to change the self-identity of the test-taker; instead, that change occurs on a more unconscious level, by means of the very language of the test. Ian Hacking would call this a "looping effect," insofar as "people classified in a certain way tend to conform to or grow into the ways that they are described."[105]

Because Baron-Cohen's book first outlines his theory of the sexed brain and then includes relevant quizzes, readers are already primed to evoke gender stereotypes, an effect that may skew their results. After reading that women are supposed to be more empathetic than men, it is likely that female readers will score better on the EQ quiz because notions about women as caring, emotional, and empathetic have already been invoked. Similarly, online versions of the test explicitly mention sex, using titles such as "How male or female is your brain?" and "Sex I.D. Find out how your mind works!"[106] On the "Sex I.D." site, which was used to gather data for a BBC television special, readers could get a "brain sex profile" in order to find out if they "think like a man or a woman." Even if gender is not explicitly mentioned, empathy is so strongly associated with femininity that it may not be required in order to elicit a priming effect, as I show below. In short, brain quizzes such as the EQ and SQ participate in a constitutive, rhetorical process with reciprocal effects.

Baron-Cohen's representative anecdotes also carry with them particular definitions of empathy, narrowing the circumference, in Burke's terms, to include only aspects of empathy that are measurable in quantitative terms. Empathy has historically been described as an emotion, and it has not always been gendered female. In rhetorical theory, it has been associated with a capacity for *feeling* emotions, not identifying them. The ancient Roman rhetorician Quintilian noted that the most effective rhetors possess a capacity to experience the emotions they seek to evoke. For Quintilian, though, empathy is also performative, since orators who can "best conceive such images will have the greatest power in moving the feelings."[107] In his formulation, empathy represents a capacity to conjure for oneself the emotional states that move the feelings, and to project those emotional states to an audience. Because the vast majority of orators at that time were men, we can surmise that empathy was not considered the unique province of women.

When it became a topic for psychological inquiry, empathy originally enjoyed a similarly broad definition, equally likely to refer to aesthetics, cognition, or embodied emotion. In 1925, Herbert Ellsworth Cory declared that dance was "the most direct elaboration of empathy (those movements by which we seek to become one with the object we contemplate)."[108] As an embodied aesthetic reaction, empathy could be directed toward objects, as well as people, as when a dancer is inspired by nature or art. Cognitive definitions of empathy used the work of Edmund Husserl, who viewed it as a method of philosophical inquiry into other minds (in German, *Einfuhlung*, or "sympathetic participation"). This definition maintained that the *actual* feelings of another are "unpresentable and unsharable" but that *meanings* of emotions could be shared to the extent that one could project his or her own feelings onto others.[109] In 1909 the psychologist Edward Titchener coined the term *empathy* as a translation of *Einfuhlung*, giving it a kinesthetic definition by referring to the way, when contemplating a physical action such as a frown or nod of the head, the body participates: "Not only do I see gravity and modesty and pride and courtesy and stateliness, but I feel or act them in the mind's muscles."[110] He later referred to this concept as motor empathy, or the mirroring of the physical behaviors of another.[111]

In the early twentieth century, it was unclear that empathy could be measured at all. The philosopher Wilbur M. Urban wrote in 1917 that the notion that one could "know" other minds was always an inference, and often a projection of one's own feeling onto others. Feeling, Urban insisted, was "unrepresentable and unsharable," so claims to know what someone else is feeling can only refer to judgments about the meaning or intentions of another.[112]

Even when researchers sought to quantify empathy, they did not find important sex differences. In 1949, Rosalie F. Dymond published the results of an initial attempt to quantify empathy, which she defined as "the imaginative transposing of oneself into the thinking, feeling and acting of another and so structuring the world as he does."[113] It is noteworthy that females did not score better on the test she devised than did males, but the females did show greater improvement on the test when given a chance to retake it.[114]

In the 1960s, Robert Hogan took up this approach, designing a new test that determined how inaccurately or accurately subjects could perceive emotions in others. While admitting that empathy may be a "creature of Academia," he nonetheless proceeded to define it as the "act of constructing for oneself another person's mental state." The accuracy of those constructions did not figure into Hogan's definition: "the verisimilitude of the resulting construct is not a necessary part of the concept's meaning."[115] His empathy scale drew on items from existing psychometric tests such as the Minnesota Multiphasic Personality Inventory and the California Psychological Inventory. Hogan found that, for the first time, women scored higher than men, on average, on his scale—"a point which," he remarks, "accords well with conventional wisdom on this topic."[116] It is also worth noting, though, that male psychology students scored highest on the test, along with men who were educated abroad. The average score of male participants may have been affected by the fact that they included a group of prison inmates and a group of "young delinquents," who had the lowest average scores of the group.

Skepticism about the attempt to quantify empathy continued despite the attempts by Dymond and Hogan to create an objective scale. Charles W. Hobart and Nancy Fahlberg argued in 1965 that empathy could only be measured once its definition shifted from the act of "'taking the role of the other'" (a definition given by George Herbert Mead) to the act of perceiving another's emotion, which, Hobart and Fahlberg argue, would be better termed "social perception." Although empathy cannot be measured, insofar as it involves the subjective acts of "identifying with another person and thus knowing his feelings, not by *seeing* them in *him*, but by *feeling* them in *oneself*," social perception can be measured. But this shift is problematic, they insisted, because it may actually test the opposite of empathy—the "attribution to another of one's own needs, interests, and attitudes."[117] It is possible, then, that empathy tests actually measure how typical one's attitudes and emotions are, or how well one squares with a cultural norm of emotion and feeling, rather than the extent to which one feels the emotions of others.

These tests of empathic accuracy reduce empathy to a concrete, testable skill, allowing it to be quantified and then compared to similarly quantified skills, for instance, systemizing ability. Baron-Cohen's version of the test uses this precedent, which reduces the full range of empathic activities to ones that can be tested, such as "correctly" identifying or predicting someone's state of mind.

Baron-Cohen's theory also draws on a separate strain of psychological research. In the 1970s, psychologists devised tests to determine whether individuals (and animals) possessed the ability to make inferences about someone else's intentions, or whether they had "theory of mind." The theory of mind (TOM) test was first devised by David Premack and Guy Woodruff as a way to distinguish between animal and human cognition.[118] In particular, it was meant to show that chimpanzees lack the fundamentally human ability to judge what someone else may be thinking—a necessity since animal researchers were finding that animal cognition significantly outstripped expectations and, consequently, threatened notions of human exceptionalism. In the late 1960s, Allen and Beatrix Gardner trained a chimpanzee named Washoe to use sign language. Soon, their experiments with Washoe showed that chimpanzees could learn sign language, coin new phrases, make references to self, and engage in imaginative play.[119] In a different set of experiments, Gordon G. Gallup showed that chimps could recognize themselves in the mirror.[120] Together, these and other studies were suggesting that humans were not the only animals to use symbols or to have a sense of self. As Jay Meddin concluded in 1979, "The chimpanzee evidence obviously places our symbolic nature, like the rest of our organism, back in the Darwinian order of evolutionary development—where it very clearly belongs."[121] Premack and Woodruff's study served to shore up a different distinction between humans and animals, based on a narrowed understanding of empathy as reading intentions in others.

Baron-Cohen adapted this test into one that could distinguish between autistic children and other children, which was necessary in part because, in the 1980s, children with intellectual impairments were being incorporated into schools and community support services instead of being placed in institutions. These shifts compelled experts to clarify diagnostic categories and provide psychological measures that could reliably distinguish children.[122] He argued that his TOM test would do just that: explain the lack of pretend play and the social impairments seen in autistic children but not in children with Down Syndrome (presumably chosen to stand in for other types of neurological disability).

One of the common tests for TOM formulated by Baron-Cohen involves a simple skit with two dolls, Sally and Anne. The researcher shows a child the two dolls. Sally has a ball or marble that she puts into a basket while Anne watches. When Sally leaves, Anne moves the ball into a box. When Sally returns, the researcher asks the child where Sally will look for her ball—in the basket or in the box. In order to pass the test, the child must answer "in the basket," demonstrating that he or she can understand where Sally thinks the ball is, not where the ball actually is. According to Baron-Cohen's results, children with autism perform poorly on the test, hence demonstrating their lack of TOM, whereas the majority of the children with Down Syndrome answered the question correctly.[123] Yet equating theory of mind with empathy involves a significant reduction or narrowing of what constitutes empathy. The TOM test is a test of cognitive empathy, or empathic ability, in the tradition of Dymond and Hogan, not emotional or embodied empathy. This narrow definition nonetheless comes to stand in for or efface the richer conception of empathy that appeared earlier in the history of psychology.

In *The Essential Difference*, Baron-Cohen includes a different test for empathy, the Reading the Mind in the Eyes Test (RMET), which gauges one's ability to correctly judge the emotion expressed in a series of photographs of people's eyes. In the seventh prompt, for instance, the test-taker must judge whether the correct expression is apologetic, friendly, uneasy, or dispirited.[124]

Faces, in general, hold a privileged place in psychological tests. In 1918, Herbert Sidney Langfeld, a Harvard University psychologist, conducted an experiment in which participants attempted to judge correctly the emotion depicted in a series of drawings based on photographs of an actor. Langfeld assumed that if at least 50 percent of his respondents agreed with the picture's title, that would indicate that the actor had successfully portrayed the emotion in question.[125] For Langfeld, this study only had to do with *empathy*, though, for some respondents chose to use an "empathic response" to help them interpret the images, and here Langfeld means *empathy* in the sense of embodied, motor imitation of the facial expression in question.[126]

As was the case with empathy, early tests of facial expressions of emotion did not immediately reveal sex differences. In 1924, J. P. Guilford demonstrated that participants could learn to improve the accuracy of their responses to these same prompts with training, and that men and women did not differ in their ability to correctly label the faces. To put it bluntly, Guilford asked, "What sex differences, if any, are revealed in the data? None whatever!"[127] James C. Coleman found similar results in his 1949 study, in which he observed participants in a number of situations, recorded them, and then asked others to judge which emotion was portrayed. Coleman's article contains a cautious note, warning against a number of problems raised by studies of facial expression. For one, the study of facial expressions was problematic because of "the highly artificial nature of judging emotions from facial expressions alone," the artificiality of the photos, sketches, and models themselves, and the "vague meaning" of emotional concepts and terms. Further, Coleman noted, people express emotions differently in different situations and in different cultures. Despite these misgivings, he did find that participants could usually identify emotions correctly from the motion pictures he showed them. Like Guilford, Coleman found "no major sex differences either in the expression or identification of emotions," although women were slightly superior at judging the expressions of emotions in others.[128]

What shifted between the 1920s and today? It is unlikely that men's and women's brains have changed so dramatically in less than 100 years, on a genetic or evolutionary level, that differences would emerge owing to such forces—though Baron-Cohen evokes precisely those explanations. Instead, it seems likely that the sociohistorical context surrounding such tests has changed. Cultural discourses that feminize empathic skills might lead to priming effects for test-takers. Those discourses stem at least in part from managerial discourses that, from the 1960s onward, privileged social intelligence even as they posited the importance of the knowledge worker. Those discourses may help constitute women as emotionally intelligent mind readers, priming them to perform better on tests of empathy.

Though Baron-Cohen presents women's superior empathic ability as scientifically proven, the psychological evidence for this claim has been contested at least since the 1980s. In 1983, Nancy Eisenberg and Randy Lennon's review of psychological studies of empathy showed that the tendency for women to score higher on a range of empathy tests was largely a function of the method used. Women's scores increase, the authors found, "when it is obvious what behavior or trait is being assessed" or on self-report studies wherein women might feel pressure to present themselves as more empathetic.[129] When researchers measured empathy less obtrusively (that is, by observing male and female participants react to a situation or by measuring physiological responses), sex differences disappeared. Here again, it seems that the forces of constitutive rhetoric are in play when women are reminded of their supposed superiority in empathizing before being offered a test.

More recently, William Ickes, Paul Gesn, and Tiffany Graham found that women scored higher on empathy tests when the test design made it clear that the study concerned empathy or when the study evoked gender-role expectations. The authors concluded that female participants may either "want to appear more empathetic than men" or that they "feel a greater obligation to do so."[130] Indeed, in an empirical study, Kristi Klein and Sara Hodges found that they wiped out gender differences altogether when participants were paid according to their accuracy in a test of their ability to correctly identify emotions in others.[131]

Susan E. Cross and Laura Madson propose that women's tendency to identify with empathic qualities may stem from gendered socialization.[132] Girls and women receive continual messages about their gendered abilities (caring for others, socializing, and so on), messages that tend to form part of their self-construal. Further, expressing emotions tends to be more culturally acceptable for females than for males; from a young age, boys are usually taught to control their emotions. In their psychometric analysis, Steven J. Muncer and Jonathan Ling found that sex differences on the EQ could be better understood by breaking the test into three types of empathy: social skills, cognitive empathy, and emotional reactivity. Men and women showed no differences in social skills items, some small differences in cognitive empathy, and the greatest difference in emotional reactivity. The authors explain that this last category refers primarily to the "willingness of an individual to express emotion rather than to the ability to identify mental states and respond with the correct emotion."[133] While some biological factors, such as hormones, may affect emotional reactivity, it seems plausible that socialization effects would also come into play in this last category. Note that accounts written by autistic individuals often point to high emotional reactivity, not low reactivity, especially to fears, tensions, and nervousness.

Taking those same qualities as evidence of evolution, biology, or brain "wiring" therefore overlooks the cultural frameworks that encourage those qualities. In short, testing situations are not neutral ones but, rather, rhetorical ones, where subjects are often persuaded (or primed) to answer in certain ways, often by being constituted as a particular type of subject. When the rhetorical situation evokes gender stereotypes or norms, the results of the test tend to conform to those norms. (We might ask whether gender norms similarly influence women's performance on the SQ.)

The SQ test has been revised, though, and the EQ test has not. Aside from the rhetorical situation of such tests, in which men are often primed to do poorly, one might also consider how revised questions might shift those results. The current EQ test includes such prompts as "I try to keep up with the current trends and fashions" (item 3) and "When I talk to people, I tend to talk about their experiences rather than my own" (item 37).[134] Here, too, empathizing is conflated with femininity, especially in the first example, since the term "fashion" evokes feminine interests in clothing and style, whereas the second indexes the stereotype that women are more caring. Typical men might score well on prompts such as "I try to keep up with the latest trends in cars and technology" or "When I talk to people, I tend to focus on how I might help them solve their problems." In the first case, the question would address a set of trends more in keeping with traditional masculinity, and the second offers a means of expressing caring that may fit more readily with traditional concepts of manhood. Chivalry, after all, is a cultural code that fits caring into a masculine identity based on protecting and providing for one's family.

In short, the EQ-SQ scale draws on gendered commonplaces to create a measure wherein specific traits stand in for all male and female brains. Beyond the gendering of the tests themselves, which may skew the results, the concepts in question can be difficult to pin down. As shown in figure 3.1, men and women overlap considerably on SQ scores. In fact, men score just six points (or 10 percent) higher than women do on the SQ, on average. According to Baron-Cohen, most

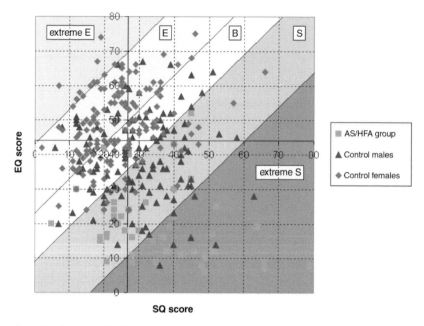

Figure 3.1. Scatter plot for Baron-Cohen's EQ-SQ test. From Simon Baron-Cohen, Rebecca C. Knick-meyer, and Matthew K. Belmonte, "Sex Differences in the Brain: Implications for Explaining Autism," *Science* 310, no. 5749 (2005): 819–823, image at 821. Reprinted with permission from AAAS.

women score about 24, while most men score about 30.[135] On the EQ, a difference of five points (or 8.3 percent) separates men and women: most women score 47, while most men score 42.[136] To argue for distinct brain "types" based on this data seems a rhetorical choice that exaggerates these similarities. If it were indeed true that men are more likely to possess a Type S brain, then we might expect a greater average difference between men's and women's scores. Instead, the measured differences between men and women could easily be the product of the tests themselves, and the ways those tests encourage participants to self-identify according to gendered norms.

Baron-Cohen's theory has proved controversial among autistic in-dividuals. Autistic women, especially, tend to find the EMB theory less than satisfactory, and they seek to widen the circumference around the term *technology*, positioning themselves as alternative representational anecdotes to the ones Baron-Cohen offers. Although many identify with the notion of systemizing, their special interests do not always fit into the male-identified repertoire of computers and technology.

Ladyrain, a person who posts on WrongPlanet, an online forum for autistic individuals, describes her interests this way:

> I don't have any mechanical or engineering aptitude at all, so probably the stereotypical obsession with door-knobs or deep-fat fryers would never cross my mind—I am knowledge-oriented more than object-oriented, although I've always had little collections of things which others find strange and 'ungirly,' and definitely know what the compulsion to have 'one of every type of something' feels like, and how hard it is to resist, even after I've lost interest in the something. I like objects for themselves, and get attached to them, I don't necessarily want to know any information about them.[137]

For ladyrain, systemizing is more a style of thinking than something attached to specific interests. She relates that she once took a systemizing approach to gardening when she decided to plant some bulbs. Rather than simply purchasing some daffodils and planting them, ladyrain writes, she "made a spreadsheet about all the different types of garden bulbs, when they flowered, how tall they grew, what soil they needed etc. etc. I wanted all the information I could get, so that I actually knew what I was doing, so I read extensively. Then I went and bought some bulbs and planted them."[138]

Similarly, a poster named nekowafer describes her style of thinking as a general pursuit of knowledge, rather than a specific type of obsession: "I've loved cats, ferrets, books, and music for a long time but I consider those pretty 'normal' and general. I will research something to death, though, and I am super detail-oriented. I will organize the CRAP out of whatever you give me, and if I don't know how to do it properly, I will research that to death."[139] Other participants have more conventional "male brain" interests that may come across, superficially, as typical female pursuits: MangoChutney writes, "I was obsessed with Friends when I was younger, and can still remember what the lines are from a lot of the earlier episodes before they've come up (although it could be because they're repeated so much here!). I love music more now, and tend to either have a huge interest in one band at a time, or on the other hand am prone to listening to the same song. Repeatedly."[140] Other interests mentioned by participants in the WrongPlanet Women's Discussion include the *Anne of Green Gables* book series, Victorian culture, bees, cursive handwriting, Garfield, Magic Nursery babies, knitting, Sailor Moon, make-up, anti-aging treatments, cooking, Martha Stewart, thrift stores, baking, and linguistics.

Yet these special interests are not necessarily read as "male brained" activities. UnderINK writes: "I think the problem is that to a psychiatrist, women are viewed as a little obsessive to begin with and they consider it natural. For instance, a woman's obsession with music, a boy band, a certain nationality of cooking or eating, a certain object (i.e.: collecting hoards and hoards of collector porcelains or Barbies), are all considered 'normal' for a woman and are not identified as an obsessive behavior."[141] When seen through the lens of typical femininity, special interests and systemizing activities may not come across as signs of autism. Although the SQ-R might pick up some of these interests, many of the items are still coded as masculine obsessions—the questions regarding financial information, wireless communication, and car engine capacity are still there. Many of the special interests outlined above by Aspie women are not reflected in the SQ-R. The EQ and SQ scales might accord with popular stereotypes about men and women, but they do not seem to align with the way autistic individuals understand themselves.

Baron-Cohen's theory does not *describe* gendered brains, then, but presents gender as a significant factor in autism's etiology, using representational anecdotes that function as reductions as much as they do representations. These anecdotes obscure much of the complexity of interests, skills, and gender that we find in autistic individuals. A more careful reading of the way autistic individuals understand gendered experiences and identity would probably yield a less dualistic model. After all, male geeks have historically been depicted as less manly than hegemonic males, while female geeks are often masculinized. Many self-identified geeks now argue for "geek" as a third gender, one neither male nor female. Perhaps the blog poster Sholf captures this dynamic best: "Being a geek is a mentally androgynous state. Girl geeks get picked on for being too manly, and guy geeks get picked on for not being manly enough. Certainly nobody ever complained about geeky guys being too manly until somebody came along and defined 'male thinking' as being geeky thinking (I bet it was a male geek)."[142] Sholf's perspective implies that the EMB theory holds sway primarily because it valorizes a style of thought that at present is economically advantageous. Baron-Cohen's theory privileges systemizing as a key skill in the contemporary knowledge economy but also expresses anxiety about the social skills that are privileged in this system—skills traditionally accorded to women.

What accompanies the knowledge economy, for some, is the "feminization of the workplace." According to Cristina Morini, cognitive capitalism "tends to prioritize extracting value from relational and emotional elements, which are more likely to be part of women's experiential baggage."[143] Perhaps this fact threatens the existing social hierarchy and produces a subconscious need to reinforce men's superiority in technical and systemizing skills, or perhaps it pathologizes individuals (often men) who do not (for whatever reason) present the kinds of social skills that are considered necessary for success. The irony in the EMB theory, though, is that, as Sholf points out, the "extreme male brained" computer geeks, formerly lampooned as 92-pound weaklings, are only now being portrayed as the epitome of a new masculinity.

Presenting Autism and Geekhood in the Twenty-first Century

The tendency to equate autism and computer geeks shows no signs of stopping. As internet technology continues to produce rapid social and economic changes, male computer geeks continue to epitomize the uncertainty felt about those changes. The texts discussed above contribute to public representations of another technology titan, Facebook founder Mark Zuckerberg. Further, these representations may influence individuals to understand themselves as autistic through self-diagnosis.

DIAGNOSING MARK

By 2012, Facebook founder Mark Zuckerberg had replaced Gates as the poster boy for the characterization of autism as epitomized by the male technogeek. Portrayals of Zuckerberg echo many of the rhetorical strategies employed earlier to diagnose Gates, but they take on an even greater valence, not only of irony and technophobia, as in "The Geek Syndrome," but also distrust and even contempt arising from technological changes, especially the rise of internet and networked technologies. In 2011 Sherry Turkle published *Alone Together*, a book exploring how networked technologies have changed social interactions. "The new technologies allow us to 'dial down' human contact," Turkle argues, "to titrate its nature and extent."[144] That same year, Nicholas Carr published *The Shallows*, which posited that internet technologies "mechanize the messy processes of intellectual exploration and even social attachment."[145] These characterizations occurred alongside a second technology bubble, this one centered around social media. As was the case in the mid-1990s, this bubble brought with it both praise of technological developments and skepticism, even fears, about the way social media tools were changing human interactions. In addition to the film *The Social Network*, two articles, in particular, constructed Zuckerberg as a new version of the stock character of the autistic computer geek. Here, Asperger's syndrome is used as a metaphor for the issues with networked technologies raised by Turkle, Carr, and others.

In "The Tech Industry's Asperger Problem," Ryan Tate constructs a different crisis from the one articulated by Silberman. The preponderance of supposedly autistic people in Silicon Valley, according to Tate's account, threatens personal privacy, not just the Silicon Valley school system, which Silberman described as being inundated with special-needs children. Tate personifies Silicon Valley companies as autistic, arguing that high rates of ASD "will come as no shock to users familiar with pedantic, apathetic, tight-lipped and self-serving tech companies."[146] By extension ASD is defined by the key features listed: pedantry, apathy, terseness, and selfishness. The article positions Zuckerberg as exemplifying those traits. Note that these traits are not included in official definitions of ASD. Instead, Tate uses the same paratactic logic as was used in "Diagnosing Bill Gates" to diagnose Zuckerberg and, by extension, social networking companies. Tate also relies on "The Geek Syndrome" (published ten years earlier) for much of his content, repackaging Silberman's concerns for a 2012 audience.

Tate begins by citing the rise of autism cases in Silicon Valley. He does not offer more recent statistics but instead cites the anecdotal evidence from "The Geek Syndrome," namely, the testimony of some unnamed "state outreach workers." Tate also cites anecdotal evidence from Peter Thiel, a venture capitalist profiled in a 2011 *New Yorker* article, who mentioned the prevalence of ASD-like behaviors in tech start-up founders. None of these statements is made by someone who has studied autism rates. Instead, they contribute to the paratactic, associative logic of the article, which links technology, autism, and characters like Zuckerberg together.

The next section of the article parallels "Diagnosing Bill Gates." Tate lists several key traits associated with ASD and then cites anecdotal evidence locating those traits in Zuckerberg. For instance, Tate notes that obsessiveness has been associated with Asperger's syndrome and then notes that Zuckerberg was "prone to spending so much time obsessing over Facebook . . . that his girlfriend insisted on a guaranteed minimum of 100 minutes of alone time together per week before she'd agree to move out to California."[147] Under the heading "Impaired Social Interaction," Tate refers to a 2010 post on a Silicon Valley Web site called Quora, in which a former Facebook employee, Yishan Wong, described Zuckerberg as having "a touch of the Asperger's," noting that Zuckerberg "just listens, sometimes while looking away from you" rather than acknowledging a co-worker's statements with typical phatic communication. Tate also refers to a 2010 interview posted online in which Zuckerberg was deemed "very awkward" and "repetitive," and an account by another start-up founder, Biz Stone (founder of Twitter), who described Zuckerberg as lacking a "sense of humor" based on a single interaction.[148] Oddly, though Tate next refers to "clumsiness" as a key Aspergian trait, he pairs that not with an anecdote about Zuckerberg's bodily habitus but with Jason Calacanis (a start-up investor) accusing Zuckerberg of being "an amoral, Asperger's like entrepreneur" based on the latter's shrewd business dealings.[149] As in "Diagnosing Bill Gates," anecdotes are presented as true indications of Zuckerberg's character. Here, though, Asperger's is falsely equated with clumsiness and amoral behavior, both associations that do not square with scientific definitions of the condition.

Whereas "Diagnosing Bill Gates" took a somewhat lighthearted approach, there is clearly an underlying thread of animosity in Tate's article. Calacanis is quoted as suggesting that, with Asperger's, "[i]t's almost as if you trade off intensity in one area for common decency and communications in another area—not that the person has a choice."[150] Tate moves from this assessment of Zuckerberg to a further association, asking: "To what extent can rampant abuse of user privacy among tech startups be traced to Asperger Disorder?" Tate employs the ironic antithesis: "Are the very Aspergers-like features that made Silicon Valley a hotbed of innovation—a relentless desire to commune with machines, a willingness to push past consumers' technological comfort zones—turning it into an antisocial, sometimes parasitic force?"[151] Tate's language echoes the fears Turkle raises about technology in *Alone Together* but links it to Asperger's syndrome in order to pathologize and label the discomfort that accompanies networked technologies.

Tate frames privacy issues as though they developed solely from the personal motivations of Zuckerberg and other technology titans, suggesting that "immoral" or "unempathetic" tech geeks might simply be ignoring their users' desires. In doing so, Tate avoids the broader context of technocapitalism, such as the tremendous competition among technology services, the need to expand those services to as broad a consumer base as possible, and the difficulties of monetizing free services by linking the free labor of users (to provide content) to targeted advertisements. All of those factors play a large role in driving privacy policies.

Tate concludes the article by laying claim to a number of other technology titans, such as Craig Newmark, founder of Craigslist; Bram Cohen, founder of BitTorent; and, of course, Bill Gates. His evidence is again paratactic or loosely associated with the characteristic it is supposed to support. Cohen, for instance, "often plays with a Rubik's Cube." Although Newmark publicly admitted that many Asperger's symptoms sounded familiar to him, he does not have an official diagnosis.

DIAGNOSING THE SELF

Across the articles considered thus far, then, we find a continued reworking of stock material and stock characters from a fairly small set of sources. We also find repeating rhetorical tropes, such as ironic antithesis, laying claim, and anecdotal evidence, as well as gendered commonplaces of autism, usually symptoms loosely associated with ASD and with technology, in particular. This stock material works to construct ASD in a very particular way, aligned with the gendered male character of the computer geek.

These rhetorical constructions of public figures are important because they may influence other individuals to understand themselves in relation to discourses of autism, neurological difference, and gender. For example, my Facebook feed announced that a number of my friends were taking the AQ test, or Asperger's quotient test, online—and sharing their results with their online friends. While personality tests have become an online staple, I found it interesting that some of my friends wanted to take this test and share the results, since I have not seen similar tests for other neurological conditions (such as attention deficit or bipolar disorder) that would "out" someone as neurodiverse. What accounts for the popularity of the AQ test, and what does it mean for the way we understand ourselves and our brains?

The very notion that a self-report quiz really tells us anything about ourselves owes its persuasiveness to psychometric testing, which developed only in the past century. Personality quizzes, whether used as psychiatric tools or as a form of entertainment, represent what Michel Foucault called "technologies of the self." These "permit individuals to effect by their own means or with the help of others a certain number of operations on their own bodies and souls, thoughts, conduct, and ways of being, so as to transform themselves in order to attain a certain state of happiness, purity, wisdom, perfection, or immortality."[152] Because they deal with the self, such individualized personality tests offer new rhetorical resources through which we understand ourselves and others, choose (or are advised to choose) careers and mates, and form identities and attitudes toward life. Surprisingly, online tests that purport to diagnose individuals with a neurological condition may help them achieve happiness or contentment. Many individuals seek an Asperger's or autism diagnosis as a way of coming to terms with difficult life experiences, such as a sense of never fitting in or always being different. For these individuals, online tools offer important sources for self-persuasion, tools that seem to help people to accept themselves and their differences—whether or not a psychologist would agree with their new label.

About.com's ASD Web site includes a special section featuring stories of self-diagnosis. These stories demonstrate how autism discourses described in this chapter become technologies of the self, tools that enable diagnoses by helping construct characters with which individuals can identify. One writer who posted on an About.com Web site, Rwinter001, wrote that he or she took "2 separate online tests that were quite extensive and both *came back positive* for aspergers [*sic*]."[153] The language this poster uses reveals that he or she sees autism as something akin to an infectious disease, for which one can test positive or negative, though the former is a psychiatric diagnosis, not something diagnosed by a medical test. That Rwinter001 uses it to refer to a mental condition signifies that these tests construct autism as something one either has or does not have—a positivist tendency that conflicts with the trend toward viewing autism as a broad spectrum shading into normalcy.

Similarly, a poster on WrongPlanet found confirmation in Baron-Cohen's EMB tests, writing: "I went to Cambridge University's Autism Research Centre web site, downloaded and printed off the AQ, FQ, EQ and SQ screening tests, then the spreadsheet that you put the answers for the AQ and EQ test into. I had one of my brothers complete all the tests according to how he saw me as I had already done my own, but not shown him the results. When I put the answers he had made into the spreadsheet, it seemed that I met all the criteria for AS."[154] This poster's language reflects the discourse of psychiatry, which tends to consider mental conditions based on a set of criteria (as in the *DSM*). This post shows that scientific materials, especially diagnostic tests, do not stay solely within the control of experts but circulate among publics, leading individuals to understand themselves and their brains in terms of psychiatric criteria.

It is important, though, that diagnoses are made in part by a process of identification between an individual and the kinds of characters understood to represent a given disorder. As Judy Segal has argued, "The person complaining to a physician of headache can expect his or her medical interview and course of treatment to be shaped in part by *the headache patient* that exists in the physician's mental cast of characters."[155] Similarly, people who self-diagnose as autistic might rely on available characterizations, especially that of the male geek. A story posted by one Greg illustrates some of the rhetorical dynamics of this self-constitution. At the age of forty, Greg became convinced that he had Asperger's syndrome after reading a review of *Adam,* a 2009 film featuring a character with Asperger's played by Hugh Dancy. Greg felt he could identify with the description of the character, and found in Asperger's syndrome an "answer" to why he "felt different and out of place in the world we live in." Promptly, Greg searched the World Wide Web for information, reading stories written by people with Asperger's syndrome and articles by professionals, with which he also identified. For six weeks he immersed himself in self-diagnosis, only to find out after a psychological assessment that he didn't have Asperger's, although he was "close to that end of the spectrum."[156] Whether or not Greg actually has it, we can see here a description of the process rhetoricians call identification. Gradually, through exposure to films, stories, and articles, Greg came to identify with the depictions of the condition that he found and began to form a self-identity in keeping with that potential diagnosis.

These examples show that autism discourses persuade readers to adopt certain self-constitutions or explanatory frameworks to help them make sense of their lives. As Electrifiedspam, a participant on WrongPlanet.net writes, "The spectrum gives me a framework to understand myself and peoples [*sic*] reactions to me. . . . 'Self-Diagnosis' has given me answers, and more importantly answers that work. It has also allowed me to predict things about myself that I never knew." Self-diagnosis not only names a self, however; it actively constitutes a self in keeping with the label. Electrifiedspam found that the diagnosis had a predictive effect, helping him or her to uncover new things about the self.[157] No details are given, but the phrasing shows that this person may have incorporated certain traits or characteristics associated with

Asperger's into his or her sense of self—regardless of whether he or she found those traits present before. Overall, self-diagnosis seems to be a rhetorical process, as is diagnosis. In the absence of a biological marker for Asperger's or autism, it becomes open to these kinds of rhetorical processes whereby individuals are assigned categories.

A Foucauldian perspective warns us, however, that "certain bodies, certain gestures, certain discourses, certain desires, come to be identified and constituted as individuals."[158] In the case of autism and Asperger's, the bodies most likely to be constituted as such tend to be male. While it is difficult to assume gender from an online handle such as Electrifiedspam, some participants on WrongPlanet and other internet sites maintain that the self-diagnostic process is more fraught for women and girls. One participant on WrongPlanet, Jessa, explains that "the psychologists I've approached have refused to evaluate me for Asperger's Syndrome because I'm female and adult."[159] The portrayals of ASD, and especially Asperger's, seem to have shaped psychologists' perceptions of the condition. Jessa's experience corroborates claims that women can remain undiagnosed because they do not fit with the dominant cultural depiction of an autistic person.

Self-diagnosis seems to offer relief to individuals such as Jessa, who seek explanations for their social difficulties and other experiences; yet disappointment can ensue when experts do not validate those diagnoses, and hence fail to validate the experiences of the people in question. From a rhetorical perspective, this phenomenon is interesting because it happens entirely through words. Nothing may change, materially speaking, if one is diagnosed with autism or Asperger's as an adult, since in many cases the individual will not necessarily seek specific treatments. Instead, the diagnosis functions as a speech act, one that shifts individuals' self-perception through rhetoric.

Presenting Computer Geeks in Science

Popular characterizations of ASD as a condition affecting males, especially males with technological aptitudes, may have also influenced scientific theories beyond Baron-Cohen's controversial theory. In particular, the male characters used to represent autism in popular discourse may influence what kinds of people are chosen for autism studies. In this section, I examine how studies of the neuroscience of autism may reflect the prominence of the male autistic character in the rhetorical culture. Neuroscientific studies of autism seek to identify differences in brain growth, activation, and function between the brains of those with autism and those without. In order to determine how notions of sex and gender inflect these studies, I examined thirty research articles published in 2010 that used functional magnetic resonance imaging (fMRI) to examine differences in brain activity and function among people with autism. Overall, this examination demonstrates that sex rarely figures as an important variable in studies of the autistic brain and that male brains tend to be taken as the default or standard. Male brains stand in for both normal *and* autistic brains, leaving female brains sidelined. This is all the more surprising given the tendency to promote sex differences between men's and women's brains in autism discourse and in neuroscience studies, as noted above. By occluding female brains in these studies, neuroscientists are in essence mapping the male autistic brain even as they purport to map the autistic brain. The male brain becomes the representative anecdote for these studies.

The first finding from my analysis is that only fourteen of the thirty studies included both male and female test subjects. The remaining sixteen studies used only male participants. In the mixed groups, female subjects were not always represented according to the 4:1 ratio estimated for autism. Eight of the fourteen studies included a proportion of female subjects approaching or exceeding the 4:1 ratio; others ranged from twenty-five to seven males for every female subject. Almost all the studies had small sample sizes, ranging from seven to forty-one individuals in the test group, so the number of female test subjects was often only one or two. Evidently, a sample size of only a handful of female autistics is unlikely to provide statistically significant indications of differences between male and female autistic brains.

Sex (or gender) also disappears from abstracts; in my sample only ten of thirty articles indicated the sex of participants in the abstracts, as opposed to the body of the article. This omission is important since many readers rely on abstracts to determine whether to read an article—or may only read the abstract. More thorough readers might look to the methods section of the article for details about how participants were selected, but only one of the articles included an explanation for the sex distribution of test subjects in the methods section. Roger Jou, Nancy Minshew, Matcheri Keshavan, and Antonio Hardan write that "the study was confined to right-handed males because the sample size was too small to accommodate for the statistical variability associated with handedness and gender."[160] Only two studies explicitly addressed sex ratio (or exclusion of females) as a limitation within their discussion sections. In their article, Dennis P. Carmody and Michael Lewis expressed the need for more females in order to increase the robustness of the results, although with nineteen male and seven female test subjects, this study actually falls in the higher range in terms of representativeness.[161] The exclusion of sex from the abstracts, methods, and discussion sections of research articles contributes to its silencing and increases the likelihood that the male autistic brain will stand in for all autistic brains.

Only one of the thirty studies considered here mentioned sex differences in the results themselves. Based on the hypothesis that individuals with autism had excessive brain growth, Cynthia Schumann et al. tracked 41 subjects (32 male; 9 female) whom they actively recruited from a broader group of 118 toddlers who began the study and were monitored for signs of developmental disorders.[162] (The 41 who were diagnosed with an ASD were matched with controls who were not.) Schumann et al. "observed significant gender differences in the longitudinal growth trajectories of several brain regions" in females, namely, more "widespread and severe" growth among females as opposed to the more localized growth patterns found in males.[163] This difference, the authors contend, might mean that females with autism are more severely affected. (Note that most of the studies in my sample recruited individuals with Asperger's syndrome or high-functioning autism, which might compound the lack of female subjects—some allege that the proportion of male to female individuals with AS may be more like 8:1 or 9:1). Schumann et al. conclude that "males and females with autism may exhibit different neuroanatomical profiles," a finding that should prompt researchers to work harder to address the disparities in sample sizes.[164]

In the remainder of the articles, sex is silenced. Perhaps the authors assume their readers already know that autism occurs more often in males than females or that the EMB theory has been advanced to account specifically for this ratio at the level of brain analysis. Yet researchers often feel compelled to offer definitions of autism itself, indicating that they do not expect their readers to be familiar with the disorder. None of the studies in question referred to the disproportionate male to female ratio in autism diagnosis—which is surprising, because one would think this would provide ready justification for the lack of female subjects.

Instead, males function as spectral characters in these studies, haunting the margins and gaps on the page. Consider the article titled "Visual

Attention in Autism Families: 'Unaffected' Sibs Share Atypical Frontal Activation" by Matthew K. Belmonte, Marie Gomot, and Simon Baron-Cohen. The article begins with evidence for "familial autism susceptibility," based on findings indicating "tantalising abnormalities" in brain activation and structure in relatives of people with autism.[165] The stated purpose of the study was to "determine whether the degree of correlation of functional activation amongst brain regions might differentiate *family members with and without ASC. Boys* with ASC, clinically unaffected *brothers* of people with ASC, and unrelated, typical controls performed a task demanding selective attention to colour and orientation."[166] In this passage, boys and brothers are substituted for family members. So the study in question relates specifically to that relationship. The authors do not explain why they chose boys and their brothers (as opposed to say, mothers and sons, girls with ASD and their sisters, or what have you). Nor do they modify their claims to address this limitation. Thus, in the discussion section, the authors conclude that "this finding of *autistic impairment* in a spatial divided attention task echoes psychophysical and electrophysiological observations of an atypical spatial distribution of visual attention *in autism.*" The limitation of the findings to males is unacknowledged. We might amend this sentence to read more accurately as follows: "This finding of *autistic impairment in boys* . . . echoes . . . observations of an atypical spatial distribution of visual attention in *boys with autism.*"[167]

The tendency for writers to state their findings in this way does not occur just in this sample, but in nearly every sample I studied. Findings were generalized to address *autism,* not autism in males. This elision is rhetorical, insofar as it leads to more persuasive statements of findings. Yet it also elides potential differences. In my sample, only Schumann's article focused on sex differences between males and females with autism. The fact that Schumann found significant differences indicates that it is important to acknowledge this difference and amend brain research that only studies males (or that studies a very small sampling of females). Given both the statistical facts (greater diagnosis in males) and the various hypotheses that connect autism to sexed processes, including more females in these studies could yield interesting and important results.

Potentially, the sexed and gendered terms in which autism is discussed deflect attention away from other possible research areas. For one, girls and women with ASDs have only recently begun to receive greater emphasis in scientific studies. While the preponderance of males with an ASD diagnosis led some researchers to understand the disorder itself as masculine or male, some researchers now claim that this gendering process has led women to be underdiagnosed. The researcher David Skuse agrees: "There is no doubt in my mind that the way we have defined autism currently biases our assessments strongly in the direction of identifying a male stereotype."[168] In other words, the male computer geek character has potentially misled researchers into taking male patterns and habits as representative of autism in general.

A number of hypotheses have been advanced to explain why women and girls might be underdiagnosed. For one, they may be better able to "pass" as normal, either because girls are expected to be shy and quiet or because they carefully observe and imitate the dress and behavior of their peers.[169] Others propose that ASDs may take different forms in girls, who may not have narrow interests and may have strong interests in language or reading, rather than math or science. Finally, some researchers theorize that girls and women may be diagnosed with other conditions such as bipolar disorder, schizophrenia, or even anorexia. On this last point, a few researchers have noticed similarities in social impairments and attention to detail in patients with anorexia nervosa and ASD. Notably, in one of these studies, David Hambrook, Kate Tchanturia, Ulrike Schmidt, Tamara Russell, and Janet Treasure found that patients with anorexia achieved high scores on Baron-Cohen's Autism Spectrum Quotient (AQ) test without scoring high on the systemizing component, associated with the male brain.[170] The authors conclude that patients with anorexia may "experience difficulties similar to those with ASDs," but they do not consider this as evidence that the AQ may be measuring something aside from autistic traits, per se.[171]

However, it seems possible that the dominant characterization of autistic individuals as male computer geeks leads researchers and practitioners to overlook females who have autistic traits because they do not present themselves in stereotypical ways. For example, an intense interest in ponies or princesses might not come across as autistic in the same way that an intense interest in sports schedules or computers might.

While sex or gender forms one prominent lens through which researchers and the public view autism, there are competing theories. Some researchers question the EMB theories for their failure to account fully for the range of symptoms that characterize autism. Elise B. Barbeau, Adrianna Mendrek, and Laurent Mottron object to the EMB theory, arguing that "the autistic brain functions differently, sometimes more like men, sometimes more like women, but we should consider that it might actually function in its own unique way."[172] One alternative understanding of autism comes from Henry Markram, Tania Rinaldi, and Kamila Markram, who hypothesize that autism might be understood as an "intense world syndrome." In their theory, autism is characterized not by an extreme male brain but by a hyperreactive and hyperplastic brain that makes the world seem overstimulating, or by "*excessive neuronal information processing and storage in local circuits of the brain.*"[173] Autistic individuals, then, may experience an excess of sensory and emotional input—not a lack thereof, as the EMB theory would have it. Symptoms such as repetitive behavior (rocking, self-stimulating behaviors such as hand-flapping, or "stimming") and withdrawal can therefore be understood as coping mechanisms that individuals use to deal with overstimulated senses.

Notably, this explanation seems to accord best with the way many autistic people describe their sensory experiences. Rachel Cohen-Rottenberg, who maintains a blog called *Journeys with Autism*, writes, "To my (autistic) mind, Intense World Syndrome theory is the closest that the scientific community has ever come to understanding autism."[174] In a post on WrongPlanet, she describes how, in her experience, sensory input "comes in faster than I can process it," so she must look away in order to "process all the 'data' coming in."[175] What may appear to be lack of empathy may be, according to her, an excess of emotional and sensory input.

Others insist that researchers have overlooked the possibility of sex-linked genetic vulnerability rather than a sexed brain as a possible cause of autism. Skuse supports this theory, which would make autism similar to other sex-linked genetic conditions. For instance, boys might be more susceptible to X chromosome defects leading to autism; girls would be protected because they possess two X chromosomes instead of one. Skuse questions whether autism spectrum conditions "should be regarded as 'the extreme of male behaviour' or as a collection of complex neurodevelopmental conditions that is more likely to manifest as a recognizable phenotype among males than females."[176] The first formulation reflects the analogical reasoning of the EMB theory, whereas the second leaves room for alternative understandings of autism as not necessarily gendered or sexed in and of itself, even if it is "recognizable" in boys more often than in girls.

By relying on the male character as representative anecdote, researchers may shift their focus toward some features of autism and away from others. While systemizing activity and lack of empathy receive great emphasis in the EMB theory, other features traditionally linked to autism, such as repetitive behavior and delays in language development, do not. As I have shown, the *kinds* of restricted interests mentioned in the EMB theory are most often interests typically associated with men. While there is nothing in the clinical description of autism that requires these interests to be in the specific areas of science, math, and technology, in the EMB theory, feminized interests are excluded. As a result, women have been marginalized in autism research, especially neuroscientific research. Further, male geeks and nerds, much like Zuckerberg in *The Social Network*, have become stock characters in television, literature, and film; most often, these characters themselves trope autistic people, mistaking the part for the whole.

CHAPTER 4

Rehearsing Gender

Autism Dads

In 1957 Leon Eisenberg published a study titled "The Fathers of Autistic Children." In the quest to single out maternal factors in autism causation, Eisenberg argued, "Father has been the forgotten man."[1] He investigated the fathers of 100 children with autism, finding a similar pattern in 85 cases: most of the fathers he identified ranked high in education and low in emotion. He illustrated this pattern with character sketches, of a surgeon, an accountant, and a would-be PhD who was a few courses shy of a degree in bacteriology. The occupation of the subject seemed relevant in all three cases but especially so in the description of Dr. R, who was "a caricature of the psychiatric stereotype of a surgeon." Eisenberg wrote that Dr. R "dealt with infected gall bladders, diseased bowels, or tumors, with little or no curiosity about the person in whom these anatomical problems were housed." His "day was thoroughly organized from the first surgical scrub to the last journal he might glance through while preparing for bed." He had achieved acclaim in the professional community, but Dr. R had left no room in his tight schedule for family life, which he "kept to the unavoidable minimum inescapable at meals and bedtime."[2] Eisenberg goes on to state that Dr. R's hobbies, such as fishing and hunting, were solitary, and that his wife was left to deal with his "contemptuous dismissal" of her problems or concerns.

Through this kind of description, Eisenberg generated a character type—fathers of autistic children—who were "obsessive, detached, and humorless individuals" and "perfectionistic to the extreme, occupied with detailed minutiae to the exclusion of concern for over-all meanings."[3] In the 1990s, as Chapter 3 showed, male computer geeks, the denizens of Silicon Valley and other high-tech centers, were similarly portrayed as the obsessively career-oriented sires of similarly obsessive children.

In other circles, fathers of autistic children are depicted as deadbeats, failing to cooperate with their wives' rigorous therapy, research, or diet regimens, to participate in support groups, or to accept their child's disability. In *Louder Than Words*, Jenny McCarthy portrays her son's father in this light, recounting instances when he failed to uphold Evan's gluten-free, casein-free diet or left her alone in the hospital with her son. McCarthy also notes that "the divorce rate in families with autistic kids is very high."[4] One Huffington Post columnist, Shelley Hendrix Reynolds, writes that divorce rates in the autism community "verg[e] on 70% within the first five years of diagnosis and 90% within the first ten." These claims, though false, tend to circulate in public discussions of autism, most often in ways that blame the divorce on the father. (Reynolds notes that her husband simply "announced that he was moving out.")[5]

Such assertions have led researchers to investigate the actual patterns of divorce in families with autistic children. Some studies show a somewhat higher divorce rate among parents with an autistic child than among parents of children without disabilities; in one study, researchers found a 25.3 percent risk of divorce in the former group versus 13.8 percent in the latter.[6] Yet other studies have found no difference in divorce rates between families with and without an autistic child. A study conducted by Brian H. Freedman, Luther G. Kalb, Benjamin Zablotsky, and Elizabeth A. Stuart found that 64 percent of children with an ASD were in families with two married parents, compared with 65.2 percent of children without an ASD.[7]

Nonetheless, the idea that autism leads to divorce persists. For example, even after these studies were released, Hannah Brown wrote on Today.com that when her son was first diagnosed with autism, her social worker told her that "80 percent of all parents of autistic children get divorced." Though untrue, this claim seemed to resonate with Brown, who, like many of her friends with autistic children, was divorced.[8]

Divorced mothers often identify the differing roles assumed by mothers and fathers of autistic children as a factor in a divorce. In a column for the Huffington Post, Elaine Hall writes that, whereas her son's autism diagnosis turned her into a "Momma Bear," her husband had a different response: "Some days, he tuned it all out and threw himself into his work. On other days, he went into 'fix-it' mode, wanting me to find the right tool—therapy, drug, doctor—to get things back to normal." Although she admits that her marriage had problems before they adopted their son, Neal, she calls herself "the ultimate caretaker, put[ting] everyone's needs and feelings before my own," and her husband "extremely critical."[9] Another mother, blogging under the pseudonym "Professor" at the Web site *The Thinking Mom's Revolution*, writes that her husband "was jealous of me, because I got to 'save' Bryce."[10] In these accounts, we see mothers taking on the mother warrior role described in Chapter 2, while fathers either withdraw or turn into "Mr. Fix-it," both roles that conflict with that of the mother.

Whether or not divorce enters the picture, it seems that autism presents more of a conflict with the traditional father's role than with the mother's role. Whereas the role of the autism mother is an extension of the concept of total motherhood applied to all mothers, that of the autism father seems to require a shift away from traditional concepts of fatherhood and masculinity. Thus, fathers must reconstruct and rehearse new roles in order to come to terms with the changes in their expectations that come after an autism diagnosis.

Perhaps because of these difficulties in assuming a new role, fathers tend to be blamed (alongside the condition itself) for their failure to actively participate in their child's care and treatment. In one About .com article, for instance, Lisa Jo Rudy offers several reasons for men's difficulties: they have fewer companions with whom to discuss their situations, they may be disappointed that they cannot relate to their sons, especially in the ways they had expected (namely, through sports), and they might view their children's behavior as a deliberate rejection of their authority.[11] Accordingly, articles about autism and fathers on About.com tend to have titles such as "How to Get Dad More Involved with His Child with Autism" and "Helping Autism Dads Connect." "By being less involved in the daily interaction with their children," Rudy states, "fathers tend to have a somewhat longer period of denial about the disability and its implications. When men do express their feelings, they tend to show anger or frustration."[12] These sources paint autism dads in largely negative terms, as individuals of poor character. As a result, fathers may struggle to gain ethos in their everyday lives—to feel confident and invested as authorities about their own children.

Increasingly, though, fathers of autistic children have begun to construct a different character in order to contest these depictions and generate authority in public discussions. For instance, in 2010 Adel Tamano offered these reflections on raising his son, Santi, in a column for the *Philippine Star*:

> I am like most men. I had typical father-and-son dreams of teaching Santi basketball (or in my case, volleyball), having him attend my alma mater, even just sharing jokes (eventually teaching him my favorite green ones when he is old enough), and watching movies together. But all these dreams were shattered when we found out that Santi had autism. An autistic child relates very differently from a typical child. So you throw all your preconceptions and expectations out the window. . . . In the end, you learn patience, sacrifice, and acceptance. In short, you learn how to truly love your child; how to be a real father.[13]

Today, books written by fathers of autistic children are plentiful. Eschewing the character of the distant father that haunted earlier autism discourse, these men tenderly describe the connections to their children, the effects on their marriages of raising a special needs child, and ultimately the transformations those experiences create in the fathers' own characters.

In this chapter I examine accounts written by fathers who use autobiographical writing to rehearse new, authoritative characters in their own lives and in public discourse. Kimberly Harrison argues that diaries can help writers work through identity challenges or to "rehearse and construct an effective ethos for turbulent times";[14] I argue here that such narratives take on a similar purpose, functioning as constitutive rhetoric that helps writers rehearse and construct an effective character as a father and to offer that character to readers.

In order to constitute this character, fathers must sometimes reject or revise other characters grounded in the commonplaces of hegemonic masculinity that emphasize male strength, success, and power and adopt new topoi of fatherhood. According to Carolyn R. Miller, there are three sources of common topics: "conventional expectation in rhetorical situations, knowledge and issues available in the institutions and organizations in which those situations occur, and concepts available in specific networks of knowledge (or disciplines)."[15] In this chapter, I show how fathers of autistic children draw on topoi related to conventional expectations of fatherhood and masculinity, topoi available within the institution of the family, and topoi available within the networks of knowledge provided by their professions. Whereas narratives written by mothers tend to take on a quest for recovery, narratives written by fathers tend to take on a quest for understanding—not simply of the child in question but of the father's own character and identity.[16]

In the first section I examine accounts by fathers who portray themselves as characters imbued with hegemonic masculine topoi of inheritance, independence, and athletics. I then discuss accounts written by fathers who drew on topoi related to the family, such as the position of fathers as "fixers" as well as the negotiation of work and family priorities. In the third section I deal with fathers who construct their characters using topoi related to their occupations or disciplines. Finally, I consider the implications of these topoi for science and policy related to autism, especially attempts to recruit fathers to participate in treatment and therapies for their children. Examining pamphlets used to advertise early childhood treatment programs, I consider how design features (fonts, images, text, and colors) may impede attempts to get more fathers engaged in their children's therapy because they fail to engage the interests and identities of autism fathers.

Rehearsing Hegemonic Masculinity

Fathers constitute their characters in part from topoi of hegemonic masculinity, or the web of concepts and commonplaces that circulate to form idealized images of manhood. As the gender scholars R. W. Connell and James W. Messerschmidt argue, it embodies "the currently most honored way of being a man."[17] Connell and Messerschmidt point out that the particular qualities associated with idealized manhood may change over time. Today, in American culture, we might posit inheritance, independence, and athletics as three of the qualities that make up hegemonic masculinity.

REFIGURING INHERITANCE

In our patriarchal society, the male line of inheritance, especially that extending from grandfathers to fathers to sons, continues to carry special meaning. This line of inheritance does not always transmit the material benefits that it does in a predominantly agricultural society or one in which only sons inherit land or property. Yet fathers still think of their sons, in particular, as inheriting symbolic and genetic materials from them: a last name, personality or appearance, athletic abilities, or special talents. In texts by autism dads, the topos of inheritance or legacy becomes a means by which men interpret the meaning of fatherhood and constitute their characters. In his book *Dads and Autism,* for instance, Emerson B. Donnell III remembers that when he found out his first child would be a son, he "was overwhelmed with the notion of carrying on a legacy."[18] Similarly, Rodney Peete linked his character to that of his father, whom he describes early in the account as an exemplary figure. Peete writes: "I was trying to figure out how my dad was such a great father and take it a step or two further. That's what each generation wants to do: build on the base that their parents created and make a better life for their own children."[19] For Peete, this vision of fatherhood failed to match up with the reality of raising his son R. J.

Likewise, the blogger Stuart Duncan writes, "A father likely sees things much more clearly [than a mother], whether it is to follow in their footsteps or to do what it is that he's always dreamed of doing. You see, quarterbacks tend to see their child being big into sports, politicians see their child becoming president one day, scientists picture their child being even smarter than they were. . . . Fathers have a vision."[20] For Duncan, this vision is "ripped away" when a child receives an autism diagnosis, which, he notes, makes many men distance themselves from their families.[21]

All of these fathers understand themselves as producing heirs who will follow in their footsteps; this topos forms a key part of a father's character. These fathers are not inventing the inheritance topos wholesale but instead are drawing on a commonplace in the rhetorical culture. We are exposed to legacies in popular magazines, television shows, books, and movies that feature a son growing up to be like his dad. In politics, Americans are familiar with the stories of the Kennedys, the Bushes, and the Romneys; in sports, those of the Mannings and Longs; in film, those of the Douglases and the Sutherlands. Fathers are encouraged to view their sons as vessels for their own hopes and dreams; sons are encouraged to enter into their fathers' occupations or to take over the family business. Disabilities challenge these fathers because they challenge the images and ideas surrounding the culturally prevalent topos of a legacy. In their narratives, fathers must rehearse alternative characters that do not fully depend on the idea of legacy or reconfigure that idea to suit the realities of their lives.

REFIGURING INDEPENDENCE

Another key element of hegemonic masculinity is independence: the normative man works a steady job to provide for his household and does not require assistance from anybody, financial or otherwise. Fathers often draw upon the topos of independence in their character rehearsals. On his blog, Duncan writes that, while some parents of autistic children might hope their child will have savant-like skills, most, like himself, only want their child "to be able to grow up happy, to be able to finish school, have friends, get a good job, have a family of their own and all those good things that many people simply take for granted."[22] For Duncan, the idea that his son Cameron might not meet those goals constitutes the hardest part of autism—harder than the emotional and financial challenges he faces, such as selling his house and moving to a new school district so that his son can attend a good school or eating ramen noodles some weeks so that he can pay for support services. Duncan's character as a father seems to be built on the topos of independence: success as a man depends on it. For one's son to fail to achieve independence presents an affront to Duncan's character, not his son's.

In his book *Breaking Autism's Barriers*, Bill Davis writes that though his hopes for a miracle cure may be improbable, he nonetheless holds out hope that his son eventually will become independent.[23] While Davis dismisses concerns about sports, he hopes for a different marker of masculinity.[24] Yet he insists that he will not be bothered if his son does not reach those goals: "People always say to be successful you have to live on your own, be married, and hold down a good job. Well, maybe my kid just can't do that."[25] Thus, Davis's writing shows a mixture of hope for independence and acknowledgment that it may not be in his son's future—and an insistence that he would accept that. Yet one gets the sense that these kinds of statements are in part attempts at self-persuasion, rehearsals of a new fatherly character that is not heavily invested in independence as a marker of success.

Similarly, the blogger Joseph Harris admits that he initially thought he had accepted that his son had autism: "I think I felt like he was still going to be able to lead a mostly typical life. I was certain that he would eventually learn to talk and read and that he might have some trouble making friends, but he would manage to have a few, that eventually he would meet a girl and fall in love and start his own family." An official diagnosis led him to question that assumption: "What if he can never be independent?" he asks.[26] Here again, independence functions as a key concern for a father, who seems to identify independence in his son as a marker of masculinity and success.

The struggles these fathers face in thinking about their sons' futures stem from the fact that independence and masculinity are deeply rooted in concepts of the liberal democratic society, one based on the agency and equality of men. The feminist scholar Eva Kittay writes that this concept of society "masks the inevitable dependencies and asymmetries that form part of the human condition—those of children, the aging and the ailing—dependencies that often mark the closest human ties."[27] Perhaps because they are socialized to identify with themselves as independent individuals, men may be challenged when confronted with a loss of independence—either for themselves or for their offspring. Studies of aging men report similar fears about losing independence, as do studies of men with disabilities. In these cases, as well, men must either reaffirm it or reconfigure it using new values.[28] A loss of independence, therefore, becomes an affront to the masculine character.

REFIGURING ATHLETIC PROWESS

Fathers also often rely on the topos of athletics. In a sense, sports symbolize bodily independence and strength—key elements of hegemonic masculinity. The athletics topos circulates in images of a father teaching his son to play catch, coaching his hockey or baseball team, and taking his son to games. Sharing in sports seems to help men develop a father character that they can deploy in their personal lives. Fathers also seem to view sports activity as crucial for their son's development of a masculine persona, perhaps because, as the sociologist Michael Messner explains, "the rule-bound structure of organized sports" functions as a context in which boys work to construct a masculine identity.[29] By taking part in sports with their sons, fathers participate in their sons' constructions of identity, but they also seem to view that participation as key to their own identities. For fathers of autistic sons, a lack of interest in sports can present a serious challenge both to their role as a father and to their masculine values.

In his book for fathers of autistic boys, Donnell describes his disappointment when his son, also named Emerson, failed to grasp the concept of ball play: "I tried to get him to play for months and months. I rolled, threw and spun softballs, whiffle-balls and kick-balls, but nothing interested him. What a heartbreaker." Donnell recounts using a system of "hardcore prompting" and "creative linking" that eventually led to ball play with his son, which gave him hope that the younger Emerson might "possibly go into some sports."[30] Here, playing with balls is represented as a natural activity for fathers and sons, coded as a strong desire on the part of the father. For a man who has built up a character based on athletic interests, it may be difficult to have a son who does not do so, who is indifferent to which team jersey to wear or which sports hero to root for.

Peete represents a particularly strong case, since his career was in athletics, perhaps the job most strongly associated with masculine identity in America. According to the legal scholar Felice M. Duffy, sports represents one of the few remaining institutions wherein male superiority is upheld without controversy. She notes that football, in particular, "provides the foundation for the ultimate old boy's network," or "the last place where men have an ultimate sense of physical superiority."[31] Indeed, successful athletes must cultivate traits of traditional masculinity, including physical strength and a "highly goal-oriented personality."[32] Peete's sport, football, reigns supreme in America perhaps in part because of the clarity it provides "between the polarities of traditional male power, strength, and violence and the contemporary fears of social feminization."[33]

Peete developed these qualities especially early in his life since, as he notes in *Not My Boy!*, his father was a college football coach. For Peete, masculinity and fatherhood are bound up in memories of his own father, who expected exceptional effort on and off the field, and, as a reward for good behavior, held out to his young son the tantalizing possibility of a visit to the football locker room. Peete went on to become a NFL quarterback, and hoped to pass along the same values to his own son. For Peete, sports build character: "Sports taught me how to work with others and how to deal with the ups and downs of friendship."[34] He believed his son R.J. would learn from team sports such essential life skills as "scheduling, timing, understanding competition, and the ability to work with other kids."[35] Like Emerson's son, R.J. was not initially interested in ball play, and like Donnell, Peete spent considerable time coaxing R.J. into engaging with sports activities. In fact, Peete provides an entire chapter on tips for encouraging autistic children to take up sports. When R.J. joins a soccer team and, eventually, scores a tie-breaking goal in the last game of the season, Peete swells with pride: "The first thing he did after that triumph, the first person he wanted to say something to, was me."[36] His son's success reinforces the new character Peete was rehearsing, that of the engaged father who is able to teach his son how to succeed on the playing field. The field seem to provide a literal commonplace, common ground on which fathers and sons can engage, and fathers of autistic boys seem to spend a significant amount of energy laying that groundwork for their relationships with their sons.

Rehearsing Family Roles

In addition to the topoi of fathers' relationships with their sons, fathers also draw on topoi related more specifically to the father's role in the family in order to rehearse their characters. Using these commonplaces, fathers can construct characters engaged in what the communication scholars John Duckworth and Patrice Buzzanell call "father work," or the "effort extended to display family prioritization," a process with material and discursive aspects.[37] Father work involves negotiating one's relation to the rest of the family and to the family as an institution or social construct. Topoi related to the institution of the family include the role of the father as breadwinner and problem-solver and "family prioritization," or putting family ahead of work. Fathers deploy them to rehearse characters of involved or engaged fathers in order to demonstrate their commitment to themselves and others.

NEGOTIATING FATHERHOOD

One of the first memoirs written by an autism father is Josh Greenfeld's three-part series of books about his son Noah. In it, Greenfeld collects journal entries he wrote about his family, beginning with Noah's birth in 1966. The diary reveals his developing character as a father and a writer. The first entries reflect his ambivalence about fatherhood. "I am not such a good daddy," he writes the day after Noah is born, when his older son, Karl, breaks a glass while his wife is still in the hospital: "I am not used to the full-time chore of baby-tending."[38] He writes, further, that fatherhood was never part of his life plan, which had previously included a stint in the army, an extended trip to Europe, and a period spent at an artists' retreat in New Hampshire: "I never dreamt that I would wind up a Westchester resident. A father. A family man with two sons."[39] Yet he wrote two days later that having a second son "pleases the male vanity" and that both of his sons "fill me with kinds of love I never dreamt possible."[40] In his diary entries, Greenfeld gradually comes to terms with his position within an institution toward which he felt ambivalent. Writing in the countercultural moment of the 1960s, he seemed somewhat bewildered at the conventional character he came to adopt.

Greenfeld's work offered one way for him to rehearse his character. In the introductory material he notes that he shaped his story "not as the professional writer I am, trained to carefully and abstractly plot ahead, but as the amateur parent I also am, thoroughly confused and beleaguered every step of the way."[41] Here, he contrasts his shaky identity as a new parent with his more established identity as a writer. However, Greenfeld's status as a writer must also shift to accommodate his family: as a new father Greenfeld takes a job, writing that he's had to end his "precarious" freelance existence, since "a family makes a realist out of any man."[42] Later, in a 1967 entry, he calls himself a "father-writer."[43] In these entries, we see Greenfeld turning to the commonplace of his work to define his character, refusing to make "father" his primary identification but instead seeking to blend it with that of "writer."

Similarly, Harris considers his father role in a post called "What Defines Me (A Discussion About Labels)." He borrows the terms "achieved status" and "ascribed status" from sociology, noting that his achieved statuses (those that result from his own choices) are "Photographer," "Father," "Husband," and "Guy who likes Reggae Music." Under "ascribed statuses," he puts "Man," "Caucasian," "Guy with a red beard," and "Father of a Child with Autism." He also notes that most individuals have a "master status," one that subsumes the others. After receiving his son's diagnosis, Harris writes, "'Father of a child with Autism' became my master status, an ascribed one, probably because it's the one that I felt (and still often feel) least suited to handle[;] it's certainly the one that challenges me the most."[44] Whereas Greenfeld struggled with the role of father—almost seeing it as ascribed—Harris struggles with the ascription "of a child with Autism." He also wonders whether, by adopting that ascribed role as his master status, he is simultaneously making his son's primary status "Autistic."

In these accounts, then, we see the topos of fatherhood being rehearsed and reconfigured, usually by combining it with something else ("writer," in Greenfeld's case, or "Father of a child with Autism," in Harris's). For these men, autism seems to present a provocation to think differently or more deeply about fatherhood as a role or an institution.

NEGOTIATING FAMILY WORK

Duckworth and Buzzanell note that, in addition to the central place of negotiating employment in "family work," fathers are increasingly expected to also be "involved parents, and nurturing caregivers."[45] Greenfeld negotiates this expectation through conflicting topoi, a kind of topical antithesis. Throughout the early diary entries, Greenfeld alternates between topoi that link fatherhood to joy and annoyance. One morning he might write, "It is always such a joy to see Karl and Noah when they first awake, when they smile and start to chatter, happy to discover the miracle of a new day." On another day, he might grumble that his sons can be "downright drags," despite their cuteness, and note that his wife has much more patience with the children than he does.[46]

Gradually, though, Greenfeld's entries come to shift between the topoi of acceptance and resistance. Some relate his begrudging acceptance of his role and of his prioritization of family: "I refuse to view his condition as a life-searing tragedy. We will do what we have to do. We will take care of him as best we can until we can no longer take care of him. We will have him in our home and find ways to live in joy with him. And when I cannot enjoy him as much as I would like to, I will love him even more."[47] Yet in other entries he admits to his ennui, even hatred for his son, calling Noah "my grim reality" and speculating about what it would mean to kill him.[48] Greenfeld's diary draws on these antithetical topoi to narrate his gradually developing sense of self as a father character.

Indeed, Greenfeld himself uses the metaphor of performance to conceptualize this process when he writes, "If Noah has proven debilitating to our dreams, he has also provided the material for a kind of realization of ourselves. It's not the realization either of us anticipated or wanted, but then one cannot predetermine the scenario one is destined—or doomed—to act out."[49] Here he confirms that he viewed fatherhood as a character to act out.

NEGOTIATING THE FATHER-AS-FIXER

While Greenfeld's books focus on a gradual acceptance of the traditional father character, other fathers take that character for granted and must revise it, especially the culturally constructed topos of the father as the fixer in the family unit. A man who posted on About.com, Bill K., sums up this tendency well: "This is a common profile among parents with an Autistic child. Successful businessman with three decades of experience in confronting adversity and overcoming it. I was not going to let my first major failure be my first born no matter what."[50] For Bill K., autism represents a failure and an affront to his hegemonic masculine identity. In the guidebook *Early Intervention and Autism*, James Ball reiterates this idea. Whereas women view dealing with autism as a "collaborative process," he notes, seeking out specialists, gathering information, and putting together a plan, dads want to fix the problem on their own: "That's what dads do. They recognize a problem, grab the required tools and rectify whatever is wrong. For dads, any situation that can't be fixed is a personal reflection of inadequacy."[51] Ball alludes to the expectations that are placed on fathers within the institution of the family via culturally constructed topoi. For the fathers featured here, that of father-as-fixer had to be revised or rejected in order for the father to take on a more productive role within the family unit.

In their books, we see Peete and Burns rehearsing or constituting those roles via rhetorical characters they take on in their narratives. In his account, Peete insists that "men want to battle a crisis, to make the plan and go after the goal with everything they have." Later he writes: "As a man, you want to be able to protect your family. You want to be able to soothe your wife. There was nothing I could say because this so-called expert had just evaluated our kid, but she'd also robbed me of all of my power."[52] Such generalizations evoke commonplaces of manhood and fatherhood; they are commonplaces in that they describe culturally available ideas about fatherhood, not necessarily actual fathers or all fathers.

Peete draws on commonplaces to characterize his actions as those of a typical husband and father. This includes his initial avoidance of his family, which he describes in the opening scene of the book: he is lounging in a leather chair at the posh Club Havana, where he used to go to escape from his wife, with whom he was "barely communicating," and his twins, including R.J., who had been recently diagnosed with autism. "I convinced myself that the Monte 2 [cigar] and Macallan [Scotch] was Daddy time," Peete writes, noting further that other fathers have likely faced a similar situation, "a time when you don't know how to be the dad your family needs."[53] He writes later that he felt an "overwhelming feeling of hopelessness," that he was a "failure as a parent" due to his inability to fix the problem, which justified his initial detachment from the family.[54] This section of the text might be read as an attempt by Peete to persuade his readers (or himself) that his actions were in keeping with those of other fathers, even if they seem selfish. The topos of father-as-fixer allows Peete to shape his character in accordance with dominant ideologies of fatherhood.

The text itself functions as a sort of conversion narrative. When his wife Robin confronts him about his behavior and issues an ultimatum, Peete must decide whether to commit to his family and his son or to leave entirely. After that event, Peete describes himself as a changed man, recounting how he had to reject some of the understandings of fatherhood on which he had constructed his character:

> [A]t first I'd mourned the vision I'd had of the kind of father I would be to R.J. And I understood that I had to let go of all the images of fatherhood that I'd received from movies and television—everyone from Ward Cleaver to Cliff Huxtable. I wanted to have as loving a relationship with R.J. as I'd enjoyed with my own dad, but I had come to terms with the fact that it couldn't be exactly the same. I couldn't simply cut and paste my dad's style of being a father onto me and my son.[55]

In other words, the topoi of traditional fatherhood had to be revised.

For Peete, the father as problem solver was replaced by family prioritization, which Duckworth and Buzzanell describe as discourses that "elevated family beyond its typically marginalized status in work-family binaries to a privileged position."[56]

Instead of characterizing himself as a fixer, Peete portrays himself as an increasingly involved father who now approaches his role with the same combination of discipline, talent, and perseverance that had earned him a high-profile athletic career. He describes his increasingly active role in his son's therapy activities, recounts how he used R.J.'s desire for routine to his advantage, and delineates his techniques for persistently engaging his son in new tasks. Making this shift required Peete to give his family's needs priority over his own and his earlier dreams for his children:

> It was only when I got myself out of that comfy leather chair and started to understand our real situation that I also understood that life had handed me an incredible opportunity. My dreams didn't have to die. In fact, they are bigger and more powerful than anything I could have imagined before. I had to let go of a lot in order to grab on to the reality of my child and of his world. I'm saying this as a man who has been humbled by the raising of his children. And through that humility, I've become a better father.[57]

In this passage Peete completes the conversion narrative, arguing that he has changed from the selfish, unrealistic father that he described in the beginning of the book to one who prioritizes family and has learned to be active and engaged. The text rehearses this role for Peete and for other fathers.

A similar type of conversion appears in Burns' book *Saving Ben*. Like Peete, Burns was highly successful in his career, although he achieved success as a businessman selling speechwriting software, rather than a football star orchestrating goals. He had built a character for himself around his success and his ability to solve problems. When Ben was diagnosed with autism, Burns writes, "I wanted him fixed as soon as possible." When the doctors' efforts failed, he continues, "someone had to act, research, step into the unknown, descend into the dungeon, rescue Ben."[58] Burns describes how he spearheaded a series of intensive treatment plans. In the start of the book, then, Burns constructs himself as a problem-solver, delineating a character in keeping with commonplaces of fatherhood but one that also borrows language from the medieval romance, much as autism mothers like Clara Claiborne Park.

Like Peete, Burns had to revise his character and reject the problem-solving topos for that of family prioritization. As he devoted more time to his son, his marriage suffered and his business foundered. His character, too, shifted: "Ben had changed me," he writes. "My ambitions had shrunk." Rather than organizing his character around his identity as a successful businessman and problem solver, he came to reconfigure his identity as a father, recognizing that the sacrifices he made may have limited his career options, but that "there are many kinds of riches, and Ben touched me in a place that cannot be untouched." Here again we see a discourse of family prioritization: Burns argues (to his readers and himself) that his choice to forgo a more lucrative career has been worth it.[59]

For some fathers, then, autism offers a way to reconfigure the father role, often leading to emotional and personal growth. A blogger called Lou writes that raising his son Diego "has completely destroyed the wall I had built around my feelings. I now allow myself to experience as well as show others a full range of emotions and I have moved past the notion that I should show indifference or stoicism."[60] Harris states, "Autism has forced me to be a better father, a better person, it has brought some amazing people into my life, it's given me a new way to define myself."[61] For Lou and Harris, constructing a father character involved revising topoi connected to the role of the father within the family, often by performing rhetorical family work. Negotiating the role of father involved coming to terms with alternative identities, as in Greenfeld's case, or rejecting the role of problem solver (for Peete and Burns) and embracing a commonplace of family prioritization. In addition, all of the writers considered in this section drew on their professional identities as topoi in their character development. Other writers take this a step further.

Refiguring Professional Identity

Given the strong link between identity and career success, fathers often apply not only the drive and dedication they apply to their careers, but often the insights of their occupations, in their encounters with autism. In such narratives, they not only construct their characters using the commonplaces of their professions but also use them to understand autism itself.

For instance, MateiCalinescu, a literary critic, writes about his son's "interesting type of memory" in a diary entry excerpted in his book *Matthew's Enigma*. He notices that Matthew tends to consider the same animal or object to be different when seen from a different angle. Thus, a cat stalking back and forth might lead Matthew to announce "'Another cat!' 'Another cat!'" For Calinescu, this episode evokes Jorge Luis Borges's story "Funes, el memorioso," which "could be seen as a detailed analysis (with that strangely rigorous logic of Borges) of infantile perception, so sensitive to issues of identity that any change in space through movement appears as a change of identity."[62] When he notices that Matthew has learned the negative function of language (no) earlier than the positive, Calinescu writes that he feels "tempted to write an essay on the primordial character of 'No.'" He notes that Matthew prefers to repeat his father's entire question rather than saying yes; notably, this might be interpreted as an early sign of autism, echolalia, but through Calinescu's lens as a postmodern literary critic, it instead becomes a philosophical question, wherein yes appears "as a concession, an acceptance, an act of submission." Later, regarding Matthew's unusual language, he ponders whether "the strange language or languages he invents may have something to do with that 'private language' which Wittgenstein considered an impossibility, given the hypothesis that any language is a channel of communication."[63] In all of these examples, Calinescu is applying his occupational topoi of language and literary theory to autism.

Calinescu recounts how he sought understanding through reading—beginning with the most recent literature, he worked backwards to Kanner's 1943 article. "Pushed by the demon of inquisitiveness," he read journal articles, memoirs by Clara Claiborne Park and Donna Williams, even Bettelheim's work, despite the warnings he received from his son's psychiatrist of its harmfulness.[64] He seeks clues in his son's language and behavior. He observes, for instance, that his son's speech was limited to the most frequent elements of daily life, which did not require the "apparently simple, but in reality highly complex and subtle expressive-affective grammar" of affection, gesture, or gaze.[65] By making these observations, Calinescu reports, he was learning how daily life, despite its apparent simplicity, was actually tremendously complicated. Despite this continued observation and research, though, he finds that his son remains a puzzle to him. In one instance, when Matthew suddenly seems to enter a regressive phase, he writes: "I have racked my mind searching in vain for a more or less plausible cause. I assembled the most circuitous, subtle, speculative-analogic, or far-fetched hypotheses, only to shoot them down as soon as I subjected them to critical attention."[66] In the end, he finds his attempts at interpretation fruitless. The frustration he feels as a result of this failure is palpable—as a literary critic, interpretation is his main mode of understanding; he can unravel the symbolic intricacies of meaning in literary texts, but he cannot easily apply the same hermeneutic practice to his son's behavior. Calinescu's work seems to fail him in his efforts to understand his son.

Roy Richard Grinker similarly draws on commonplaces of his discipline, in this case, anthropology. On the second page of his book, Grinker announces that he is "interested in the intersection between culture and illness—that is, how culture affects the way we define and classify illnesses."[67] He naturally turns to a cross-cultural approach, doing ethnographic research in India, South Africa, and South Korea and seeking a greater understanding of autism as both biological in origin and culturally inflected, comprising a group of symptoms that takes on significance in particular times and places.

With regard to his daughter Isabel, Grinker writes as someone who has already reached a point of understanding, rather than someone seeking it: "As time goes by I'm getting more comfortable with Isabel's disorder, more grateful for who she is and less mournful of the person she might have been without autism."[68] He describes Isabel's diagnosis and education from the standpoint of someone sharing his experience with readers, but not as someone searching for truth or meaning about autism. The truths he offers stem from his experiences coupled with those of other parents he has met around the world, who have turned "the hardship of raising a child with a disability into something positive, even if it means their futures are different from what they expected, or from what their families and cultures wanted."[69] Learning about other families who have autistic children seems to have helped Grinker gain this perspective. While the ostensible exigence for his book is the widespread discourse of crisis and epidemic that characterizes contemporary understandings of autism, the volume nevertheless serves as a narrative of how anthropological insights helped Grinker understand his daughter and come to terms with autism. "Isabel has challenged my assumptions about the world I thought I knew," he writes. "Through her unique personality, she's challenged my assumptions about the most elemental aspects of social life."[70] Grinker writes his book from the perspective of a father who has completed his journey of understanding, who has developed a character as a father that accepts his daughter and her condition.

Whereas Grinker seeks out insights in other cultures and settings in the present, Paul Collins approaches autism through a historical and cultural study. His *Not Even Wrong: Adventures in Autism* follows along the lines of his other books. An English professor and creative writer, Collins has written several books that profile historical figures, such as *Banvard's Folly: Thirteen Tales of People Who Didn't Change the World* (2002), *The Trouble with Tom: The Strange Afterlife and Times of Thomas Paine* (2009), and *The Book of William: How Shakespeare's First Folio Conquered the World* (2010), all of which detail the author's quest to find out more about these unique historical figures and their legacies.

Given this professional interest, it is not surprising that Collins takes a similar approach in his book about his son Morgan, using historical accounts of so-called feral children as a lens through which to consider his son. The first chapter begins with a character sketch of Morgan, told through a scene in which Collins and his wife take Morgan to see a doctor, who suggests for the first time that the boy may have developmental delays. Although he could read well and count to twenty at the age of two, Morgan's doctor noted that he seemed uninterested in people or in conversing with them.[71] Collins juxtaposes this scene with a sketch of "Peter the Wild Boy," an eighteenth-century feral boy found living in the woods in Hannover. Contemplating his notes about Peter, a subject Collins had been researching for years, led him to wonder, for the first time, whether something was wrong with Morgan.[72] Collins first relates that Peter seemed "singularly unimpressed with the prospect of fitting into human society" when he was brought before King George and presented with an opulent supper; Peter rejected the "bread and savories, eating only the nuts and beans that he could identify from the forest."[73] This scene is contrasted with Morgan's first visit to a therapist, when he refuses to respond to the therapist's attempt to engage him with colorful blocks.[74] Similarly, Collins aligns Peter's baptism in the court of the king—"the first step toward civilization"—with a scene describing his own attempts to get his son to take a shower.[75]

Collins recounts a series of these scenes before revealing the reason why they were important: "I never knew *why* I had wanted to write about Peter the Wild Boy. I'd become interested a little before Morgan turned two. . . . [L]ong before going to the doctor, before the diagnosis, before we ever imagined anything—I had been chasing a silent boy through the even greater silence of centuries, when my own boy was in front of me all along. . . . *Something* drew me to Peter, something so obvious now."[76] Peter, he learns, is now considered an early case of autism. Thus, the character study of Peter leads to insights for Collins, who seems to use them to better understand his son.

Creative nonfiction often focuses on unusual people or events, so it is not surprising that Collins draws on those topoi, using his character sketches to ask "What does it mean to be a person? To be human?"[77] Along similar lines, popular journalism tends to use provocative questions or issues, especially in reporting on science and medicine. In his book, the journalist and producer for BBC Radio Michael Blastland investigates his son's cognition and understanding in the context of a common topic of popular journalism: what it means to be human. His claim is simple: "Until you know Joe's unusual life, you won't fully understand your own." Blastland notes that his son "is a child possibly lacking almost all the philosopher's traditional definitions of what it is to be human," including criteria such as self-awareness, technological sophistication, symbolic language, and advanced reasoning ability.[78]

As a journalist trained to tease out human interest stories (and sell newspapers), he takes these musings quite far, since casting Joe as something of an alien or outsider offers a more transfixing narrative. His book employs this explanatory framework for his narrative, which centers around Joe's daily life and his reaction to transitions such as moving to a residential home, a step the Blastlands took when Joe was nine. Blastland describes Joe's reaction to this life change as "surprisingly patient bewilderment" despite the "despotic state of affairs," a reaction that leads him to question how "the rest of us make sense of the human activity raging about us."[79] Throughout, Joe offers a sort of litmus test against which Blastland measures supposedly universal human qualities or attributes; it is against the background of Joe's condition that these human traits can be identified. The upside is that Joe, according to his father, helps us appreciate "the richness of our own consciousness"—despite his brief nods to Joe's unique abilities, such as his visual acuity (for instance, being able to pick out a specific video or type of yogurt in a store).[80] It is easy to imagine this book as the kind of documentary or extended news feature about disabled people that populates the Discovery Channel, the BBC, or *60 Minutes*—human interest stories that often end up sensationalizing differences or turning into a twenty-first-century freak show. Unfortunately, Blastland's book seems to stretch the investigation so far that Joe becomes dehumanized. Autism is portrayed as a condition that renders humans into aliens or automatons, thereby denying the humanity of Joe and other autistic people.

Of course, some mothers also use topoi related to their professional expertise in their memoirs. For instance, Majia Nadesan, a communications scholar and professor at Arizona State University, draws on theories of social construction and cultural studies in *Constructing Autism: Unravelling the "Truth" and Understanding the Social* (2005). The book's introduction seems as if it could be the start of a mother warrior narrative. Nadesan describes how, "within a span of three months, my son's 'condition' was explained in terms of my mothering—my 'over-education' and excessive ministrations" and how she plunged into scientific and medical literature in attempts to understand his autism diagnosis.[81] Rather than viewing those texts through a scientific lens, though, Nadesan brought her training to bear on them, writing: "It became increasingly clear to me that autism, or more specifically, the *idea* of autism is fundamentally *socially constructed*."[82] In this way the book departs from mother warrior narratives. Instead of describing her own approaches to raising her son, she traces developments in child psychiatry, statistics, epidemiology, and personality that contributed to the very visibility of autism, its construction and performance.

Similarly, Cheri L. Florance brings her professional expertise to bear on her understanding of her son Whitney in *A Boy Beyond Reach* (2004). As a brain scientist and speech pathologist, Florance viewed her son's condition primarily through the lens of speech pathology and neurological processing. Refusing an autism diagnosis, she instead theorized that Whitney had a highly visual mind coupled with difficulties processing language. By fixing the language problems, she thought, she could also alleviate the other symptoms associated with autism, namely, social withdrawal and stereotypic behavior. The narrative traces out the implications of this theory in chronological terms, recounting the techniques she developed to work with Whitney and his progress over the course of his elementary school years. In this way, Florance's narrative mixes the quest for recovery, most common in mother's accounts, with the quest for understanding, most common in father's accounts: she is seeking to understand Whitney's difficulties and to remediate them.

For all of these parents, professional or disciplinary topoi serve inventive purposes, both for character formation and for understanding autism itself. It is clear, then, that fathers do not invent their characters with regard to their children, their families, or autism from whole cloth. Instead, they rely on available commonplaces. These may include inheritance, athletics, and independence; work life, family prioritization, or problem-solving; or professional and disciplinary identity and knowledge. The next section considers how they might prove useful for those seeking to involve fathers in autism therapies and care.

Rehearsing Fatherhood in Science and Policy

If we take their autobiographical accounts as representative, we might conclude that fathers of newly diagnosed children often struggle with their roles and may find it difficult to feel actively involved in their child's growth and development. Part of the reason for this difficulty may be that autism programs for parents draw on a different set of topoi than those that fathers embrace. For instance, Peete comments that the "special education world is run mostly by women, and a woman's touch is clear in many of the ways the institutions and interactions are organized. Some dads can feel uncomfortable trying to wedge their way into that scene." The way these programs are presented has important consequences, Peete notes, since men lose out in a big way by failing to get involved with their children's education: "They lose their position in the world, the love of their child, and a unique chance to make a difference in the lives of the people that matter to them."[83] Similarly, in her dissertation, autism researcher Jamie Winter notes that fathers' needs have not traditionally been considered in studies of early intervention treatments, perhaps because mothers are assumed to be the main participants. For instance, services may be offered during the standard nine-to-five workday (which excludes fathers and mothers who work during those hours) or they may not include the kinds of play activities fathers enjoy with their children. Winter designed a "father-focused" program for early intervention, which included flexible time arrangements and a recreational component to increase fathers' motivation.[84] Her study found that fathers were more likely to sign up for a father-focused program (as opposed to a standard package), that they were less likely to miss or cancel appointments, and that they reported higher satisfaction with the skills they learned. She cautions that autism programs for children may inadvertently discourage fathers from participating, or, at best, fail to engage them.[85]

Winter's research indicates that the design and presentation of autism interventions for children involves rhetorical considerations. Choices about what to call a program, how to describe it to parents, and what that program includes all affect whether fathers or mothers may be persuaded to participate. These questions led me to consider whether the materials distributed by intervention services inadvertently dissuade fathers from participating by drawing on topoi that appeal less to fathers than to mothers. I examined twenty brochures from autism agencies that I located by searching for "early intervention autism" and "brochure" on Google. My search yielded brochures from agencies such as Colorado Early Intervention and the National Autism Association.

In order to analyze them, I use the findings from Gloria Moss's *Gender, Design, and Marketing*, which highlights some of the gender-specific visual topoi of men's and women's design preferences. According to Moss, men prefer straight lines and shapes, fewer or darker colors, regular typography, and images of men. We might consider these elements to be visual topoi of masculinity. In contrast, women prefer rounded lines and shapes, more or brighter colors, irregular typography, and images of women.[86] We might consider these visual topoi of femininity. Of course, it is important to note that these understandings are rhetorically and culturally constructed. That is, there is nothing inherently masculine or feminine about any of these features, nor are men and women necessarily innately drawn to those features. Instead, we should view those features as recurrent elements that invoke a specific kind of audience. For instance, the same basic shaving cream formulation might be sold in a pink can featuring swirls of pastel colors for women, while the men's version might be sold in a simpler can in a dark color. Based on these tendencies, I coded each brochure for the following features: lines and shapes, colors, typography, and images.

Moss argues that men tend to prefer straight lines and angular shapes to rounded ones. Of the brochures I examined, 60 percent included rounded designs—borders, circles, and spirals embedded in backgrounds or used as callouts, or rounded logos (such as puzzle pieces or ribbons). For instance, the Early Intervention Center in Southfield, Michigan, features navy blue and yellow circles to highlight headings and key information.

Second, since Moss indicates that men tend to be drawn to fewer and darker hues, I coded for bright or primary colors (red, yellow, blue, green, purple, orange), pastels or "baby" hues, dark colors, and neutrals (black, brown, gray, white). In the brochures I examined, bright and pastel colors were common design features. Bright colors were used in 80 percent of the designs, and pastel colors were used in 60 percent. On average, brochures included five colors, excluding black and white. Surely, designers have plenty of reason to feature colorful design elements—the brochures have to do with children, and unisex designs for children often use either primary or pastel multicolor designs. Yet if the intended audience is *adults*, these design choices make less sense—especially if fathers are included in the target demographic. The designs might hail children, not adults, and especially not men.

Moss finds that men tend to prefer standard fonts to "irregular" ones. I took "irregular fonts" to mean script, cursive, or decorative fonts such as Comic Sans and Papyrus. I did not count italicized fonts if they seemed otherwise to be standard serif or sans serif fonts (such as Arial or Times New Roman). In terms of typography, 25 percent of the brochures featured script or decorative fonts. For instance, the brochure for the Saratoga County Council on Autism early intervention services features the word "Promise" or the phrase "Our Promise" five times, in a cursive font on a red background, as shown in figure 4.1.

In examining the images, I focused on photographs of people. My study yielded 129 images of people, in total. Of those, 97 were pictures of children of both genders, including babies, toddlers, and older children. Of the 32 adults shown, 9 were male and 23 were female. Thus, women represented 71 percent of the adults pictured, and men accounted for 29 percent. In most cases, the adults are implicitly figured as parents: they are shown kissing a child's cheek, looking down adoringly at a swaddled baby, or posing as in a family portrait (smiling into the camera). Women were also sometimes pictured as early intervention agents or therapists—in these cases, they are posed next to a child and focused on an activity in settings that evoke a classroom context. No men are depicted as therapists in the sample I examined.

These averages do not take into account the fact that twenty-one of the images of adults (seven men and nineteen women in various combinations) appeared in three brochures by a single agency, Early Intervention Colorado. These brochures are notable because they picture various combinations of adults with children—sometimes one parent with a child, sometimes both parents with a child, and, in one

Our Mission Statement

The Autism Council of Saratoga County serves as a collaborative resource center designed to promote the development of services and resources for individuals with Pervasive Developmental Disorders or Autism throughout their lifetime. The Autism Council of Saratoga County will strive to provide knowledge and understanding of individuals with Autism and related disabilities and serve as a critical resource to help families and care-givers find trained professionals, service providers and resources in their community. The Saratoga Council will also advocate with state and federal governments to promote public awareness on behalf of individuals with Autism .

Our Promise
to Saratoga County...

Our commitment to resources, support, awareness and advocacy.

About

Autism is a complex developmental disability that typically appears during the first three years of life and affects a person's ability to communicate and interact with others. It is defined by a certain set of behaviors and falls under the diagnostic category of a Pervasive Developmental Disorder. It is a "spectrum disorder" that affects individuals differently and to varying degrees.

You are not alone...

In Saratoga County, we organized the Council on Autism. Our goal is to provide information and education on resources, services and support to those affected by Autism. Everyone deserves a promise of support.

Our Promise

To support our residents of Saratoga County through the Council on autism is available by contacting our council representatives...

If you are a resident of Saratoga County, you can get more information about our Early Intervention Program services by contacting:

Public Health Nursing Services
31 Woodlawn Ave.
Saratoga Springs, NY 12866
(518)584-7460 (Tel.)

Or

Saratoga County Youth Bureau
152 West High Street
Ballston Spa, NY 12020
(518)884-4180 (Tel.)
(518)884-4185 (Fax.)
Website:
www.co.saratoga.ny.us/phindex.html

Promise... Promise... Promise...

Figure 4.1. Brochure of the Saratoga County Council on Autism for early intervention featuring cursive fonts. From Saratoga County Council on Autism. Reprinted with permission.

instance, a father with two children. The people shown also represent different races, including people who appear to be African American, Caucasian, Latino or Latina, and Asian American. Only one other brochure featured an image of a male adult.

If, as Moss contends, men prefer designs with photographs of other men, the remaining brochures might subtly discourage men from reading them or participating in the programs they describe. The choice of images to include may also cue men as to the type of program and who is imagined to participate. In short, these designs draw on topoi of femininity and childhood that do not square with the characters that fathers of autistic children may be constructing for themselves.

Although Moss does not discuss men's and women's reactions to pictures of children, other research suggests that such images may be more appealing to women. In 1949, Konrad Lorenz identified the features of *kindenschema*, or cuteness, which included the following:

1. A large head in proportion to the body
2. A large, protruding forehead in comparison to the rest of the face

3. Large eyes positioned below the middle line of the head
4. Short, stumpy limbs; pudgy feet and hands
5. A plump, rounded body shape
6. Soft, elastic body surfaces
7. Round, chubby cheeks
8. Clumsiness[87]

Using these qualities, researchers in the past twenty years have employed computer images of babies to judge men's and women's responses to cuteness. For instance, Janek Lobmaier et al. found that females were better than males at choosing the cuter baby picture when given a choice of two photographs that had been digitally manipulated to demonstrate a specified level of cuteness.[88] In a similar study, Reiner Sprengelmeyer et al. found that younger women outperformed women nearing or past the average age of menopause in a similar task.[89] Those who conducted these studies hypothesized that there may be a biological impulse (via hormonal influences) for women, especially young women, to be more adept at judging cuteness in infants. Note that these researchers did not ask whether individuals were drawn to the images in question, nor did they ask what feelings the images evoked. Instead, they used a more easily objectified measure, accuracy—much in the same way that Baron-Cohen employs judgments of empathic accuracy to measure empathy. Thus, these results do not necessarily explain why women would be more drawn to images of babies.

Women are not simply biologically predisposed to find babies and children cute; they are culturally conditioned to do so. Indeed, separating the two seems nearly impossible, given that females are inundated with baby dolls, encouraged to enjoy babies and children, and probably exposed to more images of children in magazines, advertising, and other media than are men. Indeed, Lorenz emphasized that the "cute response" was in part learned and could be mediated by cultural codes. Likewise, it is possible that some individuals have been conditioned to inhibit the cute response—surely, oohing and aahing over a cute baby is not generally considered a paradigmatically "masculine" activity.

When analyzed holistically, many of the brochures featured elements that can only be called juvenile, if not babyish. Take, for example, Early Intervention Colorado's *Guide I: Referral and Eligibility for Colorado Early Intervention Services.* The guide features three bright colors (blue, purple, and orange) and four pastels (pale green, lavender, peach, and pale blue). Many of the pages include pastel cartoon images of baby bottles, blocks, teddy bears, rattles, and pacifiers—topoi of babyhood. These design elements index the target "audience" for early intervention (children under two years old) but not necessarily the audience for the brochure: parents of those children. Similarly, men might be put off by the colorful puzzle pieces and linked, paperdoll-like icon of children in the brochure from the Saratoga County Council on Autism (see figure 4.1), as well as the irregular fonts.

How might designers of these brochures effectively target men, given these considerations? Moss would encourage designers to include some of the topoi of masculine design: pictures of men, fewer and darker colors, and linear designs. Following the advice of marketers who have considered the issue, they might also consider ways to ascribe gender to the product in question (in this example, early intervention services), perhaps by appealing to fundamental stereotypes about men. In her advice to marketers seeking to "gender" a product or brand, Pamela Alreck warns that crossing gender norms can be done only if "everything else about the person . . . epitomize[s] the role of someone of that sex." She uses the example of an aftershave lotion ad featuring a man and a naked baby taking a bath. This type of image could be effective, she claims, but only if the man depicted is especially masculine, such that the connotation would be that "he is so completely secure in his manhood that he can afford to show his love and tenderness for the child."[90] One can imagine, then, depicting stereotypically strong, masculine men with babies and children. Another possibility would be to depict fathers engaging in activities with their children, especially recreational activities such as sports or video games, rather than snuggling a baby, since fathers' autobiographical accounts suggest that they see those kinds of activities as especially important for their roles as fathers. Images of fathers and children engaged in sports or other male-coded activities might balance the more nurturing images often included of parents holding, cuddling with, or gazing into the faces of babies. Darker, simpler color schemes might likewise balance feminized or childish design features. Admittedly, these choices risk reifying hegemonic masculinity. Not all fathers necessarily prefer these kinds of design features, and using them might reinforce the idea that fathers are only interested in helping their children in the context of sports. Nonetheless, including more images of fathers (or male therapists) working with children, less babyish colors and designs, and more appealing descriptions of activities could help to involve more fathers in their child's care.

In terms of content, such an approach might involve addressing fathers' feelings and doubts and emphasizing the emotional gains that can come from learning to interact with their autistic children. The brochures I examined tended to speak from the authority position of the sponsoring organization, not from the position of participants (children or parents). Testimony from engaged fathers might help market early intervention programs as rewarding, especially if fathers share the frustrations and disappointments described by Donnell, Peete, and others from my analysis above. These testimonies might draw on the *commonplaces* of fatherhood I have identified in this chapter, and perhaps explain when and why they might need revising, such as the father-as-problem-solver topos that seems to frustrate many fathers.

More broadly, aside from the research conducted by Winter and a few others, little scholarship addresses ways in which fathers can play an active role in autism programs. This gap opens up possibilities for cooperative research with rhetoric and communication specialists, who might help autism researchers study how best to engage fathers. In addition to brochure design, the design of intervention programs themselves becomes rhetorical. As Winter argues, the assumptions underlying such programs may subtly persuade mothers and fathers to participate or not to participate. These include considerations of timing, location, and the kinds of activities used in the program, as well as how those programs are presented to parents. By labeling her program "father-focused," Winter may have primed fathers to respond favorably. A program called "Mommy and Me," in contrast, might discourage fathers, who would not be invoked as a target audience and would need to cross a gender boundary in order to participate.

Admittedly, there's an assumed heterosexual relationship underlying most of the preceding analysis. Aside from Burns, I encountered few narratives from homosexual fathers and none from fathers raising an autistic child with a male partner. This omission in the available research is striking in part because accounts written by autistic people often include alternative gender identifications and sexual preferences. Chapter 5 considers how autistic people understand gender, identity, and sexuality, often in ways that challenge contemporary gender theory.

CHAPTER 5

Inventing Gender

Neurodiverse Characters

As a child, Jane Meyerding found girls confusing. She simply did not understand "girltalk"—the giggling, gossiping, and secret-sharing that marks young girls' socializing.[1] "I was sailing blind," Meyerding writes, "through a world full of gender signals invisible to my gender-less self."[2] Though she did not desire to be a boy, Meyerding did not readily identify as a girl, either.

An autistic biological male named Shiva writes, similarly: "When i see 'gender' as a tick-box category on a form, i feel similarly to if, on a form asking for details of a vehicle, it asked for 'miles per gallon' when my vehicle was powered by something completely different (and that can't be measured in gallons), like say solar electricity—i just don't really consider myself to belong to the category of beings that have gender."[3]

Thus far, I have examined how gendered characters emerge in discourse about autism—either in terms of the theories about what autism is, what causes it, and how it should be treated, or in terms of the people who emerge to speak and write about it. In previous chapters, these characters have mostly conformed to hegemonic norms of male and female, masculine and feminine. For Becky Francis, these gendered characters are (to borrow Bakhtin's term) "monoglossic."[4] That is, they conform to a traditional binary gender system in which one is either male or female, masculine or feminine, and performs a gendered role that corresponds with one's sex. Yet when it comes to

accounts written by autistic people, we find a different set of characters and commonplaces: a more heteroglossic system, which includes
"plasticity, contradiction, and resistance."[5] This heteroglossic system
embraces multiple configurations of sex, gender, and sexuality.

As Kristin Bumiller has noted, a remarkable number of autistic people identify themselves as gender-neutral, androgynous, or otherwise
nontraditional in their sense of gendered identity, a factor scientists
have begun to explore.[6] Although researchers have not yet determined,
definitively, what proportion of autistic people might fall under this
category, one study by the psychiatrist Annelou L. C. de Vries and her
collaborators found that 7.8 per cent of autistic individuals surveyed
could be categorized as gender defiant.[7] Going even further, the psychiatrist Susanne Bejerot and colleagues posit that ASD may itself constitute a "gender defiant disorder." They found that "women with ASD
often display less feminine characteristics than women without ASD,
and that men with ASD often display less masculine characteristics
than men without ASD."[8] The men and women they studied were likely
to have androgynous features. Bejerot et al. argue that this evidence
contests the extreme male brain theory and could point to effects of
chemicals that disrupt the endocrine system.

While scientists may continue to explore autism and gender from a
biological perspective, here I examine how nontraditional gendered
characters form and circulate in writing by autistic people. An autistic
perspective points to the usefulness of a rhetorical model for understanding gender, one that considers it as providing a range of available
topoi through which individuals make sense of, model, and perform
a gendered character.

In this chapter, I examine accounts written by autistic people
through the lenses of rhetoric and neurodiversity. The latter refers to
a movement that argues that the "discourse of individual rights," usually applied to race, gender, ethnicity, and sexual orientation, "ought to
apply to individuals whose neurological predispositions are not typical."
In an analysis of the term *neurodiversity*, Micki McGee notes that people
on the autism spectrum have been especially active in this movement.[9]
Drawing on social models of disability, activists and practitioners argue
that autism becomes apparent owing to social norms requiring certain
kinds of communication and behavior that may be difficult for those
who process information differently.

Autistic individuals describe a range of differences they experience
in navigating the world, which may range from sensory differences

(such as high sensitivity to light or sound), synesthesia (the blending of one or more sensory inputs, such as colors with sounds), difficulty processing multiple inputs (such as speech and vision), or trouble recognizing faces. For instance, in her book *Songs of the Gorilla Nation*, the anthropologist Dawn Prince-Hughes describes autism as "a beautiful way of seeing the world," describing the thrill she gets when she encounters symmetry, as in the "lines and color of tennis courts" or the roundness of tunnels, as well as the "sense addictions" she attaches to everything from purple irises to the smell of tin boxes of Band-Aids.[10] Some autistic people also point to a greater attention to detail, an ability to focus intently on a topic, or the ability to remember visual and aural information. From this perspective, autism constitutes a different neurological make-up, one that carries with it considerable strengths even if it can present difficulties navigating a world designed for "neurotypicals," or those whose neurology accords with that of most other humans.

In terms of gender, a neurodiverse perspective may denaturalize gender norms and offer novel insights into gender as a social process. Examining gender from an autistic perspective highlights some elements as socially constructed that may otherwise seem natural and supports an understanding of gender as fluid and multidimensional. Rather than positing a single model of gender that accounts for these experiences, I show instead the range of gender theories that inform self-understanding for autistic people who identify as something other than their biologically determined sex or gender, or for people who find gender confusing or inapplicable to their experience.

As Joanne Meyerowitz points out in her study of the history of transsexuality, *How Sex Changed*, individuals "articulate[] their sense of self with the language and cultural forms available to them," using available "labels, stories, and theories to understand [one]self."[11] These components form part of what Aristotle would call the "available means" of rhetoric, the source materials that rhetors consult in constructing an argument.[12] In the case of contemporary gender forms, these topoi include scientific, feminist, social constructionist, and transgender-transsexual theories, along with public representations of gender in images, fashions, media, and the like. Autistic understandings of gender support this rhetorical model, in which individuals draw on available commonplaces in order to understand and present themselves as gendered (or alternatively gendered, or nongendered) characters. Yet, as Victoria McGeer argues, the language available to us is mostly geared to typical psychological experiences. Those whose experiences do not conform to the type must "adapt, manipulate, and perhaps outright distort the common meanings of our words in order to convey something of their own subjective experience."[13]

In order to better understand how autistic individuals use and adapt gender discourses as tools for self-understanding, I culled accounts from internet forums, blogs, and published memoirs, all of which imply not a binary concept or even a view of gender as a continuum, but something more like a copia, the rhetorical term Erasmus used to describe the practice of selecting "certain expressions and mak[ing] as many variations of them as possible."[14] *Copia* refers to a strategy of invention, a rhetorical term for the process of generating ideas. To be specific, it involves proliferation, multiplying possibilities so as to locate the range of persuasive options available to a rhetor. I find invention a fitting concept to describe autistic gendered characters.

Individuals who find themselves searching for terms with which to understand themselves now face a wide array of choices such as female-to-male (FTM) or male-to-female (MTF) transsexual, genderqueer, transgendered, femme, butch, boi, neutrois, androgyne, bi- or tri-gender, third gender, and even geek. In addition to these gendered characters, individuals may add on terms related to sexuality such as straight, gay, lesbian, pansexual, and bisexual. These terms, along with theories that inform our understandings of gender itself, form part of the available means for gender identity that autistic individuals may use. Each of these terms embeds a discursive history or genealogy and provides rhetorical options for self-expression.

Of course, not all autistic individuals identify according to a nontraditional character; many people with autism identify unproblematically as male or female (or masculine or feminine). I do not mean to suggest that the examples considered here are in any way representative of the entire population of autistic people. Some scientific studies posit that a slightly higher than average percentage of autistic people have nontraditional gender identifications and sexual preferences. However, the data drawn from these studies make conclusions problematic, in part because they each use different categories (sexual identification, gender identity, and so on) and sometimes employ problematic discourses—as in studies of Gender Identity Disorder (GID) or "gender dysphoria."

In the first part of this chapter, I examine how gendered characters serve an inventive purpose for autistic individuals: as disidentification, as a social code, as a performance of a role, and as an idiosyncratic identity. My goal is not to weigh in on whether such modes are indeed more prevalent among autistic people but to argue that their experiences are interesting because they contrast so dramatically with the binary model of sex and gender that informs the gendered theories and performances explored in earlier chapters. These texts also show how autistic enactments of gender do not simply represent disordered identifications or symptoms of autistic impairment, as psychiatric experts might have it, but may be understood as rhetorical acts. Creating gendered characters on the basis of which to act often serves a vital function for autistic people seeking a means to interact with others.

I then explore the ways scientific research, advice literature, and popular films about autism tend to close off this range of characters and reassert a binary model of gender. This section furthers John Sloop's argument that "gender/sexuality difference is persistently reaffirmed and returned to 'gender normality' on a mass cultural and ideological level."[15] In short, understanding how autistic people think about gender can offer potentially transformative insights into how gender works, but these insights are often dulled by practices of gender remediation that seek to shoehorn people into a small set of normalized gender categories.

Inventing Gender Identification and Disidentification

Autistic individuals may understand gender as a sort of disidentification. From this perspective, one relates one's own sense of gender identity to observations of available gender roles or performances and finds a lack of coherence. Such a perspective squares with the Burkean notion that "identity is not individual . . . a man 'identifies himself' with all sorts of manifestations beyond himself."[16] Gender provides one of these manifestations. Traditionally, "proper" gender identification has been considered a marker of a person's social development, and children were expected to identify unproblematically with their biological sex by the time they reached school age, although attention to alternative gender identities has lessened this expectation somewhat. We now understand that gender identification is a process that happens incrementally, and not always without conflict. The gender theorist and molecular biologist Anne Fausto-Sterling argues that gender identity is a "set of systems moving through time," one that "varies in its relative stability."[17] The experiences of the autistic individuals considered in this chapter highlight the rhetorical and fragmented nature of this process.

For some autistic people, though, gender does not easily serve as an available resource for identity. In "Growing up Genderless," Meyerding describes her "inability to identify with other women."[18] Rather than identifying as a man, as some might assume, or as a lesbian (a position Meyerding tried out in the 1970s), she finds gender incomprehensible and inapplicable to her experience. Another autistic woman, Amanda Baggs, writes on her blog that "gender is a concept that, while I understand intellectually that it is greatly important for other people, is entirely absent and incomprehensible to me."[19] Meyerding and Baggs both note a general "genderblindness," a tendency that shapes not only their perceptions of others but their own identities.

For these writers, a known disability, blindness, serves as a metaphor with which to understand an unnamed and unrecognized disability. Of course, some might object to the use of *blindness* because it is used to connote "lack of knowledge, randomness, and primitive reasoning," in the words of disability studies scholar Simi Linton. Such usage can alienate people with disabilities and also "perpetuate inaccurate information about disabled people's experience."[20] The use of "genderblind" here is somewhat ironic, given the problematic ways autism is sometimes used metaphorically to connote self-involvement or immorality.

Nonetheless, these understandings of gender—the notion of living in a nongendered way—might strike some as a utopian condition, especially feminist and gender scholars who have long argued for a more flexible system. Without a sense of gender, one cannot be susceptible to gender stereotypes or discrimination. One might conceivably feel a sense of freedom to style oneself, physically and emotionally, according to preferences not dictated by gender.

Yet not everyone finds genderblindness utopic. For some individuals, gender disorientation can be emotionally painful. Blogger Amanda Forest Vivian writes in one post: "I'm upset because I feel like there's no word to describe my gender expression and the gender expression I'm attracted to. It's probably silly to be upset about not having a word for something, but because I don't feel represented in either straight or queer communities, I do have a desire to articulate what it is that I am."[21] While academics spend significant time deconstructing terms and questioning their usefulness, for individuals, having a term to describe oneself can be tremendously important. Vivian finds the lack of such a term problematic, perhaps in part because a term might provide resources for identification. When she writes that she does not feel represented in "either queer or straight communities," she may be implying that there's a lack of identification or consubstantiality that would make it possible for her to feel accepted within those groups.

In a similar vein, the potential loss of an identificatory term can be equally troubling. One forum poster, Sleeping Chrysalid, writes that she was diagnosed with Asperger's as a child but has come to identify herself primarily as someone who is transgendered. On learning of a possible connection between the two, she panicked: "I am constantly plagued by the thought that my identity crisis may just be a result of aspergers [*sic*]. . . . It is crushing to hear that aspergers is characteristic of the male brain. My brain has many other female charactersitics [*sic*]. I can think about my feelings. I can write beautiful essays and I am doing just as well in english [*sic*] as I am doing in math."[22] This passage illustrates that Sleeping Chrysalid had built up an identity around the notion that she possessed a brain with "female characteristics." She sorted a number of her abilities into that category, such as her writing and English skills (gendered female) as opposed to math skills (gendered male). The possibility of disrupting this plan was frightening, since it would mean reshaping an orientation built up through rhetorical resources and now broken. Reorienting an identity based on Asperger's syndrome would require Sleeping Chrysalid to pick up the pieces and find new connections, new resources of identification.

Despite the difficulties of orienting oneself to a stable gender category, the topic of gender provides a point of identification for autistic individuals with nontraditional gender identities. On message boards and blogs, they share experiences with alternative gender self-concepts in ways that might be confirmatory. Bryan Crable notes that this kind of interactional rhetoric can be crucial to establishing a secure identity. Internet communication can provide a source for interactional rhetoric, or "*discourse aimed at gaining another's cooperation in the creation or defense of the rhetor's desired identity*" that is not otherwise available to individuals who might be isolated from others like them.[23] Posts on one popular internet site for autistic people, WrongPlanet.net, often take the form of identity confirmation, starting with a question like "Is anyone else here . . . ?" (followed by "transsexual," a "girly girl," or what have you). The string of responses usually tends to second this identity. For instance, when one participant posted the question, "Does anyone else here have Aspergers and are gay," he received the response, "We have an entire LGBT subforum."[24] Or, more simply, when one poster asked "Anyone else here not interested in relationships?" she received the simple response "You are not alone."[25] In short, online fora can offer resources and support for alternative self-identities that might be lacking elsewhere. These Web sites provide opportunities for interactional rhetoric that confirms and validates identities.

Although many autistic individuals find gender itself confusing, a point of disidentification as much as identification, that does not necessarily mean that they identify with the opposite sex. Indeed, women who write about their experiences with gender often protest against the assumption that they are "male-brained." This assumption follows from Baron-Cohen's extreme male brain theory of autism, which posits that autistic individuals demonstrate hyper-developed male attributes such as a propensity for systematic thinking, computers, and numbers, and a lack of female attributes, identified as social and empathizing skills. For example, although women may identify a number of perseverations, or intense interests, they do not always connect those to a male-type brain. In an online discussion published in *Women from Another Planet*, posters called Jane and Mary Margaret noted their ongoing relationship with animals; Diane and Wendy talked about their interest in cats; Kalen revealed her passion for computers, and Coa and Toni described their love for reading novels.[26] None of these (except computers) capture the kinds of male-associated systemizing activities listed in the extreme male brain theory; in fact, many of them could be seen as examples of empathizing activities, depending on one's perspective.

Indeed, the writers argue that they "are fully capable of empathy," a skill they exhibit by listening and observing carefully, by overlooking social categories and stereotypes, and applying empathy not just to humans but also to animals, plants, and inanimate objects. Mary Margaret writes, for instance, that she finds "most of humanity is ignorant for not hearing and seeing what is around them"—the rocks and trees, machines, and other people "without voices," such as the Alzheimer's patients with whom she works.[27] In *Songs of the Gorilla Nation*, Prince-Hughes describes her close connection to her "gorilla family," which she first encountered at a zoo and later studied as an anthropology graduate student. "These gorillas," she writes, "so sensitive and so trapped, were mirrors for my soul. . . . Because the gorillas were so like me in so many ways, I was able to see myself in them, and in turn I saw them—and eventually myself—in other human people." She writes passionately about how gorillas are misunderstood, portrayed as savage murderers or "caricatures of fully formed humanity," denied the empathic understanding traditionally accorded only to humans.[28] Indeed, these writers offer an expanded notion of empathy, one that addresses the broader spiritual concerns that are often lost in the neurotypical world (or sought out in high-priced yoga classes or mindfulness retreats). This form of identification seems to operate along alternative lines of affiliation, with gender being one of the least important resources for identity.

GENDER AS RESOURCE OF AMBIGUITY

Indeed, for some individuals, gender ambiguities are not necessarily negative; instead, they offer resources for thinking about gender in new ways. Autistic experiences with gender offer what Burke calls "*resources* of ambiguity," heuristics for thinking about gender as something other than a binary. As Burke writes, "It is in the areas of ambiguity that transformations take place."[29] He might also point out that it is precisely *because* gender is ambiguous that humans are motivated to advance what the communication scholars Kevin R. McClure and Kristine M. Cabral refer to as "rhetorical construction of realities," in this case, of genders.[30]

Writers sometimes situate themselves between available gender terms. Shiva writes that, though he appears unambiguously male because of his facial hair, large feet, and low voice, he also has long hair and self-identifies as not having "any sort of 'internal' gender identity whatsoever."[31] Jean Miller notes that she doesn't, either: "I myself live a somewhat femme life but it feels in some sense detachable, a costume. I was an androgynous kid and most clearly perceive the world in a non-gendered way."[32] While Shiva situates himself as a "third gender" between male and female, Miller positions herself between femme and androgynous or nongendered. Both of these writers find an alternative, ambiguous position from which to understand themselves.

Similarly, Lindsay, who maintains a blog called Autist's Corner, describes her "persona and self-concept" as more masculine than her clothing and appearance might indicate. For Lindsay, the distinction between her persona and her appearance offers a way to understand one's gender as both masculine and feminine, not one or the other. Feminized items of clothing and jewelry do not necessarily symbolize femininity, in Lindsay's case, either: "I've got a particular fascination with shiny objects, so when I wear lots and lots of gaudy jewelry, especially rings (which I often do), I often hypnotize myself looking at them as my hands move through the air. I also like to wear long, trailing skirts, the movement of which I find soothing."[33] Yet Lindsay recognizes that her clothing choices might be read as feminine even if her persona is not.

Reflections by autistic women who have become mothers also provide resources for ambiguity. Although Miller never expected to become a mother, finding that she did not identify with that socially constructed role, on conceiving she soon found that her "maternal pessimism gave way to wonder and ecstasy."[34] She encountered difficulties in the first few weeks of caring for her son Adrian because she found it difficult to assume the gendered role of mother given her own sensory and emotional needs. Yet she also recounts how she gradually learned to interpret his needs (some of which she attributes to her son's reactions to overstimulation).[35] Family relationships, then, provide a resource for thinking about gendered roles in an alternative way. Miller developed a different understanding of herself as a mother, one that did not entirely conform to mainstream representations.

In addition, autistic women find points of ambiguity between the culturally constructed identity of an autistic person—stereotypically a male—and their own interests and identities. Women often point out differences they've noticed between themselves and males with an ASD. One poster on the Web site WrongPlanet started a forum topic by asking whether others' "collecting habits or special interest areas/obsessions differ from the male stereotypes that are perpetuated in the assessment process."[36] The title of the forum, "So, I don't collect toy dinosaurs or stamps," reflects the presumption in autism diagnosis that autistic people will display interests in specific kinds of male-oriented activities. On another thread, posters considered their experiences in relation to Baron-Cohen's extreme male brain theory of autism. While some noted that they related better to men than to women, most also identified ways in which they did not fit the theory. For example, a poster using the name Revolutionrock-nroll wrote, "I think I'm more compassionate/empathetic towards others than the average male but less than the average female—in terms of caring about/relating to other people."[37] Another wrote that while she finds it hard to understand other women, and may seem less stereotypically feminine than most women, her choices of dress and appearance depend more on sensory issues than on any desire to reject femininity or "being girly."[38] Through interactional rhetoric, these participants seem to find resources for forging alternative gender identities together.

Inventing Gendered Social Codes

Other individuals tend to argue for gender as an in-built condition or an ability to recognize gendered social codes. In particular, some rely on neurological explanations grounded in metaphors of circuitry and wiring common to contemporary discourses about the brain. "My nervous system seems to be configured differently," Susan Golubock writes in her poem "Different on the Inside."[39] Meyerding writes that her wiring didn't allow her to identify with other girls, that she lacked "the social code capacity programmed into their brains." Here, Meyerding describes social interaction as a "basic operating system"—one that women and girls are expected to be especially good at operating.[40] For these writers, gender forms part of a built-in mental computer, an operating system one either has or does not have that allows one to understand, interpret, and perform gender appropriately.

At first glance, this language seems to echo the approach offered by Baron-Cohen and others who posit differences between male and female brains, who similarly rely on informatic metaphors of wiring and code. Further, such understandings may seem to contradict feminist views of gender as socially constructed or stylized repetition. Yet Golubock and Meyerding do not claim that they possess male brains. It is not a female brain that they lack but, rather, the "social code capacity" to recognize gender as an important variable. This view actually calls into question the notion that gendered behavior is necessarily connected to sex. If femininity were naturally connected to femaleness, women such as Golubock and Meyerding would not find it so hard to perform correctly. Their ways of talking about gender signify, instead, that gender is a sociorhetorical system into which individuals are drawn, but not without some requisite neurological orientation (whether innate or acquired). By recognizing gender (and being taught to do so), most become individuals who inhabit gender. Individuals with autism may not recognize gender in the first place or may learn to do so later in life.

One reason for this may be linguistic. Although not all autistic people have language delays as children, some do. Since gender depends on rhetorical and linguistic factors, language delays may also delay a developing sense that boy and girl, blue and pink, trucks and dolls are typically linked in discourse as well as social acts. Without words for "boy" and "girl," one might not develop a gendered sense of "appropriate" behaviors. Alternatively, the sensory processing differences many autistic individuals describe may inhibit a sense of gender—which essentially involves grouping individuals into two categories based on assumptions about what lies beneath their clothing. Autistic individuals may focus on other elements, or they may focus primarily on minor details (the color or texture of someone's clothing or hair rather than the general category of "boy clothes" or "girl clothes"), missing the forest for the trees, so to speak. For this reason, they may not completely participate in the sociorhetorical system that produces (and often mandates) binary sex or gender roles.

Given their difficulties understanding gender, rather than incorporating gendered norms reflexively or automatically into their identities, these writers had to carefully study gender as a set of codes or signals. Autistic women often describe how they gradually learned about the social expectations tied up with femaleness and femininity. Judy Singer notes that "it is women who are more often the social gatekeepers who scrutinize our manners, care more for them than for our minds, and want to keep us out of the club." She attributes a range of social roles to the average or neurotypical woman, such as "taking a precise reading of all the social currents of a given moment . . . sniffing out the exact social dress code that precisely fits the moment in history . . . or reading all the social cues in a group."[41] By identifying gender expectations as socially constructed roles, Singer develops an explanatory framework that helps autistic women interpret their difficulties in identifying with a gender. One might argue that Singer stereotypes neurotypical women here—certainly, not all women of any kind are adept at reading social cues or spotting the latest fashion trends. Singer points out, however, that, in the aggregate, these skills are socially assigned to the female role (rather than located in their brains). Any woman who fails to develop these skills might be read as less feminine or may be excluded from female groups.

On her blog, Vivian writes that the term *women* is a code for a range of attributes that she does not find applicable to herself: "attracted to men, mostly spends time with other women, socially sensitive, emotional in a particular way. . . . People use the word 'women' as a code word when they are talking about abortion and birth control, which are things I support, but which are *not* things that personally affect me. I'm not against the people the word 'women' stands for, but I don't feel particularly attached to them either."[42] As a signifier, *women* evokes a range of associated behaviors, concepts, beliefs, and debates— a representational system with which biological women are meant to identify. Vivian's confusion about gender identity means that she does not identify with the symbol "woman" in discourse any more than she does with the identity position.

Finding an appropriate term with which to identify may seem a futile project if one does not fit into the traditional (and limited) categories available for gender expression. Yet naming, Burke notes, is important for self-identity as a rhetorical project. Indeed, he writes: "The mere failure of a vocabulary to draw all lines to the right places is to a degree malignly persuasive (and all vocabularies naming social and political relations in the large must err somewhat in this respect)."[43] The "malign persuasion" in question might be the fact that lacking a term or word with which to identify might persuade people that they do not fit, that they are anomalous or that they lack a gender identity. Hence, it is understandable that people such as Vivian may continue to search for terms with which to identify, even temporarily.

Inventing Gendered Performances

For autistic individuals, gender may also constitute a performance in a rather literal sense: gendered characters offer them roles to play in their daily lives. Currently, theorists often define gender as a performance in a more metaphorical sense, as *performativity*, what Judith Butler has called "an identity tenuously constituted in time— an identity instituted through a *stylized repetition of acts*."[44] For Butler, this performance is not simply voluntary, like taking on a new role in a play, but an embodied *effect* of continued acting according to social norms. Sometimes, autistic women write about their gender identity in this vein. In an online comment, Lindsay states that her own hypothesis is that "gender is essentially a continuous improvised performance of a role whose nature is never explicitly communicated to you, and whose script you have to pick up from subtle social cues, starting in childhood. It's probably the single most intensively-socialized thing humans do, and the one whose 'rules' are the least explicit. Since autistic people are notoriously resistant to socialization, it just makes sense that we wouldn't pick up as much of the gender programming as NTs [neurotypicals] do."[45] Lindsay's understanding of gender echoes Butler's argument that gender can be understood as a performance—not one that can be simply turned on or off, but one that is embedded in mental and bodily habits driven by social representations.

Notably, though, some autistic women write about gender as quite literally a performance. Butler insists that one cannot put on or take off gender as though it were simply a costume or role. Yet conscious performance of a gendered character can become a coping strategy, an attempt to get along in social situations that feel false to the performer, even if it can "pass" as real to others. For example, Vivian describes her favored gender role as Manic Pixie Dream Girl: "My voice is kind of soft and little-girl-ish, I am solicitous to the point of sometimes going too far, I interject, I tease."[46] Nathan Rabin, who coined the role's name, describes this stock film character as one that is used primarily to further a plot focused on a male character. Her quirkiness and zest for life help "teach broodingly soulful young men to embrace life and its infinite mysteries and adventures."[47] We might identify Manic Pixie Dream Girl as the type of gendered character played by the female leads in *Almost Famous* (Penny Lane, played by Kate Hudson), *Yes Man* (Allison, played by Zooey Deschanel), *Eternal Sunshine of the Spotless Mind* (Clementine Kruczynski, played by Kate Winslet), and *50 First Dates* (Lucy Whitmore, played by Drew Barrymore). The female lead, in each case, plays a quirky, unusual, provocative woman—a free spirit who transforms the male lead's life. She may have some kind of neurological condition: in *50 First Dates*, Drew Barrymore plays an amnesiac whom Adam Sandler must woo, from scratch, each day; in *Eternal Sunshine of the Spotless Mind*, Clementine has had her memory erased in order to forget her previous relationship with the lead male character, played by Jim Carrey. In short, the Manic Pixie Dream Girl is a stock character used as a vector for a male character's personal development.

Yet this character provides Vivian with a culturally legible performance of gender. Vivian recognizes this performance as precisely that: "I know I act like a silly little kid, but I couldn't talk in class or make friends without it. *I need someone to be*."[48] This role does not seem like one Vivian has made up out of nowhere; instead, it seems to be an amalgam of her observations of others (in life and in film) and the expectations required of women in different social situations. Her language shows that she does not view her chosen role as fully embodied, a product of repeated stylized acts that she has imbibed since childhood. Instead, she views Manic Pixie Dream Girl much more as a performance, a rhetorical device and a coping mechanism: the role offers "the only acceptable way for a girl to be weird" and "the only way of synthesizing my AS into a reasonably acceptable personality."[49]

For some writers, gendered performances are enacted in part through clothing choices. Women in online forums often relate that, on one hand, they were put off by the dress codes mandated by mainstream gender roles but that, on the other, they enjoyed using clothing to perform alternate roles. Scholars in rhetoric have noted that dress can serve as a rhetoric directed at outside audiences, as was the case with early women suffragists examined by Carol Mattingly in *Appropriate[Ing] Dress*, or the carefully articulated and repurposed gang colors Ralph Cintrón identifies in *Angels' Town*.[50] What is at stake in the case of autistic self-identity and dress, though, seems to be something more like the kinds of personal, material rhetorics identified in Karen A. Foss and Sonja K. Foss's *Women Speak*. Foss and Foss locate rhetorical acts in a wide range of women's activities, including needlework, photography, graffiti, interior design, and baking.[51]

Individuals who post on WrongPlanet.net's discussions of fashion often identify with particular gendered characters. For instance, a poster named HarraArial recounts her "huge interest in alternative fashion (Victorian Gothic, Steampunk, and Lolita all come to mind)."[52] Each of those styles might constitute a character HarraArial can perform while wearing that type of clothing. Another poster, CockneyRebel, prefers "Vintage, unisex Mod fashions," while Pinkbowtiepumps describes her style as "mod, victorian and 50s housewife" combined.[53] We might also note that the screen names these participants adopt may also reflect a rhetorical, interactional impulse; each one seems chosen to convey a particular identity or performance thereof, such as "50s housewife" or "mod." (CockneyRebel might reflect the British origin of the 1960s Mod subculture.)

In other cases, clothing choices might be read by an audience in a particular way, reflecting what Francis calls the "adressivity" of gender,[54] but used by the individual for other purposes. Prince-Hughes describes her 1980s-era wardrobe as follows: "I wore leather jackets because their weight and thickness calmed me; dark glasses, sometimes even at night, because they cut out some of the stimulation to my nervous system; and heavy boots that made me feel secure and grounded as I clomped around in them."[55] While others might have seen her as performing a Punk identity, for Prince-Hughes the performance was more embodied; she was performing and experiencing security through her clothing. All of these individuals have found that clothing serves a range of purposes, sometimes connected to a gender identity, and at other times connected to sensory or emotional performances.

Donna Williams provides a good example of gender as a rhetorical performance because she has written about her developing identity extensively, in a series of four memoirs. In the first, *Nobody Nowhere*, Williams describes how she performed gendered roles as a coping mechanism. As a child she developed two different roles, Willie and Carol, which allowed her to interact with others. Willie, who emerged by the time Williams was three, was a pugnacious, impish boy, her defense mechanism against perceived threats: "Willie became the self I directed at the outside world, complete with hateful glaring eyes, a pinched-up mouth, a rigid corpselike stance, and clenched fists."[56] Shortly thereafter, Carol emerged. A bubbly, bouncy flirt, Carol was her tool for interacting with classmates, adults, and later, boyfriends: "Carol was everything that people liked. Carol laughed a lot. Carol made friends . . . Carol could act relatively normal. Smiling, sociable, giggly, she made the perfect dancing doll."[57] Williams did not exactly choose these roles consciously; instead, they emerged as personalities forged from parts of people she had observed (real and imaginary). These characters were called into play in different rhetorical situations. When Williams felt called to present herself as a good girl, to interact cheerfully with others, Carol might be called into play; when threatened, Willie might emerge. Both characters are "stylized repetitions," in Butler's sense, but they seem to be experienced as performances and not as entirely incorporated into a self.

Williams drew on both female and male characters to help her make her way in the world. In *Everyday Heaven*, she reflects on how these roles related to her gender: "As Willie, I felt male; as Carol, I felt female; as myself, I felt neutral. Willie was the embodiment of logic, my left-brain thinking unable to integrate with my right brain thinking that I associated with Donna and self. Carol was my imitation of girls and a social façade of 'normality.'"[58] In her blog, Williams notes that because she grew up "face blind" (she had difficulty seeing and remembering faces) and "meaning deaf" (she had trouble interpreting what others were saying) her gender identity was delayed.[59] Carol and Willie were roles she developed, on top of what she describes as a neutral self-concept, in order to cope with the demands of the outside world. They were characters she could evoke in a performance of self. For Williams, gender was a rhetorical device that could be deployed, depending on the context, to act in accordance with societal expectation.

Perhaps because she was used to this, Williams extended that performance to include sexuality. As a teenager, she writes, she performed as Carol in order to avoid homelessness, tolerating "domestic prostitution" in a series of abusive relationships. Later, she experimented with heterosexual and homosexual relationships, almost as though she were trying on sexual orientations the way she had tried on Willie and Carol. After a negative experience with a male partner, she sought out a female partner, noting the "almost male sexuality" she felt when encountering women at a lesbian bar. When that relationship ended, she realized that "lesbian" was not the proper term for her sexual orientation: "Perhaps I was bisexual. Perhaps I just chose human beings and it didn't matter too much about their gender."[60] The role of lesbian gave Williams a way to act on her attraction to a human being who happened to be a woman, a role to enact. Ultimately, though, Williams married a man and came to describe herself as a "monogamous genderqueer bisexual happily living in a straight marriage who generally feels like a gay man in a woman's body."[61] In order to come to terms with herself as a person, Williams had to reject the roles she had taken on as coping mechanisms, and to invent other terms with which to describe her self-concept.

These examples both confirm and challenge a feminist understanding of gender as performance, as Butler proposes, or as something one *does* rather than something one is, a view advanced by West and Zimmerman.[62] On one hand, Vivian and Williams both view gender as a sort of stylized performance, which seems to confirm these feminist understandings of gender. On the other, neither Vivian nor Williams seems to view gender as fully incorporated into their identities, bodies, or minds—unlike the feminist theorists arguing that ritualized performances of gender materialize as layers of embodied habits and actions. Instead, they tend to view gendered characters almost as theater—costumes to be taken on or taken off depending on the situation.

Inventing Idiosyncratic Genders

Other writers draw on a collection of terms to express an idiosyncratic view of gender and sexuality. These terms provide an alternative framework to help autistic individuals with nontraditional gender identities to affirm an individualized character.

In *Songs of the Gorilla Nation*, Prince-Hughes writes that "having autism underpinned much of my gender identity or lack thereof." She rejects the idea that "autistic people simply don't have sexuality"; instead, she insists, "it is different and takes more time to unravel."[63] Her autobiography recounts, in part, the process by which she came to understand her gender and her sexuality.

First, she describes how commonplaces drawn from gay, lesbian, and feminist communities helped her understand herself. As a teenager she used the term "queer" for inventive purposes in order to develop her burgeoning sense of character and identity: "I thought about the definition of 'queer' and concluded that in the broad sense I qualified under that category. I had no overtly sexual feelings for anyone, male or female, but I had to admit a desire to be near some women because they made me feel good." Later, she used discourses available in the feminist atmosphere of the 1970s and 1980s, committed to "searching out my own internal intimacies without outside influence." She joined a local gay and lesbian group, subscribed to *Psychology Today* and the monthly newsletter of the National Organization for Women, and drew on ideas about gender diversity to consider whether "one could be 'lesbian' in one's orientation to the world but choose to never have sex."[64]

Later, Prince-Hughes used commonplaces (verbal and otherwise) that she encountered when she began dancing at a female-owned strip club. During that period, she writes, she began to confront her sexuality: "I watched erotic videos, read all kinds of manuals, listened to women talk in the dressing room offstage about the things they really liked in a lover, and grilled them about what worked and what didn't." Using these "protocols" in her encounters with women, she gained a reputation that attracted more than a few takers. Yet she eventually realized that she had mistaken sexual interest on the part of these women for love and the desire for a relationship, though she herself did not love these women, feel fulfilled by the relationship, or necessarily want a relationship. Drawing on available discourses of romance such as popular movies, Prince-Hughes writes, she believed that it was her duty to move from initial attraction to a long-term relationship. She also used topoi of hegemonic femininity as a point of differentiation: "I knew I did not want to choose a subservient role in a relationship, that I wanted to be an intellectual, and that I wanted someone to respect me, support me in reaching my goals. I had always associated these needs with masculinity."[65] Accordingly, Prince-Hughes took on the masculine character in a relationship, becoming a chivalrous caretaker—only to find herself often in the position of being taken advantage of by women simply seeking material or physical comfort.

As an adult, Prince-Hughes writes, she realized that "being and . . . sexuality were unique and not readily classified." However, these ideas only became available when she read about more deconstructive approaches to gender that encourage "un-labeling" of sex and gender-based identities. In addition, by studying gorillas, she gained a new vocabulary of identity. After one encounter with a male silverback gorilla, for instance, Prince-Hughes writes, she "began to see that the core of my being was a great deal like this male core: looking on from the outside, blank-faced, with a deep and abiding need to protect and comfort in a world where my ways of feeling and acting no longer had context." This realization helped her understand human men and relinquish her fear of them, realizing that human men, like the gorillas she observed, were constantly confronting the unrelenting vicissitudes of modern life, "unable to protect their families" and railing against their ineptitude.[66] Prince-Hughes's evolving sense of gender and sexual identity, then, moved through a series of topoi from queer to lesbian to idiosyncratic.

Williams is not alone in applying queer terminology to her self-understanding. These terms provide an alternative framework to help autistic individuals with nontraditional gender identities to understand themselves in a positive manner, to affirm an identity rather than a lack or fault. Queer and trans understandings of gender provide some writers with alternative concepts and terms from which to craft an identity.

A number of autistic writers describe identity types that they have tried on. Vivian writes that she experimented with a range of terms, including "butch" and "trans," but eventually rejected those terms as unsuitable. She has settled on another term: "If I can get away with using the word 'faggy' without being a gay man, that's the best word to describe my gender expression and the gender expression I'm attracted to."[67]

Whereas Vivian finds terms drawn from lesbian, gay, bisexual, and transgendered (LGBT) communities useful, others are drawn to the discourses made available by a growing community of individuals who define themselves as asexual. People with disabilities are often stereotyped as lacking in sexuality, an idea that disability studies scholars have worked hard to unpack. However, it is as important to valorize asexuality as it is to affirm sexuality, since both are valid and important identificatory positions for individuals with autism. One blogger, who uses the pseudonym Thevenerablecortex, writes that being involved with a college LGBT community did not work, "on the grounds that I, as an asexual, didn't feel that I fit-in with a group which was (in large part) defined by its deviation from the canons of sexual 'normalcy.'"[68] Another blogger writes, "I sometimes identify as an asexual lesbian . . . but I'm not really 100% sure that's the right label either, so I don't use it that much."[69] For these bloggers, "asexual" serves as the best available term with which to identify, but this term does not always coincide with those used in autistic or LGBT communities.

Thus, autistic individuals may draw from a wide range of terms with which to understand their gender and sexuality. The availability of these terms means that those who do not identify as simply male or female, gay or straight, have alternatives. But terms do more than that. According to Burke, "names embody attitudes; and implicit in the attitudes there are the cues of behavior."[70] For him, attitudes are incipient actions, and in them lies "the realm of 'symbolic action' par excellence."[71] In this case, then, names provide resources for symbolic actions that individuals use to understand themselves and others, to affirm identity, or to cope in relationships. Assuming the term "bisexual" might lead one to experiment with different kinds of sexual relationships, while the term "trans" might lead one to experiment with cross-gender clothing or behaviors.

Nonetheless, other individuals refuse such terminology altogether, such as this poster on an LGBT discussion group for people with autism: "i'd say i was more intergendered than transgendered. basically, i don't feel like a 'man' i don't feel like a 'woman' and don't really want to be identified as either one . . . i'm sort of a neutral mishmash of masculine and feminine."[72] Another poster offers a similar refusal to choose: "More than feeling female (or male) I feel like me. I (and everyone else) shouldn't be seen as a gender but as an individual whose traits are her or his own, period."[73] And a third poster writes: "I've never seen any purpose for genders. They don't reflect anything real, since they take 'this sex is likely to do this' and turn it into a set of rules, making 'likely' into 'has to.' . . . And I don't identify as either because of that. It's abitrary [*sic*] and doesn't fit anything about me."[74] By rejecting gender, these individuals seem to be echoing gender theorist Kath Weston's call for a "zero concept" of gender, one that refuses to fix genders or to offer alternatives simply by multiplying the number of gender categories in our list. For Weston, naming genders "fixes as it nominalizes, encouraging people to look once again to bodies, to the visual, as gender's ultimate referent."[75] Weston warns that categories of gender are easily commodified and ranged into a continuum, with "masculine" and "feminine" securely holding up the terminal points. The possibility of a "zero concept," the nongendered or ungendered, refuses this ordering principle, thereby making possible an understanding of gender as copia—an unordered collection of gendered concepts, including the nongendered. Rejecting gender might also be understood as an idiosyncratic interpretation, one that does not bow to cultural norms or discourses.

The profusion of terms used affirms the rhetorical utility of copia. By generating a range of possibilities, participants can rhetorically constitute possible identities for themselves and others. While gender theorists might privilege the moment of disidentification, individuals who participate in these discussions seem to want to find a stasis point of some kind. Terms for gender identity seem to offer these points of identification, even if they do not square up with mainstream, binary notions of gender.

Although these findings cannot be taken as representative of autistic individuals as a whole, their diversity does support an expanded concept of autistic gender identity that pushes past a gender continuum toward a copia, in which terms can be tried on and appropriated, discarded, and invented, while still being understood as embodied and constructed. The above sections indicate five possible rhetorical functions of gender: as disidentification, as a resource for ambiguity, as a social code or symbolic order, as performance, or as idiosyncrasy. Note that any individual might draw on and enact any combination of these gendered processes at any one time—they are not mutually exclusive. For instance, one person might disidentify with traditional notions of femininity and draw instead on elements of clothing and behavior as resources of ambiguity; another person might consciously perform a traditional gender role as a coping mechanism, even as she struggles to interpret the social codes that make that gender role natural for others. All of these gendered processes function as rhetorical resources for self-creation.

Autistic understandings of gender challenge feminist and gender theorists to consider gender as a rhetoric, one that is not simply discursive but material, embodied, neurological, and fundamentally multiple. Such a perspective does not preclude a feminist analysis of, in Bumiller's terms, autism's relationship with gendered organizations of labor, authority, and citizenship, nor does it preclude critiquing the tendency for autistic individuals to be pushed to conform to gender roles. Nonetheless, it does encourage scholars of gender and feminist theories to include autistic perspectives, not just critiques of neurodiversity or autism discourses, in theorizing about sex and gender more broadly.

Incorporating autistic perspectives helps further denaturalize sex and gender not only as fluid concepts but as resources for rhetorical acts of self-fashioning. Paying attention to individuals with neurological conditions, in particular, helps denaturalize models of gender that might, in some cases, be better termed neurotypical models, since they sometimes presume an innate ability to decode and model an appropriate gendered character or, on the contrary, celebrate conscious acts of resistance to normalizing models. For autistic individuals, for instance, performing a stereotyped gendered character may be very much an act of resistance and survival.

Inventing Gender as Disorder in Scientific Discourses

Whereas autistic individuals offer a copia of available terms, theories, and self-understandings of gender, scientific studies tend to impose a less capacious model for understanding autistic gender identity. Most studies of this phenomenon employ the problematic psychiatric terms "gender dysphoria" or "gender identity disorder" (GID). Both terms imply that a failure to identify with one's biological sex constitutes a disorder or lack.

Gender identity disorder was introduced into the *Diagnostic and Statistical Manual* of the APA in 1996. In the *DSM-V*, GID was renamed "gender dysphoria." The term may seek to lessen the stigma attached to the old term, but the definitions given still reflect a binary notion of gender, defining the condition most fundamentally as incongruence between "one's experienced/expressed gender and assigned gender."[76] In children, this incongruence depends on observations of the child's preferences for clothing, play, and the like; in adults it depends more on the individual's stated understanding of his or her gender (such as a strong desire to be the opposite gender in some way).[77] Nonetheless, by continuing to include gender dysphoria in the manual at all, the APA reaffirms the normalcy of a binary gender system in which individuals are expected to conform to their biologically indicated gender. Those who fail to do so must have a psychiatric condition. By employing the logic and terminology of the

DSM, researchers exploring gender identity in autistic people tend to confirm that binary system.

The *DSM* definition of gender dysphoria sets up an either/or system: one is either feminine or masculine, either female or male. Sex, gender, and sexuality merge together in the criteria. In children, for instance, GID is indicated by "cross-gender" behaviors, such as dressing in girls' clothing (for boys) or playing with trucks (for girls). This criterion indexes gender (masculinity or femininity). But researchers also pay attention to sexual attraction, especially in adolescents and adults, in whom desires for the same sex seem to confirm a GID diagnosis. Desire to *be* the opposite sex confirms GID—which refers to sex. Within this framework, there is little room for being nongendered, androgyne, or genderqueer. Instead, individuals are remediated into one role or another—either through behavioral interventions aimed at reinforcing the biological sex and its corresponding gender or through sexual reassignment, often recommended when those behavioral interventions fail.

In a study conducted by Annelou de Vries et al., the researchers provide notes about each individual, when the gender dysphoria presented, and whether it persisted. For younger children, GID was considered a possibility if the child demonstrated "inappropriate" gender behavior, as was the case for a toddler boy who was "fascinated by mermaids, fairy tales, dolls, ballet, dressing-up." Although this boy's fascination was mitigated in later years, his interest in ballet and theater was classified as a cross-gender interest. Another boy's "obsessive dressing up" was reduced by a behavioral program, but he was "still wearing high heels" at age ten.[78] In these studies, researchers imply that children with autism and a gender identity disorder are marked as in need of gender intervention, in addition to the many other kinds of interventions to which they are exposed.

The kinds of interventions offered are not specified in de Vries et al., but they are described briefly in a case study by N. M. Mukkades et al., in which two Turkish boys with gender identity issues are profiled. In each case, the behavioral modification approaches involved encouraging the boy to identify with his father and to separate from his mother—a model clearly linked to psychoanalytic views of the child's love object.[79] In both cases, such attempts were largely ineffective; one boy expressed a continual desire to be a bride, the other, a mother.

The features that are considered markers of cross-gender identification vary by culture. In the European study by de Vries et al., they included interests in fairy tales, dolls, and dress-up. The Turkish study noted that one boy enjoyed playing with his female relatives' scarves, using them to make skirts.[80] And in a Japanese study, the authors profile a boy who "spoke in a girlish manner and covered his mouth with a hand when he laughed, as female individuals commonly do." This boy enjoyed cute characters from television cartoons and "always painted cute girls surrounded with many lovely hearts and flowers."[81] Although all of these authors cast these feminine behaviors in these boys as inappropriate, the kinds of behaviors are to some extent culturally determined. In each case, the children in question are portrayed as seeking out the mannerisms, dress, and habits of the "ideal woman."

Whereas individuals with autism are sometimes portrayed as being oblivious to culture and communication, these boys were clearly drawing from mainstream gender depictions. The Japanese case, for example, clearly reflects a culturally specific form of femininity called *kawaisa*, one that emphasizes cuteness in dress, comportment, handwriting, and appearance. In Japan, cute culture provides what Brian McVeigh calls "a socionormative commentary about how women should behave, especially vis-à-vis men."[82] Children who engage in these "cross-gender" behaviors clearly do partake of cultural messages, then, and incorporate them into their self-expression. Commodified depictions might have the advantage for children that they trope or simplify gender, providing clear-cut roles, habits, and expectations to model.

Nonetheless, all of these studies seemed to discount any possibility that ambiguous gender behaviors might be permissible in these children. Most take the notion of cross-gender identification, embedded in the *DSM*, as their framework. For this reason, I found no scientific studies that explored gender with the level of complexity expressed in the reflections posted on blogs and forums.

Most important, individuals writing about their own experiences tend to consider their gender identity as an integral part of themselves, but scientific studies often seek to explain away gender dysphoria as a symptom of autism. In their study of GID in Swedish individuals, M. Landén and P. Rasmussen caution that in some cases what might appear as gender dysphoria might actually be an expression of obsessive-compulsive behavior associated with autism. For example, an individual might display a wish to demonstrate "desire for a beloved person" through imitation.[83] Along these lines, a case study conducted by Williams, Allard, and Sears reported that one boy enjoyed holding Barbie dolls, but that he seemed most interested in the texture of their hair. The writers hypothesize that "the feminine preoccupations of these children with autism may have resulted from an inherent predisposition toward unusual interests combined with the boys' social environment," concluding that these behaviors are less likely to be related to "issues of gender identity roles/confusion."[84] Explaining away nonconformist gender behaviors may help reassure parents, but it seems that researchers seem uncomfortable with recognizing alternative gender identifications as valid, perhaps because scientific discourse does not offer appropriate language with which to express ambiguity.

Similarly, some argue that gender incongruence among autistic individuals may be an adaptation. In their profile of a forty-one-year-old man with Asperger's syndrome who expressed cross-gender identification, Gerard Gallucci et al. hypothesize that "because one of the hallmark features of autism is a deficit in social functioning and difficulty relating to others, the cross-gender role may be a means of adapting to stressful developmental issues such as conventual sexual relationships," and they hold out hope for pharmacologic and psychotherapeutic treatments that might alleviate this condition. These authors also connect alternative gender presentations with obsessive-compulsive traits, pathologizing gender difference as a psychiatric problem.[85] Here again, gender ambiguity is posited as a problem or disorder to be remediated.

In another case, a study of a girl who expressed interest in being a boy and who refused to wear female clothing, Bernd Kraemer et al. argue that the girl may have adopted a male gender identity in part as a way to better integrate her low empathizing and high systemizing skills. While the fact that a number of boys express feminized interests goes against the EMB theory of autism, in this case, the writers find that GID is "thrown into doubt" because the subject's highly developed logical thinking and dearth of emotionality were hallmarks of autism. Because these features tend to be culturally linked to masculinity, the authors conclude that they "may have led to a subjective consciousness in our patient of being male."[86] Clearly, these authors are invoking the EMB theory of autism as a possible explanation of this girl's cross-gender identification.

As is often the case with such studies, autistic individuals have little, if any, voice. In keeping with a behaviorist model of psychiatry, researchers, in Charles Bazerman's terms, "exclude introspection or any other attempt to gain knowledge of the subject's internal processes or sensations."[87] Bazerman argues that the rhetoric of psychiatry, in general, tends toward "the objectification of the subject," so that those under study seem more and more like objects than people.[88] We do not learn, then, why the children in question preferred cross-gender toys or dress. Instead, the researchers supply explanations to support or refute existing theories about autism and gender identity, including a model that assumes cross-gender identification is a disorder to be remediated.

Inventing Gender in Therapy Groups

In June 2010 the *Riverside Press-Enterprise* published an urgent call for girly paraphernalia on behalf of Capable Girls Group, a social group for girls with developmental disabilities: "We are seeking donations of new and unused hair brushes, combs, make-up, hair styling products, glitter spray, perfume, lotions, costume jewelry, scarves, hats, plain T-shirts, address books, nail polish, nail polish remover, and make-up bags," the spokesperson, Lisa Marie Dryan, stated. The goal, according to this report, was to start a new program that would allow "Teen girls with some level of developmental delay [to] learn about normal teen activities such as fashion, make-up, manicures, pedicures and more." They were also seeking "professional estheticians, stylists and fashion experts" to help out.[89] In short, the girls with developmental delay needed assistance to learn the normative, gendered codes of teenage appearance and dress.

Popular advice literature and related publications routinely discipline autistic gender identity. As Sloop argues in his study of rhetoric and gender, "transgressive bodies that do not fit existing categories are forced, or disciplined, into those categories."[90] Bumiller notes that autistic people, especially, are often "explicitly taught about the relevance of gender performance" to dating.[91] More broadly, though, autistic girls, in particular, are taught topoi of gender performance, in general—not just in order to get a date, but in order to fit in at school. Literature aimed at autistic girls emphasizes topoi of personal appearance, fashion, and beauty as key elements of a normalized identity. Further, these texts propose that a fashionable, gender-typical image can lead to social acceptance, self-confidence, and popularity. In this way, they present a rhetorical curriculum of femininity, a persuasive effort to discipline unruly autistic gender expressions.

In order to do so, these texts first position autistic women as lacking in femininity, measured especially in terms of appearance and dress. These assessments are made not by autistic girls but usually by their mothers or by the authors, who position themselves as unproblematically feminine. Consider the example of *Girls Growing up on the Spectrum: What Parents and Professionals Should Know About the Pre-teen and Teenage Years,* a handbook for parents and their daughters on all manner of concerns, from handling peer groups at schools to dealing with puberty. The authors, Shana Nichols, Gina Marie Moravcik, and Samara Pulver Tetenbaum, draw on their experiences leading workshops for autistic girls.

The fashion section of the book offers anecdotes that position autistic girls as frumpy, unkempt social ignoramuses in need of remediation. When girls first arrive at the group meetings the authors lead, they are "not all anti-fashion or fashion-clueless"—but they are clearly assessed by the leaders for their needs for fashion intervention. Some may be wearing "fashionable but somewhat inappropriate clothing" (for instance, belly-baring or tight-fitting) and others may be disheveled and not well groomed, in "track pants, running shoes, baggy T-shirts, and sweatshirts."[92] Those who are not dressed in a "casual, fashionable manner" are presumably the targets of the intensive fashion curriculum.

Girls Growing up on the Spectrum offer strategies to help caregivers (usually mothers) remediate their daughters' gender and fashion troubles, the same techniques the authors used in group meetings. They propose that mothers and daughters spend time doing "social anthropology" work, examining fashion magazines, catalogs, television shows, and teens at the mall in order to determine what clothes are in style. Although the writers insist the goal is for the girls to experience less teasing and to feel more confident, it is hard not to see the rhetoric of gender disciplining at work here. The book described workshops such as trips to the mall or the nail salon, attending separate sessions on fashion, accessories, and makeup, and studying *Seventeen* magazine and *Cosmo Girl* for cues to typical gendered presentation and behaviors. The book also includes a list of concrete goals for these girls to master, such as the ability to go to a store and choose appropriate clothing, to accessorize, and to have a personal style.[93]

These abilities become markers of gender discipline; in order to demonstrate it, autistic girls must learn to present themselves as typical girls or women, a presentation measured visually. The authors point out a variety of possible styles or gendered characters: a girl may dress "sporty, casual, trendy, alternative, dressy, preppy, glam, grungy, goth, rocker, punk, urban, bohemian, chic, etc.," but each of these characters must be carefully cued to styles available to girls in popular culture.[94] These alternatives, then, are not really alternatives, since choosing any one of those styles to emulate would still require careful study of social gender norms for a particular clique. From this remedial gender text, autistic girls learn that they will be judged based on their conformity to a set of gender ideals. The authors state that girls can choose from a number of appropriate styles, but "tomboy," "dyke," and "butch" are not among them. Presumably, these choices would not be appropriate and would lead autistic girls to be stigmatized.

One comment on Amazon.com's review page demonstrates how an autistic individual interpreted this approach to gender remediation. The commenter, "Sam," writes:

> I wonder if my mom read this, because I have been fighting her attempts to gender-condition me my whole life. . . . I am sick of the social expectations that are put on me because I am [a] girl. I am expected to be sweet, caring, talkative, empathetic but I am none of those things. . . . I just had to say something, because if a mother or caregiver reads this book, and decides to try to turn thier [sic] "tomboy" around, into a giry [sic] girl, it should be a crime.[95]

This commenter declares that, since childhood she has struggled against gender remediation, an imposed system of behavior and dress that did not square with her own desires.

The emphasis on achieving (or approximating) normal femininity in these texts seems to come from a well-intentioned desire to help autistic girls fit in. Yet this desire is fraught with assumptions about friendship that take neurotypical popular kids as the norm and that fetishize popularity as an end in itself.

Scholars trace the current manifestations of teenage popularity to trends beginning about the end of World War II, when the terms *adolescent* and *teenager* gained currency, high school began to be understood as fundamental for most children, and marketers began to see this new demographic group as a goldmine. From that time on, teens began to be targeted, in earnest, with messages about popularity, appearance, and the like, prompted in part by magazines such as *Seventeen*. The cheesy 1950s educational films promoting good hygiene, manners, and dating habits formed part of that trend.

These trends only intensified in the years that witnessed a rise in autism and Asperger's diagnoses. Teens were a shrinking demographic from the 1970s to the 1990s, but by the early 1990s their numbers once again grew, and they are now considered a powerful market force. It is little wonder that high school film and television shows such as *Glee, Degrassi: The Next Generation, Gossip Girl,* and *High School Musical* emerged. Coupled with the glut of teen clothing stores, teen music idols, and the like, these shows create a mainstream image of teenage life that is centered around high school class wars, appearance, and issues that are especially likely to affect popular kids (having two dates on the same day, for instance, or being tempted to take drugs at a party featuring letter-jacketed jocks). Scholars who study popularity in teenagers, such as Francis, argue that gender performance constitutes an important factor, with popular girls, in particular, learning to draw on "tropes of gendered performance," such as an interest in fashion and celebrity or a flirtatious personality, to give an impression of a stable, conforming gender identity.[96] Handbooks such as *Girls Growing up on the Spectrum* paper over the fact that all teens are, to a certain degree, performing characters, and holds up a monoglossic, rigid role of hegemonic femininity as the only one to which autistic girls should aspire.

Coinciding with the rise of all things teenager has been the practice of including children with disabilities in regular classrooms. This practice, usually termed "inclusive education" or "mainstreaming," began in earnest in the years following the Education for All Handicapped Children Act and Public Law 94–142, which guaranteed a free, appropriate public education to each child with a disability in every state and locality across the country. Both were passed in 1975. By 2007, the U.S. Department of Education reported that "the majority of children with disabilities are now being educated in their neighborhood schools in regular classrooms with their non-disabled peers."[97]

Mainstream education offers many pedagogical advantages for children with disabilities. Yet once included in regular classrooms, they face a set of challenges related to popularity or fitting in, a common topic of advice manuals for children and teenagers with autism (and other disabilities). For example, in an article titled "Fitting in: Tips for Promoting Acceptance and Friendships for Students with Autism Spectrum Disorders in Inclusive Classrooms," E. Amanda Boutot includes a chart of "popular versus unpopular characteristics." Under "popular" characteristics, she includes "wearing trendy clothing," "displaying leadership skills," being "good at academics (girls) or athletics (boys)," and having "good social skills." Under "unpopular" characteristics, she lists "being from low socioeconomic status," "playing alone," being "poor students (girls) or athletes (boys)," and "display[ing] inappropriate or extreme behaviors."[98] The author presents these elements rather unproblematically as plain facts of school life—in order to be popular, one must possess the qualities listed in the first column and avoid those in the last.

Most often, conforming to rules about popularity also means conforming to gender expectations. Boutot's chart insists that boys must be good at sports and girls must be good at school, but other qualities, such as what counts as trendy clothing or good social skills, also depend on gender norms. For instance, the need for trendy clothing is usually impressed on girls, especially, as a requirement for popularity. Girls may require more expensive clothing, a greater variety of items, and more investment in shopping for those items than is expected of boys. Similarly, the social skills that convey popularity are gender-specific and not always positive. For example, those expected for girls may include gossiping, flirting with boys, and subtly snubbing other girls, while boys may be expected to be good at telling jokes, mocking less popular boys, or teasing girls. All of these expectations involve rather superficial matters of appearance and behavior, and they also represent barriers for individuals with disabilities and others who do not fit the list of desired qualities.

Contemporary disability theory reminds us that disabilities depend heavily on socially constructed barriers. For example, stairs become a problem for people who use wheelchairs when no ramps are provided. A similar critique would point out that social impairments similarly depend on socially constructed norms of behavior. For example, in a materialistic society obsessed with appearance, it is not surprising that clothing choices represent a key element of fitting in. As a socially constructed norm, fashion offers a barrier, not only for those who are uninterested in fashion, cannot afford the latest styles or have trouble applying the oft-changing rules of fashion appropriately. These strictures apply, especially, to women, but increasingly to men as well. In a society that provided more leeway for acceptable gendered behaviors and interests, autistic individuals might not find fitting in as desirable or difficult.

Mainstream advice texts seldom take this approach to autism and social status. An example appears in the book *Asperger's and Girls*. In "Girl to Girl: Advice on Friendship, Bullying, and Fitting In," Lisa Iland shares some of the strategies she uses as a consultant on teen issues, arguing that "social skills attained in teen years are essential life skills for college and workplace success." She focuses her advice on "creating appeal and image," "understanding where to fit in," "meeting social expectations," and "overcoming bullying and mean girls." Throughout, she emphasizes that girls should focus on mainstreaming their image in order to become part of the "girl middle-class," rather than limiting themselves by refusing to conform. She describes how typical girls use "image profiling" to determine where another girl fits in a social hierarchy using markers such as brands, accessories, and hairstyles to determine whether they should befriend that girl.[99]

Rather than confronting teen hierarchies or counseling girls to find a niche group based on shared interests, Iland advises starting with the low-ranking "unique/unusual groups" and then attempting to move up to the "middle/mainstream" group, and eventually, the vaunted "popular/elite group," if possible.[100] In order to do so, girls should inform themselves about "Boys, fashion, shopping, movies, and music" by watching MTV or by consulting Wikipedia to bone up on the latest in teen pop culture.[101]

My aim here is not to question whether inclusive education is a good thing for children with autism but to interrogate the logic of popularity that remains intact in discourse about fitting in. It puts the onus on the autistic student (like any other), who must struggle to conform to a schema that excludes them, and many other kids, who do not fit the mold. Gender disciplining forms a large part of this calculus. Remediation discourses seek to leave school hierarchies intact, rather than challenging teachers, administrators, and others to disrupt the popularity and gender ideals that penalize unusual children of all kinds, not just students with disabilities. In this way, a discourse of mainstreaming that emphasizes fitting in without changing the institution into which students with disabilities are placed falls short of full accommodation. We might draw a parallel to discourses of liberal feminism, which stress inclusion and representation of women in institutions, versus a model of radical feminism, which stresses the need for those institutions to be changed in order to accommodate women as well as men.

Advice books also offer a rather simplistic view of childhood and adolescent social groups and of appropriate gendered behavior. For example, the idea that school groups fall into an elite, middle, and lower group simplifies what may often be a more complex arrangement, avoiding mention of ethnicity and race, class, region, or specific interests (such as drama or student council).

Autistic individuals offer a range of perspectives on this issue. Many argue that the goal of fitting in with mainstream society does not interest them. In the same volume as Iland's article, Temple Grandin argues that autistic children should be encouraged to find others who share their interests, however obscure, rather than trying to reform their own interests around those of the majority. In her essay "For Me, a Good Career Gave Life Meaning," Grandin explains that her friendships have emerged via shared interests: "In high school it was horses and later in life it was friends in the construction industry. We had a good time because we built things together."[102] She writes that she feels happiest when working on projects, not when socializing with other people—a fact educators and psychologists may find difficult to understand. Focusing on social skills, she argues, is important, but often ends up trying "to make us into something that we are not." Instead, she argues, educators and psychologists should encourage autistic individuals to develop their intellectual lives: "One parent wanted to take her child out of computer science class to make him more social. The irony is that computer science class was probably the one place her child had friends and a social life."[103] In a similar ironic turn, Jennifer McIlwee Myers writes that the desire to cure someone with "a 'disability' that makes them less interested in social activities" by making them more social is equivalent to "curing broken legs through a regimen of jogging."[104] These approaches uphold sociability as a path toward friendship, love, and career success, overlooking the alternatives carved out by individuals focused on specialized interests, hobbies, or projects.

The emphasis on social skills seems even more pronounced when the child in question is female. While geek masculinity has become an acceptable, sometimes privileged, gender construct, geek femininity remains marginalized. The reasons for this marginalization lie in entrenched gender ideals. Sherrie A. Innes agues that "mainstream American society has a deeply rooted fear of brilliant women."[105] While brainy women are increasingly common in popular culture, they usually face difficulties with peer groups, dating, and social acceptance as a trade-off for their intellectual superiority.

Given dominant depictions of female popularity and the perils of female nerddom, it is not surprising that advice literature emphasizes social skills, popularity, and fashion for girls, especially. Yet autistic women seem happy with a range of social situations—many have satisfying romantic relationships, while others (like Grandin) are content to remain unattached and maintain passionate investment in their careers. As Myers contends, the "societal obsession" with dating can hurt girls with autism and Asperger's syndrome; instead, girls should be "encouraged from an early age to look at dating and marriage realistically, factually, and logically"—starting with questioning whether they really want these things.[106]

Autistic individuals also warn that autistic teenagers are especially vulnerable to sexual abuse and exploitation. In their book *Autism-Asperger's and Sexuality: Puberty and Beyond,* Jerry and Mary Newport describe how, upon maturing, autistic women might find themselves objects of male attention and a potential path toward popularity. Mary writes: "Puberty helped in some respects [re: social skills] because I became sexy. I did everything to cultivate my looks. My peers' reactions began to change in the ninth grade. I was not ridiculed as much. However, puberty was hard because adults were having sex with me, offering me marijuana, etc. . . . My 'popularity' was an illusion and became one of the saddest parts of my life."[107]

Williams, similarly, describes a series of relationships in which she lived with men who provided her a place to live outside her abusive family home in exchange for sex, often taking advantage of the voluble and docile character Carol, who was eager to please.[108] Advice that emphasizes social skills, popularity, and fitting in to gender roles may encourage girls to consider themselves objects of male attention and desire. Such advice might risk overlooking the tendency for autistic girls to fall prey to sexual abuse or violence.

In sum, mainstream advice (especially advice not written by autistic people) often seeks to shore up normative gender roles for autistic individuals, especially for girls. In this way, it disciplines gender through a process of remediation, often in ways that limit the potentially transformative insights that might be gleaned from autistic individuals and their experiences. No one theory of gender accounts for this range of insights; instead, we might draw from autistic people an understanding of gender as identification, as a neurological condition or capacity, as performance, and as idiosyncratic. Together, these elements might be understood as copia or congeries—a heaping up of theories, names, and qualities that range far beyond simple binaries (male-female, masculine-feminine, nature-culture, and symbolic-embodied).

Conclusions

Gender, Character, and Rhetoric

It may seem curious that I have, until now, said relatively little about Temple Grandin, perhaps the most well-known autistic person in the world. It was a portrait of Grandin in Oliver Sacks's *An Anthropologist on Mars* that brought autism and Asperger's syndrome to popular attention in 1994. In 2010 the television network HBO profiled Grandin in a biopic starring Claire Danes, who won an Emmy, a Screen Actor's Guild award, and a Golden Globe for her portrayal. Grandin has published more than ten books, appears regularly in mainstream media and television outlets, and travels the country giving talks at autism conferences and events. Yet as I wrote this book, I had trouble determining where to profile her in my discussion of autism and gender, in part because Grandin is a rhetorical character. Not only is she a prominent speaker on all things autism-related, one who contributes to popular understandings of autism, but she is herself in some ways a rhetorical construction, given how often she has been portrayed in books, articles, and now, film. As such, Grandin's image, writing, and character coincide with many of the gendered factors I have explored in this book.

For one, Grandin herself has supported arguments connecting autistic abilities with computers and technology, arguments featured in Chapter 3. In 2006, for instance, she told Ira Flatow in an NPR interview, "I feel very strongly that if you got rid of all of the autistic genetics you're not going to have any scientists. There'd be no computer people.

You'd lose a lot of artists and musicians. There'd be a horrible price to pay."[1] In *The Way I See It,* Grandin writes that she fits the mold of the extreme male brain: "As a child I hated dolls and loved to build things. As an adult, I worked in the construction industry. Many activities that girls normally like, I hated."[2] Even aside from her own statements, Grandin might serve as a ready example of the EMB, given that she holds a PhD in animal science and that her day job involves designing complex animal chutes for slaughterhouses. As a rhetorical character, she is often used to support claims about fundamental human abilities, not just autism. For instance, Goleman, one of the promoters of social intelligence, uses Grandin as an example of the difficulties faced by individuals who lack the ability to participate in the "ordinary social world."[3]

However, Grandin might also fit in my discussion of gender identity and autistic difference in Chapter 5. She embodies an alternative gender performance, openly presenting herself as a celibate woman and dressing in a style inspired by her early experiences handling livestock. A UK report notes "the rather masculine cowgirl style she favours—dark grey jeans and an embroidered grey shirt with a red silk neckerchief and a cow-shaped belt buckle."[4] She is portrayed, then, as gender-defiant: "The mental sufferings of doomed livestock are more accessible to her than the preliminary advances of an amorous man," notes Lawrence Osborne in his book, *American Normal.*[5] In a popular culture saturated with assumptions about sexuality (even if the directions of sexual interest are somewhat more open than before), a celibate woman represents a curiosity, if not a subject for gender disciplining.

Grandin also vexes experts by wondering aloud whether vaccines may play a role in autism, saying: "You might be getting some kind of susceptibility, you know, that goes with genetics, where maybe they have a very difficult time metabolizing some of these toxins out."[6] She regularly addresses parents at autism conferences, and she lends her authority to the autism mothers featured in Chapter 2 by supporting a range of interpretations and theories, without singling out one. From her biographical accounts we learn that Grandin's mother, Eustacia Cutler, was an early example of an autism mother, one who rejected an early diagnosis of infant schizophrenia brought on by psychosocial trauma in favor of intensive therapy.[7]

In short, Grandin's example highlights some of the myriad ways gendered characterizations inform understandings of autism. My goal in this book has been to explore these and other gendered characters involved in autism discourse. They serve both as resources for those seeking to understand autism in popular and public discourses, and as sites of authority for mothers, fathers, scientists, and autistic persons. To conclude, I offer some of the implications of this study, in terms of autism, in terms of rhetorical studies of health and gender, and in terms of rhetorical theory more broadly.

Implications for Autism

New research findings about autism appear every day in my inbox, thanks to a Google alert I set up when I began researching this book. These findings range from new evidence of genetic factors to potential environmental triggers, new therapeutic techniques, and estimates of autism's prevalence. Despite this range of research, answers about autism's etiology seem a long way off, let alone pharmaceutical treatments that might alleviate autism's symptoms. Surely, when and if those answers arrive, we will see further debate about the desirability of medical interventions, especially from autistic people, many of whom warn against the potential for eugenic technologies such as pre-term screening and selective abortion of autistic fetuses.

For now, though, autism remains, and likely will remain, a rhetorical disorder with some prominence in public discussion for years to come. By calling it a rhetorical disorder, I do not mean to deny the reality of autism as a lived condition; instead, I am pointing out that it (like any condition) is understood and even experienced through rhetorical frameworks that shape realities of different individuals. As I have shown, mothers, fathers, scientists, and autistic individuals participate in different rhetorical constructions of autism, and gender often plays an important role in shaping the contours of what autism is and what it means for those individuals.

This insight yields some important implications for public debate. For one, gendered authority informs the rhetorical stances taken by mothers, fathers, and scientists engaged in debates about the causes and treatment of the condition. Part of the reason for a disconnect between scientific authorities and some parents, especially mothers, seems to stem from the paternalistic model of authority employed by scientists to quash theories about the role of vaccines in autism. This model risks coming across as condescending, and it fails to find connections with a maternal style of emotional persuasion.

In addition, gendered constructions of autism have material effects. Bumiller notes that "a gender-based theory of autism grossly oversimplifies the enormous complexity of the autistic condition, including its range of atypical sensory, physical, psychological, and perceptual manifestations."[8] In particular, this book demonstrates that by portraying autism via gendered characters, scientists may exclude individuals from scientific study. In my research, I found that

- mothers are often excluded from fMRI studies seeking to locate neuroanatomical indicators of autism,
- fathers are often excluded from studies of attachment or of interventions and treatment plans,
- autistic females are often excluded from general neuroscience and genetic studies of autism (or otherwise become research "orphans"—despite a spate of studies seeking to identify differences in diagnosis and presentation of autism in females),
- fathers may be subtly discouraged from participating in therapy programs, and
- alternative gender identities in autistic people are pathologized as gender dysphoria or gender identity disorder, with some autistic individuals undergoing gender remediation to fit with "typical," hegemonic gendered characters or genres.

Most important, autistic people themselves tend to be silenced in all of these cases, despite their potential to provide important insights.

Although some parents of autistic children and some autistic individuals have made their way onto the committees that determine funding for scientific studies, participatory research models seem scarce outside of social scientific research. Aside from adding stakeholders to committees, the psychologists Elizabeth Pellicano and Marc Stears note, "public engagement often consists of no more than the dissemination of research findings," an approach that "presumes that science does not need to be shaped or influenced by participation itself."[9] In other words, stakeholders may participate in early stages of research, by approving funding for particular projects, or later on, by receiving information about study results. But they seldom participate in what goes on in between; power still lies in the hands of researchers and funding agencies.

A gender perspective also reminds us to pay attention to power, to ask who is encouraged to participate and who is left out, and to gauge how those omissions affect scientific knowledge.[10] The knowledge that participants bring with them may not always involve gender, per se, but may involve expertise drawn from their experiences—as autistic people or as those who care for them. For instance, some parents have long insisted that their children developed autism after a year or two of normal development, but researchers tended to dismiss those claims. Only recently have researchers begun to investigate whether a subgroup of autistic children may regress developmentally, validating parents' anecdotal observations.[11] To take another example, autistic people often describe their conditions in terms of sensory processing difficulties, but researchers have only recently begun to explore autism from this perspective.

By including stakeholders as participants in research, gender blinders might be removed or at least recognized. For instance, imagine that participants in a study of a new autism therapy were invited to offer their input into the research design. Would someone ask why no fathers were asked to participate? Would family relationships other than a heterosexual, nuclear family be mentioned? Or, in the case of a neuroimaging study, would someone ask why only males were participating? These are all cases in which an outsider's perspective might prove valuable. As scholars of feminist science studies have argued, including individuals from marginalized groups can often contribute new perspectives, thereby increasing the rigor and objectivity of a study.[12]

Implications for Rhetorics of Health and Medicine

Autism is not the only condition that might be better understood through an analysis of the gendered rhetorics that shape it. Gendered characters play a prominent role in public discourses about health, especially in the case of conditions like autism, for which scientific information is lacking. For instance, veterans returning from wars in Iraq and Afghanistan have reported a set of physiological and psychological symptoms that they attribute to exposures to depleted uranium, chemical weapons, oil fires, and vaccines. Faced with symptoms such as fatigue, sleep disturbances, gastrointestinal problems, and neurological issues, some veterans lobbied to gain medical recognition for their injuries under the rubric of Gulf War Syndrome (GWS), or what the Veterans Administration (VA) prefers to call multisymptom illness related to "service in the Southwest Asia theater of military operations during the first Gulf War starting August 2, 1990 through the conflict in Iraq."[13] According to the National Academy of Sciences

(NAS), the symptoms of GWS have no known cause, no objective findings on clinical examination, no diagnostic biomarkers, no known tissue pathology, and no curative therapy.[14] Despite these difficulties, the NAS concluded in 2009 that sufficient evidence existed for an association between service in the Gulf War and Chronic Fatigue Syndrome (CFS), though the nature of that relationship was unclear.[15] Based on its review of the evidence, the VA states that "the evidence for an association between multisymptom illnesses and specific exposures, such as PB [pyridostigmine bromide], pesticides, and combinations thereof, is not equal to or greater than the evidence against such an association."[16] The VA nonetheless provides full compensation for those illnesses based on Title 38, Section 117 of the United States Code, providing benefits to veterans of Gulf War service. Undiagnosed and medically unexplained illnesses (including CFS and multisymptom illness) are included in that provision.

One explanation for the relative success of Gulf War veterans in gaining some measure of recognition for their suffering may be because GWS is bound up in rhetorics of masculinity and the character of the war veteran. The anthropologist Susie Kilshaw writes that GWS symbolizes a transformation in these men's lives, from "the epitome of militarised masculinity" to "embodying a lack of virility and manliness."[17] This loss of masculinity seems compelling to public audiences and, presumably, to decision makers. Some veterans have argued that the syndrome has prevented them from resuming their masculine role as breadwinner or has harmed their romantic and sexual lives. One symptom that garnered attention was a reported burning sensation or discomfort during sex. Kilshaw argues that this symptom owes its popularity to culturally loaded associations between semen and masculinity; toxic semen stands in for toxic masculinity.[18] Popular media outlets helped promote the idea that service in the Gulf conflicts caused these unexplained symptoms, perhaps because it proved provocative for viewers.

Kilshaw and others remain skeptical that GWS constitutes a biological illness, rather than a culturally constructed narrative of postwar trauma. For Kilshaw, the syndrome is fundamentally rhetorical: veterans tell similar stories about their illnesses, and those narratives become a shared genre that, in turn, constructs the experiences of veterans.[19] It is not my place here to weigh in on the relative merits of a biological or cultural view of GWS, although insights from medical humanities tell us that all illnesses are shaped by an interaction of biological and cultural factors.

My point is that when such stories emerge about unexplained illnesses, gender often plays a key role within them. The parallels to autism are striking; like GWS, autism remains a poorly explained condition, from a scientific standpoint, so gendered narratives carry much of the persuasive weight in public discourses about them.

Whereas characterizations of toxic or troubled masculinity support narratives of GWS, fibromyalgia and CFS are usually positioned as feminized disorders and, outside of the military context, sufferers still find their experiences delegitimized or explained away as psychosomatic.[20] The CFS sufferer becomes another type of gendered character; typically, a lazy housewife. A number of explanations for CFS have been proffered, including biological causes, such as chronic viral infections or exposures to toxins, and psychological ones, such as hypochondria, depression, anxiety, and perfectionism. Because the majority of sufferers are women, CFS has been cast as a modern-day neurasthenia or hysteria. Without a clear biological marker, CFS remains, like autism, open to debate, with gender playing a salient role.

To take up another case, young boys have become the face for Attention Deficit and Hyperactivity Disorder (ADHD), a condition that evokes considerable debate about boys, education, and modern life. As is the case with autism, GFS, and CFS, ADHD lacks coherent biological markers. In an article in the *British Journal of Psychiatry*, Sami Timimi argues that, since no definitive tests or biological markers exist for ADHD, it is difficult to ascertain exactly how many children have the disorder—epidemiological studies have yielded prevalence rates ranging from 0.5 to 26 percent of children.[21] By medicalizing ADHD, she argues, experts "script a potentially life-long story of disability and deficit," creating unnecessary dependence on doctors and pharmaceutical drugs.[22]

This disorder is just one of the factors identified in a perceived "boy crisis" that began in the early twenty-first century. Like autism, ADHD is understood in part through topoi about boys and girls. Although it is a psychiatric diagnosis, it indexes broad cultural shifts, including the feminization of labor and education. In *Boys Adrift* the psychologist Leonard Sax argues that contemporary schools privilege girls, who mature earlier, can sit still longer, and are driven to please authorities. For Sax, ADHD represents the pathologization of boys' difficulties in school, which stem primarily from their later development and, possibly, from chemicals that disrupt the endocrine system.[23] Another author, Peg Tyre, argues that boys are being overdiagnosed with ADHD in part because the popular depiction of the disorder captures a range of normal behaviors such as a common decline in school motivation among middle school-aged boys.[24]

All of these examples demonstrate that gender commonplaces and psychiatric or medical conditions intersect, especially in cases of medical and scientific uncertainty. In these cases, studying gender should be a key concern in the area of study Londa Schiebinger and Robert Proctor call "agnotology," or the cultural production of ignorance, since it is possible that gendered commonplaces impede rather than clarify scientific inquiry and treatment for these kinds of disorders.[25]

Implications for Gender

By focusing on rhetorical functions of gender, this study offers a way to examine gender that moves beyond questions about what gender is or what it does. Instead, this study models a view of gender as enacted rhetorically via language, embodied performances, and scientific practices that draw on gendered characters and commonplaces. As a rhetoric, gender functions in numerous ways: it can be interpreted, performed, presented, rehearsed, and invented.

First, as interpreted, typified gendered characters provide a heuristic for understanding other kinds of phenomena, namely, illnesses and neurological conditions. In the 1950s and 1960s, some autism researchers drew on culturally available characters of womanhood, especially the mother role, to offer theories about autism. Mother-blaming involved interpreting a topos of woman and applying it to a condition. Those who view Chronic Fatigue Syndrome as a symptom of neurotic womanhood are similarly interpreting gendered characters within a framework of illness.

Gendered characters function similarly in other kinds of debates, as well. To take one case, discussions about contemporary sex role behaviors often rely on evolutionary biological studies of animal populations, especially primates. In those studies, researchers interpret the sex roles of animal groups, hypothesize about what ancient human societies might have been like, and then apply those interpretations to contemporary human societies. Repeatedly, the conclusions from this type of research depend on interpretations of sex and gender characters. Feminist researchers have argued that these studies often import contemporary understandings of sex and gender and apply them to animal groups (one level of interpretation), and then reverse the process, applying understandings of animal sex roles to humans. For instance, in evolutionary terms women have historically been characterized as passive, coy, and homebound, leading to conceptions of women the gatherer and man (aggressive, sexually promiscuous, and adventurous) the hunter.[26] In turn, theories that ground rape in evolutionary adaptations interpret contemporary men's characters through a culturally constructed image of prehistoric man as competing among other men for status, resources, and control over women.[27] Gender scholars have, of course, critiqued these tendencies in sociobiology and elsewhere; here I am simply claiming that the rhetorical function of interpretation can enrich rhetorical theories of gender, in general, by showing how gendered characters work as an heuristic in scientific research.

Second, gender as performed names the more common approach of identifying how individuals deploy masculine and feminine characters in persuasive contexts. In this book I have argued that mothers of autistic children often deploy femininity in the form of maternal appeals, especially in ongoing debates about vaccines. Scientists, in turn, often deploy masculinity as a rhetorical strategy, in the particular form of a paternalist, "father-knows-best" type of character. Rhetorical scholars, especially scholars of feminist historiography, have mostly focused on the ways women have used femininity rhetorically. To name just a few studies, Carol Mattingly has detailed the self-presentation of the Women's Christian Temperance Union, which included choices of dress, decorations for speaking events, and appropriate feminine ethos, or persona.[28] Shirley Wilson Logan has shown that African American women speaking in the nineteenth century took pains to present themselves through the schema of middle-class "true womanhood," an ideology stressing propriety, moral superiority, and piety.[29] Studies of the characters men draw on include Robert A. Nye's work on masculine honor culture in scientific societies, replete with male bonding rituals such as smoking, drinking, and profanity.[30] A notable study of an alternative gender performance is Mattingly's study of Mary Walker, a doctor who dressed in male attire and received considerable attention for it in the nineteenth century.[31] In addition to rhetorical studies, feminist theorists have also explored these alternatively gendered performances, especially Judith Butler, Judith Halberstam, and many others.[32] We might hope to see more rhetorical studies of nonhegemonic gendered characters (female masculinity, drag, androgyny, and the like) in future work, especially work that examines how these identities or characters intersect with illness or neurodiversity.

Third, gender as presented refers to the practice of theorizing a condition such as autism using a gendered stock character or icon, and then using that stock character to represent a cultural moment or era. In the case of autism, male computer geeks in articles about the so-called Silicon Valley or Geek Syndrome are often used to comment on the perils of a technological era. A related example might be the presentation of HIV/AIDS as a condition affecting homosexual males. When taken as stock characters symbolizing the illness, gay men highlight certain risk factors while obscuring others. As a result, gay men have been stigmatized, while other groups may be led to underestimate the risk of contracting the disease.[33] The stock character of the gay male HIV/AIDS patient is often used to comment on perceived hedonism of gay communities, a clearly homophobic interpretation that, like the Geek Syndrome, seems more invested in a critique of a community or social context than in the condition itself. More broadly, gendered characters have often come to represent entire historical moments, such as the flapper of the 1930s or the Gibson Girl of the late nineteenth and early twentieth centuries. These characterizations constitute idealized versions of femininity or masculinity but also come to epitomize a cultural era in ways that might draw attention away from the cultural conditions affecting individuals who do not fit that prototype.

Fourth, gender can be rehearsed in and through language, including acts of self-persuasion. Such is the case in accounts written by fathers of autistic children, many of whom develop a conception of masculinity and fatherhood by reconfiguring and meshing with culturally available characters. In their memoirs, these men constitute their own characters in large part through their words, as they come to terms with how autism has affected their lives as fathers.

To some extent, the men discussed in this book participate in a broader rehearsal of masculinity and fatherhood, a "New Macho" that, some argue, now compels men to present themselves as active, engaged fathers and as more emotionally connected than previous generations of men—in part because of economic conditions that have rendered men especially vulnerable to unemployment.[34] Other rhetorical studies of gender rehearsals include Sarah Hallenbeck's argument that the bicycle precipitated new gender rehearsals for late nineteenth-century women, in part by enabling new forms of movement, dress, and action among women riders.[35] Similarly, Bo Wang has examined how Chinese women inserted themselves into political discussions during the May Fourth movement in the early twentieth century, leading to new characterizations of womanhood as well.[36] Overall, though, we have plenty of studies of how gender roles have been conserved and disciplined, but comparatively few examine how gender roles can be changed through rhetorical rehearsals.[37]

Finally, we can understand gender as a process of invention. My study of autistic concepts of gender shows that, rather than fixing gender in one place, some autistic people participate in an ongoing attempt to multiply the range of gendered characters, topoi, performances, and presentations available to them. Of course, it is important not to exaggerate the transformative potential or the ease of such inventions. After all, autistic people, like many others, are disciplined into normative gender presentations, in part by support groups such as the Capable Girls Group that encourage hegemonic gender identities and behaviors. Nonetheless, the very availability of a list of potential gender concepts beyond masculinity and femininity indicates that rhetorical actions can widen the range of options available to all individuals.

In rhetorical studies, we might examine how individuals come to understand their own gender and that of those around them. If we understand identity as a rhetorical process, as Burke, Dana Anderson, and others encourage us to do, then we might expect rhetorical theories to offer insights into how gendered identities are invented.[38] I prefer this term to "formation," since it implies that genders are not formed once and then forgotten. Invention, in contrast, implies that genders are in flux, "tenuously constituted in time," as Butler warns, though they are not entirely within conscious control.[39]

In the post-feminist era, we are often tempted to disregard gender as a significant cultural factor. Despite major shifts in the workplace, in childcare, and in family composition, all of which seem to lessen gender differences and increase gender diversity, we also live in a time when emphasized masculinity and femininity continue to shape our conceptions of ourselves, our brains, and our bodies. Autism offers an especially pertinent example of how these forces interact in ways that have significance for scientific and medical knowledge, for theories of gender, and for the experiences of autistic people and those who love them.

Implications for Rhetorical Theory

This study has demonstrated that the rhetorical importance of character ranges far beyond ethos, or credibility. Characters perform important epistemological functions, as well as constitutive and persuasive ones. That is, characters are performed by individuals for rhetorical effect, but they also circulate in discourse that creates knowledge, constitutes individual identities, and reinforces (or challenges) cultural stereotypes. Thinking of character not only in the sense of credibility but also in the sense of a stock character enables this range of richer rhetorical investigation.

For one, this study shows how characters arise out of material, cultural, and economic contexts. The refrigerator mother emerged from the confluence of psychological studies, popular childrearing texts, shifting gender roles, family structures, and childcare arrangements, and cultural conflicts over the role of women in the workplace. The autistic geek emerged from a different material and discursive network, including major shifts in the United States economy, technological change, and changes in the role of the traditional hegemonic male. Thus, characters offer condensed sites for examining social, political, and economic change from a rhetorical perspective.

I have also shown how characters perform important epistemological functions. Depending on how autism is characterized, researchers direct their attention toward different factors, research methods, and treatment strategies. Gender forms a significant element of those characters, but we might also consider how elements of class, race, sexual orientation, age, and location carry epistemological consequences when characters shape knowledge practices. For instance, in the United States, services such as Medicaid and Social Security have been portrayed in political discourse as services used primarily by "takers," "welfare queens," or "victims" who do not pay federal income tax or otherwise contribute to the nation. These characterizations affect political decisions, but they also limit public knowledge about who actually uses government services, such as low-income working families or senior citizens who have paid into the system already. Thus, characters offer a lens through which to examine epistemology, or knowledge formation, from a rhetorical perspective.

By writing about autistic individuals and character, I have also shown how stock characters serve inventive purposes for individuals. While identity is often understood as dependent on certain attributes (namely race, class, gender, sexual orientation), my study demonstrates that individuals often draw on stock characters to invent (and reinvent) an identity. The reflections of autistic individuals offer one rich resource for understanding this process, but we might also study how others rely on stock characters (directly or indirectly) for this purpose. Clearly, teenagers draw on stock characters as they rehearse possible identities (from, say, Goth to skate punk to prep), but so do performers, politicians, and professors, to name a few. Stock characters may sometimes serve as explicit resources for invention, but they may also work more subtly and unconsciously. Thus, characters offer one way for rhetoric scholars to study the process of identity formation.

Finally, throughout this text I have employed rhetorical vocabulary that seems to have fallen out of use, such as effectio (descriptions of physical appearance), notatio (description of a character's nature), prosopopoeia (impersonation of a character), prosopographia (character sketches), and conformatio (characterizations used to generate belief and authority). I have also drawn on ancient terms such as the topos, or commonplace, to better illustrate the rhetorical constitution and circulation of characters. These rhetorical terms offer a tool kit for character construction and for studying character rhetorically. Given the breadth of character as a rhetorical concept, these terms offer important resources for students of rhetoric, albeit ones less often taught than the neo-Aristotelian concepts of ethos, pathos, logos, and the like. Thus, by reinvigorating the study of character and its attendant terminology, we open up new vistas for rhetorical theory and pedagogy.

* * *

As I write this conclusion, President Barack Obama is championing a new brain mapping project, one in which autism figures prominently as a problem to be solved, part of the new frontier of knowledge and intervention that is promised by the latest attempt to channel government funds into a scientific growth area. Presumably, the project will help identify the inner workings of the brain, as well as the possibilities for treatment of brain-based conditions. In the excited flurry of information about the project, pundits are naming autism, alongside Alzheimer's disease and Parkinson's disease, as a disorder that may finally be "solved" by brain science. The brain is being positioned as the next, best frontier of scientific inquiry, and those with neurodiverse brains are being positioned as the primary targets.

The gendered characters examined in this study are in part responsible for the ease with which autism is identified as a target for the new brain project. Given this latest round of hype over neuroscientific research, it is important to understand how public and scientific discourse about the brain functions—in part by invoking characters that are interpreted, performed, presented, rehearsed, and invented through rhetorical action. The character of the autism mother pushing for new treatments, of autistic individuals as the offspring of inept geeks, and of the disengaged, deadbeat autism father all help position autism as a problem to be remediated.

Yet by developing and circulating new characters, rhetors can also enact social and political change. By forwarding alternative characters—autistic people who are capable self-advocates, parents who are accepting of their children's differences—individuals can shift public perceptions and gain a voice in decision making. Those involved in other kinds of rights movements (such as women's rights or civil rights) have had to generate alternatives to the often stereotyped, demeaning characters used to limit their opportunities and to justify oppression. Autistic individuals involved in the neurodiversity movement similarly seek to gain fundamental rights, in part by contesting the stock characters of autistic people that circulate in the media and in popular discourse. By studying the transformative potential of other characters, rhetoric scholars can generate new insights into how such social and political change can occur.

Notes

Introduction. Autism's Gendered Characters

1. Centers for Disease Control, "Autism Spectrum Disorder—Data and Statistics."

2. Heilker and Yergeau, "Autism and Rhetoric," 486.

3. Lucaites and Condit, "Re-constructing Narrative Theory," 94.

4. Jordan, *Recruiting Young Love*, xvi.

5. Ibid., xvii.

6. The *Rhetorica ad Herennium* defines *effectio* as "representing and depicting in words clearly enough for recognition the bodily form of some person" and *notatio* as "describing a person's character by the definite signs which, like distinctive marks, are attributes of that character" (Cicero 1981, 4.1.63). George Puttenham defines *prosopographia* as description of "the visage, speech and countenance of any person absent or dead" in *Arte of English Poesie*, 200. On *prosopopoeia,* in which "we display the thoughts of our opponents, as they themselves would do in a soliloquy,' see Quintilian, *Institutes of Oratory* (9.2.30). Puttenham defines *prosopopoeia* as attribution of human qualities to "dombe creatures or other insensible things" (200), making it similar to personification; Cicero describes character description as part of *conformatio* in *De Inventione* (1.24).

7. Keränen, *Scientific Characters*, 5.

8. Ibid., 7.

9. Keränen divides character into three components: *ethos*, voice, and persona. By using the term *character*, I am indexing those elements of character,

but I also pay attention to characters as culturally available means of persuasion. The term "stock character" best describes my definition of character, for the purposes of this analysis.

10. Glenn, *Rhetoric Retold*, 12.

11. Silverman, *Understanding Autism*, 6.

12. Murray, *Representing Autism*, 140.

13. Ibid., 140.

14. A. C. Carlson, "Role of Character in Public Moral Argument," 50.

15. Farrell, *Norms of Rhetorical Culture*, 277, emphasis in original.

16. Perelman and Olbrechts-Tyteca, *New Rhetoric*, 20–21.

17. C. Miller, "Aristotelian *Topos*," 132, 142.

18. Hasian, "Judicial Rhetoric," 251.

19. Ibid., 259–60.

20. Herbert, "Large Brains in Autism," 418.

21. Minshew and Keller, "Nature of Brain Dysfunction," 124.

22. Eapen, "Genetic Basis of Autism," 226.

23. Yates, "Unravelling the Genetics of Autism," 359.

24. Eapen, "Genetic Basis of Autism," 226.

25. American Psychiatric Association, "Pervasive Developmental Disorders."

26. American Psychiatric Association, "Autism Spectrum Disorder."

27. Murray, *Autism*, 13.

28. Castel, *Psychiatric Society*, 175. For critiques of the rhetoric of the *DSM* more broadly, see Stuart A. Kirk and Herb Kutchins, *The Selling of the* DSM: *The Rhetoric of Science in Psychiatry* (New York: Aldine de Gruyter, 1992); and Lucille Parkinson McCarthy and Joan Page Gerring, "Revising Psychiatry's Charter Document," *Written Communication* 11 (1994):147–92.

29. Carpenter, "Disability as Socio-Rhetorical Action," par. 1.

30. Siebers, *Disability Theory*, 8.

31. Tammet, *Born on a Blue Day*, 2–3.

32. Baggs, "Up in the Clouds," par. 15.

33. Sue Rubin describes difficulties with coordinating physical movements in Biklen, *Autism and the Myth of the Person Alone*, 84; Donna Williams describes some of her dietary, sensory, and processing difficulties, such as "severe reactive hypoglycemia," "sensory-perceptual shutdowns," and "occasional compulsive and involuntary tic-like urges to self-abuse," in *Everyday Heaven* (Kindle ed.), loc. 1078/2510.

34. Heilker and Yergeau, "Autism and Rhetoric," 487.

35. Ibid., 490.

36. Herbert, "Autism," 355, emphasis in original.

37. See, e.g., Rimland and Baker, "Brief Report."

38. D. Williams, *Everyday Heaven* (Kindle ed.), loc. 1078.

39. Grandin, *Emergence*, 112.

40. L. Carlson, *Faces of Intellectual Disability*, 93.

41. Nadesan, *Constructing Autism,* 3.

42. Ibid., 3.

43. Grinker, *Unstrange Minds,* 241.

44. L. Carlson, *Faces of Intellectual Disability,* 97.

45. Stevenson, Harp, and Gernsbacher, "Infantilizing Autism," par. 2.

46. Hacking, *Social Construction of What?* 121.

47. Rubin, "Traffic in Women."

48. Butler, *Bodies That Matter,* 1.

49. Fausto-Sterling, "Bare Bones of Sex," 1499.

50. Butler, *Gender Trouble,* 6.

51. Butler, *Bodies That Matter,* 187; West and Zimmerman, "Doing Gender," 126.

52. Although the range of this scholarship is too broad to cover in full, other notable texts include Karlyn Kohrs Campbell's *Man Cannot Speak for Her,* Cheryl Glenn's *Rhetoric Retold,* Shirley Wilson Logan's *"We Are Coming,"* and Mattingly's *Well-Tempered Women,* to name just a few.

53. Jensen, *Dirty Words,* 77.

54. A. C. Carlson, *Crimes of Womanhood,* 1.

55. Sloop, *Disciplining Gender,* 27.

56. See Bazerman, *Shaping Written Knowledge;* Gross, *Rhetoric of Science;* Mudry, *Measured Meals;* and Shea, *How the Gene Got Its Groove,* to name a few.

57. See, e.g., Harding, *Whose Science?;* Schiebinger, *Nature's Body;* Keller, *Reflections.*

58. Mudry, *Measured Meals,* 8.

59. Here I am following an approach advocated by Elizabeth Parthenia Shea in *How the Gene Got Its Groove,* 8.

60. Bleuler, *Theory of Schizophrenic Negativism,* 20.

61. Kanner, "Autistic Disturbances," 247. Clearly, these terms are not appropriate today, since they reflect bigoted views of people with intellectual disabilities, and I use them here only because it is important to be specific about the rhetorically constructed categories used by psychologists in that period.

62. Eyal, *Autism Matrix,* 129.

63. Kanner, "Autistic Disturbances," 217.

64. For more on the Nazi program of racial hygiene and the Kaiser Wilhelm Institute, see Macrakis, *Surviving the Swastika;* and M. Adams, Garland, and Weiss, "Human Heredity and Politics."

65. Schmuhl, *Kaiser Wilhelm Institute,* 181–182.

66. Ibid., 215.

67. Ibid., 216.

68. Ronen et al., "From Eugenic Euthanasia to Habilitation," 119.

69. Ibid., 119.

70. Largent, *Breeding Contempt,* 11.

71. Ibid., 2, 3.

72. Ibid., 1.

73. American Association for the Study of the Feeble-Minded, "Report of the Committee on Classification of the Feeble-Minded," 61.

74. Ibid., 62.

75. Ibid., 61.

76. Eugenics Record Office, *Report of the Committee,* 17.

77. L. Carlson, *Faces of Intellectual Disability,* 58–59.

78. Ibid., 64.

79. Ibid., 68–69.

80. Trent, *Inventing the Feeble Mind,* 23.

81. Kerlin, *Mind Unveiled,* 22 (emphasis in original), 33, 76.

82. Goddard, "Kallikak Family," 18. Of the remaining 337 individuals, 46 were "found normal," while the rest Goddard considered "unknown or doubtful."

83. Ibid., 50.

84. Ibid., 77.

85. Ibid., 90.

86. Martin A. Elks has argued that the photographs included in the report relied on rhetorical conventions in the depiction of poverty and mental disability. For instance, family members were often photographed outside dilapidated homes rather than, say, against a backdrop of trees. The homes themselves signaled poverty, which was linked rhetorically with mental disability. See Elks, "Believing Is Seeing"; "Visual Indictment."

87. While neither Kanner nor Asperger included photographs in their original articles, it has since become possible to identify a set of topoi in photographic depictions of autism, including visual metaphors of fragmentation and imprisonment. See Sarrett, "Trapped Children," 147–149.

88. Goddard, "Kallikak Family," 77.

89. Ibid., 87.

90. Ibid., 73.

91. Ibid., 87.

92. Ibid., 18, 21–22.

93. McDonagh, *Idiocy,* 100.

94. Carey, *On the Margins of Citizenship,* 63.

95. McDonagh, *Idiocy,* 96.

96. Goddard, "Kallikak Family," 80.

97. Neumärker, "Leo Kanner," 207.

98. Kanner, "Autistic Disturbances," 247, emphasis in original.

99. Ibid., 227, 231, 236, 232.

100. Ibid., 223–224.

101. Ibid., 225.

102. Ibid., 218–219.

103. Ibid., 250.

104. Ibid.

105. Asperger, "'Autistic Psychopathy,'" 40.

106. Ibid., 41.

107. Ibid.

108. Ibid., 84.

109. See, e.g., Rossi, "Women in Science"; Rossiter, *Women Scientists in America.*

110. See, e.g., Haraway, *Modest_Witness;* Keller, *Reflections.*

111. See, e.g., Schiebinger, *Nature's Body.*

112. Keller, "Gender/Science System," 241.

113. Martin, "The Egg and the Sperm."

114. Sontag, *Illness as Metaphor,* 30.

115. Lorber, *Gender and the Social Construction of Illness,* 132.

116. Siebers, *Disability Theory.*

117. Trent, *Inventing the Feeble Mind,* 2.

118. Ibid., 2.

119. Titchkosky, *Reading and Writing Disability Differently,* 7, 9.

120. Rocque, "Science Fictions," par. 7.

121. Shapiro, "Disability Rights," 59–60.

122. Garland-Thomson, "Feminist Disability Studies," 1564.

123. Herndl, *Invalid Women,* 25, 30.

124. Wilson, "Fighting Polio Like a Man," 119.

125. Soulières et al., "Level and Nature of Autistic Intelligence."

126. Lewiecki-Wilson, "Rethinking Rhetoric," 161.

127. Alcoff, "Problem of Speaking for Others," 7.

128. Stevenson, Harp, and Gernsbacher, "Infantilizing Autism."

129. Yergeau, "That's Just Your Autism Talking."

130. Scholars in rhetoric and composition have drawn attention to these issues recently. For instance, Margaret Price's book *Mad at School* challenges us to consider the ableist assumptions embedded in our pedagogical practices. Traditional classrooms require practices that may be difficult for students with mental disabilities, such as "real-time unfolding of events," "impromptu communication," "in-person contact," and "a strong social element" (61).

131. Hird, "Gender's Nature," 359.

Chapter 1. Interpreting Gender

1. Simpson, *Refrigerator Mothers.*

2. Pollak, *Creation of Doctor B.*

3. Severson, Jodlowski, and Aune, "Bruno Bettelheim," 69.

4. Grinker, *Unstrange Minds,* 81.

5. For other examples of cases wherein mothers, in particular, have been blamed for childhood psychiatric conditions, see Ehrenreich and English, *For Her Own Good*, "Motherhood as Pathology," 231–294.

6. R. Oppenheim, "They Said Our Child Was Hopeless," 23.

7. Bettelheim, *Empty Fortress*, 69.

8. Ibid., 71.

9. Ibid., 95.

10. Ibid., 156–157.

11. Ibid., 239.

12. Ibid., 96.

13. Ibid., 157.

14. Ibid., 158.

15. Ibid., 242, 239.

16. Ibid., 96.

17. Ibid., 158.

18. Ibid., 158–159.

19. Ibid., 241.

20. Ibid., 239.

21. A. C. Carlson, "Role of Character," 49.

22. M. Klein, *Selected Melanie Klein*, 184–185.

23. Ribble, "Disorganizing Factors," 460.

24. Ibid., 459.

25. Ribble, "Clinical Studies," 156.

26. Ibid., 156.

27. Bettelheim, *Empty Fortress*, 239.

28. Ribble, "Clinical Studies," 156.

29. Ribble, "Disorganizing Factors," 461.

30. Ibid., 460.

31. Goldfarb, "Effects of Early Institutional Care," 106.

32. Ibid., 107.

33. Ibid., 108.

34. Ibid., 129.

35. Bretherton, "Origins of Attachment Theory," 760.

36. Bowlby, *Maternal Care and Mental Health*, 11.

37. Ibid., 13.

38. Ibid., 11.

39. Hilgartner, *Science on Stage*, 51.

40. Bretherton, "Origins of Attachment Theory," 761.

41. "That Woman in Gray Flannel," SM114; Tolchin, "Vacations from Parenthood?" SM106.

42. Kanner, "Early Infantile Autism," 217.

43. Kanner and Eisenberg, "Early Infantile Autism," 8.

44. Ibid., 9.

45. Ibid., 10.
46. Ibid.
47. Apple, *Perfect Motherhood.*
48. Morse, *Care and Feeding of Children*, 9, 30, 31, 45, 32.
49. Ladd-Taylor, *Mother-Work*, 10.
50. Kanner, "Convenience and Convention," 301.
51. Ibid., 301.
52. Ibid., 305.
53. Ibid., 301, 302.
54. Ibid., 303.
55. Ibid., 301.
56. Ehrenreich and English, *For Her Own Good*, 241.
57. Goodspeed, Mason, and Woods, *Child Care and Guidance*, 54.
58. Bowlby, *Maternal Care and Mental Health*, 11.
59. Anthony, "Experimental Approach," 220.
60. Kanner, "Autistic Disturbances," 219, 229.
61. Anthony, "Experimental Approach," 213.
62. Friedan, *Feminine Mystique*, 413.
63. Ibid., 415.
64. Quoted in Simpson, *Refrigerator Mothers*, at 24:16.
65. Mandell et al., "Race Differences."
66. Stehli, *Sound of a Miracle*, 26–27.
67. Rimland, *Infantile Autism*, 38.
68. DesLauriers and Carlson, *Your Child Is Asleep*, 77.
69. Ibid., 74.
70. Park, *Siege*, 3.
71. Ibid., 12.
72. Park uses the name "Elly," a pseudonym, throughout *The Siege* but reveals in an epilogue that Elly's real name is Jessy.
73. R. Oppenheim, "They Said Our Child Was Hopeless," 58.
74. Hacking, "How We Have Been Learning to Talk About Autism," 509.
75. A. C. Carlson, "Role of Character in Public Argument," 50.
76. Phelan, "Imagining," 243.
77. Burke, *Counter-Statement*, 61.
78. Ibid., 61, 154, emphasis in original.
79. Hume, "Romance," 139.
80. Frye, *Anatomy of Criticism*, 193.
81. Kanner, "Autistic Disturbances," 242, emphasis in original.
82. Ibid., 249.
83. Park, *Siege*, 13, 28.
84. Burke, *Counter-Statement*, 58.
85. Jameson, "Magical Narratives," 140.
86. Park, *Siege*, 5–6.

87. Broderick and Ne'eman, "Autism as Metaphor," 469.

88. Ibid., 466.

89. Park, *Siege*, 33; Kanner, "Autistic Disturbances," 217.

90. Park, *Siege*, 11, 32. Note that Park's use of the terms *retardation* and *retarded* reflects common usage at the time, but these terms are no longer considered appropriate to describe those with intellectual disabilities.

91. Kanner, "Autistic Disturbances," 247.

92. Licia Carlson notes that depictions of ID as either static (hence beyond improvement) or dynamic (hence amenable to treatment) have been used rhetorically in different time periods to support specific education methods, institutionalized care, and interventions into the lives of the intellectually disabled. See *Faces of Intellectual Disability*, 43–45.

93. Frye, *Anatomy of Criticism*, 187.

94. Hume, "Romance," 133–135.

95. Burke, *Counter-Statement*, 124.

96. Park, *Siege*, 141.

97. Ibid., 143–144.

98. Ibid., 180–182, emphasis in original.

99. Ibid., 185.

100. Ibid.

101. Burke, *Counter-Statement*, 31, emphasis in original.

102. Ibid.

103. Park, *Siege*, 51, emphasis in original.

104. Ibid., 286.

105. Ibid., 138.

106. Lucaites and Condit, "Re-constructing Narrative Theory," 98.

107. Charland, "Constitutive Rhetoric," 148.

108. Ibid., 537.

109. Park, *Siege*, 189–90.

110. Lovaas, "Behavioral Treatment," 6.

111. Ibid., 8.

112. Broderick, "Autism as Rhetoric," under "Rhetorical Moment #1."

113. Brownlow, "Presenting the Self," 14, emphasis in original.

114. Johnson and Crowder, *Autism*, 22.

115. Maurice, *Let Me Hear Your Voice*, 16.

116. Ibid., 52.

117. Ibid., 13.

118. Ibid., 98, emphasis in original.

119. Ibid., 80.

120. Ibid., 79.

121. Ibid., 82.

122. Johnson and Crowder, *Autism*, 45, 96.

123. Maurice, *Let Me Hear Your Voice*, 16.

124. Ibid., 287. Maurice's younger son, Michel, was also diagnosed with autism and similarly lost his diagnosis after ABA. For the sake of concision, I have focused on Maurice's experiences with her older daughter, Anne-Marie.

125. Johnson and Crowder, *Autism*, 162–163.

126. Maurice, *Let Me Hear Your Voice*, 71, 131.

127. Broderick, "Autism as Rhetoric," under "Rhetorical Moment #2."

128. Dawson, "Misbehaviour," under "8. Science-based claims, or articles of faith?"

129. Welch and Mark, *Holding Time*, 19.

130. Tustin, "Revised Understandings," 586–587.

131. D. Oppenheim, Koren-Karie, Dolev, and Yurmiya, "Maternal Insightfulness"; Seskin et al., "Attachment and Autism."

132. Seskin et al., "Attachment and Autism," 949.

133. Ainsworth and Bell, "Attachment."

134. Federal Interagency Forum on Child and Family Statistics, *America's Children in Brief*, 18.

135. See Haltigan et al., "Brief Report" (which included eighty-one mothers and four fathers); Chow, Haltigan, and Messinger, "Dynamic Infant-Parent Affect Coupling" (thirty-six mothers and two fathers); and Cullen-Powell, Barlow, and Cushway, "Exploring a Massage Intervention" (thirteen mothers and one father).

136. Chow, Haltigan, and Messinger, "Dynamic Infant-Parent Affect Coupling," 103, emphasis added.

137. Benson et al., "Assessing Expressed Emotion," 78, emphasis added.

138. Ibid., 79.

Chapter 2. Performing Gender

1. J. McCarthy, speech at "Green Our Vaccines Rally."

2. See, e.g., Specter, *Denialism*, 58; Mooney and Kirshenbaum, *Unscientific America*, 14–15.

3. Wolf, "Is Breast Really Best?" 615.

4. Wakefield et al., "Ileal-Lymphoid-Nodular Hyperplasia."

5. Dominus, "Crash and Burn of an Autism Guru"; Cox, "Doctor Who Started Vaccine, Autism Debate in Ethics Row."

6. Showalter, *Hystories*, 11. Note that autism should not itself be considered hysteria. Those involved in the vaccine debate generally have children who received autism diagnoses. However, the vaccine debate echoes tendencies in debates about Gulf War Syndrome, Chronic Fatigue Syndrome, and the like, in that advocates seek out alternative explanations, including environmental pollution, endocrine disruption, and gastrointestinal disorders.

7. Schwarze, "Environmental Melodrama," 247.

8. Offit, *Autism's False Prophets*, 211.

9. Specter, *Denialism,* 101.

10. Wolf, "Is Breast Really Best?" 615.

11. Hamilton, *Treatise of Midwifery,* 162.

12. L. Carlson, *Faces of Intellectual Disability,* 71.

13. Total motherhood is one way to describe this phenomenon, but other terms have been offered, including what Douglas and Michaels call "the new momism" (*Mommy Myth,* 4) and Hays calls "intensive mothering" *(Cultural Contradictions of Motherhood,* 4).

14. Rose, *Politics of Life Itself,* 3.

15. Ibid., 23.

16. Malacrida, *Cold Comfort,* 37, 39.

17. Henderson and Peterson, "Introduction: Consumerism in Health Care," 1.

18. Democratic Leadership Council, "Health Care Quality."

19. O'Mara, "Your Child's First Healer."

20. "ADHD: Complementary/Alternative Treatments," *Parenting.com.*

21. "Autism Spectrum Disorders: At the Doctor," *Parenting.com.*

22. Malacrida, *Cold Comfort,* 13.

23. Butler, "Performative Acts," 520, emphasis in original.

24. See, e.g., C. Nichols, "Responsibilities of Woman," 127.

25. Kerber, "Republican Mother," 205.

26. Tonn, "Militant Motherhood," 2.

27. Fisher, "Vaccines," par. 4.

28. Ibid., par. 6.

29. Ibid., par. 21.

30. Wolf, "Is Breast Really Best?" 615.

31. Fisher, "Vaccines," under "Conclusion."

32. Keller, *Reflections on Gender and Science,* 52.

33. Nye, "Medicine and Science," 67.

34. Medical Hypotheses, "Aims and Scope."

35. Hyland, *Hedging,* 150.

36. Bernard et al., "Autism," 462.

37. Ibid., 464, emphasis added.

38. Ibid., 462.

39. Ibid., 467, emphasis added.

40. Ibid., emphasis added.

41. Lynch, *What Are Stem Cells?* (Kindle ed.), loc. 100/4651.

42. SafeMinds, "Executive Board."

43. Bernard, "Remarks to the US House of Representatives Committee."

44. Ibid., emphasis added.

45. Ibid.

46. Redwood, "Testimony Before the Subcommittee." 1.

47. Ibid., 3.

48. Ibid., 12.
49. Perelman and Olbrechts-Tyteca, *New Rhetoric*, 16.
50. Heller, *Vaccine Narrative*, 5.
51. Beck, *Power in the Global Age*, 102, emphasis in original.
52. Ibid., 105.
53. C. Adams, *Real Boy*, 4.
54. Whiffen, *Child's Journey*, 3.
55. J. McCarthy, *Louder Than Words*, 66.
56. Whiffen, *Child's Journey*, 48.
57. C. Adams, *Real Boy*, 45.
58. Ibid., 7.
59. Whiffen, *Child's Journey*, 48.
60. C. Adams, *Real Boy*, 79.
61. Whiffen, *Child's Journey*, 77.
62. C. Adams, *Real Boy*, 191.
63. Ibid., 188.
64. Whiffen, *Child's Journey*, 62.
65. C. Adams, *Real Boy*, 189–190.
66. Hammerback, "Creating the New Person," 18.
67. C. Adams, *Real Boy*, 259.
68. J. McCarthy, *Louder Than Words*, 138–139, emphasis in original.
69. Whiffen, *Child's Journey*, 47.
70. Ibid., 91.
71. J. McCarthy, *Louder Than Words*, 159, 195.
72. Hopefaithbelieve, "Jenny's New Book."
73. Reviews of *A Child's Journey out of Autism*.
74. Ibid.
75. Ibid.
76. Reviews of *A Real Boy: A True Story of Autism*.
77. Alyric, "Katie Wright: Autism Speaks['] Liability."
78. K. Greenfeld, "Autism Debate," 2.
79. Boehme, "Acceptance Is Not Giving Up."
80. Boehme, "An 'Autism Mom's' Open Letter to Jenny McCarthy."
81. Chew, "Confessions of a Former Warrior Mom."
82. Movius, "Opening the Window."
83. Dawson, "Bettelheim's Worst Crime," par. 1.
84. Fitzpatrick, "Ghost of the 'Refrigerator Mother.'"
85. Ehrenreich and English, *For Her Own Good*, 241.
86. Arranga, "Autism and the Abdication of Responsibility," 4.
87. Ibid., 4.
88. Silverman, *Understanding Autism*, 3, 21.
89. Ibid., 6.
90. Tommey and Arranga, "Autism Mothers Unite," 57.

91. See Gentleman, "Attention-Grabbing Antics."

92. Burt, "About."

93. Pollock, *Telling Bodies*, 1.

94. Ibid., 4.

95. "Could an Epidural Have Contributed to My Son's Autism?"

96. "What I Believed."

97. Lucy, "Cease Therapy."

98. Pollock, *Telling Bodies*, 69.

99. Lori, "Autism Vaccination Connection."

100. "What I Believed."

101. "Milestones—12–18 Months."

102. Lori, "Who Do You Trust," emphasis in original.

103. K.M.R., "Vaccination Debate."

104. Maryann, "They Get Me So Mad."

105. Lori, "Run Toward Hope."

106. Lucy, "About."

107. Parikh, "Judging Autism."

108. Novella, "August Is Vaccine Awareness Month"; McNeil, "Book Is Rallying Resistance to the Antivaccine Crusade."

109. Offit, *Autism's False Prophets*, 185.

110. Ibid., 203.

111. Ibid., 206.

112. Quoted in Kalb, "Stomping Through a Medical Minefield."

113. Ibid., par 5.

114. Ibid., par. 7.

115. Perelman and Olbrechts-Tyteca, *New Rhetoric*, 17.

116. Centers for Disease Control, "Vaccines & Immunizations."

117. Ibid.

118. Hackett, "Risk, Its Perception and the Media."

119. Weinstein et al., "Risk Perceptions," 150–151.

120. Mudry, *Measured Meals*, 2.

121. Lay, *Rhetoric of Midwifery*, 78.

122. Burton, "Ruining It for the Rest of Us."

123. Pho, "Losing the Anti-Vaccine Fight."

124. Orac, "Anti-Vaccine Movement."

125. Novella, "August Is Vaccine Awareness Month," under "The Bad."

126. Davies, Chapman, and Leask, "Antivaccination Activists on the World Wide Web," 24.

127. Shapin and Shaffer, *Leviathan and the Air-Pump*, 67.

128. Gross, *Rhetoric of Science*, xxvii, emphasis in original.

129. Offit, *Deadly Choices*, xi–xiii.

130. Ibid., xiv–xv.

131. Offit, *Autism's False Prophets*, xi–xv.

Chapter 3. Presenting Gender

1. Neal, "Review: *The Social Network*," par. 4.

2. Morgenstern, "'Social Network': Password Is Perfection," par. 3; D. Carr, "Film Version of Zuckerberg Divides Generations," par. 9.

3. Stevens, "Joyless Dweeb," par. 3.

4. Sragow, "Fear, Self-Loathing, and Facebook," par. 9.

5. Tate, "Tech Industry's Asperger's Problem."

6. Coates, "Famous People with Asperger Syndrome."

7. Quoted in Garloch, "Living the Autistic Life," under "Is it realistic to expect most people with autism to accomplish what you have?"

8. Nadesan, *Constructing Autism*, 3–4.

9. Ibid., 132.

10. Perelman and Tyteca, *New Rhetoric*, 116.

11. Ibid., 118.

12. Bush, "Decade of the Brain," 29553.

13. Rafinski, "Brain Scans Offer Picture of Mental Illnesses," 1A. In a notable evocation of mother-blaming, the article begins with the statement "Mom, you're off the hook," referring to the potential for brain scans to finally prove that bad parenting does not cause mental illness.

14. Brothers, "Males and Females"; Reuters, "It's True"; Siegfried, "Female Brain."

15. Moir and Jessel, *Brain Sex*; Blum, *Sex on the Brain*; Gray, *Men Are from Mars*.

16. The tendency to put brain types into preexisting molds did not go unchallenged by feminists. Ellen Goodman warned in a 1995 syndicated column that articles and books emphasizing gender difference were leading to resegregation: "The more similar our real lives, the more we seem to focus on the separateness of our emotional workings and biological wirings." See Goodman, "Worlds Apart," B3. In 1996, Celeste Condit published her critique of the tendency for such findings to concretize and exaggerate differences between male and female brains—a critique she originally submitted to *Science* magazine and then published in *Rhetoric Society Quarterly* when *Science* refused to publish it. See Condit, "How Bad Science Stays That Way." Yet twelve years later, neuroscientists Nicole C. Karafyllis and Gotlind Ulshöfer lamented that neurorhetorics still tends to construct brain differences along well-worn paths of gender and sex. See Karafyllis and Ulshöfer, "Introduction: Intelligent Emotions," 8. The authors point to studies that work rhetorically by assigning gender to brains, often in ways that either exaggerate differences between men and women or that constitute the very differences they hope to identify.

17. Wing, "Asperger's Syndrome," "Continuum of Autistic Characteristics," and "Autistic Continuum."

18. Asperger, "Autistic Psychopathy," 84.

19. Sacks, "Anthropologist on Mars," 115, 121.

20. Drucker, *The Effective Executive*, 3.

21. Morini, "The Feminization of Labour in Cognitive Capitalism," 50.

22. Castells, *The Rise of the Network Society*, 77.

23. Quoted in Goodnight and Green, "Rhetoric, Risk, and Markets," 122.

24. Ibid., 122.

25. Ibid., 123–124.

26. The notion of social intelligence was put forward decades earlier, shortly after the intelligence quotient (IQ) was itself introduced and during a time when men and women were leaving the farm and factory for a range of white-collar jobs in the city. From the start, the idea was linked to vocational aptitudes and interests—much like the IQ, which was tightly integrated with military planning and the rise of scientific management. In 1920, psychologist E. L. Thorndike used the term "social intelligence" in an article in *Harper's Magazine*, noting that it was one of three core types of intelligence (the other two being mechanical and abstract intelligence). See Thorndike, "Intelligence and Its Uses," 228.

27. H. Gardner, *Frames of Mind*.

28. Salovey and Mayer, "Emotional Intelligence," 189, emphasis in original.

29. Daniel Goleman, *Working with Emotional Intelligence*, 3.

30. Howe, *Pink Collar Workers*.

31. For Yann Moulier Boutang, cognitive capitalism is marked by the virtualization of the economy; the manipulation of numerical data; and innovation grounded in interactive cognitive processes of social cooperation and tacit knowledge (among other qualities). See *Cognitive Capitalism*, 50–51. My argument here is not that such a system exists, in reality—I'll leave that to others to argue. Instead, I argue that these assumptions do underlie the positioning of the male autistic computer geek as an icon of contemporary culture.

32. Davis, *Breaking Up (At) Totality*, 108.

33. Elmer-DeWitt and Farley, "Diagnosing Bill Gates," 25.

34. Ibid., 108.

35. Jarratt, *Rereading the Sophists*, 28.

36. Elmer-DeWitt and Farley, "Diagnosing Bill Gates," 25.

37. Oldenberg, "Rethinking Reagan's Closing Statement," 7.

38. Elmer-DeWitt and Farley, "Diagnosing Bill Gates," 25.

39. Seabrook, "E-mail from Bill," 56.

40. "Diagnosing Bill Gates"; Seabrook, "E-mail from Bill," 51.

41. Seabrook, "E-mail from Bill," 48.

42. Grandin, *Thinking in Pictures*, 214–215.

43. Pryal, "The Genre of the Mood Memoir," 495.

44. Burke, "Four Master Tropes," 426.

45. Burke, *Permanence and Change*, 104.

46. To take the Original Geek Test, go here: http://www.innergeek.us/geek-test.html.

47. Silberman, "Geek Syndrome," pars. 10–11.

48. Jentsch, "On the Psychology of the Uncanny," 8.

49. Ibid., 8, emphasis in original.

50. Silberman, "Geek Syndrome," pars. 38–39.

51. Burck, "Boundless Age," 101.

52. Silberman, "Geek Syndrome," pars. 11, 19, 12, 22.

53. Abraham, "Is There a Geek Syndrome?" pars. 13, 33.

54. Silberman, "Geek Syndrome," par. 1.

55. Abraham, "Is There a Geek Syndrome?" pars. 1–2.

56. Ibid., pars. 2–3.

57. Silberman, "Geek Syndrome," par. 2.

58. Jentsch, "On the Psychology of the Uncanny," 13.

59. Abraham, "Is There a Geek Syndrome?" par. 30.

60. Burke, *Grammar of Motives*, 59.

61. Ibid., 77.

62. Nash and Bonesteel, "Geek Syndrome," pars. 5, 9.

63. Windham, Fessel, and Grether, "Autism Spectrum Disorders," 186.

64. For example, Hoekstra et al., "Heritability of Autistic Traits," 375.

65. BBC News, "Autism Link to Geek Genes," under "Too Many Genes."

66. Arky, "Touch and Autism," par. 4.

67. Baron-Cohen, *Essential Difference*, 6.

68. Bumiller, "Quirky Citizens," 973.

69. Tannen, *You Just Don't Understand*, 16–17.

70. Gray, *Men Are from Mars*, 9–10.

71. Ibid., 11.

72. Ibid., xxxi.

73. Ibid., xxx.

74. Baron-Cohen, *Essential Difference*, 8, 11.

75. Ibid., 9.

76. Ibid., 8, emphasis in original.

77. Ibid., 69, 47.

78. Connell, *Gender and Power*, 183.

79. Connell and Messerschmidt, "Hegemonic Masculinity," 832.

80. Baron-Cohen, *Essential Difference*, 49.

81. Tannen, *You Just Don't Understand*, 27.

82. Baron-Cohen, *Essential Difference*, 13.

83. Ibid., 17.

84. Burke, *Permanence and Change*, 107.

85. Baron-Cohen, *Essential Difference*, 155.

86. Ibid., 157–161.

87. Ibid., 158.

88. Seabrook, "E-mail from Bill," 48.

89. Ibid., 60, emphasis in original.

90. Baron-Cohen, *Essential Difference,* 211, 215, 210.

91. Kiesler, Sproull, and Eccles, "Pool Halls, Chips, and War Games," 460.

92. Cooper, "Being the 'Go-To Guy,'" 380.

93. Light, "When Computers Were Women," 469.

94. On gendered technologies, see Sorensen and Berg, "Genderization of Technology," 152.

95. Oldenziel, *Making Technology Masculine,* 20.

96. Ibid., 23.

97. Ibid., 43. On the gendered assumptions informing definitions of technology, see also Durack, "Gender, Technology, and the History of Technical Communication," 35–43.

98. Oldenziel, *Making Technology Masculine,* 19. This applies to issues of gender as well as to race, class, and nationality. The continued underrepresentation of people of color in science and engineering attests to the social construction of technology as *white* as well as *masculine.* Non-Western, non-white technologies, which include innovations in mathematics, metallurgy, medicine, transportation, textiles, pottery, furniture, architecture, agricultural techniques, and the like, have also been excluded from definitions of technology. For a review of the racist and Eurocentric assumptions undergirding mainstream histories of science and technology, see Harding, *Whose Science? Whose Knowledge?,* chap. 9.

99. Wheelwright et al., "Predicting Autism Spectrum Quotient (AQ)," 49.

100. Ibid., 55.

101. Ibid., 49.

102. Ibid., 53.

103. Hammerback, "Creating the 'New Person,'" 18.

104. Fine, *Delusions of Gender,* 9.

105. Hacking, *Rewriting the Soul,* 21.

106. The Guardian, "How Male or Female Is Your Brain?"; BBC News, "Sex I.D."

107. Quintilian, "Institutes of Oratory," 6.2.29.

108. Cory, "Interactions of Beauty and Truth," 394.

109. Urban, "Knowledge of Other Minds," 281.

110. Titchener, *Lectures,* 21.

111. Ibid., 185.

112. Urban, "Knowledge of Other Minds," 282.

113. Dymond, "Scale for the Measurement of Empathic Ability," 127.

114. Ibid., 130.

115. Hogan, "Development of an Empathy Scale," 308.

116. Ibid., 313.

117. Hobart and Fahlberg, "Measurement of Empathy," 596–597, emphasis in original.

118. Premack and Woodruff, "Does the Chimpanzee Have a Theory of Mind?"

119. R. Gardner and B. Gardner, *Structure of Learning*.

120. Gallup, "Chimpanzees."

121. Meddin, "Chimpanzees, Symbols, and the Reflective Self," 108.

122. See Eyal, *Autism Matrix*, Chapter 4 for more on how deinstitutionalization of the mentally retarded led to increased diagnoses of autism and other mental conditions.

123. Baron-Cohen, Leslie, and Frith, "Does the Autistic Child Have a 'Theory Of Mind'?," 42.

124. Baron-Cohen, *Essential Difference*, 189. To take the Reading the Mind in the Eyes test, go to http://glennrowe.net/baroncohen/faces/eyestest.aspx.

125. Langfeld, "Judgment of Emotions," 173.

126. Ibid., 178–179.

127. Guilford, "An Experiment," 202.

128. Coleman, "Facial Expressions of Emotion," 1.

129. Eisenberg and Lennon, "Sex Differences," 124.

130. Ickes, Gesn, and Graham, "Gender Differences in Empathic Accuracy," 102.

131. Klein and Hodges, "Gender Differences," 727.

132. Cross and Madson, "Models of the Self," 9.

133. Muncer and Ling, "Psychometric Analysis," 1117.

134. Baron-Cohen, *Essential Difference*, 201, 204.

135. Ibid., 216.

136. Ibid., 207.

137. Ladyrain, Comment on "AS Women and Special Interests."

138. Ibid.

139. Nekowafer, Comment on "AS Women and Special Interests."

140. MangoChutney, Comment on "AS Women and Special Interests."

141. UnderINK, Comment on "AS Women and Special Interests."

142. Sholf, Comment on "Extreme Male Brain Hypothesis."

143. Morini, "Feminization of Labour," 40.

144. Turkle, *Alone Together*, 15.

145. N. Carr, *Shallows*, 218.

146. Tate, "Tech Industry's Asperger Problem," par. 1.

147. Ibid., under "Diagnosing Zuckerberg."

148. Ibid., under "Impaired Social Interaction."

149. Ibid., under "Clumsiness."

150. Ibid.

151. Ibid., under "A Broader Issue."

152. Foucault, "Technologies of the Self," 18.

153. Rwinter001, "Online Tests Helped Me Self-Diagnose," emphasis in original.

154. Adversarial, Comment on "Wrong Asperger's Self-Diagnosis."

155. Segal, *Health and the Rhetoric of Medicine,* 40, emphasis in original.

156. Greg, "A Lot Like the Movie Adam."

157. Electrifiedspam, Comment on "Wrong Asperger's Self-Diagnosis."

158. Foucault, *Power/Knowledge,* 98.

159. Jessa, Comment on "Why Can't I Get Diagnosed."

160. Jou et al., "Cortical Gyrification," 1463.

161. Carmody and Lewis, "Regional White Matter," 760.

162. Schumann et al., "Longitudinal Magnetic Resonance Imaging Study," 4420.

163. Ibid., 4425.

164. Ibid.

165. Belmonte, Gomot, and Baron-Cohen, "Visual Attention," 259.

166. Ibid., 260, emphasis added. The abbreviation ASC stands for Autism Spectrum Conditions, a term more prevalent in the United Kingdom.

167. Ibid., 270, emphasis added.

168. Quoted in Bazelon, "What Autistic Girls Are Made Of."

169. Ernsperger and Wendel, *Girls Under the Umbrella,* 11.

170. Hambrook et al., "Empathy, Systemizing, and Autistic Traits," 337.

171. Ibid., 338.

172. Barbeau, Mendrek, and Mottron, "Are Autistic Traits Autistic?" 27.

173. Markram, Rinaldi, and Markram, "Intense World Syndrome," 77, emphasis in original.

174. Cohen-Rottenberg, "Intense World Syndrome."

175. Cohen-Rottenberg, Comment on "Do Some Aspies Have Lots of Empathy?"

176. Skuse, "Is Autism Really a Coherent Syndrome in Boys, or Girls?" 36.

Chapter 4. Rehearsing Gender

1. L. Eisenberg, Fathers of Autistic Children," 715.

2. Ibid., 717.

3. Ibid., 721. Notably, Eisenberg declares that this perfectionism actually works against the occupational success of the scientists in the group, none of whom he ranked as "a major contributor to his field" (721). This point seems to contradict the now widespread assumption that many scientists and engineers from Albert Einstein to Alan Turing to Bill Gates, can be diagnosed as autistic, given descriptions of their extreme focus and general social ineptitude.

4. McCarthy, *Louder Than Words,* 128.

5. Reynolds, "Genie in a Bottle," pars. 19, 4.

6. Hartley et al., "Relative Risk and Timing of Divorce," 452.

7. Freedman et al., "Relationship Status Among Parents," 543.

8. Brown, "Divorce After Autism," par. 5.

9. Hall, "Divorce and Autism," pars. 4–6.

10. Professor, "Divorce and the Special Needs Parent," par. 3.

11. Rudy, "Is Autism Toughest on Dads?" par. 9.

12. Rudy, "How to Get Dad More Involved," par. 1.

13. Tamano, "How My Autistic Son Taught Me Fatherhood," par. 4–5.

14. Harrison, "Rhetorical Rehearsals," 243.

15. C. Miller, "Aristotle's 'Special Topics' in Rhetorical Practice and Pedagogy," 67.

16. This is not to say that fathers do not take part in the vaccine movement described in Chapter 2. Indeed, some fathers, including Mark Blaxill and J. P. Handley, have been very active in that movement. Notably, though, these fathers have written books that take on the vaccine issue from an argumentative standpoint and not an autobiographical one. For instance, Blaxill's book, *The Age of Autism* (New York: MacMillan, 2010), written with Dan Olmsted, takes a historical approach, tracing previous illnesses caused by mercury and connecting them with the authors' hypothesis that autism derives from mercury poisoning.

17. Connell and Messerschmidt, "Hegemonic Masculinity," 832.

18. Donnell, *Dads and Autism*, 24.

19. Peete and Morton, *Not My Boy!* 16.

20. Duncan, "Father Friday-@Autismfather," pars. 2–3.

21. Duncan, "Autism, Fathers, The Future and Denial," pars. 7–8.

22. Duncan, "Hardest Part of Autism," par. 6.

23. B. Davis, *Breaking Autism's Barriers*, 397.

24. Ibid., 379.

25. Ibid., 394.

26. Harris, "How I Feel Today," par. 1.

27. Kittay, *Love's Labor*, 14.

28. Smith et al., "'I've Been Independent for so Damn Long!'" 333; Gershick and Miller, "Coming to Terms," 187.

29. Messner, "Masculinities and Athletic Careers," 75.

30. Donnell, *Dads and Autism*, 101–102.

31. Duffy, "Twenty-Seven Years Post Title IX," 73.

32. Ibid., 323.

33. Ibid., 319.

34. Peete and Morton, *Not My Boy!* 175.

35. Ibid., 176.

36. Ibid., 188.

37. Duckworth and Buzzanell, "Constructing Work-Life Balance and Fatherhood," 569.

38. J. Greenfeld, *Child Called Noah*, 7.

39. Ibid., 10.

40. Ibid., 10–11.

41. Ibid., 6.

42. Ibid., 11.

43. Ibid., 21.

44. Harris, "What Defines Me," pars. 2–5.

45. Duckworth and Buzzanell, "Constructing Work-Life Balance and Fatherhood," 569.

46. Ibid., 26, 22, 32.

47. Ibid., 60.

48. J. Greenfeld, *Place for Noah*, 300–301.

49. Ibid., 302.

50. Bill K, Comment on "Is Autism Toughest on Dads? Your Opinion Requested," par. 3.

51. Ball, *Early Intervention and Autism*, 37.

52. Peete and Morton, *Not My Boy!* 3, 32–33.

53. Ibid., 2–3.

54. Ibid., 33.

55. Ibid., 50.

56. Duckworth and Buzzanell, "Constructing Work-Life Balance and Fatherhood," 565.

57. Peete and Morton, *Not My Boy!* 231.

58. Burns, *Saving Ben*, 29, 32.

59. Ibid., 101, 153.

60. Lou, "Emotional Reactions to Autism," par. 5.

61. Harris, "Insha'Allah," par. 3.

62. Calinescu, *Matthew's Enigma*, 2.

63. Ibid., 5, 18.

64. Ibid., 31.

65. Ibid., 35.

66. Ibid., 61, 57.

67. Grinker, *Unstrange Minds*, 2.

68. Ibid., 34.

69. Ibid., 198.

70. Ibid., 284.

71. Collins, *Not Even Wrong*, 8.

72. Ibid., 10.

73. Ibid., 16.

74. Ibid., 17–18.

75. Ibid., 23.

76. Ibid., 58.

77. Ibid., 34.

78. Blastland, *Only Boy in the World*, 1, 7.

79. Ibid., 86.

80. Ibid., 194.

81. Nadesan, *Constructing Autism*, 1.

82. Ibid., 2, emphasis in original.

83. Peete and Morton, *Not My Boy!* 227.

84. Winter, "Father Involvement in Parent Training," 19–20.

85. Ibid., 82–84.

86. Moss, *Gender, Design and Marketing*, 172.

87. Quoted in Genosko, "Natures and Cultures of Cuteness," under section I.

88. Lobmaier et al., "Female and Male Responses to Cuteness," 20.

89. Sprengelmeyer et al., "Cutest Little Baby Face," 153.

90. Alreck, "Commentary: A New Formula for Gendering Products and Brands," 10.

Chapter 5. Inventing Gender

1. Meyerding, "Growing up Genderless," 158.

2. Ibid., 164.

3. Shiva, "Gender Identity," par. 6.

4. Francis, "Gender Monoglossia," 3.

5. Ibid., 4.

6. Bumiller, "Quirky Citizens," 977.

7. De Vries et al., "Autism Spectrum Disorders in Gender Dysphoric Children," 932.

8. Bejerot et al., "Extreme Male Brain Revisited," 119.

9. McGee, "Neurodiversity," 12.

10. Prince-Hughes, *Songs of the Gorilla Nation*, 2.

11. Meyerowitz, *How Sex Changed*, 12, 37.

12. Aristotle, *Rhetoric*, I.2.26–27.

13. McGeer, "Thought and Talk of Individuals with Autism," 527.

14. Erasmus, *On Copia of Words and Ideas*, 17.

15. Sloop, *Disciplining Gender*, 12.

16. Burke, *Attitudes Toward History*, 263.

17. See Fausto-Sterling, "Dynamic Development of Gender Variability," 405–406.

18. Meyerding, "Growing up Genderless," 157.

19. Baggs, "This Is Not the Post I Started out Writing," par. 7.

20. Linton, *Claiming Disability* (Kindle ed.), loc. 1868, 2040/3359.

21. Vivian, "I'm So Butch I Wear Nightgowns," par. 5.

22. Sleeping Chrysalid, "Coexistence of Gender Variance and Autism."

23. Crable, "Rhetoric, Anxiety, and Character Armor," 3, emphasis in original.

24. Angelik, "Gay with Aspergers."

25. Catster29, "Anyone Else Here Not Interested in Relationships?"

26. J. Miller, "Differences," 45–46.

27. Ibid., 54.

28. Prince-Hughes, *Songs of the Gorilla Nation*, 3.

29. Burke, *Grammar of Motives*, xix, emphasis in original.

30. McClure and Cabral, "Clarifying Ambiguity and the Undecidable," 77.

31. Shiva, "Gender Identity," par. 5.

32. J. Miller, "Differences," 38.

33. Lindsay, "Gender Variance in Autism," par. 7.

34. J. Miller, "Mommie Wyrdest," 192.

35. Ibid., 194.

36. Whirlingmind, "So, I Don't Collect Toy Dinosaurs or Stamps . . ."

37. Revolutionrocknroll, Comment on "What Does It Mean to You to Be a Woman with Asperger's?"

38. Rattus, Comment on "What Does It Mean to You to Be a Woman with Asperger's?"

39. Golubock, "Different on the Inside," 63.

40. Meyerding, "Growing up Genderless," 158–159.

41. Singer, "Foreword: Travels in Parallel Space," xii.

42. Vivian, "Geekazoid," par. 2.

43. Burke, "Persuasion, Identification, and Dialectical Symmetry," 336.

44. Butler, *Gender Trouble*, 179, emphasis in original.

45. Lindsay, "Gender Variance in Autism," par. 9.

46. Vivian, "I'm a Fake Person," par. 2.

47. Rabin, "Bataan Death March of Whimsy Case File #1," par. 7.

48. Vivian, "I'm a Fake Person," par. 6, emphasis added.

49. Vivian, "From June 2009," pars. 5–6.

50. Mattingly, *Appropriate[Ing] Dress*; Cintrón, *Angels' Town*, 11.

51. Foss and Foss, *Women Speak*.

52. HarraArial, Comment on "Do U Care About Fashion (Girls Only)?"

53. CockneyRebel, "What Women Like Most in Fashion?"; Pinkbow-tiepumps, Comment on "Fashion Style?"

54. Francis, "Gender Monoglossia, Gender Heteroglossia," 9.

55. Prince-Hughes, *Songs of the Gorilla Nation*, 79.

56. D. Williams, *Nobody Nowhere*, 11.

57. Ibid., 19.

58. D. Williams, *Everyday Heaven*, 117–118.

59. D. Williams, "Face Blindness in Autism and Beyond." Linton would point out the irony of these terms, as well. See Linton, *Claiming Disability* (Kindle ed.), loc. 2040/3359.

60. D. Williams, *Everyday Heaven*, 118–119, 132.

61. D. Williams, "Being a Gay Man in a Woman's Body," par. 17.

62. West and Zimmerman, "Doing Gender," 126.

63. Prince-Hughes, *Songs of the Gorilla Nation*, 59, 58.

64. Ibid., 54, 58.

65. Ibid., 80, 83, 59.

66. Ibid., 59, 58, 130, 131.

67. Vivian, "I'm So Butch I Wear Nightgowns," par. 3.

68. Thevenerablecortex, "Of Sex and Loneliness," par 2.

69. The Third Glance, "On (A)sexuality," par. 5.

70. Burke, *Attitudes*, 4.

71. Burke, *Grammar of Motives*, 243.

72. "Is Anybody Here Who Has Autism and Is Transgender?"

73. Ibid., emphasis in original.

74. Ibid.

75. Weston, *Gender in Real Time*, 44.

76. American Psychiatric Association, "Proposed Revision: Gender Dysphoria in Adolescents and Adults."

77. American Psychiatric Association, "Proposed Revision: Gender Dysphoria in Children."

78. De Vries et al., "Autism Spectrum Disorders," 933.

79. Mukaddes, "Gender Identity," 530.

80. Ibid., 531.

81. Tateno, Tateno, and Saito, "Comorbid Childhood Gender Identity Disorder," 238.

82. McVeigh, "Commodifying Affection," 292.

83. Landén and Rasmussen, "Gender Identity Disorder," 171.

84. P. Williams, Allard, and Sears, "Case Study," 641.

85. Gallucci, Hackerman, and Schmidt, "Gender Identity Disorder," 39.

86. Kraemer et al., "Comorbidity of Asperger Syndrome," 295.

87. Bazerman, *Shaping Written Knowledge*, 270.

88. Ibid., 271.

89. Dean, "Social Education," C8.

90. Sloop, *Disciplining Gender*, 14.

91. Bumiller, "Quirky Citizens," 978.

92. S. Nichols, Moravcik, and Tetenbaum, *Girls Growing up on the Autism Spectrum*, 148.

93. Ibid., 152.

94. Ibid., 151.

95. Sam, "Horrible Generalizations."

96. Francis, "Gender Monoglossia, Gender Heteroglossia," 7.

97. United States Department of Education, Office of Special Education and Rehabilitative Services, "History: Twenty-Five Years of Progress in Educating Children with Disabilities through Idea," 2.

98. Boutot, "Fitting In," 157.

99. Iland, "Girl to Girl," 34–37.

100. Ibid., 38–39.

101. Ibid., 50.

102. Grandin, "For Me, a Good Career Gave Life Meaning," 149.

103. Ibid., 150.

104. Myers, "Aspie Do's and Dont's," 100.

105. Innes, "Who Remembers Sabrina?" 2.

106. Myers, "Aspie Do's and Don'ts," 92.

107. Newport, Newport, and Bolick, *Autism-Asperger's and Sexuality*, 29–30.

108. D. Williams, *Nobody Nowhere*, 87.

Conclusion

1. Flatow, "Conversation with Temple Grandin."

2. Grandin, *The Way I See It*, 245.

3. Goleman, *Social Intelligence*, 140.

4. Mulkerrins, "Temple Grandin," par. 2.

5. Osborne, *American Normal*, 6.

6. Flatow, "Conversation with Temple Grandin."

7. Cutler, *Thorn in My Pocket*, 34.

8. Bumiller, "Quirky Citizens," 973.

9. Pellicano and Stears, "Bridging Autism," 6.

10. See Harding, *Whose Science? Whose Knowledge?*

11. Rogers, "Developmental Regression," 139.

12. See Harding, *Whose Science? Whose Knowledge?*

13. United States Department of Veterans Affairs, "Gulf War Veterans' Illnesses."

14. Committee on Gulf War and Health, "Gulf War and Health," ix.

15. Ibid., 214.

16. United States Department of Veterans Affairs, "Determinations Concerning Illnesses Discussed in National Academy," under "Multisymptom Illness."

17. Kilshaw, *Impotent Warriors*, 184.

18. Ibid., 183.

19. Ibid., 127.

20. See Ware, "Suffering and the Social Construction of Illness," note to p. 6. Ware writes that "the tendency in professional medicine to discount

the complaints of women means that gender must also be examined as part of an analysis of illness experience in chronic fatigue syndrome."

21. Timimi, "ADHD Is Best Understood as a Cultural Construct."

22. Ibid., 8–9.

23. Sax, *Boys Adrift*, 99.

24. Tyre, *Trouble with Boys*, 111.

25. Proctor and Schiebinger, "Agnotology," 6.

26. Zihlman, "Paleolithic Glass Ceiling," 100; Sperling, "Baboons with Briefcases," 16.

27. For one such argument, see Thornhill and Palmer, *Natural History of Rape*, 54.

28. Mattingly, *Well-Tempered Women*, chap. 3.

29. Logan, *"We Are Coming,"* 112.

30. Nye, "Medicine and Science," 76.

31. Mattingly, *Appropriate[Ing] Dress*, 92.

32. See Butler, *Gender Trouble;* Halberstam, *Female Masculinity.*

33. See Scott, *Risky Rhetoric,* 39.

34. See Romano and Dokoupil, "Men's Lib."

35. Hallenbeck, *Writing the Bicycle.*

36. Wang, "Inventing a Discourse of Resistance," 68.

37. On gender conservatism, see Johnson, *Gender and Rhetorical Space;* Sloop, *Disciplining Gender.*

38. Burke, *Permanence and Change;* Anderson, *Identity's Strategy.*

39. Butler, "Performative Acts," 519.

Bibliography

Abraham, Carolyn. "Is There a 'Geek' Syndrome?" *Globe and Mail* (Toronto), 19 October 2002. http://www.uoguelph.ca/oaar/G&M-2002-oct-19.html (accessed May 1, 2012).

Adams, Christina. *A Real Boy: A True Story of Autism, Early Intervention, and Recovery*. New York: Berkley, 2005.

Adams, Mark B., Garland E. Allen, and Sheila Faith Weiss. "Human Heredity and Politics: A Comparative Institutional Study of the Eugenics Record Office at Cold Spring Harbor (United States), the Kaiser Wilhelm Institute for Anthropology, Human Heredity, and Eugenics (Germany), and the Maxim Gorky Medical Genetics Institute (USSR)." *Osiris* 20, no. 1 (2005): 232–262.

"ADHD: Complementary/Alternative Treatments." Parenting.com. http://www.parenting.com/health-guide/adhd-attention-deficit-hyperactivity-disorder/complementary-alternative-treatments (accessed February 26, 2013).

Adversarial. Comment on "Wrong Asperger's Self-Diagnosis," *Wrong Planet.net,* July 9, 2005. http://www.wrongplanet.net/postp249281.html &highlight=#249281 (accessed May 30, 2011).

Ainsworth, Mary D. Salter, and Silvia M. Bell. "Attachment, Exploration, and Separation: Illustrated by the Behavior of One-Year-Olds in a Strange Situation," *Child Development* 41, no. 1 (1970): 49–67.

Alcoff, Linda Martín. "The Problem of Speaking for Others." *Cultural Critique* 20 (1991–1992): 5–32.

Alreck, Pamela L. "Commentary: A New Formula for Gendering Products and Brands." *Journal of Product and Brand Management* 3, no. 1 (1994): 6–18.

Alyric. "Katie Wright: Autism Speak's Liability," *A Touch of Alyricism,* February 22, 2009. http://alyric.blogspot.com/2009/02/katie-wright-autism -speaks-liability.html (accessed May 30, 2011).

American Association for the Study of the Feeble-Minded. "Report of the Committee on Classification of the Feeble-Minded." *Journal of Psycho-Asthenics* 15 (1910): 61–62. Hathi Trust Digital Library. http://hdl.handle.net .libproxy.lib.unc.edu/2027/njp.32101065978239 (accessed February 13, 2013).

American Psychiatric Association. "Autism Spectrum Disorder." In *Diagnostic and Statistical Manual of Mental Disorders,* 5th ed. Washington, DC: American Psychiatric Association, 2000. Psychiatry Online (accessed September 2, 2013).

———. "Pervasive Developmental Disorders." In *Diagnostic and Statistical Manual of Mental Disorders,* 4th ed., Text Revision. Washington, DC: American Psychiatric Association, 2000. Psychiatry Online (accessed September 2, 2013).

———. "Gender Dysphoria in Adolescents and Adults." In *Diagnostic and Statistical Manual of Mental Disorders,* 5th ed. Washington, DC: American Psychiatric Association, 2000. Psychiatry Online (accessed September 2, 2013).

———. "Gender Dysphoria in Children." In *Diagnostic and Statistical Manual of Mental Disorders,* 5th ed. Washington, DC: American Psychiatric Association, 2000. Psychiatry Online (accessed September 2, 2013).

Anderson, Dana. *Identity's Strategy: Rhetorical Selves in Conversion.* Columbia: University of South Carolina Press, 2007.

Angelik. "Gay with Asperger's," *WrongPlanet.net,* February 28, 2011. http:// www.wrongplanet.net/postt153364.html (accessed May 30, 2011).

Anthony, James. "An Experimental Approach to the Psychopathology of Childhood: Autism." *British Journal of Medical Psychology* 31, nos. 3–4 (1958): 211–225.

Apple, Rima D. *Perfect Motherhood: Science and Childrearing in America.* New Brunswick: Rutgers University Press, 2006.

Aristotle, *The Rhetoric and Poetics of Aristotle.* Translated by W. Rhys Roberts and Ingram Bywater. New York: Modern Library, 1984.

Arky, Beth. "'Touch' and Autism." *Child Mind Institute.* Last modified January 30, 2012. http://www.childmind.org/en/posts/articles/2012–1–31-fox-show -touch-mixed-response-autism-advocates (accessed February 22, 2013).

Arranga, Teri. "Autism and the Abdication of Responsibility." *Autism File USA* 31 (2009): 4.

Asperger, Hans. "Autistic Psychopathy in Childhood." In *Autism and Asperger Syndrome,* edited by Uta Frith, 37–92. Cambridge: Cambridge University Press, 1991.

"Autism Spectrum Disorders: At the Doctor." *Parenting.com*. http://www
.parenting.com/health-guide/autism-spectrum-disorders/doctor (accessed February 26, 2013).

Baggs, Amanda. "This Is Not the Post I Started out Writing," *Nico*, November
17, 2009. https://ballastexistenz.wordpress.com/2009/11/17/this-is-not
-the-post-i-started-out-writing/ (accessed May 30, 2011).

———. "Up in the Clouds and Down in the Valley: My Richness and Yours."
Disability Studies Quarterly 30, no. 1 (2010). http://dsq-sds.org/article/view/
1052/1238 (accessed February 24, 2013).

Ball, James. *Early Intervention and Autism: Real-Life Questions, Real-Life Answers.*
Arlington, TX: Future Horizons, 2008.

Barbeau, Elise B., Adrianna Mendrek, and Laurent Mottron. "Are Autistic
Traits Autistic?" *British Journal of Psychology* 100, no. 1 (2009): 23–28.

Baron-Cohen, Simon. *The Essential Difference: Male and Female Brains and the
Truth about Autism.* New York: Basic, 2003.

Baron-Cohen, Simon, Alan M. Leslie, and Uta Frith. "Does the Autistic Child
Have a Theory of Mind?" *Cognition* 21, no. 1 (1985): 37–46.

Bazelon, Emily. "What Autistic Girls Are Made Of." *New York Times*, August
5, 2007. http://www.nytimes.com/2007/08/05/magazine/05autism-t
.html (accessed May 30, 2011).

Bazerman, Charles. *Shaping Written Knowledge.* Madison: University of Wis-
consin Press, 1988.

BBC News. "Autism Link to 'Geek Genes.'" *BBC News Health*, August 14,
2002. http://news.bbc.cauk/2/hi/health/2192611.stm (accessed May 8,
2012).

———. "Sex I.D. Find out How Your Mind Works." *BBC News Science*. http://
www.bbc.co.uk/science/humanbody/sex/add_user.shtml (accessed May
30, 2011).

Beck, Ulrich. *Power in the Global Age: A New Global Political Economy.* Cambridge, UK; Malden, MA: Polity, 2005.

Bejerot, Susanne, Jonna M. Eriksson, Sabina Bonde, Kjell Carlström, Mats B.
Humble, and Elias Eriksson. "The Extreme Male Brain Revisited: Gender
Coherence in Adults with Autism Spectrum Disorder." *British Journal of
Psychiatry* (2012): 201:116–123. doi:10.1192/bjp.bp.111.097899.

Belmonte, Matthew K., Marie Gomot, and Simon Baron-Cohen. "Visual
Attention in Autism Families: 'Unaffected' Sibs Share Atypical Frontal
Activation." *Journal of Child Psychology and Psychiatry and Allied Disciplines*
51, no. 3 (2010): 259–276.

Benson, Paul Robert, Dave Daley, Kristie L. Karlof, and Dorothy Robison. "Assessing Expressed Emotion in Mothers of Children with Autism: The Au-
tism-Specific Five Minute Speech Sample." *Autism* 15, no. 1 (2011): 65–82.

Bernard, Sallie. "Remarks to the US House of Representatives Committee
on Government Reform Hearing, 'Mercury in Medicine: Are We Taking

Unnecessary Risks?'" July 18, 2000. http://www.whale.to/v/bernard.html (accessed February 22, 2013).

Bernard, S., A. Enayati, L. Redwood, H. Roger, and T. Binstock. "Autism: A Novel Form of Mercury Poisoning." *Medical Hypotheses* 56, no. 4 (2001): 462–471.

Bettelheim, Bruno. *The Empty Fortress: Infantile Autism and the Birth of the Self.* New York: Free Press, 1967.

Biklen, Douglas. *Autism and the Myth of the Person Alone.* New York: New York University Press, 2005.

Blastland, Michael. *The Only Boy in the World: A Father Explores the Mysteries of Autism.* New York: Marlowe, 2006.

Blaxill, Mark, and Dan Olmsted. *The Age of Autism: Mercury, Medicine, and a Man-Made Epidemic.* New York: MacMillan, 2010.

Bleuler, Eugen. *The Theory of Schizophrenic Negativism.* Translated by William A. White. New York: Journal of Nervous and Mental Disease Publishing Company, 1912.

Blum, Deborah. *Sex on the Brain: The Biological Differences Between Men and Women.* New York: Penguin, 1997.

Boehme, Julie [beadbrain, pseud.]. "Acceptance Is Not Giving Up," *Autism Co-Parent,* January 1, 2009. http://beadbrainautism.blogspot.com/2009/01/acceptance-is-not-giving-up.html (accessed May 30, 2011).

———. "An 'Autism Mom's' Open Letter to Jenny McCarthy," November 12, 2007. http://autism.about.com/b/2007/11/12/an-autism-moms-open -letter-to-jenny-mccarthy.htm (accessed February 15, 2013).

Boutot, E. Amanda "Fitting In: Tips for Promoting Acceptance and Friendships for Students with Autism Spectrum Disorders in Inclusive Classrooms." *Intervention in School and Clinic* 42, no. 3 (2007): 156–161.

Bowlby, John. *Child Care and the Growth of Love.* Baltimore: Penguin, 1953.

———. *Maternal Care and Mental Health.* Geneva: World Health Organization, 1952.

Bretherton, Inge. "The Origins of Attachment Theory: John Bowlby and Mary Ainsworth." *Developmental Psychology* 28, no. 5 (1992): 759–775.

Broderick, Alicia. "Autism as Rhetoric: Exploring Watershed Rhetorical Moments in Applied Behavior Analysis Discourse." *Disability Studies Quarterly* 31, no. 3 (2011). http://dsq-sds.org/article/view/1674/1597 (accessed February 23, 2013).

Broderick, Alicia A., and Ari Ne'eman. "Autism as Metaphor: Narrative and Counter-narrative." *International Journal of Inclusive Education* 12, nos. 5–6 (2008): 459–476.

Brothers, Joyce. "Males and Females Inhabit Separate Brain Hemispheres." *Star-Ledger* (Newark, NJ), November 9, 1997, 11.

Brown, Hannah. "Divorce After Autism: Going It Alone." *Today.com*, April 2, 2012. http://www.today.com/moms/divorce-after-autism-going-it-alone -624517 (accessed February 13, 2013).

Brownlow, Charlotte. "Presenting the Self: Negotiating a Label of Autism." *Journal of Intellectual & Developmental Disability* 35, no. 2 (2010): 14–21.

Buchanan, Lindal. *Regendering Delivery: The Fifth Canon and Antebellum Women Rhetors*. Carbondale: Southern Illinois University Press, 2005.

Bumiller, Kristin. "Quirky Citizens: Autism, Gender, and Reimagining Disability." *Signs* 33, no. 4 (2008): 967–991.

Burck, Gilbert. "The Boundless Age of the Computer." *Fortune*, March 1964, 100–111.

Burke, Kenneth. *Attitudes Toward History*. 3d ed. Berkeley: University of California Press, 1984.

———. *Counter-Statement*. 2d ed. Berkeley: University of California Press, 1968.

———. "Four Master Tropes." *Kenyon Review* 3, no. 4 (1941): 421–438.

———. *A Grammar of Motives*. Berkeley: University of California Press, 1969.

———. *Permanence and Change*. 3d ed. Berkeley: University of California Press, 1984.

———. "Persuasion, Identification, and Dialectical Symmetry." *Philosophy and Rhetoric* 39, no. 4 (2006): 333–339.

Burns, Dan E. *Saving Ben: A Father's Story of Autism*. Denton: University of North Texas Press, 2009.

Burt, Jules. "About." *HighHeelHike.com*. http:/www.highheelhike.com (accessed July 23, 2012).

Burton, Susan. "Ruining It for the Rest of Us." *This American Life*. Episode 370. http://www.thisamericanlife.org/radio-archives/episode/370/ruining -it-for-the-rest-of-us?act=1.

Bush, George H. W. Proclamation. "Decade of the Brain, 1990–1999, Proclamation 6158." *Federal Register* 55, no. 140 (1990): 29553.

Butler, Judith. *Bodies That Matter: On the Discursive Limits of Sex*. New York: Routledge, 1993.

———. *Gender Trouble: Feminism and the Subversion of Identity*. New York: Routledge, 1990.

———. "Performative Acts and Gender Constitution: An Essay in Phenomenology and Feminist Theory." *Theatre Journal* 40, no. 4 (1988): 519–631.

Calinescu, Matei. *Matthew's Enigma*. Translated by Angela Jianu. Bloomington: Indiana University Press, 2009.

Campbell, Karlyn Kohrs. *Man Cannot Speak for Her*. Vol. 1, *A Critical Study of Early Feminist Rhetoric*. New York: Greenwood, 1989.

Carey, Allison C. *On the Margins of Citizenship: Intellectual Disability and Civil Rights in Twentieth-Century America*. Philadelphia: Temple University Press, 2009.

Carlson, A. Cheree. *The Crimes of Womanhood: Defining Femininity in a Court of Law.* Urbana: University of Illinois Press, 2009.

———. "The Role of Character in Public Moral Argument: Henry Ward Beecher and the Brooklyn Scandal." *Quarterly Journal of Speech* 77, no. 1 (1991): 38–52.

Carlson, Licia. *The Faces of Intellectual Disability: Philosophical Reflections.* Bloomington: Indiana University Press, 2010.

Carmody, Dennis P., and Michael Lewis. "Regional White Matter Development in Children with Autism Spectrum Disorders." *Developmental Psychobiology* 52, no. 8 (2010): 755–763.

Carpenter, Rick. "Disability as Socio-Rhetorical Action: Towards a Genre-Based Approach." *Disability Studies Quarterly* 31, no. 3 (2011). http://dsq-sds .org/article/view/1666/1605 (accessed February 10, 2013).

Carr, David. "Film Version of Zuckerberg Divides Generations." *New York Times,* October 3, 2010, http://www.nytimes.com/2010/10/04/business/media/ 04carr.html (accessed February 23, 2013).

Carr, Nicholas. *The Shallows: What the Internet Is Doing to Our Brains.* New York: Norton, 2011.

Castel, Françoise. *The Psychiatric Society.* Edited by Robert Castel and Anne Lovell. Translated by Arthur Goldhammer. New York: Columbia University Press, 1982.

Castells, Manuel. *The Rise of the Network Society.* 2d ed. Oxford: Blackwell, 2000.

Catster29. "Anyone Else Here Not Interested in Relationships?" *WrongPlanet .net,* February 13, 2010. http://www.wrongplanet.net/postt119391.html (accessed February 23, 2013).

Centers for Disease Control. "Autism Spectrum Disorder—Data and Statistics." March 29, 2012. http://www.cdc.gov/NCBDDD/autism/data.html (accessed July 3, 2012).

———. "Concerns about Autism." June 26, 2012. http://www.cdc.gov/vaccine safety/Concerns/Autism/Index.html (accessed February 15, 2013).

———. "Possible Side-effects from Vaccines." August 29, 2012. http://www .cdc.gov/vaccines/vac-gen/side-effects.htm (accessed February 15, 2013).

———. "Vaccines and Immunizations." August 29, 2012. http://www.cdc .gov/vaccines/ (accessed February 15, 2013).

———. "Vaccines and Preventable Diseases." March 14, 2012. http://www .cdc.gov/vaccines/vpd-vac/default.htm (accessed February 15, 2013).

Charland, Maurice. "Constitutive Rhetoric: The Case of the *Peuple Québécois.*" *Quarterly Journal of Speech* 73, no. 2 (1987): 133–150.

Chew, Kristina. "Confessions of a Former Warrior Mom," *Blisstree,* September 24, 2008. http://blisstree.com/feel/confessions-of-a-former-warrior-mom/ (accessed February 25, 2013).

Chow, Sy-Miin, John D. Haltigan, and Daniel S. Messinger. "Dynamic Infant-Parent Affect Coupling During the Face-to-Face/Still-Face." *Emotion* 10, no. 1 (2010): 101–114.

Cicero, Marcus Tullius. *De Inventione*. Translated by H. M. Hubbell. Cambridge: Harvard University Press, 1976.

———. *Rhetorica Ad Herennium*. Translated by Harry Caplan. Cambridge: Harvard University Press, 1981.

Cintrón, Ralph. *Angels' Town: Chero Ways, Gang Life, and the Rhetorics of the Everyday*. Boston: Beacon, 1997.

Coates, L. "Famous People with Asperger Syndrome or Similar Autistic Traits." http://www.asperger-syndrome.me.uk/people.htm (accessed February 23, 2013).

CockneyRebel. Comment on "What Women Like Most in Fashion," *WrongPlanet.net*, April 9, 2011. http://www.wrongplanet.net/postt157411.html (accessed February 23, 2013).

Cohen-Rottenberg, Rachel [neshamaruach, pseud.]. Comment on "Do Some Aspies Have Lots of Empathy?" *WrongPlanet.net*, October 30, 2008. http://www.wrongplanet.net/postt81427.html (accessed February 23, 2013).

———. "The Intense World Syndrome Theory of Autism," *Journeys with Autism: Reports from Life on the Spectrum*, June 2, 2009. http://www.journeyswithautism.com/2009/06/02/intense-world-syndrome/ (accessed May 30, 2011).

Coleman, James. "Facial Expressions of Emotion." *Psychological Monographs* 63, no. 1 (1949): 1–36.

Collins, Paul. *Banvard's Folly: Thirteen Tales of People Who Didn't Change the World*. New York: Picador, 2001.

———. *The Book of William: How Shakespeare's First Folio Conquered the World*. New York: Bloomsbury, 2009.

———. *Not Even Wrong: Adventures in Autism*. New York: Bloomsbury, 2004.

———. *The Trouble with Tom: The Strange Afterlife and Times of Thomas Paine*. New York: Bloomsbury, 2005.

Committee on Gulf War and Health. "Gulf War and Health: Volume 8: Update of Health Effects of Serving in the Gulf War." Washington, DC: National Academies Press, 2010.

Condit, Celeste. "How Bad Science Stays That Way: Brain Sex, Demarcation, and the Status of Truth in the Rhetoric of Science." *Rhetoric Society Quarterly* 26, no. 4 (1996): 83–109.

Connell, Raewyn W. *Gender and Power: Society, the Person, and Sexual Politics*. Cambridge, UK: Polity, 1987.

Connell, R. W., and James W. Messerschmidt. "Hegemonic Masculinity: Rethinking the Concept." *Gender and Society* 19, no. 6 (2005): 829–859.

Cooper, Marianne. "Being the Go-to Guy: Fatherhood, Masculinity, and the Organization of Work in Silicon Valley." *Qualitative Sociology* 23, no. 4 (2000): 379–405.

Cory, Herbert Ellsworth. "The Interactions of Beauty and Truth." *Journal of Philosophy* 22, no. 15 (1925): 393–402.

"Could an Epidural Have Contributed to My Son's Autism?" *Recovering Nicholas,* January 2, 2008. http://recoveringnicholas.com/2008/01/02/could-an-epidural-have-contributed-to-my-sons-autism/ (accessed February 23, 2012).

Coulter, Harris L., and Barbara Loe Fisher. *A Shot in the Dark: Why the P in the DPT Vaccine May Be Hazardous to Your Child's Health.* New York: Penguin, 1991.

Cox, Lauren. "Doctor Who Started Vaccine, Autism Debate in Ethics Row." *ABC News.com,* February 1, 2010. http://abcnews.go.com/Health/AutismNews/autism-british-doctor-andrew-wakefield-started-autism-vaccine-debate-ethics-debacle/story?id=9713197 (accessed February 23, 2013).

Crable, Bryan. "Rhetoric, Anxiety, and Character Armor: Burke's Interactional Rhetoric of Identity." *Western Journal of Communication* 70, no. 1 (2006): 1–22.

Cross, Susan E., and Laura Madson. "Models of the Self: Self-Construals and Gender." *Psychological Bulletin* 122, no. 1 (1997): 5–37.

Cullen-Powell, L. A., J. H. Barlow, and D. Cushway. "Exploring a Massage Intervention for Parents and Their Children with Autism: The Implications for Bonding and Attachment." *Journal of Child Health Care* 9, no. 4 (2005): 245–255.

Cutler, Eustacia. *A Thorn in My Pocket: Temple Grandin's Mother Tells the Family Story.* Arlington, TX: Future Horizons, 2004.

Davies, P., S. Chapman, and J. Leask. "Antivaccination Activists on the World Wide Web." *Archives of Disease in Childhood* 87, no. 1 (2002): 22–25.

Davis, Bill. *Breaking Autism's Barriers: A Father's Story.* London: Jessica Kingsley, 2001.

Davis, D. Diane. *Breaking up (at) Totality: A Rhetoric of Laughter.* Carbondale: Southern Illinois University Press, 2000.

Dawson, Michelle. "Bettelheim's Worst Crime," September 9, 2003. http://www.sentex.net/~nexus23/md_01.html (accessed February 23, 2012).

———. "The Misbehaviour of Behaviourists: Ethical Challenges to the Autism-ABA Industry," January 18, 2004. http://www.sentex.net/~nexus23/naa_aba.html (accessed February 23, 2012).

Dean, Jennifer. "Social Education Aim of Center's New Girls Group." *Riverside Press-Enterprise,* July 24, 2010, C8.

Democratic Leadership Council. "Health Care Quality: Consumer Empowerment," May 16, 1997. http://www.dlc.org/ndol_ci3ce9.html?kaid=111&subid=138&contentid=638 (accessed February 25, 2013).

DesLauriers, Austin M., and Carole F. Carlson. *Your Child Is Asleep: Early Infantile Autism.* Homewood, IL: Dorsey, 1969.

De Vries, Annelou L. C., Ilse L. J. Noens, Peggy T. Cohen-Kettenis, Ina A. van Berckelaer-Onnes, and Theo A. Doreleijers. "Autism Spectrum Disorders in Gender Dysphoric Children and Adolescents." *Journal of Autism and Developmental Disorders* 40, no. 8 (2010): 930–936.

Dominus, Susan. "The Crash and Burn of an Autism Guru." *New York Times Sunday Magazine,* April 20, 2011. http://www.nytimes.com/2011/04/24/magazine/mag-24Autism-t.html (accessed February 24, 2013).

Donnell, Emerson B. *Dads and Autism: How to Stay in the Game.* Califon, NJ: Altruist, 2008.

Douglas, Susan J., and Meredith W. Michaels. *The Mommy Myth.* New York: Free Press, 2004.

Drucker, Peter F. *The Effective Executive.* New York: Harper Collins, 2009.

Duckworth, John D., and Patrice M. Buzzanell. "Constructing Work-Life Balance and Fatherhood: Men's Framing of the Meanings of Both Work and Family." *Communication Studies* 60, no. 5 (2009): 558–573.

Duffy, Felice M. "Twenty-Seven Years Post Title IX: Why Gender Equity in College Athletics Does Not Exist." *Quinnipac Law Review* 19, no. 1 (2000): 67–124.

Duncan, Stuart. "Autism, Fathers, the Future and Denial," *Autism from a Father's Point of View,* February 16, 2013. http://www.stuartduncan.name/autism/autism-fathers-the-future-and-denial/ (accessed February 20, 2013).

———. "Father Friday-@Autismfather," *ManyHatsMommy,* April 22, 2011. http://manyhatsmommy.com/2011/04/22/father-friday-autismfather/ (accessed February 23, 2013).

———. "The Hardest Part of Autism—Looking to the Future," *Autism from a Father's Point of View,* June 4, 2010. http://www.stuartduncan.name/autism/the-hardest-part-of-autism-looking-to-the-future/ (accessed February 23, 2013).

Durack, Katherine T. "Gender, Technology, and the History of Technical Communication." In *Central Works in Technical Communication,* edited by Johndan Johnson-Eilola and Stuart A. Selber, 35–43. New York: Oxford University Press, 2004.

Dymond, Rosalind F. "A Scale for the Measurement of Empathic Ability." *Journal of Consulting Psychology* 13, no. 2 (1949): 127–133.

Eapen, Valsamma. "Genetic Basis of Autism: Is There a Way Forward?" *Current Opinion in Psychiatry* 24, no. 3 (2011): 226–236.

Ehrenreich, Barbara, and Deidre English. *For Her Own Good: Two Centuries of the Experts' Advice to Women.* 2d ed. New York: Anchor, 1978, 2005.

Eisenberg, Leon. "The Fathers of Autistic Children." *American Journal of Orthopsychiatry* 27, no. 4 (1957): 715–724.

Eisenberg, Nancy, and Randy Lennon. "Sex Differences in Empathy and Related Capacities." *Psychological Bulletin* 94, no. 1 (1983): 100–131.

Electrifiedspam. Comment on "Wrong Asperger's Self Diagnosis," *Wrong Planet.net*, May 14, 2010. http://www.wrongplanet.net/postxf14980-0-75.html (accessed May 30, 2011).

Elks, Martin A. "Believing Is Seeing: Visual Conventions in Barr's Classification of the Feeble-Minded." *Mental Retardation* 42, no. 5 (2004): 371–382.

———. "Visual Indictment: A Contextual Analysis of the Kallikak Family Photographs." *Mental Retardation* 43, no. 4 (2005): 268–280.

Elmer-DeWitt, Philip, and Christopher John Farley. "Diagnosing Bill Gates." *Time*, January 24, 1994, 25.

Erasmus, Desiderius. *On Copia of Words and Ideas: De Utraque Verborum Ac Rerum Copia*. Translated by Herbert Rix and Donald King. Milwaukee: Marquette University Press, 1999. eBook Collection (EBSCOhost), *EBSCOhost* (accessed February 22, 2013).

Ernsperger, Lori, and Danielle Wendel. *Girls Under the Umbrella of Autism Spectrum Disorders: Practical Solutions for Addressing Everyday Challenges*. Shawnee Mission, KS: Autism Asperger, 2007.

Eugenics Record Office, *Bulletin No. 10A: Report of the Committee to Study and to Report on the Best Practical Means of Cutting Off the Defective Germ-Plasm in the American Population. I. The Scope Of The Committees Work*. Long Island, NY: Cold Spring, 1914. National Information Resource on Ethics and Human Genetics. http://dnapatents.georgetown.edu/resources/Bulletin10A.pdf (accessed February 10, 2013).

Eyal, Gil. *The Autism Matrix*. New York: Polity, 2010.

Farrell, Thomas B. *Norms of Rhetorical Culture*. New Haven: Yale University Press, 1993.

Fausto-Sterling, Anne. "The Bare Bones of Sex: Part 1—Sex and Gender." *Signs* 30, no. 2 (2005): 1491–1527.

———. "The Dynamic Development of Gender Variability." *Journal of Homosexuality* 59, no. 3 (2012): 398–421.

Federal Interagency Forum on Child and Family Statistics. *America's Children in Brief: Key National Indicators of Well-Being, 2012*. Washignton, DC: United States Government Printing Office, 2012.

Fine, Cordelia. *Delusions of Gender: How Our Minds, Society, and Neurosexism Create Difference*. New York: Norton, 2010.

Fisher, Barbara Loe. "Vaccines: Finding a Balance Between Public Safety and Personal Choice." U.S. House Government Reform Committee, August 3, 1999. http://www.whale.to/vaccines/fisher.html (accessed February 23, 2013).

Fitzpatrick, Michael. "The Ghost of the Refrigerator Mother." *Spiked Online,* November 24, 2008. http://www.spiked-online.com/index.php/site/article/5961 (accessed February 23, 2013).

———. "An Open Letter to Gordon Brown." *Spiked Online,* April 14, 2009. http://www.spiked-online.com/index.php?/site/article/6541 (accessed February 23, 2013).

Flatow, Ira. "A Conversation with Temple Grandin," 20 January, 2006, *NPR Science Friday,* http://www.npr.org/templates/story/story.php?storyId" =5165123 (accessed February 23, 2013).

Florance, Cheri L. *A Boy Beyond Reach.* London: Simon and Schuster, 2004.

Flynn, Elizabeth A. "Composing as a Woman." *College Composition and Communication* 39, no. 4 (1988): 423–435.

Foss, Karen A., and Sonja K. Foss. *Women Speak: The Eloquence of Women's Lives.* Prospect Heights, IL: Waveland, 1991.

Foucault, Michel. *Power/Knowledge: Selected Interviews & Other Writings, 1972–1977,* edited by Colin Gordon. Translated by Colin Gordon, Leo Marshall, John Mepham, and Kate Soper. New York: Pantheon, 1980.

———. "Technologies of the Self." In *Technologies of the Self: A Seminar with Michel Foucault,* edited by Luther H. Martin, Huck Gutman, and Patrick H. Hutton, 16–49. Amherst: University of Massachusetts Press, 1988.

Francis, Becky. "Gender Monoglossia, Gender Heteroglossia: The Potential of Bakhtin's Work for Re-Conceptualising Gender." *Journal of Gender Studies* 21, no. 1 (2012): 1–15.

Freedman, Brian H., Luther G. Kalb, Benjamin Zablotsky, and Elizabeth A. Stuart. "Relationship Status among Parents of Children with Autism Spectrum Disorders: A Population-Based Study." *Journal of Autism and Developmental Disorders* 42, no. 4 (2012): 539–548.

Friedan, Betty. *The Feminine Mystique.* New York: Norton, 1963.

Frye, Northrop. *The Anatomy of Criticism: Four Essays.* Princeton: Princeton University Press, 1957.

Gallucci, Gerard, Florence Hackerman, and Chester W. Schmidt. Jr. "Gender Identity Disorder in an Adult Male with Asperger's Syndrome." *Sexuality and Disability* 23, no. 1 (2005): 35–40.

Gallup, Jr., Gordon G. "Chimpanzees: Self-Recognition." *Science* 167, no. 3914 (1970): 86–87.

Gardner, Howard. *Frames of Mind: The Theory of Multiple Intelligences.* New York: Basic, 2011.

Gardner, R. Allen, and Beatrix T. Gardner. *The Structure of Learning: From Sign Stimuli to Sign Language.* Mahwah, N.J.: Erlbaum, 1998.

Garland-Thomson, Rosemarie. "Feminist Disability Studies." *Signs* 30, no. 2 (2005): 1557–1587.

Garloch, Karen. "Living the Autistic Life." *Charlotte Observer*, October 19, 2010. http://www.charlotteobserver.com/2010/10/19/1771354/living-the-autistic-life.html (accessed February 25, 2013).

Genosko, Gary. "Natures and Cultures of Cuteness." *Invisible Culture: An Electronic Journal for Visual Culture*, no. 9 (2005). www.rochester.edu/in_visible_culture/Issue_9/issue9_genosko.pdf (accessed February 25, 2013).

Gentleman, Amelia. "Attention-Grabbing Antics for Autism." *Guardian*, April 6, 2010. http://www.guardian.co.uk/society/2010/apr/07/autism-campaign-wonderbra-posters (accessed February 23, 2013).

Gershick, Thomas J., and Adam S. Miller. "Coming to Terms: Masculinity and Physical Disability." In *Men's Health and Illness: Gender, Power and the Body*, edited by Donald Sabo and David Frederick Gordon, 183–204. Thousand Oaks, CA: Sage, 1995.

Glenn, Cheryl. *Rhetoric Retold: Regendering the Tradition from Antiquity Through the Renaissance*. Carbondale: Southern Illinois University Press, 1997.

Goddard, Henry Herbert. *The Kallikak Family: A Study in the Heredity of Feeble-Mindedness*. New York: MacMillan, 1912. http://digitalarchive.gsu.edu/cgi/viewcontent.cgi?article=1006&context=col_facpub (accessed February 25, 2013).

Goldfarb, William. "The Effects of Early Institutional Care on Adolescent Personality." *Journal of Experimental Education* 12, no. 2 (1943): 106–129.

Goleman, Daniel. *Emotional Intelligence*. New York: Bantam, 1995.

———. *Social Intelligence: The New Science of Human Relationships*. New York: Random House Digital, 2006.

———. *Working with Emotional Intelligence*. New York: Bantam, 1998.

Golubock, Susan. "Different on the Inside." In *Women from Another Planet? Our Lives in the Universe of Autism*, edited by Jean Kearns Miller, 63–72. Fairfield, CA: AuthorHouse, 2003.

Goodman, Ellen. "Worlds Apart in Public Discourse, the Sexes Return to Separate and Unequal." *Pittsburgh Post-Gazette*, March 15, 1995, B-3.

Goodnight, G. Thomas, and Sandy Green. "Rhetoric, Risk, and Markets: The Dot-Com Bubble." *Quarterly Journal of Speech* 96, no. 2 (2010): 115–140.

Goodspeed, Helen Crandall, Esther R. Mason, and Elizabeth L. Woods. *Child Care and Guidance*. Philadelphia: Lippincott, 1948. http://catalog.hathitrust.org/Record/006796848 (accessed February 25, 2013).

Grandin, Temple. *Emergence: Labeled Autistic*. With Margaret M. Scariano. Novato, CA: Arena Press, 1986.

———. "For Me, a Good Career Gave Life Meaning." In *Asperger's and Girls*. 147–150. Arlington, TX: Future Horizons, 2006.

———. *Thinking in Pictures: My Life with Autism*. 2d ed. New York: Vintage, 2006.

————. *The Way I See It: A Personal Look at Autism & Asperger's*. 2d ed. Arlington, TX: Future Horizons, 2011.

Gray, John. *Men Are from Mars, Women Are from Venus: A Practical Guide for Improving Communication and Getting What You Want in Your Relationships*. New York: Harper Collins, 1992.

Greenfeld, Josh. *A Child Called Noah: A Family Journey Continued*. New York: Holt, Rinehart and Winston, 1972.

————. *A Place for Noah*. New York: Holt, Rinehart and Winston, 1978.

Greenfeld, Karl Taro. "The Autism Debate: Who's Afraid of Jenny McCarthy?" *Time*, February 25, 2010. http://www.time.com/time/magazine/article/0,9171,1968100,00.html (accessed February 25, 2013).

Greg. "A Lot Like the Movie Adam," *About.com*, "Autism Spectrum Disorders," March 1, 2010. http://autism.about.com/u/sty/adultsaspergersyndrom1/selfdxst/A-Lot-Like-the-Movie-Adam.htm (accessed May 30, 2011).

Grinker, Roy Richard. *Unstrange Minds: Remapping the World of Autism*. New York: Basic, 2007.

Gross, Alan G. *The Rhetoric of Science*. 2d ed. Cambridge: Harvard University Press, 1996.

Guilford, J. P. "An Experiment in Learning to Read Facial Expression." *Journal of Abnormal and Social Psychology* 24 (1929): 191–202.

Hackett, Allison Jane. "Risk, Its Perception and the Media: The MMR Controversy." *Community Practitioner* 81, no. 7 (2008): 22–25.

Hacking, Ian. "How We Have Been Learning to Talk About Autism: A Role for Stories." *Metaphilosophy* 40, nos. 3–4 (2009): 499–516.

————. *Rewriting the Soul: Multiple Personality and the Sciences of Memory*. Princeton: Princeton University Press, 1995.

————. *The Social Construction of What?* Cambridge: Harvard University Press, 1999.

Halberstam, Judith. *Female Masculinity*. Durham, NC: Duke University Press, 1998.

Hall, Elaine. "Divorce and Autism: Avoidable or Inevitable?" *The Huffington Post*, April 30, 2012. http://www.huffingtonpost.com/elaine-hall/divorce-and-autism_b_1460498.html (accessed February 20, 2013).

Hallenbeck, Sarah O. Writing the Bicycle: Women, Rhetoric, and Technology in Late Nineteenth-Century America. PhD diss., University of North Carolina, Chapel Hill, 2009.

Haltigan, John, Naomi V. Ekas, Ronald Seifer, and Daniel S. Messinger. "Brief Report: Attachment Security in Infants at-Risk for Autism Spectrum Disorders." *Journal of Autism and Developmental Disorders* 41 no.7 (2010): 962–967.

Hambrook, David, Kate Tchanturia, Ulrike Schmidt, Tamara Russell, and Janet Treasure. "Empathy, Systemizing, and Autistic Traits in Anorexia Nervosa: A Pilot Study." *British Journal of Clinical Psychology* 47, no. 3 (2008): 335–339.

Hamilton, Alexander. *A Treatise of Midwifery*. Edinburgh: Charles Elliot, 1785. Eighteenth Century Collections Online, pt. 1, Gale/Cengage Learning.

Hammerback, John. "Creating the New Person: The Rhetoric of Reconstitutive Discourse." *Rhetoric Review* 20, nos. 1/2 (2001): 18–22.

Haraway, Donna. *Modest_Witness@Second_Millenium.Femaleman©_Meets_Onco-mouse™*. New York: Routledge, 1997.

Harding, Sandra. *Whose Science? Whose Knowledge? Thinking from Women's Lives*. Ithaca, NY: Cornell University Press, 1991.

HarraArial. Comment on "Do U Care About Fashion?" *WrongPlanet.net*, September 26, 2010. http://www.wrongplanet.net/postxf134818-0-15.html (accessed February 25, 2013).

Harris, Joseph. "How I Feel Today," *Another Autism Dad*, August 26, 2010. http://anotherautismdad.blogspot.com/2010/08/how-i-feel-today.html (accessed February 20, 2013).

———. "Insha'Allah," *Another Autism Dad*, January 10, 2011, http://another autismdad.blogspot.com/2011/01/inshaallah.html (accessed January 10, 2011).

———. "What Defines Me (A Discussion About Labels)," *Another Autism Dad*, March 2, 2011. http://anotherautismdad.blogspot.com/2011/03/what -defines-me-discussion-about-labels.html (accessed February 20, 2013).

Harrison, Kimberly. "Rhetorical Rehearsals: The Construction of Ethos in Confederate Women's Civil War Diaries." *Rhetoric Review* 22, no. 3 (2003): 243–263.

Hartley, Sigan L., Erin T. Barker, Marsha Malick Seltzer, Frank Floyd, Jan Greenberg, Gael Orsmond, and Daniel Bolt. "The Relative Risk and Timing of Divorce in Families of Children with an Autism Spectrum Disorder." *Journal of Family Psychology* 24, no. 4 (2010): 449–457.

Hasian, Marouf, Jr. "Judicial Rhetoric in a Fragmentary World: 'Character' and Storytelling in the Leo Frank Case." *Communication Monographs* 64, no. 3 (1997): 250–269.

Hays, Sharon. *The Cultural Contradictions of Motherhood*. New Haven: Yale University Press, 1996.

Heilker, Paul, and Melanie Yergeau. "Autism and Rhetoric." *College English* 73, no. 5 (2011): 485–497.

Heller, Jacob. *The Vaccine Narrative*. Nashville: Vanderbilt University Press, 2008.

Henderson, Sara, and Alan Peterson. "Introduction: Consumerism in Health Care." In *Consuming Health: The Commodification of Health Care*, edited by Sara Henderson and Alan Peterson, 1–10. New York: Routledge, 2002.

Herbert, Martha R. "Autism: A Brain Disorder, or a Disorder That Affects the Brain?" *Clinical Neuropsychiatry* 2, no. 6 (2005): 354–379.

———. "Large Brains in Autism: The Challenge of Pervasive Abnormality." *Neuroscientist* 11, no. 5 (2005): 417–440.

Herndl, Diane Price. *Invalid Women: Figuring Feminine Illness in American Fiction and Culture, 1840–1940.* Chapel Hill: University of North Carolina Press, 1993.

Hilgartner, Stephen. *Science on Stage: Expert Advice as Public Drama.* Stanford: Stanford University Press, 2000.

Hird, Myra J. "Gender's Nature: Intersexuality, Transsexualism and the Sex/Gender Binary." *Feminist Theory* 1, no. 3 (2000): 347–364.

Hobart, Charles W., and Nancy Fahlberg. "The Measurement of Empathy." *American Journal of Sociology* 70, no. 5 (1965): 595–603.

Hoekstra, Rosa A., Meike Bartels, Catharina J. H. Verweij, and Dorret I. Bomsma. "Heritability of Autistic Traits in the General Population." *Archives of Pediatric and Adolescent Medicine* 161, no. 4 (2007): 372–377.

Hogan, Robert. "Development of an Empathy Scale." *Journal of Consulting and Clinical Psychology* 33, no. 3 (1969): 307–316.

Hopefaithbelieve. "Jenny's New Book," *Recovering Boys,* March 31, 2009. http://recoveringty.blogspot.com/2009/03/jennys-new-book.html (accessed May 30, 2011).

"How Male or Female Is Your Brain?" *The Guardian.* http://www.guardian.co.uk/life/news/page/0,12983,937443,00.html (accessed February 25, 2013).

Howe, Louise Kapp. *Pink Collar Workers: Inside the World of Women's Work.* New York: Putnam, 1977.

Hume, Kathryn. "Romance: A Perdurable Pattern." *College English* 36, no. 2 (1974): 129–146.

Hyland, Ken. *Hedging in Scientific Research Articles.* Amsterdam; Philadelphia: John Benjamins,1998.

Ickes, William, Paul R. Gesn, and Tiffany Graham. "Gender Differences in Empathic Accuracy: Differential Ability or Differential Motivation?" *Personal Relationships* 7, no. 1 (2000): 95–109.

Iland, Lisa. "Girl to Girl: Advice on Friendship, Bullying, and Fitting In." In *Asperger's and Girls.* 33–63. Arlington, TX: Future Horizons, 2006.

Innes, Sherrie A. "Who Remembers Sabrina? Intelligence, Gender, and the Media." In *Geek Chic: Smart Women in Popular Culture,* edited by Sherrie A. Innes, 1–9. New York: Palgrave Macmillan, 2007.

"Is Anybody Here Who Has Autism and Is Transgender?" May 27, 2009, *WrongPlanet.net,* May 27, 2009. http://www.wrongplanet.net/postt99839.html (accessed February 25, 2013).

Jack, Jordynn. *Science on the Home Front: American Women Scientists in World War II.* Champaign-Urbana: University of Illinois Press, 2009.

Jameson, Fredric. "Magical Narratives: Romance as Genre." *New Literary History* 7, no. 1 (1975): 135–163.

Jarratt, Susan. *Rereading the Sophists: Classical Rhetoric Refigured.* Carbondale: Southern Illinois University Press, 1991.

Jensen, Robin E. *Dirty Words: The Rhetoric of Public Sex Education, 1870–1924.* Urbana: University of Illinois Press, 2010.

Jentsch, Ernst. "On the Psychology of the Uncanny (1906)." *Angelaki* 2, no. 1 (1995): 7–16.

Jessa. Comment on "Why Cant I Get Diagnosed," *WrongPlanet.net,* September 25, 2009. http://www.wrongplanet.net/postp2398750.html &highlight=#2398750 (accessed February 25, 2013).

Johnson, Carol, and Julia Crowder. *Autism: From Tragedy to Triumph.* Wellesley, MA: Branden, 1994.

Johnson, Nan. *Gender and Rhetorical Space in American Life, 1866–1910.* Carbondale: Southern Illinois University Press, 2002.

Jordan, Mark D. *Recruiting Young Love: How Christians Talk About Homosexuality.* Chicago: University of Chicago Press, 2011.

Jou, Roger J., Nancy J. Minshew, Matcheri S. Keshavan, and Antonio Y. Hardan. "Cortical Gyrification in Autistic and Asperger Disorders: A Preliminary Magnetic Resonance Imaging Study." *Journal of Child Neurology* 25, no. 12 (2010): 1462–1467.

K, Bill. Comment on "Is Autism Toughest on Dads? Your Opinion Requested," *About.com,* "Autism Spectrum Disorders," December 3, 2008. http://autism.about.com/b/2008/12/03/is-autism-toughest-on-dads-your-opinion-requested.htm (accessed February 25, 2013).

Kalb, Claudia. "Stomping Through a Medical Minefield." *Newsweek* October 25, 2008, 62.

Kanner, Leo. "Autistic Disturbances of Affective Contact." *Nervous Child* 2 (1943): 217–250.

———. "Convenience and Convention in Rearing Children." *Scientific Monthly* 59, no. 4 (1944): 301–306.

———. "Early Infantile Autism." *Journal of Pediatrics* 25, no. 3 (1944): 211–217.

———. "Problems of Nosology and Psychodynamics of Early Infantile Autism." *American Journal of Orthopsychiatry* 19 (1949): 416–426.

Kanner, Leo, and Leon Eisenberg. "Early Infantile Autism, 1943–1955." In *Psychopathology: A Source Book,* edited by Charles F. Read, 3–14. Cambridge: Harvard University Press, 1958. Originally published in *The American Journal of Orthopsychiatry* 25 (1956): 556–566.

Karafyllis, Nicole C., and Gotlind Ulshöfer. "Introduction: Intelligent Emotions and Sexualized Brains—Discourses, Scientific Models, and Their Interdependencies." In *Sexualized Brains: Scientific Modelling of Emotional Intelligence from a Cultural Perspective,* edited by Nicole C. Karafyllis and Gotlind Ulshöfer, 1–49. Cambridge, MA: MIT Press, 2008.

Keller, Evelyn Fox. "The Gender/Science System, or, Is Sex to Gender as Nature Is to Science?" In *The Science Studies Reader,* edited by Mario Biagioli, 234–242. New York: Routledge, 1999.

———. *Reflections on Gender and Science.* New Haven: Yale University Press, 1985.

Keränen, Lisa. *Scientific Characters: Rhetoric, Politics, and Trust in Breast Cancer Research.* Tuscaloosa: University of Alabama Press, 2010.

Kerber, Linda. "The Republican Mother: Women and the Enlightenment— an American Perspective." *American Quarterly* 28, no. 2 (1976): 187–205.

Kerlin, Isaac Newton. *The Mind Unveiled; or, a Brief History of Twenty-Two Imbecile Children.* Philadelphia, U. Hunt & Son, 1858. Archive.org. http://archive .org/details/mindunveiledorbrookerl (accessed February 23, 2013).

Kiesler, Sara, Lee Sproull, and Jacquelynne S. Eccles. "Pool Halls, Chips, and War Games: Women in the Culture of Computing." *Psychology of Women Quarterly* 9, no. 4 (1985): 451–462.

Kilshaw, Susie. *Impotent Warriors: Gulf War Syndrome, Vulnerability and Masculinity.* New York: Berghahn, 2009.

Kirk, Stuart A., and Herb Kutchins. *The Selling of DSM: The Rhetoric of Science in Psychiatry.* New York: Aldine de Gruyter, 1992.

Kittay, Eva Feder. *Love's Labor: Essays on Women, Equality, and Dependency.* New York: Routledge, 1999.

Klein, Kristi J. K., and Sara D. Hodges. "Gender Differences, Motivation, and Empathic Accuracy: When It Pays to Understand." *Personal and Social Psychology Bulletin* 27, no. 6 (2001): 720–730.

Klein, Melanie. *The Selected Melanie Klein.* Edited by Juliet Mitchell. New York: Simon and Schuster, 1987.

K.M.R. "Vaccination Debate," *Justin's Recovery Wish,* May 21, 2009. http:// justinsrecoverywish.blogspot.com/2009/05/vaccination-debate.html (accessed July 2, 2012).

Kraemer, Bernd, Aba Delsignore, Ronnie Gundelfinger, Ulrich Schnyder, and Urs Hepp. "Comorbidity of Asperger Syndrome and Gender Identity Disorder." *European Child and Adolescent Psychiatry* 14, no. 5 (2005): 292–296.

Ladd-Taylor, Molly. *Mother-Work: Women, Child Welfare, and the State, 1890– 1930.* Urbana: University of Illinois Press, 1994.

Ladyrain. Comment on "AS Women and Special Interests," *WrongPlanet .net,* August 26, 2010. http://www.wrongplanet.net/postt135988.html (accessed February 26, 2013).

Landén, M., and P. Rasmussen. "Gender Identity Disorder in a Girl with Autism—a Case Report." *European Child and Adolescent Psychiatry* 6, no. 3 (1997): 170–173.

Langfeld, Herbert Sidney. "The Judgment of Emotions from Facial Expressions." *Journal of Abnormal Psychology* 13, no. 3 (1918): 172–184.

Largent, Mark A. *Breeding Contempt: The History of Coerced Sterilization in the United States.* New Brunswick: Rutgers University Press, 2008.

Lay, Mary M. *The Rhetoric of Midwifery: Gender, Knowledge, and Power.* New Brunswick: Rutgers University Press, 2000.

Lewiecki-Wilson, Cynthia. "Rethinking Rhetoric Through Mental Disabilities." *Rhetoric Review* 22, no. 2 (2003): 156–67.

Light, Jennifer S. "When Computers Were Women." *Technology and Culture* 40, no. 3 (1999): 455–483.

Lindsay. "Gender Variance in Autism: How Much of It Is Just Sensory?" *Autist's Corner,* August 12, 2008. http://autistscorner.blogspot.com/2008/08/gender-variance-in-autism-how-much-of.html (accessed February 26, 2013).

Linton, Simi. *Claiming Disability: Knowledge and Identity.* Kindle ed. New York: New York University Press, 1998.

Lobmaier, Janek S., Reiner Sprengelmeyer, Ben Wiffen, and David I. Perrett. "Female and Male Responses to Cuteness, Age and Emotion in Infant Faces." *Evolution and Human Behavior* 31 (2010): 16–21.

Logan, Shirley Wilson. *"We Are Coming": The Persuasive Discourse of Nineteenth-Century Black Women.* Carbondale: Southern Illinois University Press, 1999.

Lorber, Judith. *Gender and the Social Construction of Illness* 2nd ed. Lanham, MD: Altamira, 2002.

Lori. "Autism Vaccination Connection," April 24, 2012. http://www.dylansautismrecovery.blogspot.com/2012/04/autism-vaccination-connection.html (accessed February 26, 2013).

———. "Run Toward the Hope," September 11, 2011. http://www.dylansautismrecovery.blogspot.com/2011/09/run-toward-hope.html (accessed February 26, 2013).

———. "Who Do You Trust?" October 7, 2011. http://www.dylansautismrecovery.blogspot.com/2011/10/who-do-you-trust.html (accessed February 26, 2013).

Lou. "Emotional Reactions to Autism," *Our Life with Diego,* December 20, 2010. http://ourlifewithdiego.blogspot.com/2010/12/our-life-as-special-needs-family.html (accessed February 20, 2013).

Lovaas, O. Ivar. "Behavioral Treatment And Normal Educational And Intellectual Functioning in Young Autistic Children." *Journal of Consulting and Clinical Psychology* 55, no. 1 (1987): 3–9.

Lucaites, John Louis, and Celeste Michelle Condit. "Re-constructing Narrative Theory: A Functional Perspective." *Journal of Communication* 35, no. 4 (1985): 90–108.

Lucy. "About," *Alex's Journey out of Autism.* http://alexautismoysurecuperacion.wordpress.com/about/ (accessed February 26, 2013).

———. "Cease Therapy," *Alex's Journey out of Autism.* http://alexautismoysurecuperacion.wordpress.com/cease-therapy/ (accessed February 26, 2013).

Lynch, John Alexander. *What Are Stem Cells? Definitions at the Intersection of Science and Politics.* Kindle ed. Tuscaloosa: University of Alabama Press, 2011.

Maccoby, Eleanor E., ed. *The Development of Sex Differences.* Stanford: Stanford University Press, 1966.

Macrakis, Kristie. *Surviving the Swastika: Scientific Research in Nazi Germany.* Oxford: Oxford University Press, 1993.

Malacrida, Claudia. *Cold Comfort: Mothers, Professionals, and Attention Deficit Disorder.* Toronto: University of Toronto Press, 2003.

Mandell, David S., John Listerud, Susan E. Levy, and Jennifer A. Pinto-Martin. "Race Differences in the Age at Diagnosis among Medicaid-Eligible Children with Autism." *Journal of the American Academy of Child and Adolescent Psychiatry* 41, no. 12 (2002): 1447–1453.

MangoChutney. Comment on "AS Women and Special Interests," *Wrong Planet.net,* September 4, 2010. http://www.wrongplanet.net/postt135988.html (accessed February 26, 2013).

Markram, Henry, Tania Rinaldi, and Kamila Markram. "The Intense World Syndrome—an Alternative Hypothesis for Autism." *Frontiers in Neuroscience* 1, no. 1 (2007): 77–96.

Martin, Emily. "The Egg and the Sperm: How Science Has Constructed a Romance Based on Stereotypical Male-Female Roles." *Signs* 16, no. 3 (1991): 485–501.

Maryann. "They Get Me So Mad—Biomedical Works!" *Matthew's Puzzle,* June 8, 2012. http://www.matthewspuzzle.com/2012/06/biomedical.html (accessed February 26, 2013).

Mattingly, Carol. *Appropriate[Ing] Dress: Women's Rhetorical Style in Nineteenth-Century America.* Carbondale: Southern Illinois University Press, 2002.

———. *Well-Tempered Women: Nineteenth Century Temperance Rhetoric.* Carbondale: Southern Illinois University Press, 1998.

Maurice, Catherine. *Let Me Hear Your Voice: A Family's Triumph over Autism.* New York: Ballantine, 1994.

McCarthy, Jenny. *Louder Than Words: A Mother's Journey in Healing Autism.* New York: Penguin, 2008.

———. Speech at "Green Our Vaccines" Rally, June 4, 2008, *YouTube,* June 4, 2008. http://www.youtube.com/watch?v=ob1fycxZIwI (accessed February 26, 2013).

McCarthy, Lucille Parkinson, and Joan Page Gerring. "Revising Psychiatry's Charter Document." *Written Communication* 11, no. 2 (1994): 147–192.

McClure, Kevin R., and Kristine M. Cabral. "Clarifying Ambiguity and the Undecidable: A Comparison in Burkean and Derridean Thought." *Qualitative Research Reports in Communication* 10, no. 1 (2009): 72–80.

McDonagh, Patrick. *Idiocy: A Cultural History.* Liverpool: Liverpool University Press, 2008.

McGee, Micki. "Neurodiversity." *Contexts* 11, no. 3 (2012): 12–13.

McGeer, Victoria. "The Thought and Talk of Individuals with Autism: Reflections on Ian Hacking." *Metaphilosophy* 40, nos. 3–4 (2009): 517–530.

McNeil, Donald G., Jr. "Book Is Rallying Resistance to the Antivaccine Crusade." *New York Times*, January 12, 2009.

McVeigh, Brian. "Commodifying Affection, Authority and Gender in the Everyday Objects of Japan." *Journal of Material Culture* 1, no. 3 (1996): 291–312.

Meddin, Jay. "Chimpanzees, Symbols, and the Reflective Self." *Social Psychology Quarterly* 42, no. 2 (1979): 99–109.

Medical Hypotheses. "Aims and Scope." http://www.journals.elsevier.com/medical-hypotheses/ (accessed February 26, 2013).

Messner, Michael. "Masculinities and Athletic Careers." *Gender and Society* 3, no. 1 (1989): 71–88.

Meyerding, Jane. "Growing up Genderless." In *Women from Another Planet? Our Lives in the Universe of Autism*, edited by Jean Kearns Miller, 157–70. Fairfield, CA: AuthorHouse, 2003.

Meyerowitz, Joanne. *How Sex Changed: A History of Transsexuality in the United States*. Cambridge: Harvard University Press, 2002.

"Milestones—12–18 Months." *Recovering Nicholas*, October 7, 2007. http://recoveringnicholas.com/2007/10/07/milestones-12–18-months/ (accessed February 26, 2013).

Miller, Carolyn R. "Aristotle's 'Special Topics' in Rhetorical Practice and Pedagogy." *Rhetoric Society Quarterly* 17, no. 1 (1987): 61–70.

———. "The Aristotelian *Topos*: Hunting for Novelty." In *Rereading Aristotle's Rhetoric*, edited by Alan G. Gross and Arthur E. Walzer, 130–146. Carbondale: Southern Illinois University Press, 2000.

Miller, Jean Kearns. "Differences." In *Women from Another Planet? Our Lives in the Universe of Autism*, edited by Jean Kearns Miller, 19–60. Fairfield, CA: AuthorHouse, 2003.

———. "Mommie Wyrdest." In *Women from Another Planet? Our Lives in the Universe of Autism*, edited by Jean Kearns Miller, 191–196. Fairfield, CA: AuthorHouse, 2003.

Minshew, Nancy J., and Thomas A. Keller. "The Nature of Brain Dysfunction in Autism: Functional Brain Imaging Studies." *Current Opinion in Neurology* 23, no. 2 (2010): 124–130.

Moir, Anne, and David Jessel. *Brain Sex: The Real Difference Between Men and Women*. New York: Dell, 1991.

Mooney, Chris, and Sheril Kirshenbaum. *Unscientific America: How Scientific Illiteracy Threatens Our Future*. New York: Basic, 2009.

Morgenstern, Joe. "Social Network: Password Is Perfection." *Wall Street Journal*, October 1, 2010, D3.

Morini, Cristina. "The Feminization of Labour in Cognitive Capitalism." *Feminist Review*, 87 (2007): 40–59.

Morse, John Lovett. *The Care and Feeding of Children.* Cambridge: Harvard University Press, 1914.

Moss, Gloria. *Gender, Design and Marketing: How Gender Drives Our Perception of Design and Marketing.* Farnham, UK: Gower, 2009.

Moulier Boutang, Yann. *Cognitive Capitalism.* Cambridge, UK: Polity, 2011.

Movius, Kate. "Opening the Window: When a Child Is Diagnosed with Autism, Everything Changes, Including a Mother's Sense of Herself." *Los Angeles Magazine,* September 1, 2010, 134.

Mudry, Jessica J. *Measured Meals: Nutrition in America.* Albany: SUNY Press, 2009.

Mukaddes, N. M. "Gender Identity Problems in Autistic Children." *Child: Care, Health and Development* 28, no. 6 (2002): 529–532.

Mulkerrins, Jane. "Temple Grandin: Autistic Woman Who Became Leading Animal Behaviour Expert." *Daily Mail (UK),* March 26, 2011. http://www.daily mail.co.uk/home/you/article-1368868/Temple-Grandin-Autistic-woman -leading-animal-behaviour-expert.html (accessed February 26, 2013).

Muncer, Steven J., and Jonathan Ling. "Psychometric Analysis of the Empathy Quotient (EQ) Scale." *Personality and Individual Differences* 40, no. 6 (2006): 1111–1119.

Murray, Stuart. *Autism.* New York: Routledge, 2011.

———. *Representing Autism: Culture, Narrative, Fascination.* Liverpool: Liverpool University Press, 2008.

Myers, Jennifer McIlwee. "Aspie Do's and Don'ts: Dating, Relationships, and Marriage." In *Asperger's and Girls,* 89–116. Arlington, TX: Future Horizons, 2006.

Nadesan, Majia Holmer. *Constructing Autism: Unravelling the Truth and Understanding the Social.* New York: Routledge, 2005.

Nash, J. Madeleine, and Amy Bonesteel. "The Geek Syndrome." May 6, 2002, *Time .com.* http://www.time.com/time/magazine/article/0,9171,1002365,00 .html (accessed February 26, 2013).

Neal, Matt. "Review: *The Social Network.*" *The Standard,* November 1, 2010. http://www.standard.net.au/story/786471/review-the-social-network/ (accessed February 26, 2013).

Nekowafer. Comment on "AS Women and Special Interests," *WrongPlanet.net,* September 23, 2010. http://www.wrongplanet.net/postxf135988-0-15 .html (accessed February 26, 2013).

Neumärker, K.-J. "Leo Kanner: His Years in Berlin, 1906–1924: The Roots of Autistic Disorder." *History of Psychiatry* 14, no. 2 (2003): 205–218.

Newport, Jerry, Mary Newport, and Teresa Bolick. *Autism-Asperger's and Sexuality: Puberty and Beyond.* Arlington, TX: Future Horizons, 2002.

Nichols, Clarina Howard. "The Responsibilities of Woman." In *Man Cannot Speak for Her.* Vol. 2, *Key Texts of the Early Feminists,* edited by Karlyn Kohrs Campbell, 123–44. New York: Greenwood, 1989.

Nichols, Shana, Gina Marie Moravcik, and Samara Pulver Tetenbaum. *Girls Growing up on the Autism Spectrum: What Parents and Professionals Should Know About the Pre-Teen and Teenage Years*. London: Jessica Kingsley, 2009.

Novella, Steven. "August Is Vaccine Awareness Month—Who Knew?" *Neurologica*, August 20, 2009. http://theness.com/neurologicablog/index .php/august-is-vaccine-awareness-month-who-knew/ (accessed February 26, 2013).

Nye, Robert A. "Medicine and Science as Masculine 'Fields of Honor.'" *Osiris* 12, no. 1 (1997): 60–79.

Offit, Paul A. *Autism's False Prophets: Bad Science, Risky Medicine, and the Search for a Cure*. New York: Columbia University Press, 2008.

———. *Deadly Choices*. New York: Basic, 2010.

Oldenburg, Christopher. "Rethinking Reagan's Closing Statement: The Rhetorical Anecdote, Synecdoche, and Ethotic Argument." *Conference Papers— National Communication Association* (January 2009): 1. *Communication & Mass Media Complete*, EBSCOhost (accessed February 26, 2013).

Oldenziel, Ruth. *Making Technology Masculine: Men, Women and Modern Machines in America, 1870–1945*. Amsterdam: Amsterdam University Press, 1999.

O'Mara, Peggy. "Your Child's First Healer." *Mothering.com*, no. 52 (January/ February 2009). http://www.mothering.com/your-childs-first-healer (accessed May 30, 2011).

Oppenheim, David, Nina Koren-Karie, Smadar Dolev, and Nurit Yirmiya. "Maternal Insightfulness and Resolution of the Diagnosis Are Associated with Secure Attachment in Preschoolers with Autism Spectrum Disorders." *Child Development* 80, no. 2 (2009): 519–527.

Oppenheim, Rosalind C. "They Said Our Child Was Hopeless." *Saturday Evening Post*, June 17, 1961, 23, 56, 58.

Orac. "The Anti-Vaccine Movement: Is It Too Late for Scientists to Bridge the Gap Between Evidence and Fear?" *Respectful Insolence*, May 27, 2009. http:// scienceblogs.com/insolence/2009/05/the_anti-vaccine_movement _is_it_too_late.php (accessed February 26, 2013).

Osborne, Lawrence. *American Normal: The Hidden World of Asperger Syndrome*. New York: Copernicus, 2002.

Parikh, Rahul K. "Judging Autism." *Salon.com*, February 19, 2009. http://www .salon.com/env/vital_signs/2009/02/19/autism_and_vaccines/index. html (accessed February 26, 2013).

Park, Clara Claiborne. "Elly and the Right to Education." *Phi Delta Kappan* 55, no. 8 (1974): 535–537.

———. *The Siege: The First Eight Years of an Autistic Child*. Boston: Little, Brown, 1967.

Peete, Rodney, and Danelle Morton. *Not My Boy! A Father, a Son, and One Family's Journey with Autism*. New York: Hyperion, 2010.

Pellicano, Elizabeth, and Marc Stears. "Bridging Autism, Science and Society: Moving Toward an Ethically Informed Approach to Autism Research." *Autism Research* 4, no. 4 (2011): 271–282.

Perelman, Chaïm, and Lucie Olbrechts-Tyteca. *The New Rhetoric: A Treatise on Argumentation*. Notre Dame: University of Notre Dame Press, 1969.

Phelan, James. "Imagining a Sequel to Wayne C. Booth's *The Rhetoric of Fiction*—Or a Dialogue on Dialogue." *Comparative Critical Studies* 7, nos. 2–3 (2010): 243–255.

Pho, Kevin. "Losing the Anti-Vaccine Fight, and What We Should Do Next," *KevinMD*, June 8, 2009. http://www.kevinmd.com/blog/2009/06/losing -the-anti-vaccine-fight-and-what-we-should-do-next.html (accessed February 26, 2013).

Pinkbowtiepumps. Comment on "Fashion Style?" *WrongPlanet.net*, March 1, 2010. http://www.wrongplanet.net/postx118354–15–0.html (accessed February 26, 2013).

Pollak, Richard. *The Creation of Doctor B: A Biography of Bruno Bettelheim*. New York: Touchstone, 1998.

Pollock, Della. *Telling Bodies Performing Birth: Everyday Narratives of Childbirth*. New York: Columbia University Press, 1999.

Premack, David, and Guy Woodruff. "Does the Chimpanzee Have a Theory of Mind?" *Behavioral and Brain Sciences* 1, no. 4 (1978): 515–526.

Price, Margaret. *Mad at School: Rhetorics of Mental Disability and Academic Life*. Ann Arbor: University of Michigan Press, 2011.

Prince-Hughes, Dawn. *Songs of the Gorilla Nation: My Journey Through Autism*. New York: Harmony, 2004.

Proctor, Robert, and Londa Schiebinger. "Agnotology: A Missing Term to Describe the Study of the 'Cultural Production of Ignorance,'" In *Agnotology: The Making and Unmaking of Ignorance*, edited by Robert Proctor and Londa Schiebinger, 1–33. Stanford: Stanford University Press, 2008.

Professor. "Divorce and the Special Needs Parent." *The Thinking Mom's Revolution*, January 21, 2013. http://thinkingmomsrevolution.com/divorce -and-the-special-needs-parent (accessed February 26, 2013).

Pryal, Katie Rose Guest. "The Genre of the Mood Memoir and the Ethos of Psychiatric Disability." *Rhetoric Society Quarterly* 40, no. 5 (2010): 479–501.

Puttenham, George. *The Arte of English Poesie*. 1590. Charlottesville, VA: University of Virginia Library, 1994. http://etext.virginia.edu/toc/modeng/ public/PutPoes.html (accessed February 26, 2013).

Quintilian. 2006. *Institutes of Oratory*. Edited by Lee Honeycutt. Translated by John Selby Watson. http://rhetoric.eserver.org/quintilian/ (accessed February 26, 2013).

Rabin, Nathan. "The Bataan Death March of Whimsy Case File #1: Elizabethtown," *The AV Club*, January 25, 2007. http://www.avclub.com/articles/

the-bataan-death-march-of-whimsy-case-file-1-eliza,15577/ (accessed February 26, 2013).

Rafinski, Karen. "Brain Scans Offer Picture of Mental Illnesses." *Miami Herald,* April 27, 1997, 1A.

Rattus. Comment on "What Does It Mean to You to Be a Woman With Asperger's?" November 9, 2012. http://www.wrongplanet.net/postt214911 .html (accessed February 22, 2013).

Redwood, Lyn. "Testimony Before the Subcommittee on Human Rights and Wellness Committee on Government Reform U.S. House of Representatives." http://www.whale.to/a/redwood.pdf (accessed February 26, 2013).

Reuters. "It's True: Sexes Don't Think Alike; Study Finds Male and Female Brain Activity Differs in Areas Considered Important to Emotions, Perceptions." *Rocky Mountain News,* January 27, 1995, 41A.

Reviews of *A Child's Journey out of Autism.* http://www.amazon.com/Childs-Journey-out-Autism-Familys/product-reviews/1402218389/ (accessed 13 February, 2013).

Reviews of *A Real Boy: A True Story of Autism.* http://www.amazon.com/ Real-Boy-Autism-Intervention-Recovery/product-reviews/B000EPFVE6/ ref=dp_top_cm_cr_acr_txt?showViewpoints=1 (accessed February 13, 2013).

Revolutionrocknroll. Comment on "What Does It Mean to You to Be a Woman with Asperger's?" November 9, 2012. http://www.wrongplanet. net/postt214911.html (accessed February 22, 2013).

Reynolds, Shelley Hendrix. "Genie in a Bottle." *The Huffington Post,* July 24, 2007. http://www.huffingtonpost.com/shelley-hendrix-reynolds/genie -in-a-bottle_1_b_57628.html (accessed February 20, 2013).

Ribble, Margarethe A. "Clinical Studies of Instinctive Reactions in New Born Babies." *American Journal of Psychiatry* 95, no. 1 (1938): 149–160.

———. "Disorganizing Factors of Infant Personality." *American Journal of Psychiatry* 98, no. 3 (1941): 459–463.

Rimland, Bernard. *Infantile Autism: The Syndrome and Its Implications for a Neural Theory of Behavior.* New York: Appleton-Century-Crofts, 1964.

Rimland, Bernard, and Sidney M. Baker. "Brief Report: Approaches to the Development of Effective Treatments for Autism." *Journal of Autism and Developmental Disorders* 26, no. 2 (1996): 237–241.

Rocque, Bill. "Science Fictions: Figuring Autism as Threat And Mystery in Medico-Therapeutic Literature." *Disability Studies Quarterly* 30, no. 1 (2010). http://dsq-sds.org/article/view/1064/1231 (accessed February 10, 2013).

Rogers, Sally J. "Developmental Regression in Autism Spectrum Disorders." *Mental Retardation and Developmental Disabilities Research Reviews* 10, no. 2 (2004): 139–143.

Romano, Andrew, and Tony Dokoupil. "Men's Lib." *Newsweek,* September 20, 2010. http://www.thedailybeast.com/newsweek/2010/09/20/why-we-need -to-reimagine-masculinity.html (accessed February 26, 2013).

Ronen, Gabriel M., Brandon Meaney, Bernard Dan, Fritz Zimprich, Walter Stögmann, and Wolfgang Neugebauer. "From Eugenic Euthanasia to Habilitation of Disabled Children: Andreas Rett's Contribution." *Journal of Child Neurology* 24, no. 1 (2009): 115–127.

Rose, Nikolas S. *The Politics of Life Itself: Biomedicine, Power, and Subjectivity in the Twenty-First Century.* Princeton: Princeton University Press, 2007.

Rossi, Alice. "Women in Science: Why So Few?" *Science* 148, no. 3674 (1965): 1196–1202.

Rossiter, Margaret W. *Women Scientists in America: Struggles and Strategies to 1940.* Baltimore: Johns Hopkins University Press, 1982.

Rubin, Gayle. "The Traffic in Women: Notes on the 'Political Economy' of Sex," in *Toward an Anthropology of Women,* edited by Rayna Reiter, 157–210. New York: Monthly Review Press, 1975.

Rudy, Lisa Jo. "Helping Autism Dads Connect," *About.com,* "Autism Spectrum Disorders," June 14, 2008. http://autism.about.com/b/2008/06/14/ helping-autism-dads-connect.htm (accessed February 26, 2013).

———. "How to Get Dad More Involved," *About.com,* "Autism Spectrum Disorders," March 13, 2009. http://autism.about.com/od/family issuesandautism/f/fatherinvolved.htm (accessed February 26, 2013).

———. "Is Autism Toughest on Dads? Your Opinion Requested," *About.com,* "Autism Spectrum Disorders," December 3, 2008. http://autism.about .com/b/2008/12/03/is-autism-toughest-on-dads-your-opinion-requested .htm (accessed February 26, 2013).

Rwinter001. "What Made Me Suspect I Have Asperger Syndrome," *About.com,* "Autism Spectrum Disorders," January 2, 2009. http://autism.about.com/u/sty/ adultsasperger'syndrom1/selfdxst/My-Self-Diagnosis.htm (accessed February 26, 2013).

Sacks, Oliver. "An Anthropologist on Mars." *New Yorker,* December 27, 1993, 106–125.

SafeMinds, "Executive Board," *SafeMinds.org,* February 14, 2013, http:// www.safeminds.org/about/executive-board.html.

Salovey, Peter, and John D. Mayer. "Emotional Intelligence." *Imagination, Cognition and Personality* 9, no.3 (1989–1990): 185–211.

Sam. "Horrible Generalizations," Review of *Girls Growing Up on the Autism Spectrum,* August 15, 2010. http://www.amazon.com/Girls-Growing-Autism-Spectrum -Professionals/product-reviews/1843108550 (accessed February 26, 2013).

Sarrett, Jennifer C. "Trapped Children: Popular Images of Children with Autism in the 1960s and 2000s." *Journal of Medical Humanities* 32, no. 2 (2011): 141–153.

Sax, Leonard. *Boys Adrift: The Five Factors Driving the Growing Epidemic of Unmotivated Boys and Underachieving Young Men.* New York: Basic, 2007.

Schiebinger, Londa. *Nature's Body: Gender in the Making of Modern Science.* Boston: Beacon, 1993.

Schmuhl, Hans-Walter. *The Kaiser Wilhelm Institute for Anthropology, Human Heredity, and Eugenics, 1927–1945: Crossing Boundaries.* Boston: Springer, 2008.

Schumann, Cynthia M., Cinnamon S. Bloss, Cynthia Carter Barnes, Graham M. Wideman, Ruth A. Carper, Natacha Akshoomoff, Karen Pierce, et al. "Longitudinal Magnetic Resonance Imaging Study of Cortical Development Through Early Childhood in Autism." *Journal of Neuroscience* 30, no. 12 (2010): 4419–4427.

Schwarze, Steven. "Environmental Melodrama." *Quarterly Journal of Speech* 92, no. 3 (2006): 239–261.

Scott, J. Blake. *Risky Rhetoric: AIDS and the Cultural Practices of HIV Testing.* Carbondale: Southern Illinois University Press, 2003.

Seabrook, John. "E-Mail from Bill." *New Yorker*, January 10, 1994, 48–52, 54–61.

Segal, Judy. *Health and the Rhetoric of Medicine.* Carbondale: Southern Illinois University Press, 2005.

Seskin, Lynn, Eileen Feliciano, Gil Tippy, Ruby Yedloutschnig, Mark K. Sossin, and Anastasia Yasik. "Attachment and Autism: Parental Attachment Representations and Relational Behaviors in the Parent-Child Dyad." *Journal of Abnormal Child Psychology* 38, no. 7 (2010): 949–960.

Severson, Katherine DeMaria, Denise Jodlowski, and James Arnt Aune. "Bruno Bettelheim, Autism, and the Rhetoric of Scientific Authority." In *Autism and Representation*, edited by Mark Osteen, 65–77. New York: Routledge, 2007.

Shapin, Steven, and Simon Schaffer. *Leviathan and the Air-Pump: Hobbes, Boyle and the Experimental Life.* Princeton: Princeton University Press, 1985.

Shapiro, Joseph P. "Disability Rights as Civil Rights: The Struggle for Recognition." In *The Disabled, the Media, and the Information Age*, edited by Jack A. Nelson, 59–67. Westport, CT: Greenwood, 1994.

Shea, Elizabeth Parthenia. *How the Gene Got Its Groove: Figurative Language, Science, and the Rhetoric of the Real.* Albany: SUNY Press, 2008.

Shiva. "Gender Identity," *Biodiverse Resistance*, December 31, 2007. http://biodiverseresistance.blogspot.com/2007/12/gender-identity.html (accessed February 26, 2013).

Sholf. Comment on "Extreme Male Brain Hypothesis," *WrongPlanet.net*, June 27, 2008. http://www.wrongplanet.net/postxf70120-0-0.html&sid=08a6 8dd33c48c6ac9b5cf5a56384f441 (accessed February 26, 2013).

Showalter, Elaine. *Hystories: Hysterical Epidemics and Modern Culture.* New York: Columbia University Press, 1997.

Siebers, Tobin. *Disability Theory.* Ann Arbor: University of Michigan Press, 2008.

Siegfried, Tom. "Female Brain Structurally Different from Male Brain." *New Haven Register*, December 20, 1990.

Silberman, Steve. "The Geek Syndrome." *Wired,* December 2001. http://www.wired.com/wired/archive/9.12/aspergers_pr.html (accessed February 26, 2013).

Silverman, Chloe. *Understanding Autism: Parents, Doctors, and the History of a Disorder.* Princeton: Princeton University Press, 2012.

Simpson, David E., dir. *Refrigerator Mothers.* Kartemquin Films, 2002.

Singer, Judy. "Foreword: Travels in Parallel Space: An Invitation." In *Women from Another Planet? Our Lives in the Universe of Autism,* edited by Jean Kearns Miller, xi–xvi. Fairfield, CA: AuthorHouse, 2003.

Skuse, David H. "Is Autism Really a Coherent Syndrome in Boys, or Girls?" *British Journal of Psychology* 100, no. 1 (2009): 33–37.

Sleeping Chrysalid. "Coexistence of Gender Variance and Autism," *Laura's Playground,* December 9, 2010. http://www.lauras-playground.com/forums/index.php?showtopic=8865&st=20 (accessed February 26, 2013).

Sloop, John M. *Disciplining Gender: Rhetorics of Sex Identity in Contemporary U.S. Culture.* Amherst: University of Massachusetts Press, 2004.

Smith, James A., Annette Braunack-Mayer, Gary Wittert, and Megan Warin. "'I've Been Independent for So Damn Long!': Independence, Masculinity and Aging in a Help Seeking Context." *Journal of Aging Studies* 21, no. 4 (2007): 325–335.

Sontag, Susan. *Illness as Metaphor and Aids and Its Metaphors.* New York: Picador, 2001.

Sørensen, Knut H., and Anne-Jorunn Berg. "Genderization of Technology Among Norwegian Engineering Students." *Acta Sociologica* 30, no. 2 (1987): 151–171.

Soulières, Isabelle, Michelle Dawson, Morton Ann Gernsbacher, and Laurent Mottron. "The Level and Nature of Autistic Intelligence II: What About Asperger Syndrome?" *PLoS ONE* 6, no. 9 (2011): e25372. doi:10.1371/journal.pone.0025372.

Specter, Michael. *Denialism: How Irrational Thinking Hinders Scientific Progress, Harms the Planet, and Threatens Our Lives.* New York: Penguin, 2009.

Sperling, Susan. "Baboons with Briefcases: Feminism, Functionalism, and Sociobiology in the Evolution of Primate Gender." *Signs* 17, no. 1 (1991): 1–27.

Sprengelmeyer, R., D. I. Perrett, E. C. Fagan, R. E. Cornwell, J. S. Lobmaier, A. Sprengelmeyer, H. B. M. Aasheim, et al., "The Cutest Little Baby Face: A Hormonal Link to Sensitivity to Cuteness in Infant Faces." *Psychological Science* 20, no. 2 (2009): 149–154.

Sragow, Michael. "Fear, Self-Loathing, and Facebook." *Baltimore Sun*, September 30, 2010.

Stehli, Annabel. *The Sound of a Miracle: A Child's Triumph over Autism.* New York: Doubleday, 1991.

Stevens, Dana. "Joyless Dweeb," *Slate.com*, October 3, 2010. http://www .slate.com/id/2269091/ (accessed February 26, 2013).

Stevenson, Jennifer L., Bev Harp, and Morton Ann Gernsbacher. "Infantilizing Autism." *Disability Studies Quarterly* 31, no. 3 (2011). http://dsq-sds. org/article/view/1675/1596 (accessed September 2, 2013).

Tamano, Adel. "How My Autistic Son Taught Me Fatherhood." *Phillipine Star (Manila)*, June 20, 2010.

Tammet, Daniel. *Born on a Blue Day: A Memoir of Asperger's and an Extraordinary Mind.* London: Hodder & Stoughton, 2006.

Tannen, Deborah. *You Just Don't Understand: Women and Men in Conversation.* New York: Ballantine, 1991.

Tate, Ryan. "The Tech Industry's Asperger's Problem: Affliction or Insult?" *Gawker,* March 1, 2012. http://gawker.com/5885196/the-tech-industrys-asperger-problem-affliction-or-insult (accessed February 26, 2013).

Tateno, Masaru, Yukie Tateno, and Toshikazu Saito. "Comorbid Childhood Gender Identity Disorder in a Boy with Asperger Syndrome." *Psychiatry and Clinical Neurosciences* 62, no. 2 (2008): 238.

"That Woman in Gray Flannel: A Debate." *New York Times,* February 12, 1956, SM114.

The Third Glance. "On (A)sexuality," *The Third Glance,* January 3, 2013. http://thethirdglance.wordpress.com/2012/01/03/on-asexuality/ (accessed February 22, 2013).

Thevenerablecortex. "Of Sex and Loneliness," *Voxcorvegis,* January 6, 2013. http://voxcorvegis.wordpress.com/2013/01/06/of-sex-and-loneliness/ (accessed February 22, 2013).

Thorndike, E. L. "Intelligence and Its Uses." *Harper's Magazine,* December 1919, 227–235.

Thornhill, Randy, and Craig T. Palmer. *A Natural History of Rape: Biological Bases of Sexual Coercion.* Cambridge, MA: MIT Press, 2001.

Timimi, Sami. "ADHD Is Best Understood as a Cultural Construct." *British Journal of Psychiatry* 184, no. 1 (2004): 8–9.

Titchener, Edward Bradford. *Lectures on the Experimental Psychology of the Thought-Processes.* New York: MacMillan, 1909.

Titchkosky, Tanya. *Reading and Writing Disability Differently: The Textured Life of Embodiment.* Toronto: University of Toronto Press, 2007.

Tolchin, Martin. "Vacations from Parenthood?" *New York Times,* November 13, 1960, SM106.

Tommey, Polly, and Teri Arranga. "Autism Mothers Unite Worldwide." *Autism File USA* 33 (2009): 57.

Tonn, Mari Boor. "Militant Motherhood: Labor's Mary Harris "Mother" Jones." *Quarterly Journal of Speech* 82, no. 1 (1996): 1–21.

Trent, James W. *Inventing the Feeble Mind: A History of Mental Retardation in the United States.* Berkeley: University of California Press, 1994.

Turkle, Sherry. *Alone Together: Why We Expect More from Technology and Less from Each Other*. New York: Basic, 2011.

Tustin, Frances. "Revised Understandings of Psychogenic Autism." *International Journal of Psychoanalysis* 72, no. 4 (1991): 585–591.

Tyre, Peg. *The Trouble with Boys: A Surprising Report Card on Our Sons, Their Problems at School, and What Parents and Educators Must Do*. New York: Three Rivers, 2009.

UnderINK. Comment on "AS Women and Special Interests," *WrongPlanet .net*, September 24, 2010. http://www.wrongplanet.net/postt135988.html (accessed February 26, 2013).

United States Department of Education, Office of Special Education and Rehabilitative Services. "History: Twenty-Five Years of Progress in Educating Children with Disabilities Through IDEA." Washington, D.C.: United States Department of Education, 2007.

United States Department of Veterans Affairs. "Determinations Concerning Illnesses Discussed in National Academy Reports on Gulf War and Health, Volumes 4 and 8." *Federal Register* 76, no. 72 (2011): 21099–21107. http://www.gpo.gov/fdsys/pkg/FR-2011-04-14/html/2011-8937.htm.

———. "Gulf War Veterans' Illnesses," September 5, 2013. http://www.publichealth.va.gov/exposures/gulfwar/.

Urban, Wilbur M. "The Knowledge of Other Minds and the Problem of Meaning and Value." *Philosophical Review* 26, no. 3 (1917): 274–296.

Vivian, Amanda Forest. "From June 2009," *I'm Somewhere Else*, April 7, 2011. http://adeepercountry.blogspot.com/2011/04/from-june-2009.html (accessed February 26, 2013).

———. "Geekazoid," *I'm Somewhere Else*, October 13, 2009. http://adeepercountry.blogspot.com/2009/10/geekazoid.html (accessed February 26, 2013).

———. "I'm a Fake Person," *I'm Somewhere Else*, October 20, 2009. http://adeepercountry.blogspot.com/2009/10/im-fake-person.html (accessed February 26, 2013).

———. "I'm So Butch I Wear Nightgowns," *I'm Somewhere Else*, November 25, 2009. http://adeepercountry.blogspot.com/2009/11/im-so-butch-i-wear-nightgowns.html (accessed February 26, 2013).

Wakefield, A. J., S. H. Murch, A. Anthony, J. Linnell, D. M. Casson, M. Malik, M. Berelowitz, et al. "Ileal-Lymphoid-Nodular Hyperplasia, Non-Specific Colitis, and Pervasive Developmental Disorder in Children." *Lancet* 351, no. 9103 (1998): 637–641.

Wang, Bo. *Inventing a Discourse of Resistance: Rhetorical Women in Early Twentieth-Century China*. PhD diss., University of Arizona, 2005.

Ware, Norma C. "Suffering and the Social Construction of Illness: The Delegitimation of Illness Experience in Chronic Fatigue Syndrome." *Medical Anthropology Quarterly* 6, no. 4 (1992): 347–361.

Weinstein, Neil D., Abbie Kwitel, Kevin D. McCaul, Renee E. Magnan, Meg Gerrard, and Frederick X. Gibbons. "Risk Perceptions: Assessment and Relationship to Influenza Vaccination." *Health Psychology* 26, no. 2 (2007): 146–151.

Welch, Martha G., and Mary Ellen Mark. *Holding Time.* New York: Simon & Schuster, 1989.

West, Candace, and Don H. Zimmerman. "Doing Gender." *Gender & Society* 1, no. 2 (1987): 125–151.

Weston, Kath. *Gender in Real Time: Power and Transience in a Visual Age.* New York: Routledge, 2002.

"What I Believed Caused My Son's Autism," *Recovering Ty,* May 24, 2008. http://recoveringty.blogspot.com/2008/05/what-i-believed-caused-my -sons autism.html (accessed July 2, 2012).

Wheelwright, S., S. Baron-Cohen, N. Goldenfeld, J. Delaney, D. Fine, R. Smith, L. Weil, and A. Wakabayashi. "Predicting Autism Spectrum Quotient (AQ) from the Systemizing Quotient-Revised (SQ-R) and Empathy Quotient (EQ)." *Brain Research* 1079, no. 1 (2006): 47–56.

Whiffen, Leeann. *A Child's Journey out of Autism: One Family's Story of Living in Hope and Finding a Cure.* Naperville, IL: Sourcebooks, 2009.

Whirlingmind. "So, I Don't Collect Toy Dinosaurs or Stamps . . .," *Wrong Planet.net,* August 7, 2012. http://www.wrongplanet.net/postt206036.html (accessed Feburary 22, 2013).

Williams, Donna. "Being a Gay Man in a Womans Body," *Donna Williams Blog,* June 30, 2009. http://blog.donnawilliams.net/2009/06/30/being-a-gay -man-in-a-womans-body/ (accessed Feburary 26, 2013).

———. *Everyday Heaven: Journeys Beyond the Stereotypes of Autism.* London: Jessica Kingsley, 2004.

———. "Face Blindness in Autism and Beyond," *Donna Williams Blog,* April 2, 2006. http://blog.donnawilliams.net/2006/04/02/face-blindness/ (accessed Feburary 26, 2013).

———. *Nobody Nowhere: The Extraordinary Autobiography of an Autistic.* New York: Avon, 1992.

Williams, Patricia Gail, Anna Mary Allard, and Lonnie Sears. "Case Study: Cross-Gender Preoccupations in Two Male Children with Autism." *Journal of Autism and Developmental Disorders* 26, no. 6 (1996): 635–642.

Wilson, Daniel J. "Fighting Polio Like a Man: Intersections of Masculinity, Disability, and Aging." *Gendering Disability,* edited by Bonnie Smith and Beth Hutschison, 119–133. New Brunswick: Rutgers University Press, 2004.

Windham, Gayle C., Karen Fessel, and Judith K. Grether. "Autism Spectrum Disorders in Relation to Parental Occupation in Technical Fields." *Autism Research* 2, no. 4 (2009): 183–191.

Wing, Lorna. "Asperger's Syndrome: A Clinical Account." *Psychological Medicine* 11, no. 1 (1981): 115–129.

————. "The Autistic Continuum." In *Mental Health in Mental Retardation: Recent Advances and Practices*, edited by Nick Bouras, 108–125. New York: Cambridge University Press, 1994.

————. "The Continuum of Autistic Characteristics." In *Diagnosis and Assessment in Autism*, edited by Eric Schopler and Gary B. Mesibov, 91–110. New York: Plenum, 1988.

Winter, Jamie Michelle. Father Involvement in Parent Training Interventions for Children with Autism: Effects of Tailoring Treatment to Meet the Unique Needs of Fathers. PhD diss., University of California, San Diego, 2005.

Wolf, Joan B. "Is Breast Really Best? Risk and Total Motherhood in the National Breastfeeding Awareness Campaign." *Journal of Health Politics, Policy, and Law* 32, no. 4 (2007): 595–636.

Yates, Darran. "Neurogenetics: Unravelling the Genetics of Autism." *Nature Reviews Neuroscience* 13, no. 6 (2012): 359.

Yergeau, Melanie. "That's Just Your Autism Talking (And Other Phrases That Shouldn't Appear in an Autism Essay)" *AspieRhetor*, December 27, 2011. http://aspierhetor.com/2011/12/27/thats-just-your-autism-talking-and -other-phrases-that-shouldnt-appear-in-an-autism-essay/ (accessed February 26, 2012).

Zihlman, Adrienne. "The Paleolithic Glass Ceiling: Women in Human Evolution." In *Women in Human Evolution*, edited by Lori D. Hager, 91–113. New York: Routledge, 1997.

Index

anti-vaccination movement (*continued*):
rhetoric of, 67–68, 74–75, 102; in
scientific journals, 77; scientific rhetoric of, 75–79; scientists' response
to, 95–96; strategies for countering,
102; tactics of, 102; threats from,
103–4; total motherhood in, 75; in
United Kingdom, 67; villains/victims
in, 68
Apple, Rima, 43
Applied Behavioral Analysis (ABA),
56–57, 59; difference in, 60; rhetoric of, 57
Aristotle, on rhetoric, 183
Arranga, Teri, 88–89
Asperger, Hans: on autism mothers, 23; autism research of, 16–17;
autistic characters of, 22; "'Autistic Psychopathy' in Childhood,"
22; during Nazi regime, 18; use of
prosopographia, 24
Asperger's and Girls (advice text),
210–11
Asperger's quotient (AQ) test, 144
Asperger's syndrome, 11; association
with male intelligence, 108, 187;
characters of, 29, 105–6, 109, 111,
210; computer geeks portrayed
with, 105–6; cross-gender identity in, 205; in *DSM-IV*, 108; fMRI
studies of, 149; rhetorical culture
of, 109, 147; self-diagnosis of, 145,
146, 147; strategies of representation for, 106; as technological metaphor, 142; television depiction of,
120; testing for, 144; transgendered
persons with, 187; versus autism,
108; women with, 140, 147
athletics: for autistic children, 162;
masculine topos of, 158, 161–62
attachment: rhetorical tradition of, 62
Attention Deficit and Hyperactivity
Disorder (ADHD), 221–22; and total motherhood, 69, 70, 71
Austist's Corner (blog), 189–90
authority: in anti-vaccination movement, 75; of autism mothers, 53–
56, 58–59, 60, 63, 75, 88, 94–95;
in autism narratives, 3–4, 6, 48–56;

gendered organization of, 201, 217;
over autism, 41–42, 217; paternalistic, 217; in rhetoric, 2–3; scientific
versus maternal, 44, 217. *See also*
ethos (rhetoric)
Autisable (blog aggregator), 105
autism: aloneness in, 51; alternative
treatments for, 10, 82; anecdotal description of, 119, 143, 144; association with maleness, 106; association
with technology, 26, 106, 215–16;
authority over, 41–42, 217; as behavioral syndrome, 10; biomedical definitions of, 10–11, 170; bodily separation theory of, 61; in brain mapping
projects, 227; causes of, 1, 10, 16,
48, 64, 65; communication problems in, 126; cultural discourses of,
26, 170, 171–72; as deficit, 57; definitions of, 6–12; diagnoses of, 2, 11–
12, 145, 208–9, 245n122; discourse
of crisis in, 170–71; early intervention programs for, 174, 175, 176–77,
180; etiology of, 31; factors influenc-
ing, 1; and feeblemindedness, 16,
17, 18, 20; fMRI studies of, 148–49,
218; geekiness as, 114–47; gendered norms of, 13; gender-neutral
rhetoric of, 63; gender ratios in, 13,
24, 149; genetic factors in, 7–8, 42,
48; genetic technologies and, 217;
hereditary theories of, 16; historical context of, 171–72; and hysteria,
237n6; infantile, 16; and intellectual
disabilities, 52; and intelligence, 23;
as intense world syndrome, 152; mating theories of, 117; media coverage
of, 30, 173; and mercury poisoning,
76–77, 79; as metaphor for self-involvement, 186; mother-child relationships in, 24, 35, 39, 48, 49, 58,
60–61; neurodiversity in, 6, 9–10,
32, 44, 182–83; neurological definitions of, 7, 218; neurophysiological
causes of, 48, 65; neuroscience of,
147–48; and obsessive-compulsive
behavior, 204; parental causation
theories, 34; photographic depictions of, 232nn86–87; physiological

JORDYNN JACK is an associate professor of English at the University of North Carolina–Chapel Hill. She is the author of *Science on the Home Front: The Rhetoric of Women Scientists during World War II.*

The University of Illinois Press
is a founding member of the
Association of American University Presses.

Composed in 10.25/13 ITC Baskerville Std
by Lisa Connery
at the University of Illinois Press
Manufactured by Thomson-Shore, Inc.

University of Illinois Press
1325 South Oak Street
Champaign, IL 61820-6903
www.press.uillinois.edu